# An Introduction to Digital Video Data Compression in Java

Fore June

An Introduction to Digital Video Data Compression in Java

CreateSpace, a DBA of On-Demand Publishing, LLC.

ISBN: 978-1456570873

# Contents

# About the Author

Fore June is an independent Internet Service Provider ( ISP ) who provides various kinds of Internet services to the public. Fore is also the author of *Windows Fan, Linux Fan*, an autobiographical book describing the adventures of and conflicts between a Windows fan and a Linux fan. Fore holds a B.Sc. degree in Physics.

# Preface

The rapid advance in computing hardware technology has sharply reduced the cost of computing, and consequently, the computing capacity of PCs has become ever more powerful. This helps the spread of video compression technology that usually requires a lot of computing power. Many multi-media workers can now learn and experiment with data compression techniques in their own PCs. In recent years this computing-intensive technology has even sought its way to low-cost embedded devices. This book grows out of the author's experience of implementing a video compression engine to be used in toys for a toy manufacturer. Video games played in a toy are at the very low-end of any multi-media products; they are implemented in embedded systems and very often a significant portion of the code is written in assembly language. The engine designer must implement the code in a way that it minimizes the storage space and computing time. To make such an implementation, one must understand thoroughly the mechanism behind the technique. It took me a long time to get familiar with the subject but after the endeavor, I enjoy the happiness of solving the problems and finishing the task. I wrote the book "An Introduction to Video Compression in C/C++" in 2009 to report and explain the techniques I have learned and used in the project. I then received encouragement from some readers that they would be grateful if I could write another similar book with programs written in java as they are more familiar with the java language. At the same time, the popularity and success of the java-based mobile OS Android revived people's interest in java. It dawned in me that writing video compression applications in java makes sense and the demand is real. Therefore, I decided to 'translate' the book into java and named it "An Introduction to Digital Video Data Compression in Java". This book is the product of the subsequent endeavor.

I am grateful to many friends who helped shape the content of this book and provided valuable information of the technology used in my video compression project. In particular, I am thankful to Mr. Richard Friedman, a Linux fan who has offered a lot of help in compiling and using many open-source tools in the project. Not only the tools have significantly shortened the development time, they have also made the code a lot more robust and efficient.

I very much hope this book is enjoyable, readable and useful to you. Above all else, I hope you could share my happiness of exploration and in turn can help others to explore this beautiful and exciting technology world and make the world better. The source code of this book can be obtained from the web site *http://www.forejune.com/jvcompress* by entering the password 'nobel_peace_prize'.

Fore June
Jan. 2011

x

# Chapter 1    Introduction

## 1.1 The Value of Knowledge

Not long after the birth of the Web, multimedia has become an inseparable part of it. As the growth of the Web accelerates, the demand of multimedia applications and the knowledge of this field explodes. Data compression is the soul of the engine that drives the rapid development of these applications. Audio and image data can be effectively transmitted across the Web or saved in a digital storage medium ( DSM ) only after they have been compressed.

Video compression can be considered as an extension of audio and image compression, whose applications go well beyond the Web. As one might have noticed, in recent years video compression products have experienced rapid growth in a variety of consumer products like iPods, iTune, mobile phones, digital cameras, TV games, and many kinds of hand-held devices. All these products have employed video compression technologies to save storage space or transmission bandwidth. Moreover, as the cost of computing drops rapidly, sophisticated video compression technologies begin to seek its way into toys, hand-held devices and many innovative low-end new consumer products that add video features to attract customers. These low-end products are usually sold in very large volume and their production cost becomes a sole factor in determining the adoption of a technology. Very often, these products are built using embedded systems and the computing power and memory space of them are relatively limited. To develop data compression programs in such an environment, one must have a thorough understanding of the technology.

After many years of research by a large number of scientists and engineers, the methodologies of producing high-quality compressed video have become mature and well known. However, surprisingly, a few years ago when we began to help implement a video compression engine in a product for a toy manufacturer, we could hardly find any literature discussing the programming and implementation of it. People who were familiar with this technology were also scarce compared to the demand of it. Therefore, a book explaining the principles and implementation of video compression could be helpful and beneficial to the workers in this field.

Even though the book presents the materials at an introductory level, some readers may still find the materials difficult, depending on their background and willingness of paying efforts in learning. But your knowledge is valuable only if you need to pay effort to gain it. Topics that are easy to you are also easy to your competitors. In the coming decades, the competition between nations will be a competition of acquiring knowledge. The more effort you pay to acquire knowledge, the wealthier and happier you will be.

Renowned management specialist Peter Drucker ( 1909 - 2005 ) had long advocated the emergence of knowledge society and the importance of knowledge workers. The social transformations from an industrial society to a knowledge society would be the most significant event of the century and its lasting legacy. Science and technology have been advancing so rapidly that manufacturing becomes irrelevant in the modern society. A DVD containing certain data that you pay twenty dollars to purchase may just cost a few cents to manufacture. Though it is very rare for the productivity between two labour workers differ by a factor more than two, the productivity of a good knowledge work can be easily a factor of 100 or higher than that of an average knowledge worker. To become proficient in a certain field, one must learn with his or her heart, overcoming difficulties, barriers and frustrations. After enduring the hard work, one would enjoy the pleasure of understanding difficult materials and acquiring valuable knowledge. While the position of a labour worker can be easily substituted by another one with little training, it is very difficult to replace a specialist of a field in the knowledge economy, for the new worker must also go through the same learning barriers and hard work to acquire the knowledge.

## 1.2 MPEG-4 and H.264 Video Compression Standards

The work on video compression was mainly developed in the 1980s by a numerous number of researchers, mostly working in universities and academic institutions. Effective and close-to-optimal generic compression models began to emerge from the researching results. These models eventually became today's compression standards, which allow different parties to develop individual applications and communicate with each other seamlessly. The standardization has been mainly done by the International Organization for Standardization ( ISO ) in cooperation with the International Telecommunications Union and the International Electrotechnical Commission ( IEC ). ISO/IEC Joint Photographic Experts' Group ( JPEG ) and Moving Picture Experts' Group ( MPEG ) produced the well-known JPEG, MPEG-1, MPEG-2 and MPEG-4 standards that form the basis of most image and video compression standards today. MPEG-4 was introduced in late 1998 and designated as a standard for a group of audio and video coding formats and related technologies under the formal standard ISO/IEC 14496. Uses of MPEG-4 include compression of AV data for web (streaming media) and CD distribution, voice (telephone, videophone) and broadcast television applications. **H.264**, also known as *MPEG-4 Part 10/AVC for Advanced Video*, is the latest video compression standard, resulting from the work of a joint project between MPEG and the Video Coding Experts Group (VCEG), a working group of the International Telecommunication Union (ITU-T) that operates in a way similar to MPEG. ITU-T has helped set a series of telecommunication standards and is the sector that coordinates telecommunications standards on behalf of ISO and IEC. H.264 is the name used by ITU-T, while ISO/IEC refers it to as *MPEG-4 Part 10/AVC* since it is presented as a new part in its MPEG-4 suite, which includes MPEG-4 Part 2, a standard used by IP-based video encoders and network cameras. It tries to improve upon the weakness of previous video compression standards including:

1. Reducing the average bit rate by 50%, compared with any other video standard for a specified video quality,
2. Using straightforward syntax specification that simplifies implementations,
3. Defining exactly how numerical calculations are to be made by an encoder and a decoder to avoid errors from accumulating,
4. Improving robustness so that transmission errors over various networks are tolerated, and
5. Increasing low latency capabilities and achieving better quality for higher latency. ( Latency refers to the time to compress, transmit, decompress and display a set of video data. )

H.264 can support a wide variety of applications with very different bit rate requirements. For example, in entertainment video applications including broadcast, satellite, cable and DVD, an H.264 encoder-decoder ( codec ) may yield a data rate between 1 to 10 Mbit/s with high latency, while for telecom services, H.264 can deliver bit rates of below 1 Mbit/s with low latency.

MPEG-4 Visual, also referred to as *MPEG-4 Part 2*, is an earlier standard developed by MPEG that has significantly different goals from H.264. Though both standards deal with video data compression, MPEG-4 Visual emphasizes on flexibility whilst H.264 stresses on efficiency and reliability. MPEG-4 Visual provides a very flexible toolkit of coding techniques and resources that allow users to code a wide range of data types including traditional rectangular frames, video objects with arbitrary shape, still images and hybrids of real-world and computer-generated synthetic visual data.

Both MPEG-4 and H.264 are 'open' international standard. The term 'open' here means any individual or organization can purchase the standards documents from ISO/IEC, or ITU-T. Sample code of implementation are also available on the Web:

*http://www.mpeg.org/MPEG/video/mssg-free-mpeg-software.html*

The documents specify exactly what is required for conforming to the standards. Ironically, any implementation of these 'standards' utilizes certain methods that fall into the scope of a number of related patents. Any software developer who implements the standards needs to pay a certain royalty fee to a number of organizations coordinated by MPEG LA, which is regarded as the 'Standard of Standards' ( *http://www.mpegla.com* ), a leading packager of patent pools for standards used in consumer electronics, as well as eCommerce, education and other technical areas. It is fairly sad to see that we have to pay royalty fees to use a 'standard'. But the world itself, being in and around us has never been perfect. We have to accept this imperfectness in order to move on. Moreover, we have the freedom of choice of using the 'standards' in our applications.

The principles and methods discussed in this book are similar to those 'standards' as they are the results of a numerous number of researchers and have been published in various scientific and technical journals. However, to avoid any possible royalty dispute, our methods deviate in many minor aspects and the implementations could be very different from the 'standard' code. Readers are free to use part or all of the code presented in this book. However, whether the implementationis have used any algorithm that falls into the scope of any patent is beyond our knowledge. If you use the code for any commercial product, you do that at your own risk.

## 1.3 This Book

This book, *An Introduction to Digital Video Data Compression in Java* is written based on the author's other book *An Introduction to Video Compression in C/C++*. The materials are discussed at an introductory level and the code is presented in Java. The implementations of more advanced topics are not included. Also, we have only considered image compression; audio compression is omitted. The programs presented are mainly for illustrating the principles of video compression and how to implement them; very often error checking and handling are not included. For the purpose of making the materials easy to understand, sometimes the parameters are hard-coded. Nevertheless, the programs can be used as a starting point for further development. More advanced topics on video data compression are presented in the last chapter without actual implementation.

We have to admit that the programs were written over a period of time and thus the notations may not be very consistent. Also, we have not optimized the code for memory usage or computing time. However, coding is always relatively the easy part compared to understanding the algorithms. All the code presented in this book can be found at the site:

*http://www.forejune.com/jvcompress/*

and you can download the programs using the password 'nobel_peace_prize'. The programs have been compiled and tested. The version of Java we have used is **1.6.0_20**. The java programs of this book reside in subdirectories with numbering reflecting the related chapter. For example, the programs discussed in Chapter 5 will be in directory **5/**. If the programs of another chapter need to use the classes developed in Chapter 5, we just need to point the CLASSPATH to **5/**. We also put most of the sample data files in the directory **data/**.

We hope you enjoy reading this book.

# Chapter 2    Elements of Information

## 2.1 What Is Information?

Basically, everyone knows that this is an information era and every day we talk about the importance of information technology and its development. Now, let us confuse you with a simple question. *What is information?* Before continuing your reading, try to answer the preceding question. Like most programmers, you may be surprised to find that after so many years of studying or working in the area of information, you really could not answer the question unless you have taken a course in information theory or have studied the subject before. To understand how data compression works, we need to first understand what information is.

Some may think that information is simply a concept and we cannot define it quantitatively. Actually, not only that we can define information, we can define it quantitatively and measure it.

Many people, including some authors of books on image compression, confuse information with data and may mistaken that information is the same as data. Actually, data is different from information. Data are used to represent information. We can have redundant data but not redundant information. We can have a large amount of data which contains very little information. For example, we can use a pseudo random number generator to generate an abundant amount of data, tens of millions of bytes. However, all these data contain very little information because if we want to transmit the information represented by these data to another person, all we need to do is to transmit the simple equation of the pseudo random number generator. The receiver can generate the huge amount of data identical to ours. As another example, when we watch news, we feel that we receive a significant amount of information if the news gives us surprises, informing us something unexpected. On the other hand, if your friend tells you that she will eat dinner tomorrow, you do not feel receiving much information as that's what you expect. For instance, consider the following two sentences,

1. India will elect her next governing party by universal suffrage.
2. China will elect her next governing party by universal suffrage.

These two sentences have exactly the same amount of data ( characters ). However, there is a big difference in information the two sentences would convey. Should the event happen, the first one does not give us any surprise and would not appear in any newspaper as that's what we would expect. However, the second one would give a big shock to the world and every newspaper would report the event; it gives us a significant amount of information. From these examples, we can see that information relates to unpredictability and surprises. It is a measure of the decrease of uncertainty or the gain of surprise of a receiver upon receiving a message. A perfectly predictable message conveys no information. To quantify the measure of information, scientists borrow the concept of entropy from physics. We know that in physics, entropy is a measure of disorder or unpredictability. In information systems, we also refer to information carried by a message as entropy. However, the use of the term entropy to describe information content is artificial. There is not much relationship between the entropy of a message and the physical entropy of a physical system.

Claude Shannon, known as the father of information theory published his landmark paper in 1948 that led to the dawn of the information era. In the paper, Shannon defined the information I(E) conveyed by an event E, measured in bits as

$$I(E) = log_2 \frac{1}{p(E)} \tag{2.1}$$

where $p(E)$ is the probability of the occurrence of the event. In other words, if $E$ is some event which occurs with probability $p(E)$ and we are informed that event E has occurred, then we say that we have received $I(E)$ bits of information given in equation (2.1). We see that when $p = 1, I = 0$. For example, if we are told that "The sun rises from the East", we do not receive any information as we are one hundred percent sure this happens. If $p(E) = 1/2$, then $I(E) = 1bit$, meaning that one bit is the amount of information we obtain when one of two possible likely outcomes is specified, like the case of examining the outcome of flipping a coin. We can also interpret I(E) given in (2.1) as the information needed to make the occurrence of E certain. Note that equation (2.1) can also be expressed as,

$$I(E) = -log_2 p(E) \tag{2.2}$$

We can also define entropy in terms of a discrete random variable $X$, with possible states (or outcomes) $x_1, ..., x_n$ as

$$H(X) = \sum_{i=1}^{n} p(x_i) log_2 \left( \frac{1}{p(x_i)} \right) = -\sum_{i=1}^{n} p(x_i) log_2 p(x_i), \tag{2.3}$$

where $p(x_i) = Pr(X{=}x_i)$ is the probability of the $ith$ outcome of $X$. Note that a random variable is not a variable in the usual sense but rather a function that maps events to numbers. To simplify our notation, henceforth, we shall write the logarithm to the base 2 of $x$ simply as $logx$, omitting the subscript on the "log".

Equation (2.3) can also be expressed as

$$H(X) = \sum_{i=1}^{n} p(x_i) I(x_i), \tag{2.4}$$

Therefore, the entropy of the discrete random variable X is the average information of its states.

## 2.2 Memory Source

Rather than using a discrete random variable to further study information, it is more intuitive and convenient to consider a model of discrete information source as shown in Figure 2-1. In the model, the source generates a sequence of symbols from a fixed finite source alphabet $X = \{x_1, x_2, ..., x_n\}$. Successive symbols are generated according to some fixed probability law.

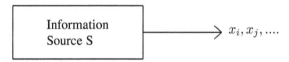

**Figure 2-1**. A discrete information source

For example, we can generate an English text message with a computer program; the alphabet $X$ consists of letters {a, b, c, d, ...} and digits { 1, 2, 3, ...}. In this model we can also view each symbol $x_i$ as a state and the alphabet $X$ as a random variable.

If the successive symbols generated from the source are statistically independent, the information source is referred to as **zero-memory source** ( or order-0 Markov source ), which is the simplest kind of sources one can have. Such an information source can be completely described by the source alphabet $X$ and the probabilities with which the symbols occur:

$$p(x_1), p(x_2), p(x_3), ....., p(x_n)$$

If symbol $x_i$ occurs, we obtain an amount of information $I(x_i)$ bits given by

$$I(x_i) = log \frac{1}{p(x_i)}$$

This means that if we receive a symbol $z$ that is very unlikely to appear, $p(z)$ is very small; $\frac{1}{p(z)}$ and thus $I(z)$ is very large. In other words, we get a lot of surprise ( information ) when we receive something totally unexpected. On the other hand, if $p(z)$ is large, $I(z)$ is small. That is, we gain little information ( surprise ) when we get something we expect.

The probability for $x_i$ to occur is simply $p(x_i)$. So the average amount of information per symbol one can receive from the source S is

$$\sum_X p(x_i)I(x_i) \quad bits$$

where we sum over the n symbols of the alphabet $X$; this average information is the entropy $H(S)$ of the zero memory source.

$$H(S) = H(X) = \sum_{i=1}^{n} p(x_i)log \frac{1}{p(x_i)} \quad bits \qquad (2.5)$$

The source gives maximum entropy $H_M(S)$ when all symbols occur with the same probability $p(x_i) = \frac{1}{n}$.

$$H_M(S) = \sum_{i=1}^{n} \frac{1}{n}log\ n = log\ n \quad bits$$

Therefore, an alphabet with 256 symbols has a maximum entropy of 8 bits, which is the maximum amount of average information per symbol that the source can generate from it.

## 2.3 Markov Memory Source

In the zero-memory model, the occurrence of each symbol is statistically independent of each other. However, in reality symbols are statistically related to each other in most cases. For example, in an English text, the probability for letter 'u' to occur is quite small. However, if we receive a letter 'q', we know that the next letter that we shall receive is very likely to be a 'u'. If we have received the letters 'democrac', there is a large chance that the next letter is a 'y'. To better study the information content of this kind of symbol sequences, we need a model in which the occurrence of a source symbol $x_i$ may depend upon $m$ preceding symbols. Such a source is referred to as an $mth$-order Markov source and is defined by specifying the occurrence of source symbols with the set of conditional probabilities

$$p(x_i/x_{k_1}, ..., x_{k_m}) \quad for \quad i = 1, 2, ..., n; \quad k_j = 1, 2, ..., n \qquad (2.6)$$

which is the probability of seeing $x_i$ after we have seen $m$ symbols.

It is often convenient to use finite state diagrams to illustrate an $mth$-order Markov source. At a given time, we can refer to the $m$ preceding symbols as the **state** of the $mth$-order Markov source at that time; as there are $n$ symbols in the alphabet, there are $n^m$ possible states. Figure 2-2 shows a state diagram of a **second-order** (i.e. $m = 2$) Markov source with binary alphabet $X = \{0, 1\}$ and conditional probabilities

$$\begin{array}{ll} p(0/00) = 0.8 & p(1/00) = 0.2 \\ p(0/01) = 0.5 & p(1/01) = 0.5 \\ p(0/10) = 0.5 & p(1/10) = 0.5 \\ p(0/11) = 0.2 & p(1/11) = 0.8 \end{array}$$

In the diagram, states are represented by circles and state transitions are indicated by arrows labeled with the corresponding conditional probabilities. ( This Figure and related examples discussed below are taken from the book *Information Theory and Coding* by **Norman Abramson**. )

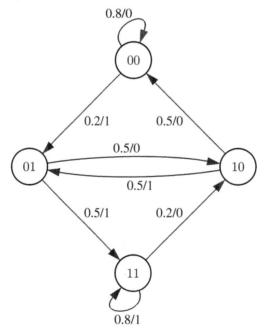

**Figure 2-2**. State diagram of a second-order Markov source with alphabet $\{0, 1\}$

In image processing, it is common to use a second or third order Markov model to predict a pixel value. That is, two or three previously occurred pixel values are used to estimate the value of a forthcoming pixel.

In many cases ( but not all ), the probability distribution over the set of states do not change with time. We refer to this kind of distribution as stationary distribution.

In these cases, when we specify the conditional symbol probabilities $p(x_i/x_{k_1}, ..., x_{k_m})$ of an $mth$-order Markov source, we also implicitly specify the $n^m$ state probabilities $p(x_{k_1}, x_{k_2}, ..., x_{k_m})$. The product of these two probabilities gives us the probability of the joint event "*the source is in the state* $(x_{k_1}, x_{k_2}, ..., x_{k_m})$ *and* $x_i$ *occurs*". That is

$$p(x_{k_1}, ..., x_{k_m}, x_i) = p(x_i/x_{k_1}, ..., x_{k_m})p(x_{k_1}, ..., x_{k_m}) \qquad (2.7)$$

The information we obtain if $x_i$ occurs while the system is in the state $(x_{k_1}, x_{k_2}, ..., x_{k_m})$ is

$$I(x_i/x_{k_1}, ..., x_{k_m}) = log\frac{1}{p(x_i/x_{k_1}, ..., x_{k_m})} \qquad (2.8)$$

and the average amount of information per symbol while the system is in the state $(x_{k_1}, x_{k_2}, ..., x_{k_m})$ is given by:

$$H(X/x_{k_1}, ..., x_{k_m}) = \sum_{X} p(x_i/x_{k_1}, ..., x_{k_m})I(x_i/x_{k_1}, ..., x_{k_m}) \qquad (2.9)$$

where the summation is over the $n$ symbols in the alphabet $X$. If we average this quantity over all the $n^m$ possible states, we obtain the average amount of information, or the entropy of the $mth$-order Markov source S.

$$H(S) = \sum_{X^m} p(x_{k_1}, ..., x_{k_m})H(X/x_{k_1}, ..., x_{k_m}) \qquad (2.10)$$

In other words, if we have a very long text consisting of $n$ symbols which can be described by such a model, then $H(S)$ of (2.10) gives us the average information per symbol of the text. For example, in a long Internet message, we can take the alphabet as the generalized ASCII code, consisting of 256 symbols or characters ( i.e. $n = 256$ ). To estimate the average information content of the message, we may take $m$ to be 4 ( i.e. using a 4-th order Markov model ). There will be totally $256^4 = 2^{32}$, about 4 billion states. We have to collect the statistics over the 4 billion states to estimate the probabilities and use them to find the entropy given in (2.10), which gives us the average information per symbol. The total information of the message is then the length of the message times $H(S)$.

Substituting (2.9) and (2.8) into (2.10) and making simplifications, we can express the entropy ( average information per symbol ) in the following form:

$$H(S) = \sum_{X^{m+1}} p(x_{k_1}, ..., x_{k_m}, x_i) \times log\frac{1}{p(x_i/x_{k_1}, ..., x_{k_m})} \qquad (2.11)$$

**Example 2-1**
Consider the Markov source of Figure 2-2, where the alphabet only consists of two symbols which are the binary digits, i.e. $X = \{1, 0\}$. Since the stationary distribution does not depend upon the initial states, we can calculate the probability for each state from the conditional symbol probabilities. One can show that the stationary distribution is:

$$p(00) = \tfrac{5}{14} \quad p(01) = \tfrac{2}{14}$$
$$p(10) = \tfrac{2}{14} \quad p(11) = \tfrac{5}{14}$$

We summarize the relevant probabilities in Table 2-1:

**Table 2-1** Probabilities for Markov Source $X = \{0, 1\}$ of Figure 2-2

| $x_{k_1}, x_{k_2}, x_i$ | $p(x_i/x_{k_1}, x_{k_2})$ | $p(x_{k_1}, x_{k_2})$ | $p(x_{k_1}, x_{k_2}, x_i)$ |
|:---:|:---:|:---:|:---:|
| 000 | 0.8 | $\frac{5}{14}$ | $\frac{4}{14}$ |
| 001 | 0.2 | $\frac{5}{14}$ | $\frac{1}{14}$ |
| 010 | 0.5 | $\frac{2}{14}$ | $\frac{1}{14}$ |
| 011 | 0.5 | $\frac{2}{14}$ | $\frac{1}{14}$ |
| 100 | 0.5 | $\frac{2}{14}$ | $\frac{1}{14}$ |
| 101 | 0.5 | $\frac{2}{14}$ | $\frac{1}{14}$ |
| 110 | 0.2 | $\frac{5}{14}$ | $\frac{1}{14}$ |
| 111 | 0.8 | $\frac{5}{14}$ | $\frac{4}{14}$ |

Note that $p(x_{k_1}, x_{k_2}, x_i) = p(x_i/x_{k_1}, x_{k_2}) \times p(x_{k_1}, x_{k_2})$. We can now calculate the average entropy of the system using (2.11):

$$H(S) = \sum_{X^3} p(x_{k_1}, x_{k_2}, x_i) log \frac{1}{p(x_i/x_{k_1}, x_{k_2})} \tag{2.12}$$

Substituting the probabilities in Table 2-1 into (2.12), we obtain

$$
\begin{aligned}
H(S) \quad &= \tfrac{4}{14} \times log\tfrac{1}{0.8} + \tfrac{1}{14} \times log\tfrac{1}{0.2} + \tfrac{1}{14} \times log\tfrac{1}{0.5} + \tfrac{1}{14} \times log\tfrac{1}{0.5} \\
&+ \tfrac{1}{14} \times log\tfrac{1}{0.5} + \tfrac{1}{14} \times log\tfrac{1}{0.5} + \tfrac{1}{14} \times log\tfrac{1}{0.2} + \tfrac{4}{14} \times log\tfrac{1}{0.8} \\
&= 0.81 \text{(bit / binary digit)}
\end{aligned}
$$

In equation (2.10), $X^m$ is the *mth* extension of the alphabet $X$, which has $n^m$ symbols, $\sigma_1, \sigma_2, ..., \sigma_{n^m}$ and each $\sigma_i$ corresponds to some sequence of $m$ $x'_k s$. One can define the $r$-th extension of an $m$-th order Markov source, where we group $r$ symbols together to form one new 'super-symbol'. If we consider each of these 'super-symbols' as a symbol, our alphabet $X$ becomes:

$$X = \{\sigma_1, \sigma_2, ..., \sigma_{n^r}\}$$

By grouping $r$ symbols together, we have considered the correlation between $r$ symbols, which can give us better estimate of the information content of a text. In reality, there could be long-range correlations between groups of symbols. To accurately calculate the average information, we actually need to consider an extremely long message and make the group as large as possible. Theoretically, the average information of a 'typical' stationary infinite text is given by the entropy rate $H(X)$, which is the limit of the joint entropy of $n$ 'symbols' averaged over n:

$$H(X) = \lim_{n \to \infty} \frac{1}{n} H(X_1, X_2, ..., X_n) \tag{2.13}$$

We may also define the entropy rate, $H(S)$ using conditional probabilities:

$$H(S) = \lim_{n \to \infty} \frac{1}{n} H(X_n | X_{n-1}, X_{n-2}, ..., X_1) \tag{2.14}$$

One can show that the two quantities defined in (2.13) and (2.14) are basically equal ( i.e. $H(S) = H(X)$ ).

What (2.14) tells us is that when reading a text, if we use a sufficiently large number of symbols to predict the forthcoming symbol, the accuracy of prediction reflects the average information of the text. If we can predict the next symbol very well, there is a lot of redundancy and the average information which is equal to the entropy rate is very small. Since $n$ tends to infinity in (2.13) and (2.14), we have exhausted the search of any long-range correlations in the text.

## 2.4 Information of Text and Kolmogorov Complexity

In the previous section, we have discussed that the average information a text contains is given by its entropy rate. The problem of this approach is that entropy rate is defined using an infinite text of symbols. We have also discussed a model of information source and some of its properties. We are interested to know how closely the model and theories relate to the physical process of information generation in real life. In practice, every text is of finite length and we can only estimate its information content using predictions based on a finite number of preceding symbols. In some situations, such an estimate can be totally off. For instance, consider a simple experiment that uses the following program, **Randtest.java** to generate 10 million integers of data using a pseudo random number generator:

```
/*
   Randtest.java : Testing compression of numbers generated by
                   psuedo random number generator
*/
import java.io.*;
import java.util.Random;

class Randtest {
  public static void main(String[] args) {

    try {
      DataOutputStream out;
      FileOutputStream fos = new FileOutputStream ( "randnums" );
      out = new DataOutputStream( fos );
      Random generator = new Random();
      for ( int i = 0; i  < 10000000; ++i ) {
        int r = generator.nextInt();
        out.writeInt ( r );
      }
      out.close();
    } catch ( Exception e ) {
      System.err.println("apply: "+e.toString() );
    }
    System.out.println("Random numbers saved in 'randnums'!");
  }
}
```

The 40 millions bytes of data are saved in the file "randnums". Now let us use the common compression utility **gzip** to compress the data, saving the output data in the file "randnums.gz" and check the file sizes:

```
$ javac Randtest.java
$ java Randtest
$ gzip -c randnums > randnums.gz
$ ls -l randnums*
-rw-r--r-- 1 user user 40000000 2010-09-12 09:37 randnums
-rw-r--r-- 1 user user 40006132 2010-09-12 09:40 randnums.gz
```

We see that the compressed file size is about the same as the original size. This implies that we were not able to compress the data and the average information of the file is 8 bits per symbol. If we calculate the entropy using Equation (2.12), we shall obtain a similar value. In other words, the file "randnums" contains about 320 million bits of information! If we need to transmit these data to a friend we need to transmit 320 million bits! We know that this could not be true because the data are generated from a simple program using a simple pseudo random number generator ( **random**() ). We can simply send our friend the program along with the pseudo random number generator, which together may contain less than 1 Kbytes of data. Our friend can then use the program to reproduce all the 320 million bits of the file "randnums". Therefore, the information that the file "randnums" contains is actually much less than 320 million bits. Does this mean that the definition of entropy rate given in (2.13) or (2.14) is inconsistent with our experience of information of data? The main reason for the inconsistency is that we have only considered a finite number of symbols in the compression process. The utility program **gzip** is based on the Ziv-Lempel algorithm which uses a finite look-ahead buffer for searching a string that matches the string under consideration. Because of the limited buffer size, all characters appear random to the encoder and the text cannot be compressed. In practice, any pseudo random number generator ( PRNG ) has a a finite period, which means that the sequence repeats itself after a certain number. Within a period, the generated numbers appear random. In general, the period of a PRNG is very long for it to have practical use. If we have generated a sequence that is much longer than the period and our compression program has used a look-ahead buffer larger than the period, the huge file will be compressed to a very small one, which is consistent with our intuition that the sequence actually contains very little information. Therefore, in some situations entropy rate may not be a good estimate of the **average** information of data as it requires an infinite number of bits of data in the measurement to give the correct result.

A more fundamental approach to estimate the information of data or text is to consider the Kolmogorov complexity, also known as algorithmic entropy, which is a measure of the computational resources required to generate the text. For example, consider the following string of length 96:

go!go!go!go!go!go!go!go!go!go!go!go!go!go!go!go!
go!go!go!go!go!go!go!go!go!go!go!go!go!go!go!go!

The string can be described by a short English Language description like, "go! 32 times" which consists of only 12 characters.

More formally, the complexity of a string is the length of the string's shortest description in some fixed universal description language. One can show that the Kolmogorov complexity of a string cannot be too much larger than the length of the string itself. Suppose **P** is a program that outputs a string **x**, then **P** is a description of **x**. The length of the program, $l(\mathbf{P})$ is essentially the complexity of the string **x**. We can now make a formal definition of Kolmogorov complexity.

Kolmogorov ( algorithmic ) complexity $K_u(x)$ of a string $x$ with respect to a universal computer $u$ is defined as

$$K_u(x) = \min_{P:u(P)=x} l(P) \tag{2.15}$$

the minimum length over all programs $P$ that print $x$ and halt.

One can show that if $K_1$ and $K_2$ are the complexity functions relative to description languages $L_1$ and $L_2$, then there exists a constant $c$, which depends only on languages $L_1$ and $L_2$, such that

$$|K_1(x) - K_2(x)| \leq c, \quad for\ all\ strings\ x \tag{2.16}$$

This implies that the effect of choosing a description language on $K$ is bounded.

One can prove that Kolmogorov complexity is the minimum number of bits into which a string can be compressed without losing information. In other words, it is the information the string contains. Therefore, a string is incompressible if its length is equal to its Kolmogorov complexity. One can also show that when the string is sufficiently long, the entropy of the string converges to the Kolmogorov complexity. Therefore, the information contained in a fractal image or a set of pseudo random numbers is very small as the data can be generated by a simple program using an algorithm.

## 2.5 Data Reversibility

By now we know that data are different from information. We can use different amount of data to represent the same piece of information. In practice, a set of data may have a lot of redundancy and data compression is achieved by getting rid of the redundancy. There are two kinds of data compression, lossless and lossy. In lossless compression, no information is lost and the exact original data set can be recovered. In lossy compression, information is lost and the original data set cannot be recovered. In other words, in lossy compression, we throw away some information in order to achieve a higher compression ratio. *What kind of information do we want to throw away?* Naturally, we want to throw away the irrelevant information and retain the important information. Given a set of data, *how do we decide on which portion of data is more important than others*? In fact, separating the relevant and irrelevant information is the state of the art of lossy data compression. The following discussion gives a brief idea how this can be done.

Suppose we want to know about the age of the people in a country of a million. We would not want to remember the age of every individual. If we just want to remember one value concerning age, we would most likely remember the average age of the population; we don't care about the age of the president or the age of any 'great leader' of the country. The average value gives us a brief idea about the population of the country. Indeed, the average value of a data set is usually the most crucial value. On the other hand, we cannot reconstruct the whole set from its average value. In other words, when we average the values of a set of data, we lose information; the process is irreversible. This is also true in the physical world. For instance, consider the case that we put a drop of red ink in a glass of water. We will see that the ink spreads over and eventually the whole glass of water becomes red. However, no matter how long we continue to observe the glass of red water, we will never see the process reverses itself and the ink pigment forms a drop again. Microscopically, the process is reversible; when an ink pigment molecule interacts with a water molecule, there is nothing that forbids them to go in one direction or the other. From the point of view of information theory, the process is reversible because we have recorded the information of every single molecule. However, macroscopically, the entropy law of physics forbids the process to be reversible. This is because when we observe the glass of water macroscopically, we observe an unaccountable number of molecules simultaneously; we are observing the average behavior of the molecules. Because of the averaging effect, information is lost in the process and thus it is irreversible.

# Chapter 3   Imaging Basics

## 3.1 Sampling and Quantization

*Sampling* is the process of examining the value of a continuous function at regular intervals. We might measure the voltage of an analog waveform every millisecond, or measure the brightness of a photograph every millimeter, horizontally and vertically. Sampling rate is the rate at which we make the measurements and can be defined as

$$Sampling\ rate = \frac{1}{Sampling\ interval}\ Hz$$

If sampling is performed in the time domain, $Hz$ is *cycles/sec*.

In the case of image processing, we can regard an *image* as a two-dimensional light-intensity function $f(x, y)$ of spatial coordinates $(x, y)$. Since light is a form of energy, $f(x, y)$ must be nonnegative. In order that we can store an *image* in a computer, which processes data in discrete form, the image function $f(x, y)$ must be digitized both spatially and in amplitude. Digitization of the spatial coordinates $(x, y)$ is referred to as *image sampling* or *spatial sampling*, and digitization of the amplitude $f$ is referred to as *quantization*. Moreover, for moving video images, we have to digitize the time component and this is called *temporal sampling*. Digital video is a representation of a real-world scene, sampled spatially and temporarily and with the light intensity value quantized at each spatial point. A scene is sampled at an instance of time to produce a *frame*, which consists of the complete visual scene at that instance, or a *field*, which consists of odd- or even-numbered lines of spatial samples. Figure 3-1 shows the concept of spatial and temporal sampling of videos.

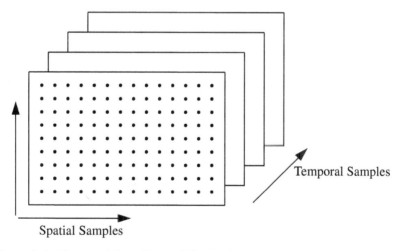

**Figure 3-1**   Temporal Sampling and Spatial Sampling

## 3.1.1 Spatial Sampling

Usually, a two-dimensional ( 2D ) sampled image is obtained by projecting a video scene onto a 2D sensor, such as an array of Charge Coupled Devices ( CCD array ) . For colour images, each colour component is filtered and projected onto an independent 2D CCD array. The CCD array outputs analogue signals representing the intensity levels of the colour component. Sampling the signal at an instance in time produces a sampled image or frame that has specified values at a set of spatial sampling points in the form of an $N \times M$ array as shown in the following equation.

$$f(x,y) \approx \begin{pmatrix} f(0,0) & f(0,1) & \dots & f(0, M-1) \\ f(1,0) & f(1,1) & \dots & f(1, M-1) \\ \cdot & \cdot & \dots & \cdot \\ \cdot & \cdot & \dots & \cdot \\ f(N-1,0) & f(N-1,1) & \dots & f(N-1, M-1) \end{pmatrix} \qquad (3.1)$$

The right image of Figure 3-2 below shows that a rectangular grid is overlaid on a 2D image to obtain sampled values $f(x,y)$ at the intersection points of the grid. We may approximately reconstruct the sampled image by representing each sample as a square picture element ( pixel ) as shown on the left image of Figure 3-2. The visual quality of the reconstructed image is affected by the choice of the sampling points. The more sampling points we choose, the higher resolution the resulted sampled image will be. Of course, choosing more sampling points requires more computing power and storage.

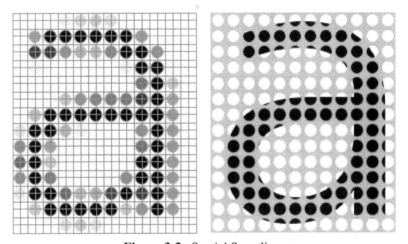

**Figure 3-2**  Spatial Sampling

## 3.1.2 Temporal Sampling

*Temporal sampling* of video images refers to the process of taking a rectangular 'snapshot' of the image signal at regular time intervals. The rate at which we take the the snapshots is the *sampling rate* and is defined as the *frame rate* or *field rate*. When we play back a sequence of frames obtained in this way at the same rate, an illusion of motion may be created. A higher frame rate produces apparently smoother motion but requires more computing power and storage to process and save the larger number of samples. Early silent films used anything between 16 and 24 frames per second ( fps ). Current television standards use sampling rate of 25 or 30 frames per second.

There are two commonly used temporal sampling techniques, *progressive* sampling and *interlaced* sampling. Progressive sampling is a frame-based sampling technique where a video signal is sampled as a series of complete frames. Film is a progressive sampling source for video. Interlaced sampling is a field-based sampling technique where the video is sampled periodically at two sample fields; half of the data in a frame ( one field ) are scanned at one time. To reconstruct the frame, a pair of sample fields are superimposed on each other ( interlaced ). In general, a field consists of either the odd-numbered or even-numbered scan lines within a frame as shown in Figure 3-3.

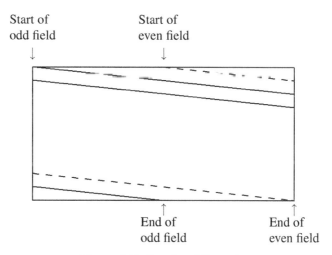

Start of
odd field

Start of
even field

End of
odd field

End of
even field

**Figure 3-3**   Interlaced Scanning

An interlaced video sequence contains a sequence of fields, each of which consists of half the data of a complete frame. The interlaced sampling technique can give the appearance of smoother motion as compared to the progressive sampling method when the data are sampled at the same rate. This is due to the "motion blur" effect of human eyes; the persistence of vision can cause images shown rapidly in sequence to appear as one. When we rapidly switch between two low quality fields, they appear like a single high quality image. Because of this advantage, most current video image formats, including several high-definition video standards, use interlaced techniques rather than progressive methods.

## 3.1.3 Quantization

*Quantization* is the procedure of constraining the value of a function at a sampling point to a predetermined finite set of discrete values. Note that the original function can be either continuous or discrete. For example, if we want to specify the temperature of Los Angels, ranging from $0^oC$ to $50^oC$, up to a a precision of $0.05^oC$, we must be able to represent 1001 possible values, which require 10 bits to represent one sample. On the other hand, if we only need a precision of $1^oC$, we only have 51 possible values requiring 6 bits for the representation. For image processing, higher precision give higher image quality but requires more bits in the representation of the samples. We will come back to this topic and discuss how to use quantization to achieve lossy image compression.

# 3.2 Color Spaces

To describe an image, we need a way to represent the color information. A gray-level image only requires one number to indicate the brightness or luminance of each spatial sample. Very often, we employ a **color model** to precisely describe the color components or intensities. A **color model** can be regarded as an abstract mathematical model that describes how colors are presented as tuples of numbers, typically as three or four values or color components; the resulting set of colors that define how the components are to be interpreted is called a **color space**. The commonly used **RGB** color model naturally fits the representation of colors by computers. However, it is not a good model for studying the characteristics of an image.

## 3.2.1 RGB Color Model

X-ray, light, infrared radiation, microwave and radio waves are all electromagnetic ( EM ) waves with different wavelengths. Light waves lie in the visible spectrum with a narrow wavelength band from about 350 to 780 nm. The retina of a human eye can detect only EM waves lying within this visible spectrum but not anything outside. The eye contains two kinds of light-sensitive receptor cells, **cones** and **rods** that can detect light.

The **cones** are sensitive to colors and there are three types of cones, each responding to one of the three primary colors, red, green and blue. Scientists found that our perception of color is a result of our cones' relative response to the red, green and blue colors. Any color can be considered as a combination of these three colors with certain intensity values. The human eye can distinguish about 200 intensities of each of the red, green and blue colors. Therefore, it is natural that we represent each of these colors by a byte which can hold 256 values. In other words, 24 bits are enough to represent the 'true' color. More bits will not increase the quality of an image as human eyes cannot resolve the extra colors. Each eye has 6 to 7 million cones located near the center of the eye, allowing us to see the tiny details of an object.

On the other hand, the **rods** cannot distinguish colors but are sensitive to dim light. Each eye has 75 million to 150 millions rods located near its corner, allowing us to detect peripheral objects in an environment of near darkness.

We can characterize a visible color by a function $C(\lambda)$ where $\lambda$ is the wavelength of the color in the visible spectrum. The value for a given wavelength $\lambda$ gives the relative intensity of that wavelength in the color. This description is accurate when we measure the color with certain physical instrument. However, the human visual system ( HVS ) does not perceive color in this way. Our brains do not receive the entire distribution $C(\lambda)$ of the visible spectrum but rather three values – the **tristimulus values** – that are the responses of the three types ( red, green and blue ) of cones to a color. This human characteristics leads to the formulation of the trichromatic theory: *If two colors produce the same tristimulus values, they are visually indistinguishable.* A consequence of of this theory is that it is possible to match all of the colors in the visible spectrum by appropriate mixing of three primary colors. In other words, any color can be created by combining red, green, and blue in varying proportions. This leads to the development of the **RGB color model**.

The RGB ( short for red, green, blue ) color model decomposes a color into three components, Red ( R ), Green ( G ), and Blue ( B ); we can represent any color by three components $R, G, B$ just like the case that a spatial vector is specified by three components $x, y, z$. If the color components $R, G$ and $B$ are confined to values between 0 and 1, all definable colors lie in a unit cube as shown in Figure 3-4. This color space is most natural for representing computer images, in which a color specification such as ( 0.1, 0.8, 0.23 ) can be directly translated into three positive integer values, each of which is represented by one byte.

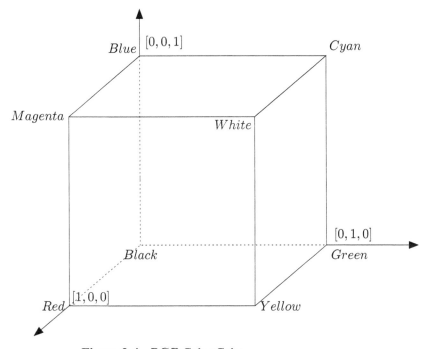

**Figure 3-4**  $RGB$ Color Cube

In this model, we express a color $C$ in the vector form,

$$C = \begin{pmatrix} R \\ G \\ B \end{pmatrix} \qquad 0 \le R, G, B \le 1 \qquad (3.2)$$

In some other notations, the authors like to consider $R$, $G$, and $B$ as three unit vectors like the three spatial unit vectors $\mathbf{i}$, $\mathbf{j}$, and $\mathbf{k}$. Just as a spatial vector $\mathbf{V}$ can be expressed as $\mathbf{v} = x\mathbf{i} + y\mathbf{j} + z\mathbf{k}$, any color is expressed as $C = (rR + gG + bB)$, and the red, green, blue intensities are specified by the values of $r$, $g$, and $b$ respectively. In our notation here, $R$, $G$, and $B$ represent the intensity values of the color components.

Suppose we have two colors $C_1$ and $C_2$ given by

$$C_1 = \begin{pmatrix} R_1 \\ G_1 \\ B_1 \end{pmatrix}, \qquad C_2 = \begin{pmatrix} R_2 \\ G_2 \\ B_2 \end{pmatrix}$$

Does it make sense to add these two colors to produce a new color $C$? For instance, consider

$$C = C_1 + C_2 = \begin{pmatrix} R_1 + R_2 \\ G_1 + G_2 \\ B_1 + B_2 \end{pmatrix}$$

You may immediately notice that the sum of two components may give a value larger than 1 which lies outside the color cube and thus does not represent any color. Just like adding two points in space is illegitimate, we cannot arbitrarily combine two colors. A linear combination of colors makes sense only if the sum of the coefficients is equal to 1. Therefore, we can have

$$C = \alpha_1 C_1 + \alpha_2 C_2 \tag{3.3}$$

when

$$0 \le \alpha_1, \alpha_2 \quad and \quad \alpha_1 + \alpha_2 = 1$$

In this way, we can guarantee that the resulted components will always lie within the color cube as each value will never exceed one. For example,

$$R = \alpha_1 R_1 + \alpha_2 R_2 \le \alpha_1 \times 1 + \alpha_2 \times 1 = 1$$

which implies

$$R \le 1$$

The linear combination of colors described by Equation (3.3) is called *color blending*.

### 3.2.2 YUV Color Model

While the RGB color model is well-suited for displaying color images on a computer screen, it is not an effective model for image processing or video compression. This is because the human visual system ( HVS ) is more sensitive to luminance ( brightness ) than to colors. Therefore, it is more effective to represent a color image by separating the luminance from the color information and representing luma with a higher resolution than color.

The YUV color model, defined in the TV standards, is an efficient way of representing color images by separating brightness from color values. Historically, YUV color space was developed to provide compatibility between color and black /white analog television systems; it is not defined precisely in the technical and scientific literature. In this model, Y is the luminance ( luma ) component, and U and V are the color differences known as chrominance or chroma, which is defined as the difference between a color and a reference white at the same luminance. The conversion from RGB to YUV is given by the following formulas:

$$\begin{aligned} Y &= k_r R + k_g G + k_b B \\ U &= B - Y \\ V &= R - Y \end{aligned} \tag{3.4}$$

with

$$0 \leq k_r, k_b, k_g$$
$$k_r + k_b + k_g = 1 \tag{3.5}$$

Note that equations (3.4) and (3.5) imply that $0 \leq Y \leq 1$ if the $R, G, B$ components lie within the unit color cube. However, U and V can be negative. Typically,

$$k_r = 0.299, k_g = 0.587, k_b = 0.114 \tag{3.6}$$

which are values used in some TV standards. For convenience, in the forthcoming discussions, we always assume that $0 \leq R, G, B \leq 1$ unless otherwise stated.

The complete description of an image is specified by Y ( the luminance component ) and the two color differences ( chrominance ) $U$ and $V$. If the image is black-and-white, $U = V = 0$. Note that we do not need another difference ( $G - Y$ ) for the green component because that would be redundant. We can consider (3.4) as three equations with three unknowns, $R, G, B$. We can always solve for the three unknowns and recover $R, G, B$. A fourth equation is not necessary.

It seems that there is no advantage of using YUV over RGB to represent an image as both system requires three components to specify an image sample. However, as we mentioned earlier, human eyes are less sensitive to color than to luminance. Therefore, we can represent the U and V components with a lower resolution than Y and the reduction of the amount of data to represent chrominance components will not have an obvious effect on visual quality. Representing chroma with less number of bits than luma is a simple but effective way of compressing an image.

## 3.2.3 YCbCr Color Model

The YCbCr color model defined in the standards of ITU (International Telecommunication Union) is closely related to YUV but with the chrominace components scaled and shifted to ensure that they lie within the range 0 and 1. It is sometimes abbreviated to YCC. It is also used in the JPEG and MPEG standards. In this model, an image sample is specified by a luminance ( Y ) component and two chrominance components ( Cb, and Cr ). The following equations convert an RGB image to one in YCbCr space.

$$Y = k_r R + k_g G + k_b B$$

$$C_b = \frac{B - Y}{2(1 - k_b)} + 0.5$$

$$\tag{3.7}$$

$$C_r = \frac{(R - Y)}{2(1 - k_r)} + 0.5$$

$$k_r + k_b + k_g = 1$$

An image may be captured in the RGB format and then converted to YCbCr to reduce storage or transmission requirements. Before displaying the image, it is usually necessary to convert the image back to RGB. The conversion from YCbCr to RGB can be done by solving for $R, G, B$ in the equations of (3.7). The equations for converting from YCbCr to

RGB are shown below:

$$R = Y + (2C_r - 1)(1 - k_r)$$

$$B = Y + (2C_b - 1)(1 - k_b)$$

$$G = \frac{Y - k_r R - k_b B}{k_g}$$

$$= Y - \frac{k_r(2C_r - 1)(1 - k_r) + k_b(2C_b - 1)(1 - k_b)}{k_g}$$

(3.8)

If we use the ITU standard values $k_b = 0.114, k_r = 0.299, k_g = 1 - k_b - k_r = 0.587$ for (3.7) and (3.8), we will obtain the following commonly used conversion equations.

$$Y = 0.299R + 0.587G + 0.114B$$
$$C_b = 0.564(B - Y) + 0.5$$
$$C_r = 0.713(R - Y) + 0.5$$

(3.9)

$$R = Y + 1.402C_r - 0.701$$
$$G = Y - 0.714C_r - 0.344C_b + 0.529$$
$$B = Y + 1.772C_b - 0.886$$

In equations (3.7), it is obvious that $0 \le Y \le 1$. It turns out that the chrominance components $C_b$ and $C_r$ defined in (3.7) also always lie within the range [0, 1]. We prove this for the case of $C_b$. From (3.7), we have

$$
\begin{aligned}
C_b &= \frac{B - Y}{2(1 - k_b)} + \frac{1}{2} \\
&= \frac{B - k_r R - k_g G - k_b B + 1 - k_b}{2(1 - k_b)} \\
&= \frac{B}{2} + \frac{-k_r R - k_g G + 1 - k_b}{2(1 - k_b)} \\
&\ge \frac{B}{2} + \frac{-k_r \times 1 - k_g \times 1 + 1 - k_b}{2(1 - k_b)} \\
&= \frac{B}{2} \\
&\ge 0
\end{aligned}
$$

Thus

$$C_b \ge 0$$

(3.10)

Also,

$$
\begin{aligned}
C_b &= \frac{B - Y}{2(1 - k_b)} + \frac{1}{2} \\
&= \frac{B - k_r R - k_g G - k_b B}{2(1 - k_b)} + \frac{1}{2} \\
&\leq \frac{B - k_b B}{2(1 - k_b)} + \frac{1}{2} \\
&= \frac{B}{2} + \frac{1}{2} \\
&\leq \frac{1}{2} + \frac{1}{2} \\
&= 1
\end{aligned}
$$

Thus

$$ C_b \leq 1 \qquad\qquad (3.11) $$

Combining (3.10) and (3.11), we have

$$ 0 \leq C_b \leq 1 \qquad\qquad (3.12) $$

Similarly

$$ 0 \leq C_r \leq 1 \qquad\qquad (3.13) $$

In summary, we have the following situation.

$$ \text{If} \qquad 0 \leq R, G, B \leq 1 $$

$$ \qquad\qquad (3.14) $$

$$ \text{then} \quad 0 \leq Y, C_b, C_r \leq 1 $$

Note that the converse is not true. That is, if $0 \leq Y, C_b, C_r \leq 1$, it does **not** imply $0 \leq R, G, B \leq 1$. A knowledge of this helps us in the implementations of the conversion from RGB to YCbCr and vice versa. We mentioned earlier that the eye can only resolve about 200 different intensity levels of each of the RGB components. Therefore, we can quantize all the RGB components in the interval [0,1] to 256 values, from 0 to 255, which can be represented by one byte of storage without any loss of visual quality. In other words, one byte ( or an 8-bit unsigned integer ) is enough to represent all the values of each RGB component. When we convert from RGB to YCbCr, it only requires one 8-bit unsigned integer to represent each YCbCr component. This implicitly implies that all conversions can be done efficiently in integer arithmetic that we shall discuss below.

## 3.3 Conversions between RGB and YCbCr

It is straightforward to write a java program to convert RGB to YCbCr or from YCbCr to RGB. We discussed in the previous section that the implementation can be effectively done in integer arithmetic. However, for clarity of presentation, we shall first discuss a floating point implementation. The java programs presented in this book are mainly for illustration of concepts. In most cases, error checking is omitted and some variable values are hard-coded.

## 3.3.1 Floating Point Implementation

The program listed below shows the conversion between RGB and YCbCr using ITU standard coefficients. It is a direct implementation of equations (3.9). The R, G, and B values, which must lie between [0,1] are hard-coded and converted to Y, Cb, and Cr, which are then converted back to R, G, and B.

Program Listing 3-1

```
/*  Rgbyccf.java
 *  Program to demonstrate the conversions between RGB and YCbCr
 *  using ITU standard coefficients.
 *  Floating point arithmetic is used.
 *  Compile: $javac rgbyccf.java
 *  Execute: $java regyccf
 */

import java.io.*;

class Rgbyccf {
  public static void main(String[] args) {
    //0 <= R, G, B <= 1, sample values
    double R = 0.3, G = 0.7, B = 0.2, Y, Cb, Cr;
    System.out.printf("\nOriginal R, G, B:\t%f, %f, %f", R, G, B );

    Y  = 0.299 * R + 0.587 * G + 0.114 * B;
    Cb = 0.564 * (B - Y) + 0.5;
    Cr = 0.713 * (R - Y) + 0.5;
    System.out.printf("\nConverted Y, Cb, Cr:\t%f, %f, %f",Y,Cb,Cr);

    //recovering R, G, B
    R = Y + 1.402 * Cr - 0.701;
    G = Y - 0.714 * Cr - 0.344 * Cb  + 0.529;
    B = Y + 1.772 * Cb - 0.886;
    System.out.printf("\nRecovered R, G, B:\t%f, %f, %f\n\n",R,G,B);
  }
}
```

The program generates the following outputs:

```
Original R, G, B:      0.300000, 0.700000, 0.200000
Converted Y, Cb, Cr:   0.523400, 0.317602, 0.340716
Recovered R, G, B:     0.300084, 0.699874, 0.200191
```

The recovered R, G, and B values differ slightly from the original ones due to rounding errors in computing and the representation of numbers in binary form.

### 3.3.2 Integer Implementation

The above program illustrates the conversion between RGB and YCbCr using floating-point calculations. However, such an implementation is not practical. Not only that rounding errors are introduced in the computations, floating-point arithmetic is very slow. When compressing an image, we need to apply the conversion to every pixel. Switching to integer-arithmetic in calculations can easily shorten the computing time by a factor of two to three. In RGB-YCbCr conversion, using integer-arithmetic is quite simple because we can always approximate a real number as a fraction between two integers. For example, the coefficients for calculating Y from RGB can be expressed as:

$$0.299 = 19595/2^{16}$$
$$0.587 = 38470/2^{16} \tag{3.15}$$
$$0.114 = 7471/2^{16}$$

The integer-arithmetic expression for Y can be obtained by multiplying the equation

$$Y = 0.299R + 0.587G + 0.114B$$

by $2^{16}$, which becomes

$$2^{16}Y = 19595R + 38470G + 7471B \tag{3.16}$$

At the same time, we quantize the R, G, and B values from [0, 1] to $0, 1, ..., 255$ which can be done by multiplying the floating-point values by 255. We also need to quantize the shifting constants 0.5, 0.701, 0.529, and 0.886 of (3.9) using the same rule by multiplying them by 255, which will become

$$0.5 \times 255 = 128$$
$$0.701 \times 255 = 179$$
$$0.529 \times 255 = 135 \tag{3.17}$$
$$0.886 \times 255 = 226$$

Actually, representing a component of RGB with integer values 0 to 255 is the natural way of a modern computer handling color data. Each pixel has three components ( R, G, and B ) and each component value is saved as an 8-bit unsigned number.

As shown in (3.9), in floating-point representation, the $C_b$ component is given by

$$C_b = 0.564(B - Y) + 0.5$$

After quantization, it becomes

$$C_b = 0.564(B - Y) + 128 \tag{3.18}$$

Multiplying (3.18) by $2^{16}$, we obtain

$$2^{16}C_b = 36962(B - Y) + 128 \times 2^{16} \tag{3.19}$$

The corresponding equation for $C_r$ is:

$$2^{16}C_r = 46727(R - Y) + 128 \times 2^{16} \tag{3.20}$$

As R, G, and B have become integers, we can carry out the calculations using integer multiplications and then divide the result by $2^{16}$. In binary calculations, dividing a value by $2^{16}$ is the same as shifting the value right by 16. Therefore, from (3.16), (3.19) and (3.20), the calculations of $Y$ and $C_b$ using integer-arithmetic can be carried out using the following piece of java code.

$$Y = (19595 * R + 38470 * G + 7471 * B) >> 16;$$
$$Cb = (36962 * (B - Y) >> 16) + 128; \tag{3.21}$$
$$Cr = (46727 * (R - Y) >> 16) + 128;$$

One should note that the sum of the coefficients in calculating $Y$ is $2^{16}$ (i.e. $19595 + 38470 + 7471 = 65536 = 2^{16}$ ), corresponding to the requirement, $k_r + k_g + k_b = 1$ in the floating-point representation.

The constraints of (3.14) and the requirement of $0 \leq R, G, B \leq 255$ implies that in our integer representation,

$$0 \leq Y \leq 255$$
$$0 \leq Cb \leq 255 \tag{3.22}$$
$$0 \leq Cr \leq 255$$

In (3.9) the $R$ component is obtained from $Y$ and $C_r$:

$$R = Y + 1.402C_r - 0.701$$

In integer-arithmetic, this becomes

$$2^{16}R = 2^{16}Y + 91881C_r - 2^{16} \times 179 \tag{3.23}$$

The value of R is obtained by dividing (3.23) by $2^{16}$ as shown below in java code:

$$R = (Y + 91881 * Cr >> 16) - 179; \tag{3.24}$$

We can obtain similar equations for G and B. Combining all these, equations of (3.9) when expressed in integer-arithmetic and in java code will take the following form:

$$Y = (19595 * R + 38470 * G + 7471 * B) >> 16;$$
$$Cb = (36962 * (B - Y) >> 16) + 128;$$
$$Cr = (46727 * (R - Y) >> 16) + 128;$$

$$\tag{3.25}$$

$$R = Y + (91881 * Cr >> 16) - 179;$$
$$G = Y - ((46793 * Cr + 22544 * Cb) >> 16) + 135;$$
$$B = Y + (116129 * Cb >> 16) - 226;$$

In (3.25), it is obvious that a 32-bit integer is large enough to hold any intermediate calculations. Program Listing 3-2 below shows its implementation. The program generates the outputs shown below.

Program Listing 3-2

```
/*  Rgbycci.java
 *  Simple program to demonstrate conversion from RGB to YCbCr and vice
 *  versa using ITU-R recommendation BT.601, and integer-arithmetic.
 *  Since Java does not have data type "unsigned char", we use "int".
 *  Compile: $javac rgbycci.java
 *  Execute: $java regycci
 */
import java.io.*;

/* Note:
 * 216 = 65536
 * kr = 0.299 = 19595 / 216
 * kg = 0.587 = 38470 / 216
 * Kb = 0.114 = 7471 / 216
 * 0.5 = 128 / 255
 * 0.564 = 36962 / 216
 * 0.713 = 46727 / 216
 * 1.402 = 91881 / 216
 * 0.701 = 135 / 255
 * 0.714 = 46793 / 216
 * 0.344 = 22544 / 216
 * 0.529 = 34668 / 216
 * 1.772 = 116129 / 216
 * 0.886 = 226 / 255
 */

class Rgbycci {
  public static void main(String[] args) {
    int R, G, B;      //RGB components
    int Y, Cb, Cr;    //YCbCr components
    //some sample values for demo
    R = 252; G = 120; B = 3;

    //convert from RGB to YCbcr
    Y = ( 19595 * R + 38470 * G + 7471 * B ) >> 16;
    Cb = ( 36962 * ( B - Y ) >> 16) + 128;
    Cr = (46727 * ( R - Y ) >> 16) + 128;
    System.out.printf("\nOriginal RGB & corresponding YCbCr values:");
    System.out.printf("\n\tR = %6d, G = %6d, B = %6d", R, G, B );
    System.out.printf("\n\tY = %6d, Cb = %6d, Cr = %6d", Y, Cb, Cr );

    //convert from YCbCr to RGB
    R = Y + (91881 * Cr >> 16) - 179;
    G = Y -( ( 22544 * Cb + 46793 * Cr ) >> 16) + 135;
    B = Y + (116129 * Cb >> 16) - 226;
    System.out.printf("\n\nRecovered RGB values:");
    System.out.printf("\n\tR = %6d, G = %6d, B = %6d\n\n", R, G, B );
  }
}
```

Outputs of Program Listing 3-2

```
Original RGB & corresponding YCbCr values:
        R =    252, G =    120, B =      3
        Y =    146, Cb =     47, Cr =    203

Recovered RGB values:
        R =    251, G =    120, B =      3
```

Again, some precision has been lost when we recover R, G, and B from the converted Y, Cb, and Cr values. This is due to the right shifts in the calculations, which are essentially truncate operations. Because of rounding or truncating errors, the recovered R, G, and B values may not lie within the range [0, 255]. To remedy this, we can have a function that check the recovered value; if the value is smaller than 0, we set it to 0 and if it is larger than 255, we set it to 255. For example,

```
if (  R < 0 )
   R = 0;
else if ( R > 255 )
   R = 255;
```

However, this check is not necessary when we convert from RGB to YCbCr. This is because from (3.14), we know that we always have $0 \leq Y, C_b, C_r \leq 1$. For any positive real number, $a$ and $0 \leq a \leq 1$ and any positive integer $I$,

$$0 \leq Round(aI) \leq Round(I) = I \quad \text{and similarly} \quad 0 \leq Truncate(aI) \leq I$$

This implies that after quantization and rounding, we always have $0 \leq Y, C_b, C_r \leq 255$.

## 3.4 YCbCr Sampling Formats

We mentioned earlier that we may represent the $C_r$ and $C_b$ components with less bits than Y without much effect on visual quality as our eyes are less sensitive to color than to luminance. This is a simple way of compressing an image. In general, people consider four adjacent pixels of an image at a time and this leads to the standards 4:4:4, 4:2:2, and 4:2:0 sampling formats, which are supported by video standards MPEG-4 and H.264.

### 4:4:4 YCbCr Sampling Formats

4:4:4 YCbCr sampling means that for every four luma samples there are four $C_b$ and four $C_r$ samples and hence the three components, $Y$, $C_b$, and $C_r$ have the same resolution. The numbers indicate the relative sampling rate of each component in the horizontal direction. So at every pixel position in the horizontal direction, a sample of each component of ( $Y$, $C_b$, $C_r$ ) exists. The 4:4:4 YCbCr format requires as many bits as the RGB format and thus preserves the full fidelity of the chrominance components.

### 4:2:2 YCbCr Sampling Formats (High Quality Color Reproduction)

4:2:2 YCbCr sampling means that the chrominance components have the same vertical resolution as the luma but half the horizontal resolution. Therefore, for every four luma samples there are two $C_b$ and two $C_r$ samples. Sometimes this format is referred to as YUY2.

## 4:2:0 YCbCr Sampling Formats (Digital Television and DVD Storage)

4:2:0 YCbCr sampling means that each of the chrominance components has half the horizontal and vertical resolution of the luma component. That is, for every four luma samples ($Y$) there are one $C_b$ and one $C_r$ samples. It is sometimes known as YV12 and is widely used in video conferencing, digital television and digital versatile disk (DVD) storage. The term "4:2:0" is rather confusing as the numbers do not reflect relative resolutions between the components and apparently have been chosen due to historical reasons to distinguish it from the 4:4:4 and 4:2:2 formats.

Figure 3-5 shows the sampling format of 4:2:0; progressive sampling is used.

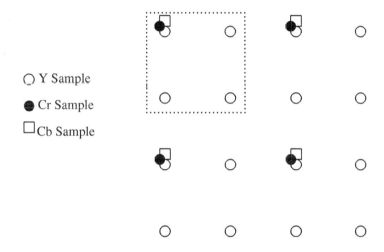

**Figure 3-5**   4:2:0 Sampling Patterns

**Example 3-1**

```
Image resolution: 1024 x 768 pixels

4:4:4 Y ,Cb, Cr resolution: 1024 x 768 samples
Total number of bits: 1024x768x8x3 = 18874368 bits

4:2:0 Y resolution: 1024 x 768 samples
4:2:0 Cb, Cr resolution: 512x384 samples (8 bits for samples)
Total number of bits: (1024 x 768 x 8) + (512 x 384 x 8 x 2)
                    = 9437184 bits

The 4:2:0 format requires half as many bits as the 4:4:4
format and the RGB format.
```

# 3.5 Measuring Video Quality

It is important to have some agreed upon methods to measure the quality of video so that we can evaluate and compare various video images presented to the viewer. However, this is a difficult and often an imprecise process and inherently subjective as there are so many factors that can influence the measurement. In general, there are two  classes of methods that people use to measure video quality: *subjective tests*, where human subjects are asked to assess or rank the images, and *objective tests*, which compute the distortions between the original and processed video sequences.

## 3.5.1 Subjective Quality Measurement

Subjective quality measurement asks human subjects to rank the quality of a video based on their own perception and understanding of quality. For example, a viewer can be asked to rate the quality on a 5-point scale, with quality ratings ranging from bad to excellent as shwon in Figure 3-6.

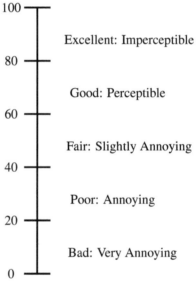

**Figure 3-6**  Example of video quality assessment scale used in subjective tests

Very often, a viewer's perception on a video is affected by many factors such as the viewing environment, the lighting conditions, display size and resolution, the viewing distance, the state of mind of the viewer, whether the material is interesting to the viewer and how the viewer interacts with the visual scene. It is not uncommon that the same viewer who observes the same video at different times under different environments may give significantly different evaluations on the quality of the video. For example, it has been shown that subjective quality ratings of the same video sequence are usually higher when accompanied by good quality sound, which may lower the evaluators' ability to detect impairments. Also, viewers tend to give higher ratings to images with higher contrast or more colorful scenes even though objective testing show that they have larger distortions in comparison to the originals.

Nevertheless, subjective quality assessment still remains the most reliable methods of measuring video quality. It is also the most efficient method to test the performance of components, like video codecs, human vision models and objective quality assessment metrics.

## 3.5.1.1 ITUR BT.500

The ITU-R Recommendation BT-500-11 formalizes video subjective tests by recommending various experiment parameters such as viewing distance, room lighting, display features, selection of subjects and test material, assessment and data analysis methods. There are three most commonly used procedures from the standard: *Double Stimulus Continuous Quality Scale ( DSCQS ), Double Stimulus Impairment Scale ( DSIS ) and Single Stimulus Continuous Quality Evaluation ( SSCQE ) .*

### Double Stimulus Continuous Quality Scale (DSCQS)

In the DSCQS method, a viewer is presented with a pair of images or short sequences X and Y, one after the other. The viewer is asked to rank X and Y by marking on a continuous line with five intervals ranging from 'Bad' to 'Excellent', which has an equivalent numerical scale from 0 to 100, like the one shown in Figure 3-6. The reference and test sequences are shown to the viewer twice in alternating fashion, the order chosen in random. The accessor does not know in advance which is the reference sequence and which is the test sequence. Figure 3-7 shows an experimental set-up that can be used for testing a video coder-decoder ( CODEC ); it is randomly assigned which sequence is X and which sequence is Y.

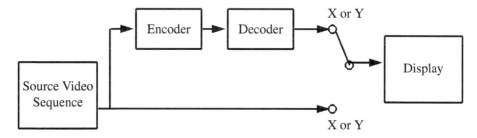

**Figure 3-7**   DSCQS Testing System

### Double Stimulus Impairment Scale (DSIS)

In the DSIS method the reference sequence is always presented before the test sequence, and it is not necessary to show the pair twice. Viewers are asked to rate the sequences on a 5-point scale, ranging from "very annoying" to "imperceptible" like the one shown in Figure 3-6. This method is more effective for evaluating clearly visible impairments, such as noticeable artifacts caused by encoding or transmission.

Both the DSCQS and DSIS methods use short sequences ( 8 - 10 sec ) in the test and this becomes a problem when we want to evaluate video sequences with long duration and quality varies significantly over time like those distributed via the Internet.

### Single Stimulus Continuous Quality Evaluation (SSCQE)

SSCQE is designed to evaluate video sequences with significant temporal variations of quality. In this method, longer sequences ( 20 - 30 minutes ) are presented to the viewers without any reference sequence. The accessors evaluate instantaneously the perceived quality by continuously adjusting a side slider on the DSCQS scale, ranging from "bad" to "excellent". The slider value is periodically sampled every 1 - 2 seconds. Using this method, differences between alternative transmission configurations can be analyzed in a more informative manner. However, as the accessor has to adjust the slider from time to time, she may be distracted and thus the rating may be compromised. Also, because of the 'recency or memory effect', it is quite difficult for the accessor to consistently detect momentary changes in quality, leading to stability and reliability problems of the results.

## 3.5.2 Objective Quality Measurement

Though subjective measurements are the most reliable method to evaluate video qualities, they are complex and expensive as human subjects are required to do the evaluation. It is a lot more convenient and cost-effective to automatically measure quality using an algorithm. Indeed, video processing system developers rely heavily on objective ( algorithmic ) measurement to access video qualities. The simplest and most widely used form of measuring the quality is Peak Signal to Noise Ratio ( PSNR ) which calculates the distortion at the pixel level. Peak Signal to Noise Ratio ( PSNR ) measures the mean squared error ( MSE ) between the reference and test sequences on a logarithmic scale, relative to the square of the highest possible signal value in the image, $(2^n - 1)^2$, where n is the number of bits per image sample. It is described by Equation (3.26):

$$PSNR_{db} = 10log_{10}\frac{(2^n - 1)^2}{MSE} \tag{3.26}$$

The mean squared error, MSE of two $M \times N$ images X and Y where one of the images is considered to be a noisy approximation of the other with sample values $X_{ij}$ and $Y_{ij}$ respectively can be calculated using the following equation:

$$MSE = \frac{1}{M \times N} \sum_{i=0}^{M-1} \sum_{j=0}^{N-1} (X_{ij} - Y_{ij})^2 \tag{3.27}$$

Though PSNR is a straightforward metric to calculate, it cannot describe distortions perceived by a complex and multi-dimensional system like the human visual system (HVS), and thus fails to give good evaluations in many cases. For example, a viewer may be interested in an object of an image but not its background. If the background is largely distorted, the viewer would still rate that the image is of high quality; however, PSNR measure would indicate that the image is of poor quality. The limitations of this metric have led to recent research in image processing that has focused on developing metrics that resembles the response of real human viewers. Many approaches have been proposed but none of them can be accepted as a standard to be used as an alternative to subjective evaluation. The search of a good acceptable objective test for images will remain a research topic for some time.

# Chapter 4    Image and Video Storage Formats

There are a lot of proprietary image and video file formats, each with clear strengths and weaknesses. The file formats are generally not a user-defined option and many of the features are specified by the vendors. This book is about video compression programming and we are not interested in exploring various file formats. However, we do need to know a few formats in order that we can carry out experiments on image or video compression using files downloaded from the Internet. Therefore, we shall discuss a couple simple standard formats and some related tools that we will use later in this book.

## 4.1 Portable Pixel Map ( PPM )

The Portable Pixel Map ( PPM ) file format is a lowest and simplest common denominator color image format. A PPM file contains very little information about the image besides basic colors and thus it is easy to write programs to process the file, which is the purpose of this format. A PPM file consists of a sequence of one or more PPM images. There are no data, delimiters, or padding before, after, or between images. The PPM format closely relates to two other bitmap formats, the PBM format, which stands for Portable Bitmap ( a monochrome bitmap ), and PGM format, which stands for Portable Gray Map ( a gray scale bitmap ).   All these formats are not compressed and consequently the files stored in these formats are usually quite large. In addition, the PNM format means any of the three bitmap formats. You may use the unix manual command **man** to learn the details of the PPM format:

$**man ppm**

The three bitmap formats can be stored in two possible representations:

1. an ASCII text representation (which is extremely verbose), and
2. a binary representation (which is comparatively smaller).

Each PPM image consists of the following (taken from unix ppm manual):

1. A "magic number" for identifying the file type. A ppm images magic number is the two characters "P6".
2. Whitespace (blanks, TABs, CRs, LFs).
3. A width, formatted as ASCII characters in decimal.
4. Whitespace.
5. A height, again in ASCII decimal.
6. Whitespace.
7. The maximum color value (*Maxval*), again in ASCII decimal.  Must be less than 65536 and more than zero.
8. Newline or other single whitespace character.
9. A raster of *Height* rows, in order from top to bottom. Each row consists of *Width* pixels, in order from left to right. Each pixel is a triplet of red, green, and blue samples, in that order. Each sample is represented in pure binary by either 1 or 2 bytes. If the *Maxval* is less than 256, it is 1 byte. Otherwise, it is 2 bytes. The most significant byte is first. A row of an image is horizontal. A column is vertical. The pixels in the image are square and contiguous.

10. In the raster, the sample values are "nonlinear." They are proportional to the intensity of the ITU-R Recommendation BT.709 red, green, and blue.

In summary, a PPM file has a header and a body, which may be created using a text editor. The header is very small with the following properties:

1. The first line contains the magic identifier "P3" or "P6".
2. The second line contains the *width* and *height* of the image in ascii code.
3. The last part of the header is the maximum color intensity integer value.
4. Comments are preceded by the symbol #.

Here are some header examples:

Header example 1

```
P6 1024 788 255
```

Header example 2

```
P6
1024 788
# A comment
255
```

Header example 3

```
P3
1024   # the image width
788    # the image height
       # A comment
1023
```

The following is an example of a PPM file in P3 format.

```
P3
# feep.ppm
4 4
15
0   0   0     0   0   0     0   0   0    15   0 15
0   0   0     0  15   7     0   0   0     0   0  0
0   0   0     0   0   0     0  15   7     0   0  0
15   0 15     0   0   0     0   0   0     0   0  0
```

You can simply use a text editor to create it; for example, copy-and-paste the content into a file named "feep.ppm", which then becomes a PPM file and can be viewed by a browser or the unix utility **xview**. When you execute the unix command,

**$ xview feep.ppm**

you should see a tiny image appear on the upper left corner of your screen along with the following messages,

```
feep.ppm is a 4x4 PPM image with 16 levels
   Building XImage...done
```

## 4.2 The Convert Utility

Once we obtain an image in PPM format, we can easily convert it to other popular formats such as PNG, JPG, or GIF using the **convert** utility, which is a member of the ImageMagick suite of tools. Conversely, if you obtain an image from other sources in another format, you may also use **convert** to convert it to the PPM format. Besides making conversion between image formats, the utility can also resize an image, blur, crop, despeckle, dither, draw on, flip, join, re-sample, and do much more. It can even create an image from text. We use the unix manual command to see the details of its usage:

   $ **man convert**

We can also run 'convert -help' to get a summary of its command options. The following are some simple examples of its usage.

```
$convert feep.ppm  feep.png
$convert house.jpg house.ppm
$convert house.jpg -resize 60% house.png
$convert -size 128x128 xc:transparent -font \
    Bookman-DemiItalic -pointsize 28 -channel RGBA \
     gaussian 0x4 -fill lightgreen -stroke green \
    -draw "text 0,20 'Freedom'" freedom.png
```

The last command creates a PNG ( Portable Network Graphics ) file named "freedom.png" from the text "Freedom". If you want to convert a PDF file to PPM, you may use the utility **pdftoppm**. You may run **"pdftoppm –help"** to find out the details of its usage.

## 4.3 Read and Write PPM Files

In this section, we present a simple java program that shows how to read and write a PPM file. We will use scalar numeric data types to read or write data to a file. In java, a scalar data type is stored in a variable that is passed by value, meaning that a copy of the data variable is made during the invocation of a method. The scalar numeric data types of java are **byte, char, short, int, long, float,** and **double**. A byte is an 8-bit signed quantity. A char is a 16 bit unsigned quantity. A short, an int, and a long are all signed data types and are 16-bit, 32-bit and 64-bit respectively. The floating point scalar data types of java are **float** and **double**. A float is a signed 32-bit IEEE-1985 floating point quantity while a double is a 64-bit IEEE floating point quantity.

Note that java does not have an unsigned byte data type. So in many cases, we use data type **byte** to read and write the color components of an image as each component only has less than 256 different values. However, when we process the data, we need to convert them to integers, keeping in mind that a negative **byte** value actually means an unsigned value larger than 127; for example, -1 represents 255.

The complete java program **Ppmdemo.java** that demonstrates the reading and writing of PPM files is shown in **Listing 4-1**; the file names and some parameters are hard-coded. We have used the Java Advanced Imaging API (JAI) to simplify some of our coding. The Java Advanced Imaging API provides a set of object-oriented interfaces that supports a simple, high-level programming model which allows images to be manipulated easily in Java applications and applets. As shown in the program, JAI is used to read in a PPM file and render the image on screen; it reads in the RGB components of the image using the method **getPixels**() and save them in the integer array *samples*[]. After rendering the image, the program opens the file "testwrite.ppm". It then outputs the PPM header to the file, converts the integer array *samples*[] to the byte array *bytes*[]. sends the byte array to the file using the method **write**().

After compiling the program with the command "$javac Ppmdemo.java", you may test it with a PPM file using a command similar to the following, which reads the image data from the PPM file "beach0.ppm" and renders the image on screen:

```
$ java Ppmdemo ../data/beach0.ppm
```

Figure 4-1 shows the rendering of such an image using the program. The resulted data are saved in "testwrite.ppm" and you may examine the image using the command "$xview testwrite.ppm". If you want to compare the data of the original file "beach0.ppm" with that of the newly created file, you may use the **diff** command:

```
$ diff testwrite.ppm ../data/beach0.ppm
```

You may find that there's no difference between the files "testwrite.ppm" and "beach0.ppm".

**Program Listing 4-1**

---

```java
/*
   Ppmdemo.java
   PPM files may either have ASCII or raw (binary) data.
   The decoder automatically determines the data format
   and reads the data accordingly. By default the encoder
   stores the image data in raw format whenever possible.
*/
import java.io.*;
import java.awt.Frame;
import java.awt.image.*;
import javax.media.jai.JAI;
import javax.media.jai.RenderedOp;
import com.sun.media.jai.codec.FileSeekableStream;
import javax.media.jai.widget.ScrollingImagePanel;
import com.sun.media.jai.codec.PNMEncodeParam;

public class Ppmdemo {
  public static void main(String[] args) throws InterruptedException {
    if (args.length != 1) {
      System.out.println("Usage: java " + "Ppmdemo" +
                                      "input_image_filename");
      System.exit(-1);
    }

    /*
     * Create an input stream from the specified file name
     * to be used with the file decoding operator.
     */
    FileSeekableStream stream = null;
    try {
      stream = new FileSeekableStream(args[0]);
    } catch (IOException e) {
      e.printStackTrace();  System.exit(0);
    }

    //First we demonstrate the reading of pnm data

    /* Create an operator to decode the image file. */
    RenderedOp image1 = JAI.create("stream", stream);

    /* Get the width and height of image. */
```

```
int width = image1.getWidth();
int height = image1.getHeight();

//allocate array to hold RGB data
int [] samples = new int[3*width*height];

Raster ras = image1.getData();
//save pixel RGB data in samples[]
ras.getPixels( 0, 0, width, height, samples );

System.out.printf("Image width=%d, height=%d\n", width, height );

/* Attach image1 to a scrolling panel to be displayed. */
ScrollingImagePanel panel=new ScrollingImagePanel(image1,width,height);

/* Create a frame to contain the panel. */
Frame window = new Frame("Displaying PPM Data");
window.add(panel);
window.pack();    window.show();
Thread.sleep( 2000 ); //sleep for two seconds
window.dispose();       //close the frame

//now, we demonstrate the writing of ppm data
String filename = "testwrite.ppm";
try {
  File f = new File ( filename );
  OutputStream out = new FileOutputStream( f );

  //First write PPM header.
  byte [] P6 = { 'P', '6', '\n' };
  out.write ( P6 );
  String s = Integer.toString ( width );
  for ( int i = 0; i < s.length(); ++i )    //write the width
    out.write ( s.charAt(i) );
  out.write ( ' ' );
  s = Integer.toString ( height );
  for ( int i = 0; i < s.length(); ++i )    //write the height
    out.write ( s.charAt(i) );
  out.write ( '\n' );
  //write color levels
  byte [] colorLevels = { '2', '5', '5', '\n' };
  out.write ( colorLevels );

  int size = 3 * width * height;
  byte [] bytes = new byte[size];
  //save the image data
  for ( int i = 0; i < size; i += 1 ){
     bytes[i] = (byte) samples[i];
  }
  out.write ( bytes );
  out.close();
} catch (IOException e) {
  e.printStackTrace();
  System.exit(0);
}
  }
}
```

**Figure 4-1** Displaying a PPM Image

## 4.4 Common Intermediate Format ( CIF )

There exists a wide variety of 'standard' video formats which would lay a heavy burden on a developer to study and understand them for encoding or decoding data saved in their formats. In practice, it is common for a party to use a utility program to capture or convert to a set of standard 'intermediate formats' before compressing or transmitting the data. The **Common Intermediate Format ( CIF )**, first proposed in the H.261 standard, is designed for the purpose of standardizing the horizontal and vertical resolutions in pixels of YCbCr video data. CIF allows easy conversions to standard television systems of PAL ( Phase Alternating Line ) and NTSC ( the National Television System Committee ). CIF is also known as **FCIF** ( Full Common Intermediate Format ); it defines a video sequence with a luminance resolution of $352 \times 288$ and a frame rate of $30000/1001 (\approx 29.97)$ fps with color encoding using YCbCr 4:2:0. Note that a CIF-image ( $352 \times 288$ ) consists of $22 \times 18$ macroblocks, each of which is a $16 \times 16$ pixel block that we shall discuss in Chapter 5. **QCIF**, meaning "Quarter CIF" defines a resolution with frame width and height halved as compared to that of CIF. Similarly, **SQCIF** ( Sub Quarter CIF ), **4CIF** ( $4 \times$ CIF ) and **16CIF** define various resolutions with CIF as the basis. Table 4-1 below summarizes these formats.

**Table 4-1**   Common Intermediate Format

| Format | Luminance Resolution ( horizontal × vertical ) | Bits / Frame (4:2:0, 8 bits/Sample) |
|---|---|---|
| CIF | $352 \times 288$ | 1216512 |
| QCIF | $176 \times 144$ | 304128 |
| SQCIF | $128 \times 96$ | 147456 |
| 4CIF | $704 \times 576$ | 4866048 |
| 16CIF | $1408 \times 1152$ | 14598144 |

The CIF formats do not use square pixels. Rather, they specify a pixel to have a native aspect rate of approximately 1.222:1 because on older television systems, a pixel aspect ratio of 1.2:1 was the standard for 525-line systems. As computer systems use square-pixel, a CIF raster has to be rescaled horizontally by about 109% in order to avoid a "stretched" appearance.

The choice of a particular CIF format depends on the application and available resources like storage and transmission capacity. For example, video conferencing requires real-time transmission of data and its applications commonly use CIF and QCIF that gives fairly good resolution but do not give an overwhelming amount of data. As standard-definition-television has higher transmission bandwidth and DVD-videos are recorded off-line, 4CIF is an appropriate format. For mobile multimedia applications, QCIF or SQCIF are appropriate as the display resolution and transmission bandwidth are limited. Column 3 of Table 4-1 shows the number of bits required to represent one uncompressed frame for each CIF format, where YCbCr 4:2:0 format and 8 bits per luma and chroma sample are used.

# Chapter 5   Macroblocks

## 5.1 Introduction

In general, a PC image or a frame with moderate size consists of many pixels and requires a large amount of storage space and computing power to process it. For example, an image of size 240 x 240 has 57600 pixels and requires $\frac{3}{2} \times 57600 = 86,400$ bytes of storage space if **4:2:0** format is used. It is difficult and inconvenient to process all of these data simultaneously. In order to make things more manageable, an image is decomposed into **macroblocks**. A macroblock is a 16 x 16 pixel-region, which is the basic unit for processing a frame and is used in video compression standards like MPEG, H.261, H.263, and H.264. A macroblock has a total of $16 \times 16 = 256$ pixels.

In our coding, we shall also process an image in the units of macroblocks. For simplicity and the convenience of discussion, we assume that each of our frames consists of an integral number of macroblocks. That is, both the width and height of an image are divisible by 16. The Common Intermediate Format ( CIF ) discussed in Chapter 4 also has a resolution of $352 \times 288$ that corresponds to $22 \times 18$ macroblocks. In addition, we shall use the **4:2:0** YCbCr format; a macroblock then consists of a $16 \times 16$ Y sample block, an $8 \times 8$ Cb sample block and an $8 \times 8$ Cr sample block. To better organize the data, we further divide the $16 \times 16$ Y sample block into four $8 \times 8$ sample blocks. Therefore, a **4:2:0** macroblock has a total of six $8 \times 8$ sample blocks; we label these blocks from 0 to 5 as shown in Figure 5-1:

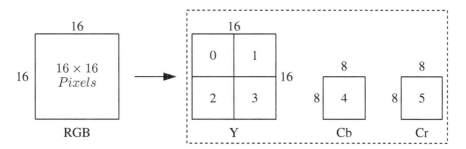

**Figure 5-1**. Macroblock of 4:2:0

## 5.2 Implementing RGB and 4:2:0 YCbCr Transformation for Video Frames

When implementing the conversion of RGB to YCbCr, we process the data in units of macroblocks. A macroblock has four $8 \times 8$ Y sample blocks, one $8 \times 8$ Cb sample block and one $8 \times 8$ Cr sample block. We assume that a frame has an integral number of macroblocks. In the **4:2:0** YCbCr format, for each RGB pixel, we make a conversion for Y but we only make a conversion for Cb and Cr for every four RGB pixels ( see Figure 3-5 ). Each group of four pixels is formed by grouping 4 neighbouring pixels. For simplicity, when calculating the Cb, and Cr components, we simply use the upper left pixel of the four and ignore the other three. ( Alternatively, one can take the average value of the four RGB pixel values when calculating the Cb and Cr values. )

Before discussing the implementation of RGB-YCbCr transformations, we would like to highlight some programming features of java that some readers may overlook or misundestand.

## Some Notes on Java Programming

Firstly, java always passes parameters by values; it does not support pass-by-reference. This means that we cannot change the value of a variable by passing it as an argument to a function.

Secondly, a java object variable is analogous to an object pointer in C++. For example, suppose we have defined a **Pixel** class:

```
class Pixel {
  int red;
  int green;
  int blue;
};
```

The java code,

```
Pixel aPixel = new Pixel();        //java
```

is the same as the C++ code,

```
Pixel *aPixel = new Pixel();       //C++
```

Basically, we can always regard a java object variable as a pointer ( address ) pointing to the object. Though we cannot change the value of a function parameter, we can change the state of the object that a function parameter points at. For example, the following function changes the value of *red*:

```
void setPixel ( Pixel p ) {
  p.red = 100;
}
```

The function sets the value of *red* of the **Pixel** object pointed by *p* to 100. On the other hand, the following piece of code does not make any change to the object.

```
void setPixel ( Pixel p ) {
  p = new Pixel();
  p.red = 100;
}
```

This is because in the function, *p* is assigned a new value, pointing to a local object. This new local pointer value will not be passed back to the calling function.

In general, most parts of a java program written for manipulating objects involve assigning pointer values rather than object values. For example, consider a statement such as the following:

```
x = objectVariable;
```

In C++, this means copying the object denoted by *objectVariable* to variable *x*. They then represent two different objects. Changing *x* will not affect *objectVariable*. However, in java, **no object-copying** occurs; the statement simply means assigning the pointer *object-Variable* to *x*. When you change the object referenced by *x*, you also change the object referenced by *objectVariable* as both of them point to the same object.

Thirdly, unlike C++, when we declare an array of objects, java does not create the objects automatically. Rather, it defines an array of pointers initialized to NULL. For example, if we want to create an array of Pixel objects, we must use the **new** operator to do the instantiation like the following:

```
class PixelArray {
  Pixel [] pa = new Pixel[16];//create an array of NULL pointers
  PixelArray(){                    //constructor
    for ( int i = 0; i < 16; ++i ) //instantiation
      pa[i] = new Pixel();
  }
}
```

Fourthly, the **round**() function of the java Math library does not work properly like that of C++. Java rounds 0.5 to 1 but it rounds −0.5 to 0 rather than −1. That is, Math.round ( 0.5 ) yields 1 but Math.round ( -0.5 ) yields 0. This asymmetry in handling positive and negative numbers may cause problems in programming in the future. Readers may need to add some extra coding to correct this defect in their programs.

Finally, we would like to explain briefly the difference between a class and an object. We believe most readers understand the difference but there may be a few who come from a different programming background and may not be familiar with terminologies of object-oriented programming (OOP). In short, a class refers to the code of a structure that performs certain tasks. A class contains both data (referred to as attributes), and functions (referred to as methods). An object is an instantiation of a class and is instantiated by the **new** keyword. This is in analogy of building a house. The blueprint that specifies the details of building a house corresponds to a class. A house built based on the blueprint corresponds to an object. Building a house consumes resources such as glass, wood and stone. In the same way, creating an object requires resources such as memory and files. We can build more than one house using the same blueprint. In a similar sense, we can create more than one object based on the same class. When we use a class name in a description, we may refer to either the class or an object depending on the context of description. Also, java functions and methods mean the same thing in this book.

## Implementation

For convenience of programming, we define four classes: the object of class **RGB** holds the RGB values of a pixel, **YCbCr** holds the YCbCr values of a pixel, and **RGB_MACRO** and **YCbCr_MACRO** hold the RGB and YCbCr sample values of a macroblock ( 16 × 16 *pixels* ) of Figure 5-1 respectively. We put all these definitions in the file "common.java", which is listed in Figure 5-2 below.

```
//common.java
class RGB {    //defines an RGB pixel
  int R;       //0 - 255
  int G;       //0 - 255
  int B;       //0 - 255
}
class YCbCr {
  int Y;       //0 - 255
  int Cb;      //0 - 255
  int Cr;      //0 - 255
}
class RGB_MACRO {  //16x16 RGB block
  RGB [] rgb;
  RGB_MACRO(){     //constructor
    rgb = new RGB[256];
    //allocate memory
    for ( int i = 0; i < 256; ++i )
      rgb[i] = new RGB();
  }
}
class YCbCr_MACRO {          //4:2:0 YCbCr Macroblock
  int [] Y = new int[256];  //16x16 (four 8x8 samples)
  int [] Cb  = new int[64]; //8x8
  int [] Cr  = new int[64]; //8x8
}
class RGBImage {
  int width;                //image width
  int height;               //image height
  RGB  [] ibuf;             //image data buffer
  //constructor
  RGBImage ( int w, int h ) {
    width = w;
    height = h;
    ibuf = new RGB[width*height];//image data buffer
    for ( int i = 0; i < width * height; ++i )
      ibuf[i] = new RGB();
  }
}
```

**Figure 5-2** Public classes for Processing Macro Blocks

We have learned in Chapter 3 how to convert an RGB pixel to YCbCr values using integer arithmetic. We define a function named **rgb2ycbcr** ( RGB $a$, YCbCr $b$ ) to convert an RGB pixel $a$ to a YCbCr pixel $b$ and a function named **rgb2y**( RGB $a$ ) to convert an RGB pixel $a$ to a Y component and returns its value as an integer. Now, we need a function to convert an entire RGB macroblock to a **4:2:0** YCbCr macroblock, which consists of four $8 \times 8$ Y sample blocks, one $8 \times 8$ Cb sample block and one $8 \times 8$ Cr sample block. The following function **macroblock2ycbcr()**, listed in Figure 5-3 does the job; the input of it is a java object variable ( pointer ) pointing to an **RGB_MACRO** object containing the data of a $16 \times 16$ RGB macroblock; the function converts the RGB values to YCbCr values and put the data in a **YCbCr_MACRO** object pointed by the object variable of the second input parameter of the function and thus the converted values will be sent back to the calling function via this parameter.

```
  /*
    Convert an RGB macro block ( 16x16 ) to
    4:2:0 YCbCr sample blocks ( six 8x8 blocks ).
  */
void macroblock2ycbcr(RGB_MACRO rgb_macro,YCbCr_MACRO ycbcr_macro)
{
    int i, j, k, r;
    YCbCr ycc = new YCbCr();

    r = k = 0;
    for ( i = 0; i < 16; ++i ) {
      for ( j = 0; j < 16; ++j ) {
        //need one Cb, Cr for every 4 pixels
        if ( ( i & 1 ) == 0 && ( j & 1 ) == 0 ) {
          //convert to Y and Cb, Cr values
          rgb2ycbcr ( rgb_macro.rgb[r], ycc );
          ycbcr_macro.Y[r] = ycc.Y;
          ycbcr_macro.Cb[k] = ycc.Cb;
          ycbcr_macro.Cr[k] = ycc.Cr;
          k++;
        } else { //only need Y component for other 3 pixels
          ycbcr_macro.Y[r] = rgb2y ( rgb_macro.rgb[r] );
        }
        r++;       //convert every pixel for Y
      }
    }
}
```

**Figure 5-3** Function for converting an RGB macroblock to 4:2:0 YCbCr Sample Blocks

In Figure 5-3, the statement "**if ( ( i & 1 ) == 0 && ( j & 1 ) == 0 ) {** " is true only when both $i$ and $j$ are even. This implies that it selects one pixel from a group of four neighbouring pixels as shown in Figure 3-5, and makes a conversion to Y, Cb, Cr; it makes a conversion of only the Y component for the other 3 pixels as we have considered the 4:2:0 YCbCr format. For example, the statement is true when

$(i, j) = (0, 0), (0, 2), ..., (2, 0), (2, 2), ..., (14, 14).$

We can similarly define a function, **ycbcr2macroblock()** to convert a YCbCr macroblock to an RGB macroblock. The following program, **RgbYcc.java** of Listing 5-1 contains all the functions we need to convert video frames from RGB to YCbCr and back. It can be compiled with the command "javac RgbYcc.java".

**Program Listing 5-1** Conversions between RGB and YCbCr

```
/*
  RgbYcc.java
  Class for converting RGB to YCbCr and vice versa.
*/

/*
  Convert from RGB to YCbCr using  ITU-R recommendation BT.601.
    Y = 0.299R + 0.587G + 0.114B
   Cb = 0.564(B - Y ) + 0.5
   Cr = 0.713(R - Y ) + 0.5

  Integer arithmetic is used to speed up calculations.
  Note:
      2^16 = 65536
```

```
        kr = 0.299 = 19595' / 2^16
        kg = 0.587 = 38470 / 2^16
        Kb = 0.114 =  7471 / 2^16
        0.5 = 128 / 255
        0.564 = 36962 / 2^16
        0.713 = 46727 / 2^16
        1.402 = 91881 / 2^16
        0.701 = 135 / 255
        0.714 = 46793 / 2^16
        0.344 = 22544 / 2^16
        0.529 = 34668 / 2^16
        1.772 = 116129 / 2^16
        0.886 = 226 / 255
*/

import java.io.*;

class RgbYcc {
  public void rgb2ycbcr( RGB rgb, YCbCr ycc )
  {
    //coefs summed to 65536 (1 << 16), so Y is always within [0, 255]
    ycc.Y = (19595 * rgb.R + 38470 * rgb.G + 7471 * rgb.B ) >> 16;
    ycc.Cb = ( 36962 * ( rgb.B - ycc.Y ) >> 16 ) + 128 ;
    ycc.Cr = ( 46727 * ( rgb.R - ycc.Y )  >> 16 ) + 128 ;
  }

  //just convert an RGB pixel to Y component
  public int rgb2y( RGB rgb )
  {
    int y;

    y = ( 19595 * rgb.R + 38470 * rgb.G + 7471 * rgb.B ) >> 16;
    return y;
  }

  //limit value to lie within [0,255]
  public RGB chop ( RGB rgb )
  {
    if (rgb.R < 0 || rgb.B < 0 || rgb.B < 0 ||
        rgb.R > 255 || rgb.B > 255 || rgb.G > 255 )
      if ( rgb.R < 0 ) rgb.R = 0;
      else if ( rgb.R > 255 ) rgb.R = 255;
      if ( rgb.G < 0 ) rgb.G = 0;
      else if ( rgb.G > 255 ) rgb.G = 255;
      if ( rgb.B < 0 ) rgb.B = 0;
      else if ( rgb.B > 255 ) rgb.B = 255;

    return rgb;
  }

/*
  Convert from YCbCr to RGB domain. Using ITU-R standard:
    R = Y + 1.402Cr - 0.701
    G = Y - 0.714Cr - 0.344Cb + 0.529
    B = Y + 1.772Cb - 0.886
  Integer arithmetic is used to speed up calculations.
*/

  public void ycbcr2rgb( YCbCr ycc, RGB rgb )
  {
```

```
    rgb.R = ycc.Y              + ( 91881 * ycc.Cr   >> 16 ) - 179;
    rgb.G = ycc.Y -(( 22544 * ycc.Cb + 46793 * ycc.Cr ) >> 16) + 135;
    rgb.B = ycc.Y   + (116129 * ycc.Cb   >> 16 ) - 226;

    rgb = chop ( rgb );      //enforce values to lie within [0,255]
}

/*
  Convert an RGB macro block ( 16x16 ) to
  4:2:0 YCbCr sample blocks ( six 8x8 blocks ).
*/

void macroblock2ycbcr ( RGB_MACRO rgb_macro, YCbCr_MACRO ycbcr_macro )
{
    int i, j, k, r;
    YCbCr ycc = new YCbCr();

    r = k = 0;
    for ( i - 0; i < 16; ++i ) {
      for ( j = 0; j < 16; ++j ) {
        //need one Cb, Cr for every 4 pixels
        if ( ( i & 1 ) == 0 && ( j & 1 ) == 0 ) {
          //convert to Y and Cb, Cr values
          rgb2ycbcr ( rgb_macro.rgb[r], ycc );
          ycbcr_macro.Y[r] = ycc.Y;
          ycbcr_macro.Cb[k] = ycc.Cb;
          ycbcr_macro.Cr[k] = ycc.Cr;
          k++;
        } else { //only need the Y component for other 3 pixels
          ycbcr_macro.Y[r] = rgb2y ( rgb_macro.rgb[r] );
        }
        r++;     //convert every pixel for Y
      }
    }
}

/*
  Convert the six 8x8 YCbCr sample blocks to RGB macroblock ( 16x16 ).
*/
void ycbcr2macroblock( YCbCr_MACRO ycbcr_macro, RGB_MACRO rgb_macro )
{
    int i, j, k, r;
    YCbCr ycc = new YCbCr();

    r = k = 0;
    for ( i = 0; i < 16; ++i ) {
      for ( j = 0; j < 16; ++j ) {
        //one Cb, Cr has been saved for every 4 pixels
        if ( ( i & 1 ) == 0 && ( j & 1 ) == 0 ) {
          ycc.Y = ycbcr_macro.Y[r];
          ycc.Cb = ycbcr_macro.Cb[k];
          ycc.Cr = ycbcr_macro.Cr[k];
          k++;
        } else {
          ycc.Y = ycbcr_macro.Y[r];
          ycc.Cb = ycbcr_macro.Cb[k];
          ycc.Cr = ycbcr_macro.Cr[k];
        }
        ycbcr2rgb ( ycc, rgb_macro.rgb[r] );
        r++;
```

```
        }
      }
    }
  }
----------------------------------------------------------------------------
```

After we have implemented the functions to convert an RGB macroblock to a YCbCr macroblock and vice versa, we can utilize these functions to convert an image frame from RGB to YCbCr and save the data. As 4:2:0 format is used, the saved YCbCr data are only half as much as the original RGB data. In our discussions, the four Y sample blocks of a YCbCr macroblock are stored in the linear array Y[256] ( Figure 5-2 ). In some cases, it is more convenient to separate the 256 Y samples into four sample blocks, each with size 64 ( = 8 × 8 ). The relation between the indexes of the linear array and the four sample blocks, labeled 0, 1, 2, and 3 is shown in Figure 5-4; the following piece of code shows how to separate the data into four 8 × 8 blocks:

```
int b, i, j, k, r;

//one macroblock has 256 Y samples
byte [] Yblock = new byte[256];

 r = 0;
//save four 8x8 Y sample blocks
for ( b = 0; b < 4; b++ ) {
  if ( b < 2 )
    k = 8 * b;                    //points to beginning of block
  else
    k = 128 + 8 * ( b - 2 );  //points to beginning of block
    for ( i = 0; i < 8; i++ ) { //one sample-block
      if ( i > 0 ) k += 16;       //advance k by 16 (one row)
      for ( j = 0; j < 8; j++ ) {
        Yblock[r] = ( byte ) ycbcr_macro.Y[k+j];
        r++;
      }
    }
}
```

The array *Yblock* saves the Y sample blocks in the order of block 0, 1, 2 and 3 as shown in Figure 5-4. In the code, *Yblock* is a **byte** array, which prepares us to write the data to a file conveniently. On the other hand, *ycbcr_macro.Y* is a 32-bit integer array and we know that *Y* is always positive and lies in the range [0, 255]. However, in java, a **byte** is an 8-bit signed value. This means that any positive value larger than 127 and smaller than 256 will become a negative number when we convert it from an **int** to a **byte**. Will this cause error in the program? The answer is **no** because in a modern computer, any number is represented as a binary number. It is the way that we interpret a binary number that gives us a signed or an unsigned value. For example, an **int** of value 255 is represented by the 32-bit number 00000000000000000000000011111111. When we cast this to a **byte**, we take the lower eight bits, 11111111. If we interpret 11111111 as a signed-number, we obtain the value −1 but if we interpret it as an unsigned-number, we obtain the value 255. Regardless of our interpretation, we are processing the binary number 11111111. So if we save this binary number in a file and read it back, we always get back the same binary number. Of course, we need to be careful in our coding so that we will not change the 8-bit

number 11111111 into the 32-bit binary number 11111111111111111111111111111111,
which also represents the value of −1.

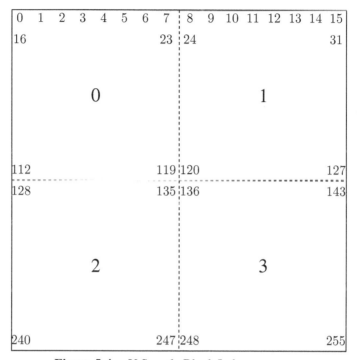

**Figure 5-4**    Y Sample Block Indexes

Program Listing 5-2 below shows the program **Encode.java** that contains the complete
code of the class **Encode** that has functions to convert an RGB frame to YCbCr and to
save the converted data in a file.  The class only has two member functions, namely,
**save_yccblocks()** and **encode()**.  The function **save_yccblock()** saves one YCbCr block
in the specified file; the function **encode()** makes use of **save_yccblocks()** and other functions of **RgbYcc** to convert a frame of RGB data to YCbCr and save the converted data in
the file.

**Program Listing 5-2** Encode Class

```
/*
  Encode.java
  Contains functions that convert an RGB frame to YCbCr and save the
  converted data.
*/

import java.io.*;

class Encode {
  //save one YCbCr macroblock.
  public void save_yccblocks(YCbCr_MACRO ycbcr_macro,DataOutputStream out)
  {
```

```java
int b, i, j, k, r;

//one macroblock has 256 Y samples
byte [] Yblock = new byte[256];

 r = 0;
//save four 8x8 Y sample blocks
for ( b = 0; b < 4; b++ ) {
  if ( b < 2 )
    k = 8 * b;                    //points to beginning of block
  else
    k = 128 + 8 * ( b - 2 );  //points to beginning of block
    for ( i = 0; i < 8; i++ ) { //one sample-block
      if ( i > 0 ) k += 16;      //advance k by 16 (length of 1 row)
      for ( j = 0; j < 8; j++ ) {
        Yblock[r] = ( byte ) ycbcr_macro.Y[k+j];
        r++;
      }
    }
}

//save one 8x8 Cb block
byte [] Cb_block = new byte[64];
k = 0;
for ( i = 0; i < 8; ++i ) {
  for ( j = 0; j < 8; ++j ) {
    Cb_block[k] = ( byte ) ycbcr_macro.Cb[k];
    k++;
  }
}

//save one 8x8 Cr block
byte [] Cr_block = new byte[64];
k = 0;
for ( i = 0; i < 8; ++i ) {
  for ( j = 0; j < 8; ++j ) {
    Cr_block[k] = ( byte ) ycbcr_macro.Cr[k];
    k++;
  }
}

//save 4 Y sample blocks, one Cb block, one Cr block in file
try {
  out.write ( Yblock );
  out.write ( Cb_block );
  out.write ( Cr_block );
} catch (IOException e) {
  e.printStackTrace();
  System.exit(0);
}
}

/*
  Convert 1 frome of RGB to YCbCr and save the converted data.
*/
public void encode ( RGBImage image, DataOutputStream out )
{
  int row, col, i, j, k, r;
  RGB_MACRO rgb_macro = new RGB_MACRO();
  //macroblock for YCbCr samples
```

```
    YCbCr_MACRO ycbcr_macro = new YCbCr_MACRO();
    RgbYcc rgbycc = new RgbYcc ();

    for ( row = 0; row < image.height; row += 16 ) {
      for ( col = 0; col < image.width; col += 16 ) {
        k = row * image.width + col;
        r = 0;
        for ( i = 0; i < 16; ++i ) {
  for ( j = 0; j < 16; ++j )
    rgb_macro.rgb[r++] = image.ibuf[k++];
  k += ( image.width - 16 );   //next row within macroblock
        }
        //convert from RGB to YCbCr
        rgbycc.macroblock2ycbcr( rgb_macro, ycbcr_macro );

        //save one YCbCr macroblock
        save_yccblocks( ycbcr_macro, out );
      } //for col
    } //for row
  }
}
```

Note that in **Encode.java** of Listing 5-2, the function **save_yccblocks()** uses **out.write()** to send 8-bit bytes to the file. In the decoding process, we will use something like **in.read()** to read one 8-bit byte back but the byte read is returned as a 32-bit integer and thus the value lies in the range [0, 255].

The corresponding code that converts a file of YCbCr data to RGB data is shown in **Decode.java** of Listing 5-3.

**Program Listing 5-3** Decode Class

```
/*
  Decode.java
  Contains functions to read YCbCr data from a file and convert from YCbCr
  to RGB.
*/
import java.io.*;

class Decode {
 /*
  Get YCbCr data from file pointed by in. Put the four 8x8 Y sample blocks,
  one 8x8 Cb sample block and one 8x8 Cr sample block into a class object
  of YCbCr_MACRO.
  Return: number of bytes read from file.
 */
  public int get_yccblocks( YCbCr_MACRO ycbcr_macro, DataInputStream in )
  {
    int r, row, col, i, j, k, n, b, c;

    byte abyte;

    n = 0;
    //read data from file and put them in four 8x8 Y sample blocks
    for ( b = 0; b < 4; b++ ) {
      if ( b < 2 )
        k = 8 * b;                        //points to beginning of block
```

```
      else
        k = 128 + 8 * ( b - 2 );   //points to beginning of block
      for ( i = 0; i < 8; i++ ) { //one sample-block
        if ( i > 0 ) k += 16;      //advance by 1 row of macroblock
        for ( j = 0; j < 8; j++ ){
   try {
              if ( ( c = in.read() ) == -1 )    //read one byte
                break;
              ycbcr_macro.Y[k+j] = c;
            } catch (IOException e) {
                e.printStackTrace();
                System.exit(0);
            }
             n++;
        } //for j
      } //for i
    } //for b

    //now do that for 8x8 Cb block
    k = 0;
    for ( i = 0; i < 8; ++i ) {
      for ( j = 0; j < 8; ++j ) {
        try {
          if ( ( c = in.read() ) == -1 )        //read one byte
            break;
          ycbcr_macro.Cb[k++] = c;
        } catch (IOException e) {
          e.printStackTrace();
          System.exit(0);
        }
        n++;
      }
    }

    //now do that for 8x8 Cr block
    k = 0;
    for ( i = 0; i < 8; ++i ) {
      for ( j = 0; j < 8; ++j ) {
        try {
          if ( ( c = in.read() ) == -1 )        //read one byte
            break;
          ycbcr_macro.Cr[k++] = c;
        } catch (IOException e) {
          e.printStackTrace();
          System.exit(0);
        }
        n++;
      }
    }
    return n;              //number of bytes read
}

/*   Read in YCbCr data from file.
 *   Convert a YCbCr frame to an RGB frame.
 *   Return RGB data via parameter image.
 */
public int decode_yccFrame ( RGBImage image, DataInputStream in )
{
  int r, row, col, i, j, k, block;
  int n = 0;
```

```
//16x16 pixel macroblock; assume 24-bit for each RGB pixel
RGB_MACRO rgb_macro = new RGB_MACRO();
YCbCr_MACRO ycbcr_macro = new YCbCr_MACRO();
RgbYcc rgbycc = new RgbYcc();
for ( row = 0; row < image.height; row += 16 ) {
  for ( col = 0; col < image.width; col += 16 ) {
    int m = get_yccblocks( ycbcr_macro, in );
    if ( m <= 0 ) { System.out.printf("\nout of data\n"); return m;}
    n += m;
    rgbycc.ycbcr2macroblock( ycbcr_macro, rgb_macro );
    k = (row * image.width + col); //points to macroblock beginning
    r = 0;
    for ( i = 0; i < 16; ++i ) {
      for ( j = 0; j < 16; ++j ) {
        image.ibuf[k].R = rgb_macro.rgb[r].R;
        image.ibuf[k].G = rgb_macro.rgb[r].G;
        image.ibuf[k].B = rgb_macro.rgb[r].B;
        k++;   r++;
      }
      k += (image.width - 16);   //points to next row of macroblock
    }
  } //for col
  } //for row
  return n;  //number of bytes read
}
}
```

In **Decode.java** of Listing 5-3, the function **get_yccblocks()**  gets YCbCr data from a file pointed by *in*; the data are organized in macroblocks, consisting of four $8 \times 8$ Y sample blocks, one $8 \times 8$ Cb sample block and one $8 \times 8$ Cr sample block. The function saves the data in a class object of YCbCr_MACRO and returns the data via the parameter *ycbcr_macro*. The function **decode_yccFrame()** uses **get_yccblocks()** to convert the YCbCr data of an image or frame to RGB, stores the RGB data in the buffer of a class object of RGBImage and returns the data via the first function parameter *image*.

## 5.3 Testing Implementation Using PPM Image

We can test the implementation presented in section 5.2 using a PPM image, the format of which has been discussed in Chapter 4. It is the simplest portable format that one can have and does not have any compression. As pointed out before, the implementation of section 5.2 only works for images with height and width divisible by 16. If you obtain a PPM image with dimensions non-divisible by 16, you need to use the "convert" utility with the "-resize" option to change its dimensions before doing the test.

Again, we simplify our code by hard-coding the file names used for testing. We put the testing files in the directory "../data/", a child directory of the parent of the directory testing programs reside. Suppose the testing file is called "beach.ppm". All we want to do is to read the RGB data of "beach.ppm", convert them to YCbCr and save the YCbCr macroblocks in the file "beach.ycc". In saving the YCbCr macroblocks, we also need to save the image dimensions for decoding. We employ a very simple format for our ".ycc" file; the first 8 bytes contain the header text, "YCbCr420"; the next two bytes contain the image width followed by another two bytes of image height; data start from the thirteenth byte.

We then read the YCbCr macroblocks back from "beach.ycc" into a buffer and convert the YCbCr data to RGB. We save the recovered RGB data in the file "beach1.ppm". The testing program **test_encode_ppm.cpp** that performs these tasks is listed in Listing 5-3.

**Program Listing 5-3**

---

```
/*
 * Test_encode_ppm.java
 * Code testing the encoding and decoding of an RGB frame to and
 * from YCbCr format. The original RGB data are saved in a PPM
 * file.  The restored RGB data are saved in another PPM file.
 */
import java.io.*;
import java.awt.Frame;
import java.awt.image.*;
import javax.media.jai.JAI;
import javax.media.jai.RenderedOp;
import com.sun.media.jai.codec.FileSeekableStream;
import javax.media.jai.widget.ScrollingImagePanel;
import com.sun.media.jai.codec.PNMEncodeParam;

public class Test_encode_ppm {
  private static byte [] header = {'Y','C','b','C','r','4','2','0'};

  public static void write_ycc_header(int width, int height,
                                             DataOutputStream out)
  {
    try {
      out.write ( header );
      out.writeInt ( width );
      out.writeInt ( height );
    } catch (IOException e) {
      e.printStackTrace();
      System.exit(0);
    }
  }

  public static int read_ycc_header( RGBImage rgbimage,  DataInputStream in)
  {
    byte [] bytes = new byte[header.length];
    try {
      in.read ( bytes );
      rgbimage.width  = in.readInt ();
      rgbimage.height = in.readInt ();
    } catch (IOException e) {
      e.printStackTrace();
      System.exit(0);
    }
    for ( int i = 0; i < header.length; ++i )
      if ( bytes[i] != header[i] )
        return -1;      //wrong header

    return 1;
  }

  public static void main(String[] args) throws InterruptedException {
    if (args.length < 3) {
      System.out.println("Usage: java " + "Test_encode_ppm" +
        " input_ppm_filename output_ycc_filename recoverd_ppm_filename\n" +
```

```
     "e.g. java Test_encode_ppm ../data/beach.ppm t.ycc t.ppm");
   System.exit(-1);
}

/*
 * Create an input stream from the specified file name
 * to be used with the file decoding operator.
 */
 FileSeekableStream stream = null;
 try {
   stream = new FileSeekableStream(args[0]);
 } catch (IOException e) {
   e.printStackTrace();
   System.exit(0);
 }

/* Create an operator to decode the image file. */
RenderedOp image = JAI.create("stream", stream);

/* Get the width and height of image. */
int width = image.getWidth();
int height = image.getHeight();

if ( width % 16 != 0 || height % 16 != 0 ) {
  System.out.println("Program only works for image dimensions divisible");
  System.out.println("by 16. Use 'convert' to change image dimension.");
  System.exit(1);
}
int [] samples = new int[3*width*height];

Raster ras = image.getData();
//save pixel RGB data in samples[]
ras.getPixels( 0, 0, width, height, samples );
RGBImage rgbimage = new RGBImage( width, height );
//copy image data to RGBImage object buffer
int isize = width * height;
for ( int i = 0, k = 0; i < isize; ++i, k+=3 ) {
  rgbimage.ibuf[i].R =  samples[k];
  rgbimage.ibuf[i].G = samples[k+1];
  rgbimage.ibuf[i].B = samples[k+2];
}

try {
  File f = new File ( args[1] );
  OutputStream o = new FileOutputStream( f );
  DataOutputStream out = new DataOutputStream ( o );
  write_ycc_header ( width, height, out );
  Encode enc = new Encode ();

  //save encoded data ( YCbCr ) in file specified by args[1]
  enc.encode ( rgbimage, out );
  out.close();
} catch (IOException e) {
   e.printStackTrace();
   System.exit(0);
}

System.out.printf("\nEncoding done, YCbCr data saved in %s\n",args[1]);

//read the YCbCr data back from file args[1] and convert to RGB
```

```
   DataInputStream in;
   Decode ycc_decoder = new Decode ();
   try {
     File f = new File ( args[1] );
     InputStream ins = new FileInputStream( f );
     in = new DataInputStream ( ins );
     if ( read_ycc_header ( rgbimage,  in ) == -1 ){
       System.out.println("Not YCC File");
       return;
     }
     /*
       Decode data: convert YCbCr data from file args[1] to RGB.
       Restored RGB data returned via parameter rgbimage.
     */
     ycc_decoder.decode_yccFrame (rgbimage, in);
   } catch (IOException e) {
     e.printStackTrace();
     System.exit(0);
   }

   /*
     Now save RGB data in PPM format in the file specified by args[2].
   */
   isize = rgbimage.width * rgbimage.height;
   byte [] P6 = { 'P', '6', '\n' };
   byte [] colorLevels = { '2', '5', '5', '\n' };
   String sw = Integer.toString ( rgbimage.width ) + " ";
   String sh = Integer.toString ( rgbimage.height ) + "\n";
   byte [] bytes = new byte[3*isize];
   for ( int i = 0, k = 0; i < isize; i++, k+=3 ){
       bytes[k] = (byte) (rgbimage.ibuf[i].R);
       bytes[k+1] = (byte) (rgbimage.ibuf[i].G);
       bytes[k+2] = (byte) (rgbimage.ibuf[i].B);
   }
   try {
       File f = new File ( args[2] );
       OutputStream o = new FileOutputStream( f );
DataOutputStream out = new DataOutputStream ( o );
       out.write ( P6 );
       out.writeBytes ( sw );
       out.writeBytes ( sh );
       out.write ( colorLevels );
       out.write ( bytes );    //save 8-bit RGB data
       out.close();
   } catch (IOException e) {
     e.printStackTrace();
     System.exit(0);
   }
   System.out.printf("Decoded data saved in %s \n", args[2] );
 }
}
```

You can now put all the java files, **common.java, Decode.java, Encode.java, Rg-bYcc.java,** and **Test_encode_ppm.java** in the same directory and compile them with the command,

```
     $javac *.java
```

The main class **Test_encode_ppm.class** is generated. You have to supply three filenames to do the test, the first being the input PPM file, the second for storing YCbCr data, and the third for saving the decoded RGB data. For example you can issue a command like the following to carry out the test:

```
$java Test_encode_ppm ../data/beach.ppm t.ycc t.ppm
```

When it is executed, it does the following:

1. reads RGB data from "../data/beach.ppm",
2. saves YCbCr data in "t.ycc", and
3. saves reconstructed RGB data in "t.ppm".

You can view the PPM files using "xview"; the command "xview ../data/beach.ppm" displays the original RGB image and the command "xview t.ppm" displays the recovered RGB image.

You should find that the two images almost look identical to each other even though we have compressed "beach.ppm" to "t.ycc" by a factor of two. If you want to find out the file sizes, you can issue the command "ls -l ../data/beach.ppm t.ycc t.ppm". Upon executing this command, you should see a display similar to the following:

```
73743   ../data/beach.ppm
73743   t.ppm
36876   t.ycc
```

The first column indicates the file sizes in bytes. As you can see, files "beach.ppm" and "t.ppm" have identical size but the file "t.ycc" that contains YCbCr data is only half the size of the file "beach.ppm" that contains RGB data.

In our experiment, the original RGB image ( beach.ppm ) is shown in Figure 5-5a and the restored RGB image ( t.ppm ) is shown in Figure 5-5b.

**Figure 5-5a**                    **Figure 5-5b**

# Chapter 6    Discrete Cosine Transform ( DCT )

## 6.1 Time, Space and Frequency Domains

Data compression techniques can be classified as *lossless* or *lossy*. In lossless compression, we can reverse the process and recover the exact original data. This technique works by exploiting and removing redundancy of data and no information is lost in the process. Typically, lossless compression is used to compress text and binary programs and compression ratios achieved are usually not very high.

In lossy compression, we throw away some information carried by the data and thus the process is not reversible. The technique can give us much higher compression ratios. *Given a set of data, what kind of information should we throw away?* It turns out that choosing the portion of information to throw away is the state-of-the-art of lossy compression. Note that in technical terms, we can have redundant data but **not** redundant information. However, we can have irrelevant information and usually this is the part of the information contained in a data set that we want to throw away. For example, when we write a story about a marathon runner, we may usually omit the part that tells the time she sleeps, the time she gets up and the time she eats without affecting the story. Given an image, we want to determine which components are not as relevant as other components and discard the less relevant components. In previous chapters, we discussed that by transforming the representation of an image from RGB to 4:2:0 YCbCr format, which separates the intensity from color components, we can easily compress an image by a factor of two without much down grading of the image quality. The underlying principles in this stage of compression is that human eyes are more sensitive to brightness than to color and in practice, we do not need to retain as much information of the color components as we need in presenting an image. However, even after this change in format, we still represent the image in the spatial domain, where a sample value depends on the positon of the two-dimensional space. That is, it is a function of the coordinates (x, y) of a two-dimensional plane. Our eyes do not have any crucial discrimination of a point at any special position in space and thus it is difficult for us to further pick the irrelevant information and throw it away if we need to. On the other hand, if we could represent the image in the frequency domain, we know that our eyes are not very sensitive to high frequency components and if we have to get rid of any information, we would like to get rid of those components first.

It turns out that in nature, any wave can be expressed as a superposition of sine and cosine waves. In other words, any periodic signals can be decomposed into a series of sine and cosine waves with frequencies that are integer multiples of a certain frequency. This is the well-known **Fourier Theorem**, which is one of the most important discoveries in the history of science and technology. It is the foundation of many science and engineer applications. Lossy image compression is one of the many applications that utilizes a transform built on top of the theorem.

## 6.2 Discrete Cosine Transform ( DCT )

Numerous research has been conducted on transforms for image and video compression. There are a few methods that are practical and popularly used. For static image compression, the Discrete Wavelet Transform ( DWT ) is the most popular method and can yield good results; it has been incorporated in the JPEG standard. Other popular methods that require less memory to operate include Karhunen-Loeve Transform ( KLT ), Singular Value Decomposition ( SVD ), and Discrete Cosine Transform ( DCT ). For video compression, DCT tends to give very good performance and has been incorporated in the MPEG standard. In this book, DCT will be the only significant transform that we shall discuss.  DCT closely relates to Discrete Fourier Transform ( DFT ). Two dimensional DCT operates on a block of $N \times M$ pixels is shown in Figure 6-1.

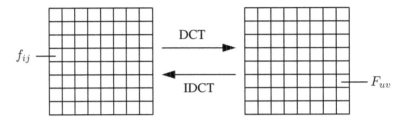

**Figure 6-1**. DCT and Inverse DCT ( IDCT )

In the figure, $f_{ij}$ are the pixel values and $F_{uv}$ are the transformed values. The transform is reversible meaning that if we discount the rounding errors occurred in arithmetic calculations, we can recover the original pixel values by reversing the transformation. The reversed transformation is known as Inverse DCT or IDCT, which is also shown in **Figure 6-1**.

The general equation for a 2D **DCT** of a block of $N \times M$ pixles with values $f_{ij}$s is defined by the following equation:

$$F_{uv} = N_u M_v \sum_{i=0}^{N-1} \sum_{j=0}^{M-1} f_{ij} cos\frac{(2j+1)v\pi}{2M} cos\frac{(2i+1)u\pi}{2N} \qquad (6.1)$$

where

$$K_r = \begin{cases} \sqrt{\frac{1}{K}} & \text{if } r = 0 \\ \sqrt{\frac{2}{K}} & \text{if } r > 0 \end{cases} \qquad (6.2)$$

and $K$ is $M$ or $N$ in (6.1).

The corresponding IDCT is given by the following equation:

$$f_{ij} = \sum_{u=0}^{N-1} \sum_{v=0}^{M-1} N_u M_v F_{uv} cos\frac{(2j+1)v\pi}{2M} cos\frac{(2i+1)u\pi}{2N} \qquad (6.3)$$

In many applications, $N = M$ and equations (6.1) and (6.2) can be expressed in matrix forms. If **f** and **F** denote the matrices $(f_{ij})$ and $(F_{uv})$ respectively, equation (6.1) can be rewritten in the following matrix form:

$$\mathbf{F} = \mathbf{R}\,\mathbf{f}\,\mathbf{R^T} \qquad (6.4)$$

where $\mathbf{R^T}$ is the transpose of the transform matrix $\mathbf{R}$. The matrix elements of $\mathbf{R}$ are

$$R_{ij} = N_i cos\frac{(2j+1)i\pi}{2N} \qquad (6.5)$$

where $N_i$ is defined in (6.2). It turns out that the inverse of $\mathbf{R}$ is the same as its transpose, i.e. $\mathbf{R}^{-1} = \mathbf{R}^{\mathrm{T}}$. (Such a matrix is an orthogonal matrix which consists of orthogonal (perpendicular) unit row and column vectors (i.e. orthonormal vectors).) Therefore, the inverse transformation, IDCT can be found by:

$$\mathbf{f} = \mathbf{R}^{\mathrm{T}}\,\mathbf{F}\,\mathbf{R} \tag{6.6}$$

### Example

Consider N = M = 4. The DCT transform matrix $\mathbf{R}$ is a $4 \times 4$ matrix. Using the fact that $cos(\pi - \theta) = -cos\theta$, $cos(\pi + \theta) = -cos\theta$ and $cos(2\pi + \theta) = cos\theta$, we obtain the following matrix:

$$\mathbf{R} = \begin{pmatrix} a & a & a & a \\ b & c & -b & -c \\ a & -a & -a & a \\ c & b & b & c \end{pmatrix} \quad where \quad \begin{aligned} a &= \tfrac{1}{2} \\ b &= \sqrt{\tfrac{1}{2}}cos\tfrac{\pi}{8} \\ c &= \sqrt{\tfrac{1}{2}}cos\tfrac{3\pi}{8} \end{aligned} \tag{6.7}$$

Evaluating the cosines, we have

$$\mathbf{R} = \begin{pmatrix} 0.5 & 0.5 & 0.5 & 0.5 \\ 0.653 & 0.271 & -0.271 & -0.653 \\ 0.5 & -0.5 & -0.5 & 0.5 \\ 0.271 & -0.653 & -0.653 & 0.271 \end{pmatrix} \tag{6.8}$$

Sometimes, DCT is referred to as Forward DCT ( FDCT ) in order to distinguish it from Inverse DCT ( IDCT ).

## 6.3 Floating-point Implementation of DCT and IDCT

A direct floating-point implementation of DCT and IDCT of an $N \times N$ block is straightforward and simple. All we need to do is to use two for-loops to do summations. Program Listing 6-1 shows the implementation. In the program, the functions **dct_direct()** and **idct_direct()** do the actual work of DCT, and IDCT respectively; they use floating point ( double ) in calculations. The functions **dct()** and **idct()** simply cast short values to double and call **dct_direct()** or **idct_direct()** to do the transformations. In the functions, the values of f[i][j] and F[u][v] correspond to $f_{ij}$ and $F_{uv}$ in equations (6.1) and (6.3) respectively; a[u] and a[v] correspond to $N_u$ and $N_v$.

**Program Listing 6-1** DCT and IDCT using Floating Point

```
/*
 * DctDirect.java
 * A straightforward implementation of DCT and IDCT for the purpose of
 * learning and testing.
 * Floating-point arithmetic is used.  Such an implementation should
 * not be used in practical applications.
 */
```

```java
class DctDirect {

  private static double PI = 3.141592653589;

  //input: f, N; output: F
  static int dct_direct( int N, double [][] f, double [][] F )
  {
    double [] a = new double[32];
    double sum, coef;
    int i, j, u, v;

    if ( N > 32 || N <= 0 ) {
      System.out.printf ("\ninappropriate N\n");
      return -1;
    }
    a[0] = Math.sqrt ( 1.0 / N );
    for ( i = 1; i < N; ++i ) {
      a[i] = Math.sqrt ( 2.0 / N );
    }
    for ( u = 0; u < N; ++u ) {
      for ( v = 0; v < N; ++v ) {
        sum = 0.0;
        for ( i = 0; i < N; ++i ) {
          for ( j = 0; j < N; ++j ) {
    coef =  Math.cos ((2*i+1)*u*PI /
                      (2*N)) * Math.cos ((2*j+1)*v*PI/(2*N));
    sum += f[i][j] * coef;
  } //for j
          F[u][v] = a[u] * a[v] * sum;
        } //for i
      } //for u
    } //for v

    return 1;
  }

  //input: N, F; output: f
  static int idct_direct( int N, double [][] F, double [][] f )
  {
    double [] a = new double[32];
    double  sum, coef;
    short i, j, u, v;

    if ( N > 32 || N <= 0 ) {
      System.out.printf ("\ninappropriate N\n");
      return -1;
    }
    a[0] = Math.sqrt ( 1.0 / N );
    for ( i = 1; i < N; ++i )
      a[i] = Math.sqrt ( 2.0 / N );

    for ( i = 0; i < N; ++i ) {
      for ( j = 0; j < N; ++j ) {
        sum = 0.0;
        for ( u = 0; u < N; ++u ) {
          for ( v = 0; v < N; ++v ) {
    coef =  Math.cos ((2*j+1)*v*PI/(2*N)) *
                            Math.cos ((2*i+1)*u*PI / (2*N));
    sum += a[u] * a[v] * F[u][v] * coef;
```

```
    } //for j
          //*(f+i*N+j) =   sum;
          f[i][j] = sum;
        } //for i
      } //for u
    } //for v
    return 1;
  }


//   change values from int to double and vice versa.
static int dct ( int N, int [][] f, int [][] F )
{
  double [][] tempx = new double[32][32];
  double [][] tempy = new double[32][32];
  int  i, j;

  if ( N > 32 || N <= 0 ) {
    System.out.printf ("\ninappropriate N\n");
    return -1;
  }
  for ( i = 0; i < N; ++i )
    for ( j = 0; j < N; ++j )
      tempx[i][j] = (double) f[i][j];

  dct_direct ( N, tempx, tempy );      //DCT operation
  for ( i = 0; i < N; ++i )
    for ( j = 0; j < N; ++j )
      F[i][j] = (int ) ( Math.floor (tempy[i][j]+0.5) );  //rounding

  return 1;
}

//   change values from int to doulbe, and vice versa.
static int idct ( int N, int [][] F, int [][] f )
{
  double [][] tempx = new double[32][32];
  double [][] tempy = new double[32][32];
  int  i, j;

  if ( N > 32 || N <= 0 ) {
    System.out.printf ("\ninappropriate N\n");
    return -1;
  }
  for ( i = 0; i < N; ++i )
    for ( j = 0; j < N; ++j )
      tempy[i][j] = (double) F[i][j];

  idct_direct ( N, tempy, tempx );  //IDCT operation
  for ( i = 0; i < N; ++i )
    for ( j = 0; j < N; ++j )
      f[i][j] = (int) Math.floor (tempx[i][j]+0.5);  //rounding

  return 1;
}

static void print_elements ( int N,  int [][] f )
{
  int i, j;
```

```
    for ( i = 0; i < N; ++i ){
      System.out.printf("\n");
      for ( j = 0; j < N; ++j ) {
        System.out.printf ("%4d, ", f[i][j] );
      }
    }
  }

  public static void main(String[] args) throws InterruptedException
  {
    int [][] f = new int[8][8], F = new int[8][8];
    int i, j, N;
    byte [][] temp = new byte[8][8];
    N = 8;

    //try some values for testing
    for ( i = 0; i < N; ++i ) {
      for ( j = 0; j < N; ++j ) {
        f[i][j] = i + j;
      }
    }

    System.out.printf("\nOriginal sample values");
    print_elements ( N, f );
    System.out.printf("\n-------------------\n");

    dct ( N, f, F );          //performing DCT
    System.out.printf("\nCoefficients of DCT:");
    print_elements ( N, F );
    System.out.printf("\n-------------------\n");

    idct ( N, F, f );          //performing IDCT
    System.out.printf("\nValues recovered by IDCT:");
    print_elements ( N, f );
    System.out.printf("\n");
  }
}
```

---

The implementation shown in Listing 6-1 is inefficient and impractical in image and video compression, which requires numerous operations of DCT and IDCT. Also, it is not a good programming practice to print out messages inside a function which is designed for other purposes. However, this program can be used for checking purposes when we later implement DCT and IDCT using more efficient methods. When the program is executed, it prints the following outputs, where $N = 8$ has been considered. The original sample values and the recovered values after going through DCT and IDCT are identical:

---

```
Original sample values
    0,    1,    2,    3,    4,    5,    6,    7,
    1,    2,    3,    4,    5,    6,    7,    8,
    2,    3,    4,    5,    6,    7,    8,    9,
    3,    4,    5,    6,    7,    8,    9,   10,
    4,    5,    6,    7,    8,    9,   10,   11,
    5,    6,    7,    8,    9,   10,   11,   12,
```

```
    6,     7,     8,     9,    10,    11,    12,    13,
    7,     8,     9,    10,    11,    12,    13,    14,
----------------------

Coefficients of DCT:
   56,   -18,     0,    -2,     0,    -1,     0,     0,
  -18,     0,     0,     0,     0,     0,     0,     0,
    0,     0,     0,     0,     0,     0,     0,     0,
   -2,     0,     0,     0,     0,     0,     0,     0,
    0,     0,     0,     0,     0,     0,     0,     0,
   -1,     0,     0,     0,     0,     0,     0,     0,
    0,     0,     0,     0,     0,     0,     0,     0,
    0,     0,     0,     0,     0,     0,     0,     0,
----------------------

Values recovered by IDCT:
    0,     1,     2,     3,     4,     5,     6,     7,
    1,     2,     3,     4,     5,     6,     7,     8,
    2,     3,     4,     5,     6,     7,     8,     9,
    3,     4,     5,     6,     7,     8,     9,    10,
    4,     5,     6,     7,     8,     9,    10,    11,
    5,     6,     7,     8,     9,    10,    11,    12,
    6,     7,     8,     9,    10,    11,    12,    13,
    7,     8,     9,    10,    11,    12,    13,    14,
```

We can see from the output that there are only a few nonzero coefficient values after DCT and they are clustered at the upper left corner. So after DCT, it becomes clear to us that the sample block **f** actually does not contain as much information as it appears and it is a lot easier to carry out data compression in the transformed domain.

The value of the DCT coefficient F(0, 0) at position (0, 0) is in general referred to as the DC value and others are referred to as AC values. This is because F(0, 0) is essentially a scaled average of all the sample values. We can easily see this if we write down the formula for calculating its value by setting $u = 0, v = 0$, and $N = M$ in Equation (6.1). That is,

$$F_{00} = \frac{1}{N} \sum_{i=0}^{N-1} \sum_{j=0}^{N-1} f_{ij} \tag{6.9}$$

where we have used the fact that $N_0 N_0 = \sqrt{\frac{1}{N}}\sqrt{\frac{1}{N}} = \frac{1}{N}$, and $cos(0) = 1$. ( $F_{00}/N$ is the exact average of all the values. ) In Chapter 2, we discussed that the average of a set of values could give us the most crucial information of the set if we are only allowed to know one single value. Therefore, the DC value of the DCT coefficients of a block of samples is the most important single value and we want to retain its value.

## 6.4 Fast DCT

As DCT is so important in signal processing, a lot of research has been done to speed up its calculations. One main idea behind speeding up DCT is to break down the summation into stages and in each stage, intermediate sums of two quantities are formed. The intermediate sums will be used in later stages to obtain the final sum. In this way, the number of calculations grows with $N log N$ rather than $N^2$ as in the case of direct DCT for an $N \times N$ sample block.

This kind of DCT is referred to as Fast DCT. In this section, we only discuss the speeding up of Forward DCT. The techniques also apply to Inverse DCT that we shall discuss later.

If we consider only small values of $N$ in the form of $N = 2^n$, it is not difficult to understand how the stage break-down is done. For instance, consider $N = 8$, which is what we need in our video compression. ( In Chapter 5, we discussed that a macroblock consists of $8 \times 8$ sample blocks. ) We can rewrite (6.1) as follows.

$$F_{uv} = a_u a_v \sum_{i=0}^{7} \sum_{j=0}^{7} f_{ij} \cos \frac{(2j+1)v\pi}{16} \cos \frac{(2i+1)u\pi}{16} \qquad (6.10)$$

with

$$
\begin{aligned}
a_0 &= \sqrt{\frac{1}{8}} = \frac{1}{2\sqrt{2}} \\
a_k &= \sqrt{\frac{2}{8}} = \frac{1}{2} \qquad \text{for } k > 0
\end{aligned}
\qquad (6.11)
$$

Equation (6.10) implies that we can express a two dimensional ( 2D ) DCT as two one-dimensional (1D ) DCT. Equation (6.10 ) can be rewritten as follows.

$$F_{uv} = a_u a_v \sum_{i=0}^{7} \overline{F}_{iv} \cos \frac{(2i+1)u\pi}{16} \qquad (6.12)$$

where

$$\overline{F}_{iv} = \sum_{j=0}^{7} f_{ij} \cos \frac{(2j+1)v\pi}{16} \qquad (6.13)$$

Aside from a multiplicative constant, Equation (6.13) can be interpreted as a 1D DCT or the DCT of one row ( the i-th row ) of samples of an $8 \times 8$ sample block. For convenience of writing, we shall suppress writing the index i; it is understood that we consider one row of samples. Also, we let

$$
\begin{aligned}
x_j &= f_{ij} \\
y_v &= \overline{F}_{iv}
\end{aligned}
\qquad (6.14)
$$

Equation (6.13) becomes

$$y_k = \sum_{j=0}^{7} x_j \cos \frac{(2j+1)k\pi}{16}, \qquad k = 0, 1, ..., 7 \qquad (6.15)$$

If we let $\theta = \frac{\pi}{16}$, we can list all the coefficients of $y_k$ ( k = 0, 1, .. 7 ) in a table as shown below.

|       | $x_0$ | $x_1$ | $x_2$ | $x_3$ | $x_4$ | $x_5$ | $x_6$ | $x_7$ |
|-------|-------|-------|-------|-------|-------|-------|-------|-------|
| $y_0$ | 1 | 1 | 1 | 1 | 1 | 1 | 1 | 1 |
| $y_1$ | $\cos(1\theta)$ | $\cos(3\theta)$ | $\cos(5\theta)$ | $\cos(9\theta)$ | $\cos(11\theta)$ | $\cos(13\theta)$ | $\cos(15\theta)$ | $\cos(15\theta)$ |
| $y_2$ | $\cos(2\theta)$ | $\cos(6\theta)$ | $\cos(10\theta)$ | $\cos(14\theta)$ | $\cos(18\theta)$ | $\cos(22\theta)$ | $\cos(26\theta)$ | $\cos(30\theta)$ |
| $y_3$ | $\cos(3\theta)$ | $\cos(9\theta)$ | $\cos(15\theta)$ | $\cos(21\theta)$ | $\cos(27\theta)$ | $\cos(33\theta)$ | $\cos(39\theta)$ | $\cos(45\theta)$ |
| $y_4$ | $\cos(4\theta)$ | $\cos(12\theta)$ | $\cos(20\theta)$ | $\cos(28\theta)$ | $\cos(36\theta)$ | $\cos(44\theta)$ | $\cos(52\theta)$ | $\cos(60\theta)$ |
| $y_5$ | $\cos(5\theta)$ | $\cos(15\theta)$ | $\cos(25\theta)$ | $\cos(35\theta)$ | $\cos(45\theta)$ | $\cos(55\theta)$ | $\cos(65\theta)$ | $\cos(75\theta)$ |
| $y_6$ | $\cos(6\theta)$ | $\cos(18\theta)$ | $\cos(30\theta)$ | $\cos(42\theta)$ | $\cos(54\theta)$ | $\cos(66\theta)$ | $\cos(78\theta)$ | $\cos(90\theta)$ |
| $y_7$ | $\cos(7\theta)$ | $\cos(21\theta)$ | $\cos(35\theta)$ | $\cos(49\theta)$ | $\cos(63\theta)$ | $\cos(77\theta)$ | $\cos(91\theta)$ | $\cos(105\theta)$ |

**Table 6-1**

Since $\theta = \frac{\pi}{16}$, we have $16\theta = \pi$. We can simplify the above table by making use of some basic cosine properties such as

$$
\begin{aligned}
\cos(\pi - \alpha) &= -\cos(\alpha)\\
\cos(2\pi - \alpha) &= \cos(\alpha)
\end{aligned}
\tag{6.16}
$$

Using (6.16), we can reduce $\cos(n\theta)$ with $n \le 8$ to a form of $\pm\cos(k\theta)$ with $k \le 7$. For example,

$$
\begin{aligned}
\cos(9\theta) &= \cos(16\theta - 7\theta) &= \cos(\pi - 7\theta) &= -\cos(7\theta)\\
\cos(35\theta) &= \cos(32\theta + 3\theta) &= \cos(2\pi + 3\theta) &= \cos(3\theta)
\end{aligned}
$$

Applying these, we can simplify Table 6-1 to Table 6-2 as shown below, where $cs$ represents *cosine*:

|        | $x_0$ | $x_1$ | $x_2$ | $x_3$ | $x_4$ | $x_5$ | $x_6$ | $x_7$ |
|--------|-------|-------|-------|-------|-------|-------|-------|-------|
| $y_0$ | 1 | 1 | 1 | 1 | 1 | 1 | 1 | 1 |
| $y_1$ | $cs(1\theta)$ | $cs(3\theta)$ | $cs(5\theta)$ | $cs(7\theta)$ | $-cs(7\theta)$ | $-cs(5\theta)$ | $-cs(3\theta)$ | $-cs(1\theta)$ |
| $y_2$ | $cs(2\theta)$ | $cs(6\theta)$ | $-cs(6\theta)$ | $-cs(2\theta)$ | $-cs(2\theta)$ | $-cs(6\theta)$ | $cs(6\theta)$ | $cs(2\theta)$ |
| $y_3$ | $cs(3\theta)$ | $-cs(7\theta)$ | $-cs(1\theta)$ | $-cs(5\theta)$ | $cs(5\theta)$ | $cs(1\theta)$ | $cs(7\theta)$ | $-cs(3\theta)$ |
| $y_4$ | $cs(4\theta)$ | $-cs(4\theta)$ | $-cs(4\theta)$ | $cs(4\theta)$ | $cs(4\theta)$ | $-cs(4\theta)$ | $-cs(4\theta)$ | $cs(4\theta)$ |
| $y_5$ | $cs(5\theta)$ | $-cs(1\theta)$ | $cs(7\theta)$ | $cs(3\theta)$ | $-cs(3\theta)$ | $-cs(7\theta)$ | $cs(1\theta)$ | $-cs(5\theta)$ |
| $y_6$ | $cs(6\theta)$ | $-cs(2\theta)$ | $cs(2\theta)$ | $-cs(6\theta)$ | $-cs(6\theta)$ | $cs(2\theta)$ | $-cs(2\theta)$ | $cs(6\theta)$ |
| $y_7$ | $cs(7\theta)$ | $-cs(5\theta)$ | $cs(3\theta)$ | $-cs(1\theta)$ | $cs(1\theta)$ | $-cs(3\theta)$ | $cs(5\theta)$ | $-cs(7\theta)$ |

**Table 6-2**

In Table 6-2, each $y_i$ is equal to the sum over k of $x_k$ times the coefficient at column k and row i. We observe that the columns possess certain symmetries; besides the first row, whenever $\cos(k\theta)$ appears in an i-th column, it also appears in another j-th column when $i + j = 7$. This implies that we can always group the i-th and j-th columns together in our summing operations to compute $(x_i \pm x_j)\cos(k\theta)$ provided $i + j = 7$. For example, we can rewrite $y_0$ and $y_2$ as follows:

$$
\begin{aligned}
y_0 &= (x_0 + x_7) + (x_1 + x_6) + (x_2 + x_5) + (x_3 + x_4)\\
y_2 &= (x_0 + x_7)c_2 + (x_1 + x_6)c_6 - (x_2 + x_5)c_6 - (x_3 + x_4)c_2
\end{aligned}
\tag{6.17}
$$

where

$$
c_k = \cos(k\theta)
$$

Once we have computed $(x_i + x_j)$ with $i + j = 7$, we can use this intermediate result in the calculations of both of $y_0$ and $y_2$. Moreover, we can continue this process recursively until we obtain the final values. For instance, let

$$
\begin{aligned}
x_i' &= (x_i + x_j), & i + j &= 7\\
x_j' &= (x_i - x_j), & i + j &= 7\\
x_i'' &= (x_i' + x_j'), & i + j &= 7/2 = 3\\
x_j'' &= (x_i' - x_j'), & i + j &= 7/2 = 3
\end{aligned}
\tag{6.18}
$$

We can rewrite $y_0$ and $y_2$ in (6.17) as follows:

$$
\begin{aligned}
y_0 &= (x_0' + x_3') + (x_1' + x_2') &&= (x_0'' + x_1'') \\
y_2 &= (x_0' - x_3')c_2 + (x_1' - x_2')c_6 &&= x_3''c_2 + x_2''c_6
\end{aligned}
\tag{6.19}
$$

We can decompose $y_4$ and $y_6$ in a similar way as $y_4$ only uses $c_4$ and $y_6$ uses only $c_2$ and $c_6$ of the cosine functions in the calculations. Equations of (6.20) shows the decomposition of $y_4$ and $y_6$:

$$
\begin{aligned}
y_4 &= (x_0' + x_3')c_4 - (x_1' + x_2')c_4 = (x_0'' - x_1'')c_4 \\
y_6 &= (x_0' - x_3')c_6 + (x_2' - x_1')c_2 = x_3''c_6 - x_1''c_2
\end{aligned}
\tag{6.20}
$$

The calucation of the other $y_k's$ ($y_1, y_3, y_5$, and $y_7$) involves four cosine functions ($c_1, c_3, c_5$ and $c_7$) and they appear to be more difficult to decompose. It turns out that these cosine functions can be expressed in terms of each other by making use of some basic cosine properties like those expressed in (6.21):

$$
\begin{aligned}
\cos(\alpha - \beta) &= \cos(\alpha)\cos(\beta) + \sin(\alpha)\sin(\beta) \\
8\theta &= \frac{8\pi}{16} = \frac{\pi}{2} \\
c_4 = \cos(4\theta) &= \sin(4\theta) = \cos(\frac{\pi}{4}) = \sin(\frac{\pi}{4}) = \frac{1}{\sqrt{2}} \\
c_1 = \cos(1\theta) &= \cos(8\theta - 7\theta) = \cos(\frac{\pi}{2} - 7\theta) = \sin(7\theta) \\
c_3 = \cos(3\theta) &= \cos(7\theta - 4\theta) = \cos(7\theta)\cos(4\theta) + \sin(7\theta)\sin(4\theta) = \frac{c_7 + c_1}{\sqrt{2}} \\
c_5 = \cos(5\theta) &= \cos(1\theta + 4\theta) = \cos(1\theta)\cos(4\theta) - \sin(1\theta)\sin(4\theta) = \frac{c_1 - c_7}{\sqrt{2}}
\end{aligned}
\tag{6.21}
$$

Making use of the identities of (6.21), we can apply the decomposition steps to all the $y_i's$. For example, we can express $y_1$ as

$$
\begin{aligned}
y_1 &= (x_0 - x_7)c_1 + (x_1 - x_6)c_3 + (x_2 - x_5)c_5 + (x_3 - x_4)c_7 \\
&= x_7'c_1 + x_6'c_3 + x_5'c_5 + x_4'c_7 \\
&= x_7'c_1 + \frac{x_6'(c_1 + c_7)}{\sqrt{2}} + \frac{x_5'(c_1 - c_7)}{\sqrt{2}} + x_4'c_7 \\
&= [x_7' + \frac{x_6' + x_5'}{\sqrt{2}}]c_1 + [x_4' + \frac{x_6' - x_5'}{\sqrt{2}}]c_7 \\
&= [x_7' + x_6'']c_1 + [x_4' + x_5'']c_7 \\
&= x_7'''c_1 + x_4'''c_7
\end{aligned}
\tag{6.22}
$$

In (6.22), the subscripts in the third and fourth recursive stages are not well-defined but their meanings should be clear. We observe that in the calculations, we often have expressions in the the following form:

$$
\begin{aligned}
c &= (a + b) \\
d &= (a - b)
\end{aligned}
\tag{6.23}
$$

The computations of (6.23) can be represented by a diagram shown in Figure 6-2, which is referred to as a butterfly computation because of its appearance. It is also a simple flow graph.

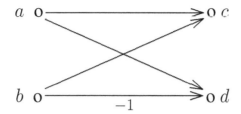

**Figure 6-2**. Flow Graph of Butterfly Computation

If we include the constants $a_k$ in our calculation of $y_k$ and let

$$C_k = c_k a_k = \frac{c_k}{2} = \frac{\cos(\theta)}{2} \quad k \geq 1, \; and$$
$$C_0 = \frac{1}{\sqrt{2}}$$

we arrive at the following flow graph. ( Note that $a_0 = \frac{1}{2\sqrt{2}} = C_4.$ )

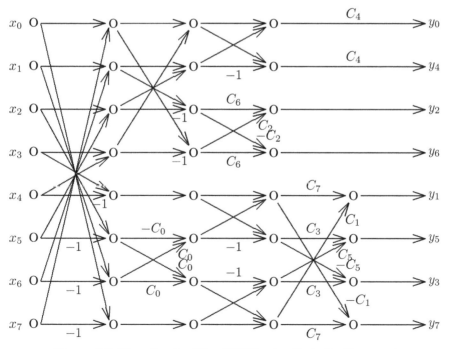

**Figure 6-3**. Flow Graph of $8 \times 8$ DCT using Butterfly Computation

We can obtain $y_k$ by tracing the paths of getting to it. For example, $y_2$ is given by

$$
\begin{aligned}
y_2 &= x_2'' C_6 + x_3'' C_2 \\
&= [x_1' - x_2'] C_6 + [x_0' - x_3'] C_2 \\
&= [(x_1 + x_6) - (x_2 + x_5)] C_6 + [(x_0 + x_7) - (x_3 + x_4)] C_2
\end{aligned}
$$

The following piece of C/C++ code shows how we can compute $y_k's$ from $x_k's$. The first for-loop does the butterfly computations $(x_i \pm x_j)$, which are the first stage operations of the flow graph shown in Figure 6-3. It then performs the eight operations of the second stage of Figure 6-3. Next, the code does the calculations of the upper-half third stage, which is also the final stage of the upper-half flow graph. The lower-half has a total of four stages; the remaining code carries out the transforms of the third and fourth stages of the lower-half flow graph of Figure 6-3:

```
for (j = 0; j < 4; j++) {  //1st stage transform, see flow-graph
    j1 = 7 - j;
    x1[j] = x[j] + x[j1];
    x1[j1] = x[j] - x[j1];
}
x[0] = x1[0] + x1[3];         //second stage transform
x[1] = x1[1] + x1[2];
x[2] = x1[1] - x1[2];
x[3] = x1[0] - x1[3];
x[4] = x1[4];
x[5] = ( x1[6] - x1[5] ) * C0;
x[6] = ( x1[6] + x1[5]) * C0
x[7] = x1[7];

y[0] = ( x[0] + x[1] )*C4; //upper-half of 3rd (final) stage,
y[4] = ( x[0] - x[1] )*C4; //  see flow-graph
y[2] = x[2] * C6 + x[3] * C2;
y[6] = x[3] * C6 - x[2] * C2;

x1[4] = x[4] + x[5];          //lower-half of third stage
x1[5] = x[4] - x[5];
x1[6] = x[7] - x[6];
x1[7] = x[7] + x[6];

y[1] = x1[4] * C7 + x1[7] * C1;//lower-half of 4th (final) stage
y[7] = x1[7] * C7 - x1[4] * C1;
y[5] = x1[5] * C3 + x1[6] * C5;
y[3] = x1[6] * C3 - x1[5] * C5;
```

This code works a lot faster than the direct implementation of DCT; most practical video coders use a similar implementation. However, for the coder to be commercially competitive, we need to go one step further. We have to use integer-arithmetic, which makes further significant speed improvement of the calculations.

# 6.5 Integer Arithmetic

In practice, we use integer arithmetic to implement a Fast DCT. To see how this works, without loss of generality, let us consider 16-bit integers and consider a simple example with a number $x = 2.75$. We cannot express this number as an integer directly, but we can imagine that there is a binary point at the right side of bit 0 of a 16-bit integer. In this imaginary format, $x$ can be represented as a bit vector with imaginary digits ( i.e. $2.75 = 2^1 + 2^{-1} + 2^{-2}$ ):

$$
\begin{array}{lcccccccccccccccccc}
bit\ position: & 15 & & & & & & 9 & 8 & 7 & 6 & 5 & 4 & 3 & 2 & 1 & 0 \\
x = & 0 & 0 & 0 & 0 & 0 & 0 & 0 & 0 & 0 & 0 & 0 & 0 & 0 & 1 & 0 & . & 1 & 1
\end{array}
$$

$$(6.24)$$

In (6.24), the 16-bit integer does not contain the two '1' bits to the right of the binary point, which is the fractional part of $x$. To retain the information of the fractional part, we can shift the whole number left by 8 bits. Shifting a number left by 8 bits is the same as multiplying it by $2^8 (= 256)$. After this shift, the binary point will be at the position between bit 8 and bit 7; the number $x(= 2.75)$ becomes an integer $x'$ as shown below:

$$
\begin{array}{lccccccccccccccccc}
bit\ position: & 15 & & & & & & 9 & 8 & & 7 & 6 & 5 & 4 & 3 & 2 & 1 & 0 \\
x' = & 0 & 0 & 0 & 0 & 0 & 0 & 1 & 0 & . & 1 & 1 & 0 & 0 & 0 & 0 & 0 & 0
\end{array}
$$

$$(6.25)$$

The value of $x$ now becomes

$$x' = 2^9 + 2^7 + 2^6 = 704$$

which is the same as $2.75 \times 256 = 704$. If we now divide $x'$ by 256, or right-shift it by 8 bits, we obtain the integer 2; that is, we have truncated the fraction part of 2.75. In many cases, we would prefer a round operation than a truncate. Rounding 2.75 gives us 3. The rounding result can be achieved by first adding 0.5 to 2.75 before the truncation. If we express 0.5 in our imaginary format and left-shift it by 8 bits, we obtain the value $128(= 2^7)$. So adding 0.5 to $x$ corresponds to the operation of adding $2^7$ to $x'$. This is illustrated in the following equations, where $x'' = x' + 0.5 \times 2^7$:

$$
\begin{array}{lccccccccccccccccccc}
bit\ position & : & 15 & & & & & & 9 & 8 & & 7 & 6 & 5 & 4 & 3 & 2 & 1 & 0 \\
x' & = 0 & 0 & 0 & 0 & 0 & 0 & 1 & 0 & . & 1 & 1 & 0 & 0 & 0 & 0 & 0 & 0 \\
+0.5 \times 2^7 & = 0 & 0 & 0 & 0 & 0 & 0 & 0 & 0 & . & 1 & 0 & 0 & 0 & 0 & 0 & 0 & 0 \\
x'' & = 0 & 0 & 0 & 0 & 0 & 0 & 1 & 1 & . & 0 & 1 & 0 & 0 & 0 & 0 & 0 & 0
\end{array}
$$

$$(6.26)$$

Obviously, when we right-shift $x''$ by 8 bits, we obtain our desired value 3. In general, we can transform real positive numbers to integers by multiplying the real numbers by $2^n$; rounding effect is achieved by adding the value $2^{n-1}$ to the results before shifting them right n bits. This is true for positive numbers but *will it be also true for negative numbers? Should we still add 0.5 to the negative number or should we subtract 0.5 from it before the truncation?* The following example sheds light on what we should do.

Most modern-day computers use two's complement to represent negative numbers. Binary numbers that can have negative values are referred to as signed numbers, otherwise they are referred to as unsigned numbers. In two's complement representation, if we right-shift an unsigned number one bit, a 0 is always shifted into the leftmost bit position. However, if we right-shift a negative signed-number, a 1 is shifted in. For example, consider the following program:

```
class Sign {
  public static void main(String[] args) throws InterruptedException
  {
      char  u = 0x8200;            //16-bit unsigned number
      short s = (short) 0x8200;    //16-bit signed number

      u >>= 1;                     //right-shift one bit
      s >>= 1;                     //right-shift one bit

      int ui = 0x0000ffff & u;     //take lower 16 bits of u
      int si = 0x0000ffff & s;     //take lower 16 bits of s
      System.out.printf("\nunsigned shift:  0x%x", ui );
      System.out.printf("\nsigned shift:    0x%x\n", si );
  }
}
```

When the program is compiled and executed, it will produce the following outputs:

```
unsigned shift:   0x4100
signed shift:     0xc100
```

The outputs show that a 1 has been shifted into $s$ ( a short, 16-bit signed number ) and a 0 has been shifted into $u$ ( a char, 16-bit unsigned number). Because of this property, in java programming, integer-division of a negative signed-number by $2^n$ is different from right-shifting it by n bits. For example,

$$-1/2 = 0 \quad but \quad -1 >> 1 \ yields \ -1$$

$$-3/2 = -1 \quad but \quad -3 >> 1 \ yields \ -2$$

Now consider the negative signed-number $y = -2.75$. Its 2s complement representation can be obtained by complementing all bits of the corresponding positive number ( 2.75 ) shown in (6.24) and adding 1 to the rightmost bit of the complemented number. Thus it has the following binary form.

| $bit\ position:$ | 15 | | | | | | 9 | 8 | 7 | 6 | 5 | 4 | 3 | 2 | 1 | 0 | | | |
|---|---|---|---|---|---|---|---|---|---|---|---|---|---|---|---|---|---|---|---|
| $y =$ | 1 | 1 | 1 | 1 | 1 | 1 | 1 | 1 | 1 | 1 | 1 | 1 | 1 | 1 | 0 | 1 | . | 0 | 1 |

$$(6.27)$$

When we round -2.75, we would like to obtain a value of -3 rather than -2 as the former is closer to its real value. Suppose we perform the same operations that we did to positive numbers discussed above, shifting it left 8 bits, adding $0.5 \times 2^7$ and then right shifting 8 bits. This situation is illustrated by following equations where $y'' = y' + 0.5 \times 2^7$.

$$
\begin{array}{lcccccccccccccccccc}
bit\ position & : & 15 & & & & & & & 9 & 8 & & 7 & 6 & 5 & 4 & 3 & 2 & 1 & 0 \\
y' & = & 1 & 1 & 1 & 1 & 1 & 1 & 0 & 1 & . & 0 & 1 & 0 & 0 & 0 & 0 & 0 & 0 \\
+0.5 \times 2^7 & = & 0 & 0 & 0 & 0 & 0 & 0 & 0 & 0 & . & 1 & 0 & 0 & 0 & 0 & 0 & 0 & 0 \\
y'' & = & 1 & 1 & 1 & 1 & 1 & 1 & 0 & 1 & . & 1 & 1 & 0 & 0 & 0 & 0 & 0 & 0
\end{array}
$$
(6.28)

When we right-shift $y''$ 8 bits, we obtain the following.

$$
\begin{array}{lccccccccccccccccccc}
bit\ position & : & 15 & & & & & & 9 & 8 & 7 & 6 & 5 & 4 & 3 & 2 & 1 & 0 \\
y'' >> 8 & = & 1 & 1 & 1 & 1 & 1 & 1 & 1 & 1 & 1 & 1 & 1 & 1 & 1 & 0 & 1 & . & 1 & 1
\end{array}
$$
(6.29)

In (6.29), $y'' >> 8$ has a value of -3 ( in 2s complement representation ) and is what we want. Therefore, we conclude that to obtain the rounding effect, we always add 0.5 (= 0.1 in binary) to the number before truncating ( right-shifting ) for both positive and negative numbers.

When we add two numbers using integer arithmetic, we must align the binary points of the two numbers before addition. If the first number has been left-shifted by n bits, the second one must also be shifted by the same amount. In our implementation of Fast DCT, we use 32-bit integers; all the coefficients $C_i$ are pre-multiplied by $1024(= 2^{10})$. After the calculations, we right-shift the integers by the same number of bits to obtain the final results. The code of the implementation of Fast DCT is listed below:

**Program Listing 6-2** : Integer-arithmetic Implementation of Fast DCT and IDCT

```
/*
  DctVideo.java
  An implementation of 8x8 DCT and IDCT for video compression.
  32-bit integer-arithmetic is assumed.
  For DCT operation:
     dct ( int [][] X, int [][] Y );
     X is the input of 8x8 array of samples; values must be within [0, 255]
     Y is the output of 8x8 array of DCT coefficients.
  For IDCT operation:
     idct ( int [][] Y, int [][] X );
     Y is the input of an 8x8 array of DCT coefficients.
     X is the output of an 8x8 array of sample values.

  compile: javac DctVideo.cpp
  To use them, create an object of the class DctVideo:
     DctVideo dct_idct = new DctVideo();
  then call the functions by:
     dct_idct.dct ( ... );
     dct_idct.idct ( ... );
*/

class DctVideo {
  private final double PI =  3.141592653589;
  private final short shift = 10;              //10 bits precision
                                               // for fixed-point arithmetic
  //at the final stage, values have been shifted twice
```

```
  private final short shift1 = 2 * shift;
  private final int fac = 1 << shift ;        //multiply all constants by 2^10
  private final int delta = 1 << (shift-1); //for round adjustment~0.5x2^10
  private final int delta1=1 << (shift1-1); //for final round adjust~0.5x2^20
  private final double a = PI / 16.0;         //angle theta

  //DCT constants; use integer-arithmetic.
  private final int c0 = (int) ( 1 / Math.sqrt ( 2 ) * fac );
  private final int c1 = (int) ( Math.cos ( a ) / 2 * fac );
  private final int c2 = (int) ( Math.cos ( 2*a ) / 2 * fac );
  private final int c3 = (int) ( Math.cos ( 3*a ) / 2 * fac );
  private final int c4 = (int) ( Math.cos ( 4*a ) / 2 * fac );
  private final int c5 = (int) ( Math.cos ( 5*a ) / 2 * fac );
  private final int c6 = (int) ( Math.cos ( 6*a ) / 2 * fac );
  private final int c7 = (int) ( Math.cos ( 7*a ) / 2 * fac );

  /*
    DCT function.
    Input: X, array of 8x8, containing data with values in [0, 255].
    Ouput: Y, array of 8x8 DCT coefficients.
  */
  void dct(int [][] X, int [][] Y)
  {
    int   i, j, j1, k;
    int [] x = new int[8], x1 = new int[8];
    int [][]  m = new int[8][8];
    /*
      Row transform
      i-th row, k-th element
    */
    for (i = 0, k = 0; i < 8; i++, k++) {
      for (j = 0; j < 8; j++)
        x[j] = X[k][j];                    //data for one row

      for (j = 0; j < 4; j++) {   //first stage transform, see flow-graph
        j1 = 7 - j;
        x1[j] = x[j] + x[j1];
        x1[j1] = x[j] - x[j1];
      }
      x[0] = x1[0] + x1[3];              //second stage transform
      x[1] = x1[1] + x1[2];
      x[2] = x1[1] - x1[2];
      x[3] = x1[0] - x1[3];
      x[4] = x1[4];
      //after multiplication, add delta for rounding,
      x[5] = ((x1[6] - x1[5]) * c0 + delta ) >> shift;
      //shift-right to undo 'x fac' to line up binary points of all x[i]
      x[6] = ((x1[6] + x1[5]) * c0 + delta ) >> shift;
      x[7] = x1[7];

      m[i][0] = (x[0]+x[1])*c4;   //upper-half of third (final) stage
      m[i][4] = (x[0] - x[1]) * c4;
      m[i][2] = x[2] * c6 + x[3] * c2;
      m[i][6] = x[3] * c6 - x[2] * c2;

      x1[4] = x[4] + x[5];              //lower-half of third stage
      x1[5] = x[4] - x[5];
      x1[6] = x[7] - x[6];
      x1[7] = x[7] + x[6];
```

```
       m[i][1] = x1[4]*c7 + x1[7]*c1;//lower-half of fourth (final) stage
       m[i][7] = x1[7] * c7 - x1[4] * c1;
       m[i][5] = x1[5] * c3 + x1[6] * c5;
       m[i][3] = x1[6] * c3 - x1[5] * c5;
    } //for i

    /*
       At this point, coefficients of each row (m[i][j]) has been multiplied
       by 2^10. We can undo the multiplication by << 10 here before doing
       the vertical transform. However, as we are using int variables,
       which are 32-bit to do multiplications, we can tolerate another
       multiplication of 2^10. So we delay our undoing until the end
       of the vertical transform and we undo all left-shift operations
       by shifting the results right 20 bits ( i.e. << 2 * 10 ).
    */
    // Column transform
    for (i = 0; i < 8; i++) {                         //eight columns

       //consider one column
       for (j = 0; j < 4; j++) {                      //first-stage operation
          j1 = 7 - j;
          x1[j] = m[j][i] + m[j1][i];
          x1[j1] = m[j][i] - m[j1][i];
       }
                                                      //second-stage operation
       x[0] = x1[0] + x1[3];
       x[1] = x1[1] + x1[2];
       x[2] = x1[1] - x1[2];
       x[3] = x1[0] - x1[3];
       x[4] = x1[4];
       //undo one shift for x[5], x[6] to avoid overflow
       x1[5] = (x1[5] + delta) >> shift;
       x1[6] = (x1[6] + delta) >> shift;

       x[5] = (x1[6] - x1[5]) * c0;
       x[6] = (x1[6] + x1[5]) * c0;
       x[7] = x1[7];

       m[0][i] = (x[0] + x[1]) * c4; //upper-half of third (final) stage
       m[4][i] = (x[0] - x[1]) * c4;
       m[2][i] = ( x[2] * c6 + x[3] * c2 ) ;
       m[6][i] = ( x[3] * c6 - x[2] * c2 );

       x1[4] = x[4] + x[5];                 //lower-half of third stage
       x1[7] = x[7] + x[6];
       x1[5] = x[4] - x[5];
       x1[6] = x[7] - x[6];

       m[1][i] = x1[4] * c7 + x1[7] * c1; //lower-half of fourth stage
       m[5][i] = x1[5] * c3 + x1[6] * c5;
       m[3][i] = x1[6] * c3 - x1[5] * c5;
       m[7][i] = x1[7] * c7 - x1[4] * c1;
    } // for i

    //we have left-shift (multiplying constants) twice
    //so undo them by right-shift
    for ( i = 0; i < 8; ++i ) {
       for ( j = 0; j < 8; ++j ) {
          Y[i][j] = ( m[i][j] + delta1 ) >> shift1; //add delta1 to round
       }
```

```
     }
   }

   /*
     Implementation of idct() is to reverse the operations of dct().
     We first do vertical transform and then horizontal; this is easier
     for debugging as the operations are just the reverse of those in dct();
     of course,it works just as well if you do the horizontal transform first.
     So in this implementation, the first stage of idct() is the final stage
     of dct() and the final stage of idct() is the first stage of dct().
   */
   void idct(int [][] Y, int [][] X)
   {
     int    j1, i, j;
     int [] x = new int[8], x1 = new int[8], y = new int[8];
     int [][] m = new int[8][8];

     //column transform
     for ( i = 0; i < 8; ++i ) {
       for (j = 0; j < 8; j++)
         y[j] = Y[j][i];

       x1[4] = y[1] * c7 - y[7] * c1;   //lower-half final stage of dct
       x1[7] = y[1] * c1 + y[7] * c7;
       x1[6] = y[3] * c3 + y[5] * c5;
       x1[5] = -y[3] * c5 + y[5] * c3;

       x[4] = ( x1[4] + x1[5] );        //lower-half of third stage of dct
       x[5] = ( x1[4] - x1[5] );
       x[6] = ( x1[7] - x1[6] );
       x[7] = ( x1[7] + x1[6] );

       x1[0] = ( y[0] + y[4] ) * c4;    //upper-half of 3rd (final) dct stage
       x1[1] = ( y[0] - y[4] ) * c4;
       x1[2] = y[2] * c6 - y[6] * c2;
       x1[3] = y[2] * c2 + y[6] * c6;

       x[0] = ( x1[0] + x1[3] );        //second stage of dct
       x[1] = ( x1[1] + x1[2] );
       x[2] = ( x1[1] - x1[2] );
       x[3] = ( x1[0] - x1[3] );

       //x[4], x[7] no change
       x1[5] = ((x[6] - x[5])*c0 + delta ) >> shift;//add delta for rounding,
       x1[6] = ((x[6] + x[5])*c0 + delta ) >> shift;// shift-right to undo
       x[5] = x1[5];                                // 'x fac' to line up x[]s
       x[6] = x1[6];

       for (j = 0; j < 4; j++) {        //first stage transform of dct
         j1 = 7 - j;
         m[j][i] = (x[j] + x[j1] );
         m[j1][i] = (x[j] - x[j1] );
       }
     } //for i

     //row transform
     for ( i = 0; i < 8; i++ ) {
       for (j = 0; j < 8; j++)
```

```
        y[j] = m[i][j] ;                    //data for one row

    x1[4] = y[1] * c7 - y[7] * c1;
    x1[7] = y[1] * c1 + y[7] * c7;
    x1[6] = y[3] * c3 + y[5] * c5;
    x1[5] = -y[3] * c5 + y[5] * c3;


    x[4] = ( x1[4] + x1[5] );          //lower-half of third stage
    x[5] = ( x1[4] - x1[5] );
    x[6] = ( x1[7] - x1[6] );
    x[7] = ( x1[7] + x1[6] );


    x1[0] = ( y[0] + y[4] ) * c4;
    x1[1] = ( y[0] - y[4] ) * c4;
    x1[2] = y[2] * c6 - y[6] * c2;
    x1[3] = y[2] * c2 + y[6] * c6;


    //undo one shift for x[5], x[6] to avoid overflow
    x1[5] = (x[5] + delta) >> shift;
    x1[6] = (x[6] + delta) >> shift;
    x[5] = (x1[6] - x1[5]) * c0;
    x[6] = (x1[6] + x1[5]) * c0;
    //x[4], x[7] no change
    x[0] = ( x1[0] + x1[3] );          //second stage transform
    x[1] = ( x1[1] + x1[2] );
    x[2] = ( x1[1] - x1[2] );
    x[3] = ( x1[0] - x1[3] );


    for (j = 0; j < 4; j++) {          //1st stage transform,see flow-graph
      j1 = 7 - j;
      m[i][j] = (x[j] + x[j1]);
      m[i][j1] = (x[j] - x[j1]);
    }
  }
  //we have left-shift (multiplying constants) twice
  for ( i = 0; i < 8; ++i ) {
    for ( j = 0; j < 8; ++j ) {
      X[i][j] = ( m[i][j] + delta1 ) >> shift1;  //round by adding delta
    }
  }
}
}
```

----------------------------------------------------------------------------

In Listing 6-2, constant *shift* has value 10 and *shift1* has value 20 which are used for shifting values. Constant *fac* is obtained by left-shift 1 by 10 and thus has a value of 1024. Integer constants $c0, c1, c2, c3, c4, c5, c6, c7$ correspond to coefficients $C_k$ in (6.23) multiplied by 1024. Constants *delta* and *delta1* are used for rounding adjustments as explained above. In the second stage transform, in calculating $x[5]$ and $x[6]$, $x1[5]$ and $x1[6]$ have been multiplied by $c0$. However, no multiplication of any $ci$ is involved in other $x[i]$'s. Therefore, to line up the binary point of all $x[i]$'s including $x[5]$ and $x[6]$, we have to right-shift the intermediate results of $x[5]$ and $x[6]$ by 10 bits, i.e.

$$x1[5] = (x1[5] + delta) >> shift;$$
$$x1[6] = (x1[6] + delta) >> shift;$$

(6.30)

At the end, because we have multiplied the constants $ci$'s twice in the intermediate calculations, we must undo the corresponding shifting operations by right-shifting the intermediate results by $shift1$ ( = 20 ). Shifting an integer 20 bits is equivalent to shifting it 10 bits twice.

The code in Listing 6-2 can be used to do Fast DCT of a practical video compression application.

## 6.6 Inverse DCT ( IDCT ) Implementation

Once we have written the code for DCT, the implementation of IDCT becomes easy. All we need to do is to reverse the steps in the DCT program. In the flow graph shown in Figure 6-3, when we traverse from left to right, we obtain the DCT; if we traverse from right to left, we obtain the IDCT. To understand why this is so, lets examine a butterfly computation, where we obtain $(c, d)$ from $(a, b)$. If we reverse the direction of the butterfly flow-graph, going from right to left, we recover $(a, b)$ from $(c, d)$ by

$$a = (c + d)/2$$
$$b = (c - d)/2$$

(6.31)

Figure 6-4 shows the reversed butterfly except that we have suppressed writing the constant $\frac{1}{2}$ in the diagram.

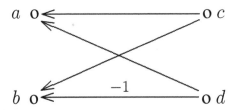

**Figure 6-4**. Flow Graph of Reversed Butterfly Computation

Basically, (6.23) and (6.31) have the same form. If we had multiplied the right side of (6.23) by $\frac{1}{\sqrt{2}}$ and solved for $c$, and $d$ to obtain (6.31), then the forms of (6.23) and (6.31) would become identical; there's no difference in going forward ( from left to right ) and going backward ( from right to left ) in the flow graph.

Another case shown in the flow graph of Figure 6-3 is of the form

$$c = aC_i - bC_j$$
$$d = aC_j + bC_i$$

(6.32)

where $C_k = cos(k\theta)$, and $\theta = \frac{\pi}{16}$. ( If the "minus" operation occurs in the second rather than the first equation of (6.32), we can simply interchange the roles of $c$, and $d$ to make it look the same as (6.32). ) It turns out that in (6.32) we always have $i + j = 8$. Therefore,

$$C_j = cos(j\theta) = cos(\frac{j\pi}{16}) = cos(\frac{(8-i)\pi}{16}) = cos(\frac{\pi}{2} - i\theta) = sin(i\theta)$$

(6.33)

and we can express the quations of (6.32) in a matrix form as shwon below.

$$
\begin{pmatrix} c \\ d \end{pmatrix} = \begin{pmatrix} cos(i\theta) & -sin(i\theta) \\ sin(i\theta) & +cos(i\theta) \end{pmatrix} \begin{pmatrix} a \\ b \end{pmatrix}
\tag{6.34}
$$

You may now recognize that the equations of (6.34) represent a rotation of $i\theta$ on a plane about the origin, which rotates the point $(a, b)$ to the point $(c, d)$. The inverse of such a transformation is a rotation of $-i\theta$ which will bring the point $(c, d)$ back to $(a, b)$. That is,

$$
\begin{pmatrix} a \\ b \end{pmatrix} = \begin{pmatrix} cos(i\theta) & +sin(i\theta) \\ -sin(i\theta) & +cos(i\theta) \end{pmatrix} \begin{pmatrix} c \\ d \end{pmatrix}
\tag{6.35}
$$

where we have used the fact that $sin(-i\theta) = -sin(i\theta)$ and $cos(-i\theta) = cos(i\theta)$. Thus, we can obtain the inverse of (6.32) by simply changing the sign of $C_j$. That is, we replace any $-C_j$ by $C_j$ and the corresponding $C_j$ by $-C_j$. So the inverse of ( 6.32) is given by

$$
a = cC_i + dC_j
$$
$$
b = -cC_j + dC_i
\tag{6.36}
$$

By doing this substitution for all $-C'_j s$ in Figure 6-3, we can obtain the flow graph for IDCT. Correspondingly, in developing the IDCT program, we start with the DCT code, starting from the bottom of the DCT function, and working our way up with the replacing strategy; the resulted code is the IDCT function. The implementation of IDCT is also shown in Listing 6-2 ( **DctVideo.java** ); the function **idct()** is straightforward implementations of what we have discussed. Both the functions **dct()** and **idct()** are ready for use for video compression.

We can compile **DctVideo.java** of Listing 6-2 using the command,

```
javac DctVideo.java
```

which generates the byte code for the class **Dctvideo.class** that can be used in a java application. We provide **Test_dct.java** listed below for you to test the DCT and IDCT routines of **DctVideo.java**. Note that the sample values must be within the range [0, 255]:

**Program Listing 6-3** : Testing DCT and IDCT routines of DctVideo.java

---

```
/*
  Test_dct.java
  For testing dct() and idct() routines in DctVideo.java.
  Compile: javac Test_dct.java
  Execute: java Test_dct
*/

public class Test_dct {
  //print one 8x8 sample block
```

```
static void print_block( int [][] X )
{
  for ( int i = 0; i < 8; ++i ){
    System.out.printf("\n");
    for ( int j = 0; j < 8; ++j ) {
      System.out.printf("%4d, ", X[i][j] );
    }
  }
}

public static void main(String[] args) throws InterruptedException
{
  int [][] X = new int[8][8], Y = new int[8][8];
  int i, j;

  //some sample data
  for ( i = 0; i < 8; ++i )
    for ( j = 0; j < 8; ++j )
      X[i][j] = 3 * i *j  + j + 1 ;

  System.out.printf("\nOriginal Data:");
  System.out.printf("\n ------------------");
  print_block ( X );

  DctVideo dct_idct = new DctVideo();

  dct_idct.dct(  X,  Y );

  System.out.printf("\n\nData after dct:");
  print_block ( Y );

  dct_idct.idct ( Y, X );

  System.out.printf("\n\nData recovered by idct:");
  System.out.printf("\n ------------------");
  print_block ( X );
  System.out.printf("\n");
  }
}
```

You may compile the program using the command "javac Test_dct.java", put the resulted file "Test_dct.class" in the same directory the file "DctVideo.class" resides, and run it with the command, "java Test_dct". You should then see the following outputs:

```
Original Data:
 ------------------
    1,    2,    3,    4,    5,    6,    7,    8,
    1,    5,    9,   13,   17,   21,   25,   29,
    1,    8,   15,   22,   29,   36,   43,   50,
    1,   11,   21,   31,   41,   51,   61,   71,
    1,   14,   27,   40,   53,   66,   79,   92,
    1,   17,   33,   49,   65,   81,   97,  113,
    1,   20,   39,   58,   77,   96,  115,  134,
    1,   23,   45,   67,   89,  111,  133,  155,

Data after dct:
  330, -209,    0,  -22,    0,   -6,    0,   -1,
```

```
-191,    124,      0,     13,      0,      4,      0,      1,
   0,      0,      0,      0,      0,      0,      0,      0,
 -20,     13,      0,      1,      0,      0,      0,      0,
   0,      0,      0,      0,      0,      0,      0,      0,
  -6,      4,      0,      1,      0,      0,      0,      0,
   0,      0,      0,      0,      0,      0,      0,      0,
  -1,      1,      0,      1,      0,      0,      0,      0,

Data recovered by idct:
------------------
   1,      2,      3,      4,      5,      6,      7,      8,
   1,      5,      9,     13,     17,     21,     25,     29,
   2,      8,     15,     22,     29,     36,     43,     50,
   1,     11,     21,     31,     41,     51,     61,     71,
   1,     14,     27,     40,     53,     66,     79,     92,
   1,     17,     33,     49,     65,     81,     97,    113,
   1,     20,     39,     58,     77,     96,    115,    133,
   1,     23,     45,     67,     89,    111,    133,    155,
------------------------------------------------------------
```

The sample outputs again show that the restored data after IDCT are the same as the original data. Also, like before, the DCT coefficients tend to cluster at the upper left corner of the $8 \times 8$ block.

# 6.7 Applying DCT and IDCT to YCbCr Macroblocks

In Chapter 5, we have discussed the down sampling of an RGB image to 4:2:0 YCbCr macroblocks. A 4:2:0 YCbCr macroblock conists of four $8 \times 8$ Y sample blocks , one $8 \times 8$ Cb sample block and one $8 \times 8$ Cr sample block. It is natural to apply the Fast DCT with $N = 8$ discussed above to each of these sample blocks. In Chapter 5, we developed a test program ( "Test_encode_ppm.java" ) that reads an RGB image in PPM format, decomposes and converts it to 4:2:0 YCbCr macroblocks, and saves the YCbCr data in a ".ycc" file. Here, we go one step further. We want to develop a test program that reads the RGB data from a PPM file, converts them to YCbCr macroblocks, applies DCT to the sample blocks, and saves the DCT coefficients in a file with extension ".dct". Our ".dct" file has a format similar to that of a ".ycc" file; the first 8 bytes consist of the header text "DCT4:2:0"; the next four bytes contain the image width followed by another four bytes of image height; data start from the seventeenth byte ( byte 16 ). The test program can also reverse the process. The reversed process consisting of reading a ".dct" file, applying IDCT to the data to recover the YCbCr macroblocks, converting YCbCr back to RGB and saving the RGB data in a PPM file.

To accomplish these, we need to add a few more functions in the classes of programs **Encode.java** and **Decode.java** discussed in Chapter 5. The following functions are added to the **Encode** class of **Encode.java**:

```
void save_one_dctblock ( int [][] Y, DataOutputStream out );
void save_dct_yccblocks( YCbCr_MACRO ycbcr_macro, DataOutputStream out );
void encode_dct ( RGBImage image, DataOutputStream out );
```

These functions are shown in Listing 6-4. Their meanings are self-explained by the code. Since the **Encode** class needs to use the functions of the **RgbYcc** class that we developed in Chapter 5, we need to setup the classpath to access the **RgbYcc** class before we compile **Encode.java**. The following command will do the job:

```
export CLASSPATH=$CLASSPATH:../5/
```

In the program, please be careful not to confuse the Y variable that we use to represent an array of DCT coefficients with the Y component of a YCbCr pixel.

**Program Listing 6-4** : Revised Encode.java

---

```
/*
   Encode.java
   Contains functions that convert an RGB frame to YCbCr, then to DCT
   coefficients which are saved in a file.  The program reads the data
   back from the file, convert them back to YCbCr and to RGB, which
   will be saved in another file.
*/
import java.io.*;

class Encode {

   //save one YCbCr macroblock.
   public void save_yccblocks(YCbCr_MACRO ycbcr_macro, DataOutputStream out)
   {
      //code has been presented in Encode.java of Chapter 5
   }

   /*
      Convert one frome of RGB to YCbCr and save the converted data.
   */
   public void encode ( RGBImage image, DataOutputStream out )
   {
      //code has been presented in Encode.java of Chapter 5
   }

   //The following functions are added in Chapter 6
   void save_one_dctblock ( int [][] Y, DataOutputStream out )
   {
      for ( int i = 0; i < 8; ++i )
         for ( int j = 0; j < 8; ++j )
            try {
               out.writeShort( Y[i][j] );  //save DCT coefficients of the block
            } catch (IOException e) {
               e.printStackTrace();
               System.exit(0);
            }
   }

   /*
    * Apply DCT to the six 8x8 sample blocks of a 4:2:0 YCbCr macroblock
    * and save the coefficients in a file pointed by out
    */
   void save_dct_yccblocks( YCbCr_MACRO ycbcr_macro, DataOutputStream out )
   {
      int b, i, j, k, r;
      int [][] X = new int[8][8], Y = new int[8][8];
      DctVideo dct_idct = new DctVideo();

      //save DCT of Y
      for ( b = 0; b < 4; b++){    //Y has four 8x8 sample blocks
```

```
    if ( b < 2 )
      r =  8 * b;                 //points to beginning of block
    else
      r = 128 + 8*(b-2);          //points to beginning of block
    k = 0;
    for ( i = 0; i < 8; i++ ){//one sample-block
      if ( i > 0 ) r += 16;    //multiply i by 16 ( length of one row )
      for ( j = 0; j < 8; j++ ) {
        X[i][j] = ycbcr_macro.Y[r+j];
      }
    }
    dct_idct.dct ( X, Y );          //DCT tranform of 8x8 block
    save_one_dctblock ( Y, out ); //save DCT coefficients of 8x8 block
  }
  k = 0;
  for ( i = 0; i < 8; ++i ) {
    for ( j = 0; j < 8; ++j ) {
      X[i][j] = ycbcr_macro.Cb[k];
      k++;
    }
  }
  dct_idct.dct ( X, Y );          //DCT of Cb 8x8 sample block
  save_one_dctblock( Y, out );
  k = 0;
  for ( i = 0; i < 8; ++i ) {
    for ( j = 0; j < 8; ++j ) {
      X[i][j] = ycbcr_macro.Cr[k];
      k++;
    }
  }
  dct_idct.dct ( X, Y );          //DCT of Cr 8x8 sample block
  save_one_dctblock ( Y, out );
}


/*
 * Convert RGB data to YCbCr, then to DCT coeffs and save DCT coeffs
 * which will be saved in a file.
 */
void encode_dct ( RGBImage image, DataOutputStream out )
{
  int row, col, i, j, k, r;

  RGB_MACRO rgbmacro = new RGB_MACRO();
  YCbCr_MACRO ycbcr_macro = new YCbCr_MACRO();//YCbCr macroblock
  RgbYcc rgbycc = new RgbYcc();

  for ( row = 0; row < image.height; row += 16 ) {
    for ( col = 0; col < image.width; col += 16 ) {
      k = row * image.width + col; //points to beginning of macroblock
      r = 0;
      for ( i = 0; i < 16; ++i ) {
        for ( j = 0; j < 16; ++j ) {
          rgbmacro.rgb[r++] = image.ibuf[k++];
        }
        k += image.width - 16;     //points to next row of macroblock
      }
      rgbycc.macroblock2ycbcr ( rgbmacro, ycbcr_macro );
      save_dct_yccblocks( ycbcr_macro, out );
    } //for col
```

```
      } //for row
   }
}
```

---

In Listing 6-4, the function **encode_dct**() converts RGB data of an image to YCbCr and makes use of the function **save_dct_yccblocks**() to convert the YCbCr samples to DCT coefficients, and save the coefficients in the specified file. The DCT coefficients are saved as 16-bit numbers. It seems that we have not achieved any data compression in the DCT transformation process; we have expanded the data instead. Actually, this is only an intermediate stage and the saved DCT data are used for testing, demonstration and explanation of concepts. As you will see later, we do not really need to save the DCT coefficients in a file. The purpose of DCT transformation is mainly to setup the data in a way that we can compress them efficiently in later stages of the compression pipeline.

The corresponding functions we need to add to **Decode.java** of Listing 5-3 of Chapter 5 to convert DCT coefficients back to YCbCr data and then to RGB include the following:

```
int get_one_dctblock ( int [][] Y, DataInputStream in );
int get_dct_yccblocks( YCbCr_MACRO ycbcr_macro, DataInputStream in );
int decode_dct ( RGBImage image, DataInputStream in );
```

These functions are shown in Listing 6-5. Again, their meanings are self-explained by the code.

**Program Listing 6-5** : Revised Decode.java

---

```
/*
  Decode.java
  Contains functions to:
     read DCT data from a file,
     carries out IDCT to obtain YCbCr macroblocks from DCT coefficients,
     convert YCbCr data to RGB, and
     read YCbCr data from a file
*/

import java.io.*;

class Decode {

  public int get_yccblocks( YCbCr_MACRO ycbcr_macro, DataInputStream in )
  {
    //code presented in Chapter 5
  }

  public int decode_yccFrame ( RGBImage image, DataInputStream in )
  {
    //code presented in Chapter 5
  }

  /*-------------------------------------------------------------
    Functions above are from Chapter 5.
```

```
    Functions below are added in Chapter 6.
    ----------------------------------------------------------------
*/

int get_one_dctblock ( int [][]  Y, DataInputStream in  )
{
  for ( int i = 0; i < 8; ++i )
    for ( int j = 0; j < 8; ++j )
        try {
          Y[i][j] = ( int ) in.readShort();
        } catch (IOException e) {
          e.printStackTrace();
          System.exit(0);
        }
  return 1;
}

int get_dct_yccblocks( YCbCr_MACRO ycbcr_macro, DataInputStream in )
{
  int r, row, col, i, j, k, n, p, block;
  int [][] Y = new int[8][8], X = new int[8][8];
  DctVideo dct_idct = new DctVideo();

  n = 0;
  //read data from file and put them in four 8x8 Y sample blocks
  for ( block = 0; block < 4; block++ ) {
    if ( get_one_dctblock( Y, in ) < 1 )
      return 0;
    dct_idct.idct ( Y, X );
    k = 0;
    if ( block < 2 )
      p = 8 * block;                //points to beginning of block
    else
      p = 128 + 8 * ( block - 2 );  //points to beginning of block
    for ( i = 0; i < 8; i++ ) {     //one sample-block
      if ( i > 0 ) p += 16;         //advance marcoblock length ( 16 )
      for ( j = 0; j < 8; j++ ) {
        ycbcr_macro.Y[p+j] = X[i][j];
        n++;
      } //for j
    } //for i
  } //for block

  //now do that for 8x8 Cb block
  k = 0;
  if ( get_one_dctblock( Y, in ) < 1 )
    return 0;
  dct_idct.idct ( Y, X );
  for ( i = 0; i < 8; ++i ) {
    for ( j = 0; j < 8; ++j ) {
      ycbcr_macro.Cb[k] = X[i][j];
      k++;
      n++;
    }
  }

  //now do that for 8x8 Cr block
  k = 0;
  if ( get_one_dctblock( Y, in ) < 1 )
    return 0;
```

```
      dct_idct.idct ( Y, X );
      for ( i = 0; i < 8; ++i ) {
        for ( j = 0; j < 8; ++j ) {
          ycbcr_macro.Cr[k] = X[i][j];
          k++;
          n++;
        }
      }
      return n;                              //number of coefficients read
    }

    /*
     *    Decode DCT coeffs to a YCbCr frame and then to RGB.
     */
    int decode_dct ( RGBImage image, DataInputStream in )
    {
      int r, row, col, i, j, k, block;
      int n = 0;
      RGB_MACRO rgb_macro=new RGB_MACRO(); //assume 24-bit for each RGB pixel
      YCbCr_MACRO ycbcr_macro = new YCbCr_MACRO(); //YCbCr macroblock
      RgbYcc rgbycc = new RgbYcc();
      for ( row = 0; row < image.height; row += 16 ) {
        for ( col = 0; col < image.width; col += 16 ) {
          int m = get_dct_yccblocks( ycbcr_macro, in );
          if ( m <= 0 ) { System.out.printf("\nout of dct data\n"); return m;}
          n += m;
          rgbycc.ycbcr2macroblock( ycbcr_macro, rgb_macro );
          k = row * image.width + col;
          r = 0;
          for ( i = 0; i < 16; ++i ) {
            for ( j = 0; j < 16; ++j ) {
              image.ibuf[k].R = rgb_macro.rgb[r].R;
              image.ibuf[k].G = rgb_macro.rgb[r].G;
              image.ibuf[k].B = rgb_macro.rgb[r].B;
              k++;   r++;
            }
            k += (image.width - 16);    //points to next row of macroblock
          }
        } //for col
      }  //for row
      return n;
    }
  }
```

Finally, the program **Test_dct_ppm.java** of Listing 6-6 performs the tasks of DCT testing on an image file. It first reads RGB data from the testing PPM file specified by args[0] and uses the function **encode_dct** () to convert the RGB data to 4:2:0 YCbCr macroblocks and then to 16-bit DCT coefficients, saving them in the file specified by args[1]. Secondly, it uses the function **decode_dct**() to read the DCT data back from the file args[1] and recovers the RGB data. The recovered RGB data are saved in the PPM file specified by args[2].

The following is an example of usage of this program:

```
java Test_dct_ppm ../data/beach.ppm t.dct t.ppm
```

After executing the program, we can check the recovered data by issuing the command "xview t.ppm". One can observe that the image of "t.ppm" is essentially identical to that of the original file, "../data/beach.ppm". The images of these two files are shown at the end of this Chapter ( Figure 6-6 ).

**Program Listing 6-6** :    Testing DCT and IDCT functions

```
/*
 * Test_dct_ppm.java
 * Program to test integer implementations of DCT, IDCT, and RGB-YCbCr
 * conversions using macroblocks. PPM files are used for testing.
 * It reads from the file specified by args[0] the RGB data, converts
 * them to 4:2:0 YCbCr macroblocks, and then to 16-bit DCT coefficients
 * which will be saved in the file specified by args[1].
 * The program then reads back the DCT coefficients from file args[1],
 * performs IDCT, converts them to YCbCr macroblocks and the to RGB data.
 * The recovered RGB data are saved in the file speicified by args[2].
 * PPM files can be viewed using "xview".
 *
 * Compile:  javac Test_dct_ppm.java
 * Execute:  e.g. java Test_dct_ppm ../data/beach.ppm t.dct t.ppm
 * Need to set classpath by: "export CLASSPATH=$CLASSPATH:../5/"
 */

import java.io.*;
import java.awt.Frame;
import java.awt.image.*;
import javax.media.jai.JAI;
import javax.media.jai.RenderedOp;
import com.sun.media.jai.codec.FileSeekableStream;
import javax.media.jai.widget.ScrollingImagePanel;
import com.sun.media.jai.codec.PNMEncodeParam;

public class Test_dct_ppm {

  //DCT file header
  private static byte [] header = { 'D', 'C', 'T', '4', ':', '2', ':', '0' };

  public static void write_dct_header( int width, int height, DataOutputStream out )
  {

    try {
      out.write ( header );
      out.writeInt ( width );
      out.writeInt ( height );
    } catch (IOException e) {
      e.printStackTrace();
      System.exit(0);
    }
  }

  public static int read_dct_header(RGBImage rgbimage,  DataInputStream in)
  {
    byte [] bytes = new byte[header.length];
    try {
      in.read ( bytes );
      rgbimage.width  = in.readInt ();
      rgbimage.height = in.readInt ();
    } catch (IOException e) {
      e.printStackTrace();
      System.exit(0);
```

```
    }
    for ( int i = 0; i < header.length; ++i )
      if ( bytes[i] != header[i] )
        return -1;         //wrong header

    return 1;
  }

  //save PPM header and RGB data
  public static int save_ppm ( RGBImage rgbimage, DataOutputStream out )
  {
    byte [] P6 = { 'P', '6', '\n' };
    byte [] colorLevels = { '2', '5', '5', '\n' };
    String sw = Integer.toString ( rgbimage.width ) + " ";
    String sh = Integer.toString ( rgbimage.height ) + "\n";

    int isize = rgbimage.width * rgbimage.height;
    byte [] bytes = new byte[3*isize];
    for ( int i = 0, k = 0; i < isize; i++, k+=3 ){
        bytes[k] = (byte) (rgbimage.ibuf[i].R);
        bytes[k+1] = (byte) (rgbimage.ibuf[i].G);
        bytes[k+2] = (byte) (rgbimage.ibuf[i].B);
    }

    try {
      out.write ( P6 );
      out.writeBytes ( sw );
      out.writeBytes ( sh );
      out.write ( colorLevels );
      out.write ( bytes );
    } catch (IOException e) {
      e.printStackTrace();
      System.exit(0);
    }

    return 1;
  }

  public static void main(String[] args) throws InterruptedException
  {
    if (args.length < 3) {
      System.out.println("Usage: java " + "Test_dct_ppm" +
        " input_ppm_filename output_dct_filename recoverd_ppm_filename\n" +
        "e.g. java Test_dct_ppm ../data/beach.ppm t.dct t.ppm");
      System.exit(-1);
    }

    /*
     * Create an input stream from the specified file name
     * to be used with the file decoding operator.
     */

    FileSeekableStream stream = null;
    try {
      stream = new FileSeekableStream(args[0]);
    } catch (IOException e) {
      e.printStackTrace();
      System.exit(0);
    }
    /* Create an operator to decode the image file. */
```

```
RenderedOp image = JAI.create("stream", stream);

/* Get the width and height of image. */
int width = image.getWidth();
int height = image.getHeight();

if ( width % 16 != 0 || height % 16 != 0 ) {
  System.out.println("Program only works for image dimensions");
  System.out.println("divisible by 16. Use 'convert' to change");
  System.out.println("image dimensions.");
  System.exit(1);
}
int [] samples = new int[3*width*height];

Raster ras = image.getData();
//save pixel RGB data in samples[]
ras.getPixels( 0, 0, width, height, samples );
RGBImage rgbimage = new RGBImage( width, height );
//copy image data to RGBImage object buffer
int isize = width * height;
for ( int i = 0, k = 0; i < isize; ++i, k+=3 ) {
  rgbimage.ibuf[i].R =  samples[k];
  rgbimage.ibuf[i].G = samples[k+1];
  rgbimage.ibuf[i].B = samples[k+2];
}
//Convert data to DCT coefficients and save them in file args[1]
try {
  File f = new File ( args[1] );
  OutputStream o = new FileOutputStream( f );
  DataOutputStream out = new DataOutputStream ( o );
  write_dct_header ( width, height, out );
  Encode enc = new Encode ();
  enc.encode_dct ( rgbimage, out );
  out.close();
} catch (IOException e) {
   e.printStackTrace();
   System.exit(0);
}

System.out.printf("\nEncoding done, DCT coeff saved in %s\n",args[1]);

//read the DCT data back from args[1] and convert to RGB
DataInputStream in;
Decode dct_decoder = new Decode ();
try {
  File f = new File ( args[1] );
  InputStream ins = new FileInputStream( f );
  in = new DataInputStream ( ins );
  if ( read_dct_header ( rgbimage,  in ) == -1 ){
    System.out.println("Not YCC File");
    return;
  }
  //To be fair in the demo, we use a new image buffer
  //Java collects any memory garbage
  //Apply IDCT
  rgbimage = new RGBImage ( rgbimage.width, rgbimage.height );
  dct_decoder.decode_dct (rgbimage, in);
  in.close();
} catch (IOException e) {
   e.printStackTrace();
```

```
      System.exit(0);
   }

   //Save recovered RGB data in file args[2] in PPM format.
   try {
     File f = new File ( args[2] );
     OutputStream o = new FileOutputStream( f );
     DataOutputStream out = new DataOutputStream ( o );
     save_ppm ( rgbimage, out ); //save PPM header and RGB data
     out.close();
   } catch (IOException e) {
     e.printStackTrace();
     System.exit(0);
   }
   System.out.printf("Decoded data saved in %s \n", args[2] );
  }
 }
 }
```

We may use the command "ls -l ../data/beach.ppm t.dct t.ppm ../5/t.ycc" to list the sizes of the original *beach* ppm file and the transformed files. If you do so, you may see something similar to the following, where the left column shows the file sizes:

```
     36880   ../5/t.ycc
     73743   ../data/beach.ppm
     73744   t.dct
     73743   t.ppm
```

We see that the file size of the DCT data is twice as large as that of the YCbCr data. This is because we have saved each DCT coefficient as a 16-bit number but each YCbCr sample value is only 8-bit. It seems that we have done something that have expanded rather than compressed the image data. Actually, the DCT is only an intermediate process. We do not really need to save any DCT coefficients. We do so here only for the purpose of testing and learning DCT. In the next chapter, we shall discuss what we shall do after the DCT step. At the moment, let us summarize what we have discussed, the encoding and decoding processes up to this point. The encoding stage consists of the following steps:

1. Converts RGB data to 4:2:0 YCbCr macroblocks. Each macroblock consists of four $8 \times 8$ Y sample blocks, one $8 \times 8$ Cb sample block, and one $8 \times 8$ Cr sample block. This step compresses the data by a factor of 2.
2. Applies DCT to each $8 \times 8$ sample block which gives an $8 \times 8$ array of 16-bit DCT coefficients. This step expands the data by a factor of 2.

On the other hand, the decoding stage consists of the following steps:

1. Applies IDCT to each $8 \times 8$ arrary of DCT coefficients to recover an $8 \times 8$ YCbCr 8-bit sample block. Reconstructs 4:2:0 YCbCr macroblocks from the sample blocks.
2. Converts YCbCr macroblocks to RGB data.

The encoding steps are shown in Figure 6-5.

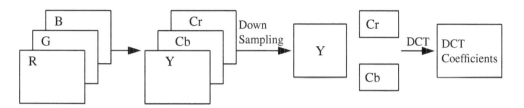

**Figure 6-5**. Encoding of RGB Data

**Figure 6-6**    Effect of down-sampling and DCT: The Original RGB Image ( left ) and The
Restored Image ( right )

# Chapter 7    Quantization and Run-level Encoding

## 7.1 Introduction

In Chapter 6, we have discussed using DCT to transform image data to the frequency domain. We have seen that DCT alone does not achieve any data compression and does not lose any information. However, the transformation usually clusters the data that allow us to carry out compression in the next stage effectively. Typically, the 'low frequency' components of the DCT coefficients of a block of image position around the DC (0,0) coefficient. As shown in the data output of Section 6.6 of Chapter 6, the nonzero DCT coefficients are clustered around the top-left (DC) coefficient and the distribution is roughly symmetrical in the horizontal and vertical directions. This special characteristics inspire people to reorder the DCT coefficients so that more consecutive zeros are lined up together and thus are easier to encode.

After DCT, the next operation in our compression pipeline involves quantization which will generate even more zeros in a DCT block as small values are approximated by a zero. After quantization, we shall reorder the data so that they can be encoded effectively using a technique called run-level encoding. The run-level values are then encoded using entropy encoding which can be Huffman encoding or arithmetic encoding. In this book, we only discuss Huffman encoding which is a lot faster than arithmetic encoding though it may yield slightly lower compression ratio. Entropy encoding generates a bit stream which is ready for transmission or storage. Figure 7-1 summarizes these encoding steps, which extend the steps shown in Figure 6-5.

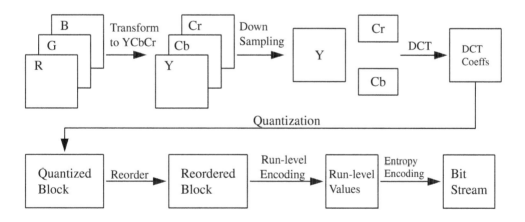

**Figure 7-1**. Encoding of RGB Image Block

Among all the stages shown in Figure 7-1, only the operations "Down Sampling" and "Quantization" are irreversible. Other stages are reversible; no information is lost in the operation. In particular, no rounding error will be introduced in the operations, "Reorder", "Run-level Encoding", and "Entropy Encoding"; the original data before each operation can be recovered exactly.

Besides "Down Sampling", compression occurs in stages "Run-level Encoding" and "Entropy Encoding". On the other hand, operations "DCT", "Quantization", and "Reorder" set up the data for these stages to compress them efficiently.

# 7.2 Quantization

We discussed in Chapter 3 that *quantization* is the procedure of constraining the value of a function at a sampling point to a predetermined finite set of discrete values. A *quantizer* maps a range of values X to a reduced range of values F. Therefore, a quantized signal can be represented by fewer bits than the original signal as the range of quantized values is smaller. To achieve high compression, we do not want to retain the full range of DCT coefficients as we did in Chapter 6 where we have used 16-bit ( i.e. data type short ) to save a DCT coefficient. In this Chapter, we discuss how to quantize DCT coefficients and represent a coefficient with significantly less bits.

Quantization can be done using a *scalar quantizer* or a *vector quantizer*. A *scaler quantizer* maps one sample of the input signal to one quantized output value. It is a special case of a *vector quantizer* which maps a group of input samples ( a 'vector' ) to an index of a codebook that contains vectors ( groups ) of quantized values. A vector quantizer in general yields better results but consumes a lot more computing power.

### 7.2.1 Scalar Quantization

An example of a simple *scalar quantizer* is an operation that rounds a real number to an integer. Obviously, the operation is a many-to-one mapping and is irreversible. Information is lost in the process; we cannot determine the exact value of the original real number from the rounded integer.

A more general example of scalar quantization is a uniform quantizer where an input value X is divided by a **quantization parameter** ( or step size ) q and rounded to the nearest integer $F_q$ as shown in Equation (7.1) below:

$$F_q = round(\frac{X}{q})  \qquad (7.1)$$

The quantized output level is given by

$$Y = F_q \times q \qquad (7.2)$$

The output levels Y are spaced uniformly with step size q. The following example shows a uniform quantizer with various step sizes.

**Example 7-1** A uniform quantizer with step sizes, 1, 2, 3, 5, and 8.

| X | Y q = 1 | Y q = 2 | Y q = 3 | Y q = 5 | Y q = 8 |
|---|---|---|---|---|---|
| -5 | -5 | -6 | -6 | -5 | -8 |
| -4 | -4 | -4 | -3 | -5 | -8 |
| -3 | -3 | -4 | -3 | -5 | 0 |
| -2 | -2 | -2 | -3 | 0 | 0 |
| -1 | -1 | -2 | 0 | 0 | 0 |
| 0 | 0 | 0 | 0 | 0 | 0 |
| 1 | 1 | 2 | 0 | 0 | 0 |
| 2 | 2 | 2 | 3 | 0 | 0 |
| 3 | 3 | 4 | 3 | 5 | 0 |
| 4 | 4 | 4 | 3 | 5 | 8 |
| 5 | 5 | 6 | 6 | 5 | 8 |
| 6 | 6 | 6 | 6 | 5 | 8 |
| 7 | 7 | 8 | 6 | 5 | 8 |
| 8 | 8 | 8 | 9 | 10 | 8 |
| 9 | 9 | 10 | 9 | 10 | 8 |
| 10 | 10 | 10 | 9 | 10 | 8 |
| 11 | 11 | 12 | 12 | 10 | 8 |
| 12 | 12 | 12 | 12 | 10 | 16 |

Figure 7-2 shows two examples of scalar quantizer. The linear scalar quantizer shown on the left shows linear mapping between input and output values. The nonlinear quantizer on the right shows a dead zone where small input values are mapped to zero.

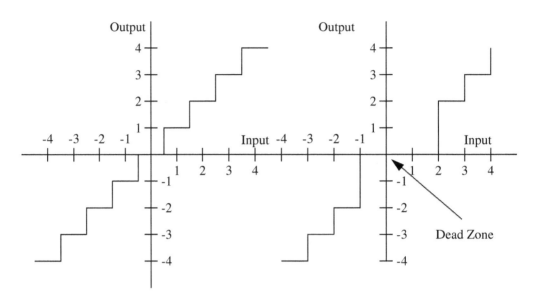

**Figure 7-2**. Linear and Non-linear Quantizers

More precisely, we can define an $N$-point scalar quantizer $Q$ as a mapping $Q : R \rightarrow C$ where $R$ is the real line and

$$C \equiv \{y_1, y_2, ...., y_N\} \subset R \qquad (7.3)$$

is the output set or codebook with size $|C| = N$. The output values, $y_i$, are referred to as output levels, output points, or reproduction values. Quite often, we choose the indexing of output values so that

$$y_1 < y_2 < ... < y_N \qquad (7.4)$$

The resolution or code rate, $r$, of a scalar quantizer is defined as $r = log_2 N$, which measures the number of bits required to uniquely specify the quantized value.

Every quantizer can be viewed as making up of two successive operations ( mappings ), an encoder, $E$, ( or forward quantizer $FQ$ ), and a decoder, $D$ ( or inverse quantizer $IQ$ ). The encoder $E$ is a mapping

$$E : R \rightarrow I \qquad (7.5)$$

where $I = \{1, 2, 3, ..., N\}$, and the decoder is the mapping

$$D : I \rightarrow C. \qquad (7.6)$$

Therefore, if $Q(x) = y_i$, then $E(x) = i$ and $D(i) = y_i$. Consequently, $Q(x) = D(E(x))$. Note that the decoder can be implemented by a table-lookup process, where the table or codebook contains the output set which can be stored with very high precision without affecting the transmission rate $R$. The decoder is also referred to as an inverse quantization and the encoder is sometimes referred to as forward quantization.

## 7.2.2 Vector Quantization

Vector quantization ( VQ ) is a generalization of scalar quantization to the quantization of a vector, an ordered set of real numbers. Speech or image samples can be grouped together to form a vector. Thus vector quantization can be regarded as a form of pattern recognition where an input pattern is "approximated" by one of a predetermined set of patterns stored in a codebook.

We can define a vector quantizer $Q$ of dimension $k$ and size $N$ as a mapping from a vector in k-dimensional Euclidean space, $R^k$, into a finite set $C$ that contains $N$ output or reconstructed vectors, called *code vectors* or *codewords*. That is,

$$Q: R^k \to C, \tag{7.7}$$

where

$$
\begin{aligned}
C &= \{y_1, y_2, ..., y_N\} \\
y_i &\in R^k \\
i &\in I \equiv \{1, 2, ..., N\}
\end{aligned}
\tag{7.8}
$$

The set $C$ is referred to as the *codebook* or the *code* with $N$ distinct elements, each a vector in $R^k$. The *resolution* or *code rate* $r$ of the vector quantizer is given by:

$$code\ rate\ r = \frac{log_2 N}{k} \tag{7.9}$$

In general, the code rate of a vector quantizer is the number of bits per vector component used to represent the input vector, indicating the accuracy or precision it can achieve with the quantizer. Note that for a given dimension $k$, the resolution is determined by the size $N$ of the codebook but not by the number of bits used to specify the code vectors stored in the codebook. Even if we specify a code vector to a very high precision, we still can have a very low resolution by using a small codebook. Typically, a codebook is loaded as a lookup table in the main memory of a computer and the number of bits used in each table entry does not affect the quantizer's resolution or bit rate.

Associated with each of the $N$ vectors in $C$ is a partition of $R^k$ into $N$ regions or *cells*, $R_i$ for $i \in I$:

$$R_i - \{\mathbf{x} \in R^k . Q(\mathbf{x}) = y_i\} \tag{7.10}$$

The $ith$ cell $R_i$ given by (7.10) is called the *inverse image* or *pre-image* of $y_i$ under the mapping $Q$ and can be denoted by:

$$R_i = Q^{-1}(y_i) \tag{7.11}$$

The application of VQ to image compression can be summarized as follows:

1. Partition an image into blocks of pixels.
2. Choose a vector from the codebook that best-approximates the current block.
3. Send the index pointing to the chosen vector to the decoder.
4. At the decoder, reconstruct an approximate copy of the original block using the chosen vector.

Figure 7-3 shows the concept of vector quantization.

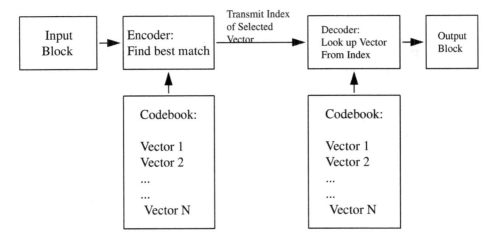

**Figure 7-3**. Vector Quantization

## 7.2.3 MPEG-4 Quantization

Video compression standard MPEG-4 allows two methods to quantize DCT coefficients. A parameter called quantizer_scale ( quantization_parameter ) is used to control how much information is discarded during the quantization process. The parameter can take values from 1 to 31 in the case of 8-bit textures and 1 to $2^{quant\_precision} - 1$ in the case of non 8-bit textures. Each frame may use a different value of quantizer_scale. The two methods are referred to as Method 2 ( basic method ) and Method 1 ( more flexible but more complex ). Method 2, which is the default method, specifies the quantization of the DC component, $F[0][0]$ using a fixed quantizer step:

$$Forward\ Quantization: F_q[0][0] = \frac{F[0][0]}{dc\_scalar}$$
$$Inverse\ Quantization: F'[0][0] = F_q[0][0] \times dc\_scalar$$

(7.12)

where $dc\_scalar$ which has a value of 8 in the short header mode and depends on the quantizer_parameter is determined from the following table:

| quantizer_parameter($Q_p$) | 1 - 4 | 5 - 8 | 9 - 24 | 25 - 31 |
|---|---|---|---|---|
| dc_scalar(luminance) | 8 | $2Q_p$ | $Q_p + 8$ | $2Q_p - 16$ |
| dc_scalar(chrominance) | 8 | $\dfrac{2Q_p + 13}{2}$ | $\dfrac{Q_p + 13}{2}$ | $Q_p - 6$ |

**Table 7-1**: MPEG-4 Quantization Parameters.

All other coefficients are rescaled as follows.

$$|F| = Q_p \times (2 \times |F_Q| + 1) \qquad \text{if } Q_p \text{ is odd and } F_Q \neq 0$$

$$|F| = Q_p \times (2 \times |F_Q| + 1) - 1 \qquad \text{if } Q_p \text{ is even and } F_Q \neq 0 \qquad (7.13)$$

$$|F| = 0 \qquad \text{if } F_Q = 0$$

where $F_Q$ is the forward-quantized coefficient and $F$ is the rescaled ( inverse-quantized ) coefficient.

In Method 1, which is also referred to as alternate quantizer, MPEG-4 uses a weighting factor to exploit properties of the human visual system ( HVS ). Since human eyes are less sensitive to some frequencies, we can quantize these frequencies with a coarser step-size, which results in a more compactly coded bit-stream and minimizes the image distortion. MPEG-4 recommends different weight matrices for the quantization of various sample blocks. The forward and inverse quantization can be described as follows.

Forward Quantization is described by the following equation ( we shall explain the meaning of intra and inter blocks in a later chapter ).

$$F_Q(u, v) = \frac{16F(u, v)}{2Q_p(W(u, v) - k \times Q_p)} \qquad (7.14)$$

where

$$k = \begin{cases} 0 & \text{for intra coded blocks} \\ sign(F_Q(u, v)) & \text{for inter coded blocks} \end{cases}$$

and

$$sign(x) = \begin{cases} -1 & \text{if } x < 0 \\ +1 & \text{otherwise} \end{cases}$$

Inverse Quantization is described by Eqaution (7.15) shown below.

$$F'(u, v) = \begin{cases} 0 & \text{if } F_Q(u, v) = 0 \\ \dfrac{(2F_Q(u, v) + k) \times W(u, v) \times Q_p}{16} & \text{if } F_Q(u, v) \neq 0 \end{cases} \qquad (7.15)$$

Users can define the weighting factors $W(u, v)$ based on their particular applications. MPEG-4 suggests some default weighting factors, which are shown in Table 7-2, where the left table ( Table 7-2a ) shows the default weighting matrix for intra-coded macroblocks and the right one presents the default weighting matrix for inter-coded macroblocks. Again, we shall explain the difference between intra-coded and inter-coded blocks in a later chapter. The tables assume that a macroblock is of size $8 \times 8$. For example, if intra-coded blocks are used, $W(0, 0) = 8$, and $W(7, 7) = 45$. On the other hand, when inter-coded blocks are used, $W(0, 0) = 16$ and $W(7, 7) = 33$.

**Table 7-2a** Intra Block Weights $W(u, v)$                    **Table 7-2b** Inter Block Weights $W(u, v)$

| $u \backslash v$ | 0 | 1 | 2 | 3 | 4 | 5 | 6 | 7 |
|---|---|---|---|---|---|---|---|---|
| 0 | 8 | 17 | 18 | 19 | 21 | 23 | 25 | 27 |
| 1 | 17 | 18 | 19 | 21 | 23 | 25 | 27 | 28 |
| 2 | 20 | 21 | 22 | 23 | 24 | 26 | 28 | 30 |
| 3 | 21 | 22 | 23 | 24 | 26 | 28 | 30 | 32 |
| 4 | 22 | 23 | 24 | 26 | 28 | 30 | 32 | 35 |
| 5 | 23 | 24 | 26 | 28 | 30 | 32 | 35 | 38 |
| 6 | 25 | 26 | 28 | 30 | 32 | 35 | 38 | 41 |
| 7 | 27 | 28 | 30 | 32 | 35 | 38 | 41 | 45 |

| $u \backslash v$ | 0 | 1 | 2 | 3 | 4 | 5 | 6 | 7 |
|---|---|---|---|---|---|---|---|---|
| 0 | 16 | 17 | 18 | 19 | 20 | 21 | 22 | 23 |
| 1 | 17 | 18 | 19 | 20 | 21 | 22 | 23 | 24 |
| 2 | 18 | 19 | 20 | 21 | 22 | 23 | 24 | 25 |
| 3 | 19 | 20 | 21 | 22 | 23 | 24 | 26 | 27 |
| 4 | 20 | 21 | 22 | 23 | 25 | 26 | 27 | 28 |
| 5 | 21 | 22 | 23 | 24 | 26 | 27 | 28 | 30 |
| 6 | 22 | 23 | 24 | 26 | 27 | 28 | 30 | 31 |
| 7 | 23 | 24 | 25 | 27 | 28 | 30 | 31 | 33 |

Listing 7-1 presents an implementation of a uniform quantizer. The implementation is simple and straightforward; the array *coef[]* holds an $8 \times 8$ sample block of DCT coefficients; *Qstep* is the quantization parameter discussed above. The code shows both forward quantization ( FQ ) and inverse quantization ( IQ ).

**Program Listing 7-1**: Implementation of Uniform Quantizer

```
class Quantizer {

  short Qstep = 12;

  //forward quantizer
  void quantize_block ( short [][]  coef )
  {
    for ( int i = 0; i < 8; i++ )
      for ( int j = 0; j < 8; j++ )
        coef[i][j] = ( short ) Math.round ( (double)coef[i][j] / Qstep );
  }

  //inverse quantize one block
  void inverse_quantize_block ( short [][] coef )
  {
    for ( int i = 0; i < 8; i++ )
      for ( int j = 0; j < 8; j++ )
        coef[i][j] = (short) ( coef[i][j] * Qstep );
  }
}
```

# 7.3 Reordering

After DCT transform and forward quantization, a sample block may have only a few nonzero coefficients and all others are zeros. It is desirable to to group zero coefficients together so that they can be represented effectively. The optimum reordering path ( scan order ) depends on the distribution of nonzero DCT coefficients. A commonly used scan order is a zigzag path starting from the DC coefficient at the top left corner of an $8 \times 8$ sample block as shown in Figure 7-4. After such a reordering, nonzero coefficients tend to cluster together at the beginning of the reordered array, followed by long sequences ( runs ) of zeros. Data consist of long runs of certain values can be efficiently encoded using a run-level coding technique that we shall discuss in the next section.

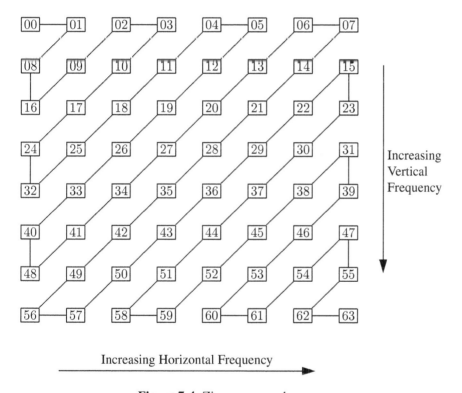

**Figure 7-4**. Zigzag scan order

Figure 7-4 shows that in a zigzag scan, sample 0 is the first element to be read, followed by sample 1, then by sample 8, sample 16, sample 9, and so on. After a zigzag scan, the indices of the original DCT coefficients are reordered as below.

|    |    |    |    |    |    |    |    |
|----|----|----|----|----|----|----|----|
| 0  | 1  | 8  | 16 | 9  | 2  | 3  | 10 |
| 17 | 24 | 32 | 25 | 18 | 11 | 4  | 5  |
| 12 | 19 | 26 | 33 | 40 | 48 | 41 | 34 |
| 27 | 20 | 13 | 6  | 7  | 14 | 21 | 28 |
| 35 | 42 | 49 | 56 | 57 | 50 | 43 | 36 |
| 29 | 22 | 15 | 23 | 30 | 37 | 44 | 51 |
| 58 | 59 | 52 | 45 | 38 | 31 | 39 | 46 |
| 53 | 60 | 61 | 54 | 47 | 55 | 62 | 63 |

Researchers have explored and tried various scanning orders but the zigzag scan remains the most commonly used scan in video compression. However, for some applications such as a field block where the coefficient distribution is often skewed, an alternate scan is more effective. In an alternate scan, the left-hand coefficients are scanned before those on the right side as shown in Figure 7-5.

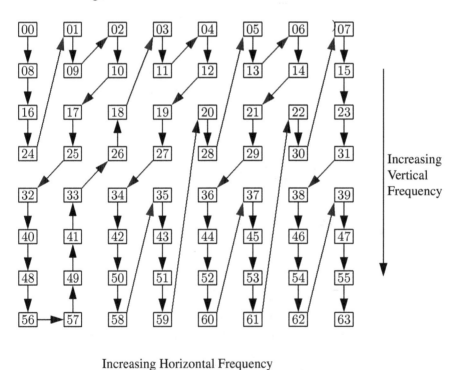

Increasing Vertical Frequency

Increasing Horizontal Frequency

**Figure 7-5**. Alternate scan order

In our subsequent discussions, we shall only use the zigzag scan. Listing 7-2 shows the implementations of such a reordering and the reverse of it. The code assumes that 64 samples are arranged in an $8 \times 8$ sample block. The one dimensional index $k$ is represented as a two-dimensional pair of integers $(i, j)$ with $i = k/8, j = k\%8$. For example, 1 is represented by $(0, 1)$, 8 by $(1, 0)$, 23 by $(2, 7)$, and so on. The function **reorder()** uses zigzag scan to rearrange the 64 sample elements stored in the $Y[][]$ array and save the reordered sampled in the array $Yr[][]$. The function **reverse_reorder()** does the opposite; it restores the original order from array $Yr[][]$ and saves the results in array $Y[][]$.

**Program Listing 7-2: Reordering**

```
class Reorder {

  int [] zigzag = {
     0,   1,   8,  16,   9,   2,   3,  10,
    17,  24,  32,  25,  18,  11,   4,   5,
    12,  19,  26,  33,  40,  48,  41,  34,
    27,  20,  13,   6,   7,  14,  21,  28,
    35,  42,  49,  56,  57,  50,  43,  36,
    29,  22,  15,  23,  30,  37,  44,  51,
    58,  59,  52,  45,  38,  31,  39,  46,
    53,  60,  61,  54,  47,  55,  62,  63
  };

  void reorder ( short [][] Y, short [][] Yr )
  {
    int k, i1, j1;
    k = 0;
    for ( int i = 0; i < 8; i++ ){
       for ( int j = 0; j < 8; j++ ){
          i1 =  zigzag[k] / 8;
          j1 = zigzag[k] % 8;
          Yr[i][j] = Y[i1][j1];
          k++;
       }
    }
  }

  void reverse_reorder ( short [][] Yr, short [][] Y )
  {
    int k, i1, j1;
    k = 0;
    for ( int i = 0; i < 8; i++ ){
       for ( int j = 0; j < 8; j++ ){
          i1 = zigzag[k] / 8;
          j1 = zigzag[k] % 8;
          Y[i1][j1] = Yr[i][j];
          k++;
       }
    }
  }
}
```

# 7.4 Run-Level Encoding

After DCT, forward quantization and reordering, we may obtain long sequences of zeros
followed by nonzero values. One of the effective methods to encode this kind of data is the
three-dimensional ( 3D ) run-level encoding. A 3D run-level codeword is represented by a
tuple ( *run, level, last* ) where *run* is the number of zeros preceding a nonzero coefficient,
*level* is the value of the nonzero coefficient, and *last* indicates if the codeword is the final one
with nonzero coefficient in the block. The following shows two examples of 3D run-level
encoding.

Input Sequence:   $1, 0, -2, 3, 0, 0, 0, 4, 5, 0, -1, 6, 0, 0, 0, ..., 0$

Output:                 $(0, 1, 0), (1, -2, 0), (0, 3, 0), (3, 4, 0), (0, 5, 0), (1, -1, 0), (0, 6, 1)$

Input Sequence:   $0, 0, 2, 0, 0, 0, 0, 1, 0, 0, -2, 0, 7, 0, 0, 0, ..., 0$

Output:                 $(2, 2, 0), (4, 1, 0), (2, -2, 0), (1, 7, 1)$

The special case the whole block containing zeros is coded by (64, 0, 1):

Input Sequence:   $0, 0, 0, ..., 0$

Output:                 $(64, 0, 1)$

Implementation of run-level encoding can be done by defining a class *run3D* comprising public members *run*, *level*, and *last* as follows. A *run3D* object can hold one run-level codeword.

```
class Run3D {
    byte   run;
    short  level;
    byte   last;
};
```

Suppose a macroblock of $8 \times 8$ DCT coefficients have been quantized, zigzag-reordered, and
saved in an array $Y[]$. Listing 7-3 presents a piece of code that can run-level-encode such a
block of 64 coefficients. The function **run_block()** accepts the $8 \times 8$ block of coefficients
saved in the array $Y[]$ as input; the outputs are the run-level codewords returned in the run3D
object array *runs[]*. Each run3D object holds the information of the tuple (*run, level, last*) that
represents a codeword.

### Program Listing 7-3: Run-level Encoding

```
class Run {
  /*
    Input: 64 quantized DCT coefficients in Y[][].
    Output: 3D run-level codewords in runs[].
  */
  void run_block ( short [][] Y, Run3D [] runs )
  {
```

```
      byte run_length = 0, k = 0;
      for ( int i = 0; i < 8; i++ ) {
        for ( int j = 0; j < 8; j++ ) {
          if ( Y[i][j] == 0  ) {
            run_length++;
            continue;
          }
          runs[k].run = run_length;
          runs[k].level = Y[i][j];
          runs[k].last = 0;
          run_length = 0;
          k++;
        }
      }
      if ( k > 0 )
        runs[k-1].last = 1;              //last nonzero element
      else {                            //whole block 0
        runs[0].run = 64;
        runs[0].level = 0;
        runs[0].last = 1;               //this needs to be 1 to terminate
      }
    }
  }
}
```

The corresponding code that recovers the block of 64 DCT coefficients from the run-level codewords is presented in Listing 7-4; the code first recovers the zeros and nonzero values from the run-level codewords saved in *runs*[] until it finds that the *last* field of the codeword is 1; after detecting the *last* field to be 1, it sets the remaining values of *Y*[] to zero.

**Program Listing 7-4: Run-level Decoding**

```
class Run {
  /*
   *    Input: 3D run-level codewords of a macroblock in runs[].
   *    Output: 64 DCT coefficients in Y[][].
   */
  void run_decode ( Run3D [] runs, short [][] Y )
  {
    int i, j, r, k = 0, n = 0;

    while ( n < 64 ) {
      for ( r = 0;   r < runs[k].run; r++ ){
        i = n / 8;
        j = n % 8;
        Y[i][j] = 0;
        n++;
      }
      if ( n < 64 ){
        i = n / 8;
        j = n % 8;
        Y[i][j] = runs[k].level;
        n++;
      }
```

```
         if ( runs[k].last != 0 ) break;
         k++;
      }
      //run of 0s to end
      while ( n < 64 ) {
         i = n / 8;
         j = n % 8;
         Y[i][j] = 0;
         n++;
      }
   }
}
```

Listing 7-5 presents the program **Test_run.java** which is a complete program that demonstrates the operations of quantization, reordering and run-level encoding and the reverse of the operations. It reads DCT coefficients from the file specified by args[0] which has saved blocks of $8 \times 8$ DCT coefficients in short ( 16-bit ) form as discussed in Chapter 6; the file of args[0] can be obtained from the PPM image file "beach.ppm" after the operations of 4:2:0 YCbCr down sampling and DCT Transformation that we have discussed in Chapter 6. The functions **get64, print_blcock,** and **print_run** are member functions of the class **Run**; **get64** gets 64 sample values from the DataInputStream *in* and put them in the two-dimensional array $Y[][]$, which will be returned to the calling function; **print_block** prints one $8 \times 8$ sample block; **print_run** prints the run-level codewords on one 64-sample block.

**Program Listing 7-5: Quantization, Reordering, and Run-level Encoding**

```
/*
   Test_run.java
   A demo program that illustrates the concepts of quantization, zigzag
   reordering and run-level encoding.  It reads DCT coefficients from the
   file specified by args[0] which has saved 8x8 blocks of DCT
   coefficients in short ( 16-bit ) form.
   Compile:  javac Test_run.java
   Execute:  e.g. java Test_run ../6/t.dct
*/

import java.io.*;

public class Test_run {

   //DCT file header
   private static byte []  header = { 'D', 'C', 'T', '4', ':', '2', ':', '0' };

   static int read_dct_header ( DataInputStream in )
   {
     byte [] bytes = new byte[header.length];
     try {
       in.read ( bytes );
       int width = in.readInt();     //not used here
       int height = in.readInt();    //not used here
     } catch (IOException e) {
        e.printStackTrace();
        System.exit(0);
```

```
    }
    for ( int i = 0; i < header.length; ++i )
      if ( bytes[i] != header[i] )
        return -1;       //wrong header

    return 1;
  }

  public static void main(String[] args) throws InterruptedException
  {
    if (args.length < 1) {
      System.out.println("Usage: java " + "Test_run" +
        " input_dct_filename \n" +
        "e.g. java Test_run ../6/t.dct");
      System.exit(-1);
    }

    Run3D [] runs = new Run3D[64];
    short [][] Y - now short[8][8];
    short [][] Yr = new short[8][8];
    for ( int i = 0, i < 64; ++i )
      runs[i] = new Run3D();
    //read the DCT data back from args[0]
    DataInputStream in;
    Quantizer quantizer = new Quantizer();
    Reorder reorder = new Reorder();
    Run run = new Run();
    try {
      File f = new File ( args[0] );
      InputStream ins = new FileInputStream( f );
      in = new DataInputStream ( ins );
      if ( read_dct_header ( in ) == -1 ){
        System.out.println("Not dct File");
        return;
      }
      String key;
      InputStreamReader converter = new InputStreamReader(System.in);
      BufferedReader keyin = new BufferedReader(converter);
      while ( run.get64 ( Y, in ) > 0 ) {        //read a block of 64 samples
        System.out.printf("\nA block of DCT coefficients:");
        run.print_block ( Y );
        quantizer.quantize_block ( Y );

        System.out.printf("\nDCT block after quantization ( Qstep = %d ):",
                                                      quantizer.Qstep );
        run.print_block ( Y );
        reorder.reorder ( Y, Yr );

        System.out.printf("\nDCT block After zigzag reorder:");
        run.print_block ( Yr );
        run.run_block ( Yr, runs );

        System.out.printf("\n3D run-level codewords of the reordered
                                        quantized DCT coeficients:");
        run.print_run ( runs );
        System.out.printf("\nHit any key to reverse the processes:");
        keyin.readLine();

        //reversing the process
        short [][] new_Y = new short[8][8];
```

```
      run.run_decode ( runs, new_Y );
      System.out.printf("\nDCT block after decode run:");
      run.print_block ( new_Y );

      reorder.reverse_reorder ( new_Y, Y );
      System.out.printf("\nDCT block after reversing reorder:");
      run.print_block ( Y );

      quantizer.inverse_quantize_block ( Y );
      System.out.printf("\nDCT block after inverse quantization:");
      run.print_block ( Y );

      System.out.printf("\nDo you want another block? ( y/n) ");
      key = keyin.readLine();
      if ( key.equals( "n" ) ) break;
    }
    in.close();
  } catch (IOException e) {
    e.printStackTrace();
    System.exit(0);
  }
 }
}
```

Listing 7-6 shows sample outputs of the program **Test_run.java**. You can see from the data that reordering and run-level encoding are reversible while quantization is not.

### Listing 7-6: Sample outputs of Test_run.java

```
A block of DCT coefficients:
    629,      -5,      -1,      -1,       1,      -1,      -2,      -1,
     -8,      -5,      -1,       0,       0,      -1,      -2,      -2,
      2,      -3,      -1,      -1,      -4,      -4,      -3,      -2,
     -3,      -4,      -3,      -1,       1,      -2,      -4,      -3,
     -1,      -6,       0,      -1,      -1,       1,       0,       0,
     -4,      -5,      -3,       0,       2,      -1,      -1,       0,
     -1,      -2,      -2,      -1,      -1,      -1,      -1,      -2,
      1,      -1,       0,       0,       0,      -2,      -2,      -1,
DCT block after quantization ( Qstep = 12 ):
     52,       0,       0,       0,       0,       0,       0,       0,
     -1,       0,       0,       0,       0,       0,       0,       0,
      0,       0,       0,       0,       0,       0,       0,       0,
      0,       0,       0,       0,       0,       0,       0,       0,
      0,       0,       0,       0,       0,       0,       0,       0,
      0,       0,       0,       0,       0,       0,       0,       0,
      0,       0,       0,       0,       0,       0,       0,       0,
      0,       0,       0,       0,       0,       0,       0,       0,
DCT block After zigzag reorder:
     52,       0,      -1,       0,       0,       0,       0,       0,
      0,       0,       0,       0,       0,       0,       0,       0,
      0,       0,       0,       0,       0,       0,       0,       0,
      0,       0,       0,       0,       0,       0,       0,       0,
      0,       0,       0,       0,       0,       0,       0,       0,
      0,       0,       0,       0,       0,       0,       0,       0,
      0,       0,       0,       0,       0,       0,       0,       0,
      0,       0,       0,       0,       0,       0,       0,       0,
3D run-level codewords of the reordered quantized DCT coeficients:
```

```
( 0,   52, 0)    ( 1,   -1, 1)

Hit any key to reverse the processes:

DCT block after decode run:
      52,        0,       -1,        0,        0,        0,        0,        0,
       0,        0,        0,        0,        0,        0,        0,        0,
       0,        0,        0,        0,        0,        0,        0,        0,
       0,        0,        0,        0,        0,        0,        0,        0,
       0,        0,        0,        0,        0,        0,        0,        0,
       0,        0,        0,        0,        0,        0,        0,        0,
       0,        0,        0,        0,        0,        0,        0,        0,
       0,        0,        0,        0,        0,        0,        0,        0,
DCT block after reversing reorder:
      52,        0,        0,        0,        0,        0,        0,        0,
      -1,        0,        0,        0,        0,        0,        0,        0,
       0,        0,        0,        0,        0,        0,        0,        0,
       0,        0,        0,        0,        0,        0,        0,        0,
       0,        0,        0,        0,        0,        0,        0,        0,
       0,        0,        0,        0,        0,        0,        0,        0,
       0,        0,        0,        0,        0,        0,        0,        0,
       0,        0,        0,        0,        0,        0,        0,        0,
DCT block after inverse quantization:
     624,        0,        0,        0,        0,        0,        0,        0,
     -12,        0,        0,        0,        0,        0,        0,        0,
       0,        0,        0,        0,        0,        0,        0,        0,
       0,        0,        0,        0,        0,        0,        0,        0,
       0,        0,        0,        0,        0,        0,        0,        0,
       0,        0,        0,        0,        0,        0,        0,        0,
       0,        0,        0,        0,        0,        0,        0,        0,
       0,        0,        0,        0,        0,        0,        0,        0,
Do you want another block? ( y/n)
```

# Chapter 8   Huffman Encoding

## 8.1 Introduction

Rather than saving the 3D run-level tuples directly, people encode them using an entropy encoder which in general yields significant compression. Entropy encoding is a reversible or lossless process; exact data can be recovered in the decoding process from the encoded data. Arithmetic coding and Huffman coding are two popular methods of entropy encoding with the former giving slightly better results and consuming more computing power. This kind of encoding is also referred to as variable-length coding ( VLC ) because the codewords representing symbols are of varying lengths. We shall only discuss the Huffman encoding method here.

The commonly used generalized ASCII code uses 8 bits to represent a character and uni-code uses 16 bits to do so; these are fixed-length codes, which are simple but inefficient in the representation. Huffman coding assigns a variable-length codeword to each symbol ( or tuple here ) based on the probability of the occurrence of the symbol. Frequently occurring symbols are represented with short codewords whilst less common symbols are represented with longer codewords; in this way we have a shorter average codeword length and thus saving space to store the codewords, leading to data compression.

We say that a code has the **prefix property** and is a prefix code if no codeword is the prefix, or start of the codeword for another symbol. A code with codewords $\{1, 01, 00\}$ has the prefix property; a code consisting of $\{1, 0, 01, 00\}$ does not, because "0" is a prefix of both "01" and "00". A non-prefix code like $\{ 1, 0, 01, 00 \}$ cannot be instantaneously decoded because when we receive a bitstream such as "001", we do not know whether it consists of $\{$ '0', '0', '1' $\}$, or $\{$ '0', '01' $\}$ or $\{$ '00', '1' $\}$. On the other hand, a prefix code can be instantaneously decoded. That is, a message can be transmitted as a sequence of concatenated codewords, without any out-of-band markers to frame the words in the message. The receiver can decode the message unambiguously, by repeatedly finding and removing prefixes that form valid codewords, which are impossible if the message is formed by a non-prefix code as shown in the above example. Prefix codes are also known as prefix-free codes, prefix condition codes, comma-free codes, and instantaneous codes.

Not only that Huffman codes are prefix codes, they are also optimal in the sense that no other prefix code can yield a shorter average codeword length than a corresponding Huffman code. It is the foundation of numerous compression applications, including text compression, audio compression, image compression, and video compression. It is a building block of many contemporary multi-media applications.

Huffman code was developed by David A. Huffman while he was a Ph.D. student at MIT, and published in the 1952 paper "A Method for the Construction of Minimum-Redundancy Codes." Huffman codes are easiest to understand and implement if we use trees to represent them though the tree concept was not used when Huffman first developed the code. Briefly, Huffman tree is a **binary tree** ( an ordered 2-ary tree ) with a weight associated with each node. Let us first consider some simple examples to understand its principles.

Consider the following two codes.

| Symbol | Code 1 | Code 2 |
|:------:|:------:|:------:|
| a | 000 | 000 |
| b | 001 | 11 |
| c | 010 | 01 |
| d | 011 | 001 |
| e | 100 | 10 |

Code 1 is a fixed-length code with codeword length 3 and Code 2 is a variable-length code. Both of them have the prefix property ( note that a fixed-length code always has the prefix property ). They can be represented by binary trees like those shown in Figure 8-1. Decoding a bitstream is simply a process of traversing the binary tree; we start from the root of the tree and go left or right based on whether the current bit examined is 0 or 1 until we reach a leaf, which is associated with a symbol; we then start from the root again and examine the next bit and so on. For example, Code 2 decodes the string "000100111" uniquely to "aecb". It is obvious that Code 2 always has a shorter average codeword length when compared to Code 1.

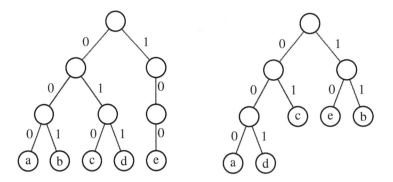

**Figure 8-1**. Binary Tree Representations of Code1 ( left ) and Code 2 ( right )

## 8.2 Huffman Codes

Consider an example that the probabilities of the occurrence of symbols are known:

| Symbol | Frequency | Code 1 | Code 2 |
|--------|-----------|--------|--------|
| a | 0.35 | 000 | 00 |
| b | 0.20 | 001 | 10 |
| c | 0.20 | 010 | 011 |
| d | 0.15 | 011 | 010 |
| e | 0.10 | 100 | 110 |

We can calculate the average lengths $\overline{L}$ of the codewords of the two codes. Obviously, Code 1 is a fixed-length code and the average length is 3. For Code 2, we need to take into account the frequency of occurrence of each symbol:

Code 1 : $\overline{L}\ = 3\ bits$

Code 2 : $\overline{L}\ = 0.35 \times 2 + 0.20 \times 2 + 0.20 \times 3 + 0.15 \times 3 + 0.10 \times 3 = 2.45\ (bits)$

$$(8.1)$$

Code 2 is a prefix code and has a significantly shorter average codeword length than that of Code 1. *But is Code 2 the best code for the given frequencies? Can we do better than Code 2, creating a code that has shorter $\overline{L}$ than Code 2?* This question can be answered by constructing a Huffman tree to obtain a Huffman code for the given symbols and frequencies. We start from a forest of trees, each of which has only one single node ( which is a root as well as a leaf ); each root consists of the symbol and the weight ( probability ) of it. In this example, we totally have five single-noded trees as shown in Figure 8-2:

**Figure 8-2**. A Forest of Single-noded Trees

Next, we merge the two trees whose roots have lowest weights and calculate the sum of the two weights. We assign the sum as the weight to the root of the merged tree. The resulted forest is shown in Figure 8-3, where we have merged two pairs of roots that have the lowest weights.

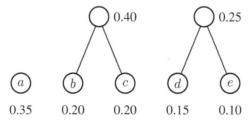

**Figure 8-3**. Merging Two Pairs of Roots with Lowest Weights

We repeat the above merging process until there is only one tree in the forest. Figure 8-4 and Figure 8-5 show two more iterations of the process. Note that for clarity of presentation, some node positions have been rearranged.

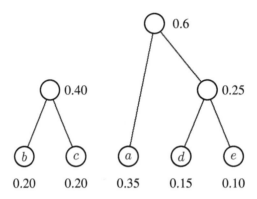

**Figure 8-4**. Merging Two More Roots with Lowest Weights

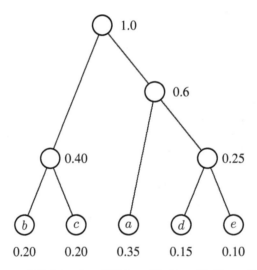

**Figure 8-5**. Merging All Trees Yields a Huffman Tree

As shown in Figure 8-5, the final single tree obtained is the Huffman tree that we need. To obtain the codeword for a symbol, we traverse the tree, starting from the root, until we arrive at a leaf, which contains the symbol; in the traversal, we generate a 0 on going left and a 1 on going right ( it works just as well if we generate a 1 on going left and a 0 on right ) as shown in Figure 8-6. The sequence of 1's and 0's parsed in the traversal from the root to the symbol is the codeword. The following table shows the Huffman code obtained from the Huffman tree of Figure 8-6.

| Symbol | Codeword | Length |
|:------:|:--------:|:------:|
| a | 10 | 2 |
| b | 00 | 2 |
| c | 01 | 2 |
| d | 110 | 3 |
| e | 111 | 3 |

The average length of the Huffman code is

$$\overline{L} = 0.35 \times 2 + 0.20 \times 2 + 0.20 \times 2 + 0.15 \times 3 + 0.10 \times 3 = 2.25 \ (bits) \qquad (8.2)$$

which is shorter than that of Code 2 ( 2.45 bits ) discussed above. Actually, one can prove that Huffman code is optimal. That is, a Huffman code always gives the shortest average code length of all prefix codes for a given set of probabilities of occurrences of symbols. ( We'll skip the proof here. )

Note that the symbols are not limited to alphabets and letters. They can be any quantitative values or even abstract objects. Note also that a Huffman decoder does not need to know the probability distribution of the symbols in order to decode them. It only needs to know the Huffman tree to decode a bit-stream consisting of codewords encoded by a Huffman code. In the decoding process, we start from the root of the tree and traverse the tree according to the 0's and 1's we read from the bit-stream until we reach a leaf to recover the encoded symbol; we then start from the root again and read in further bits for traversal to obtain the next symbol and so on. For example, suppose the following is the output bit-stream resulted from encoding a sequence of symbols using the Huffman tree of Figure 8-6:

$$00101110110 \qquad (8.3)$$

Upon decoding, we start from the tree root and first read in '0 0', reaching symbol 'b'; we then start from the root again and read in '1 0', reaching symbol 'a'; next, the bit sequence '1 1 1' gives symbol 'e'; next, '0 1' gives 'c' and finally '1 0' gives 'a'. Therefore, the encoded sequence of symbols of the bit-stream (8.3) is "b a e c a".

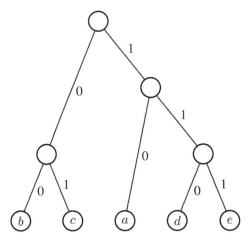

**Figure 8-6**. Traversing the Huffman Tree

# 8.3 Huffman Tree Properties

A Huffman tree can be conveniently constructed using a priority queue. A priority queue is a special queue that associates each element with a priority value. A general queue has the property of "First In First Out ( FIFO )". That is, the first element that enters the queue is the first to be removed. In other words, the first entered-element is always at the front of the queue which is the next element to be deleted. This happens in a cashier station of a supermarket; the customer who arrives first at the cashier is the first one to be served. On the other hand, a priority queue does not follow the FIFO scenario; it is the element that has the highest priority in the queue that will be deleted first. This could happen when the president of a big company meets a number of visitors; she would first meet the most important visitor before meeting other less important people. Therefore, the element at the front of a priority queue always has the highest priority and is the first one to be deleted. In other words, when an element with a priority higher than the priorities of all the elements currently in the queue enters the queue, it will be moved to the front of the queue.

In our application, we can set the priority of a node ( root of a tree ) to be the reciprocal of its weight. That is, the lower the weight, the higher the priority. As an example, in Figure 8-2, node **e** has the highest priority, followed by node **d**, and node **a** has the lowest priority. With this association, a Huffman tree can be constructed by the following steps:

1. Start with a forest consisting of single-node trees; the root of a tree contains a symbol and its weight, which is the reciprocal of its priority value.
2. Insert the roots ( nodes ) of all trees of the forest into a priority queue.
3. Delete two nodes from the priority queue; the two deleted nodes always have the least weights ( highest priorities ).
4. Merge the deleted nodes to form a new root with combined weights; insert the new root back to the priority queue.
5. Repeat steps 3 - 4 until the priority queue is empty.

In the above steps, when the priority queue is empty, a single tree is formed and it is the required Huffman tree. In the process, we assume that a root always links to the rest of the nodes of the tree.

The priority queue implementation is straightforward and intuitive. However, it is not the most efficient method. and we shall not use it here. To make more efficient or customized implementations, it is helpful to learn some properties of a Huffman tree.

Firstly, we have learned that a Huffman tree is optimal. However, it is not unique. Given a set of frequencies, we can have more than one Huffman tree that yields the optimal average codeword length; different trees can be constructed by interchanging the assignment of 0 and 1 to the left and right traversal or by merging roots with equal weights in different orders.

Secondly, all internal nodes ( non-leaves ) of a Huffman tree always have two children. The binary tree that represents Code 1 in Figure 8-1 will never occur in a Huffman tree regardless of the occurrence frequencies of the symbols.

Thirdly, if the weights of the symbols are changing, the Huffman tree needs to be recomputed dynamically. This can be done by utilizing the *Sibling Property*, which defines a binary tree to be a Huffman tree if and only if:

1. all leaf nodes have non-negative weights,
2. all internal nodes have exactly two children,
3. the weight of each parent node is the sum of its childrenś weights, and
4. the nodes are numbered in increasing order by non-decreasing weight so that siblings are assigned consecutive numbers or rank, and most importantly, their parent node must be higher in the numbering.

The *Sibling Property* is usually used in *Dynamic Huffman Coding*, where we encode a stream of symbols on the fly and the symbol statistics changes as we read in more and more symbols.

Finally, we shall prove a lemma concerning binary trees to help us simplify the implementation of a Huffman tree when we use an array to implement it. Consider a binary tree where

$n_0$ = number of leaves ( nodes of degree 0 )

$n_1$ = number of nodes of degree 1 ( nodes having one child )

$n_2$ = number of nodes of degree 2 ( nodes having two children )

**Lemma**:

For a non-empty binary tree,

$$n_0 = n_2 + 1 \tag{8.4}$$

**Proof**:

The total number of nodes in the tree is

$$n = n_0 + n_1 + n_2 \tag{8.5}$$

Except the root, a node always has a branch leading to it. Thus the total number of branches is

$$n_B = n - 1 \tag{8.6}$$

But all branches stem from nodes of degree 1 or 2, so

$$n_B = n_1 + 2 \times n_2 \tag{8.7}$$

Combining (8.6) and (8.7), we have

$$n - 1 = n_1 + 2 \times n_2 \tag{8.8}$$

yielding

$$n_0 + n_1 + n_2 - 1 = n_1 + 2 \times n_2 \tag{8.9}$$

Simplifying (8.9), we obtain

$$n_0 = n_2 + 1$$

which is the result we want to prove.

From Huffman tree properties discussed above, we know that a Huffman tree does not have any node of degree 1 ( i.e. $n_1 = 0$ ) and thus the number of internal nodes is equal to $n_2$. Also, the number of symbols is equal to the number of leaves ( $n_0$ ) in the tree. Therefore, if we have $n$ symbols, from the Lemma, we know that the corresponding Huffman tree will have $n_2 = n_0 - 1 = n - 1$ internal nodes. To save a Huffman tree, we need an entry for each of the left and right child pointers and an entry for each symbol. The total number of entries $N_T$ in the table that holds the Huffman Tree is equal to the number of pointers plus the number of symbols and is given by

$$N_T = 2 \times (n - 1) + n = 3 \times n - 2 \tag{8.10}$$

For instance, consider a Huffman tree consisting of five symbols: a, b, c, d, e as shown in Figure 8-7.

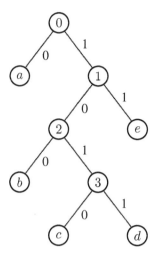

**Figure 8-7.** A Huffman Tree Consisting of Five Symbols

The following table shows the corresponding Huffman code of Figure 8-7.

| Symbol | Codeword |
|--------|----------|
| a | 0 |
| b | 100 |
| c | 1010 |
| d | 1011 |
| e | 11 |

In this example, the size of the table $N_T$ that implements the Huffman tree is

$$N_T = 3 \times 5 - 2 = 13 \tag{8.11}$$

The Huffman tree is represented by the following table ( Table 8-1 ), where traversing left gives a 0, and traversing right gives a 1 and $N_T = 13$. Note that in the table, the root is pointing at the highest table location ( $N_T - 1$ ) and when traversing the tree we move from the top of the table down to a location that contains a symbol. When we reach a location whose index is smaller than $N_T$, we know that we have reached a terminal node ( leaf ) containing a symbol.

**Table 8-1**

| Table Index | Table Content | Comments |
|---|---|---|
| 12 | 0 | left child of node 0 ( root ) |
| 11 | 10 | right child of node 0 |
| 10 | 8 | left child of node 1 |
| 9 | 4 | right child of node 1 |
| 8 | 1 | left child of node 2 |
| 7 | 6 | right child of node 2 |
| 6 | 2 | left child of node 3 |
| 5 | 3 | right child of node 3 |
| 4 | 'e' | symbol at leaf |
| 3 | 'd' | symbol at leaf |
| 2 | 'c' | symbol at leaf |
| 1 | 'b' | symbol at leaf |
| 0 | 'a' | symbol at leaf |

The following piece of java-like pseudo code shows how we traverse the table to obtain the symbols; in the code, htree[] is the table containing the Huffman tree:

```
loc = 3 * N - 3;              //start from root, N = # of symbols
do {
  loc0 = loc;                 //in is data pointer pointing to
                              //  encoded data
  if ( read_one_bit( in ) == 0 ) //a 0, go left
     loc = htree[loc0];
  else
     loc =  htree[loc0+1];   //a 1, go right

} while ( loc >= N );         //traverse until reach leaf
return htree[loc];            //return
```

Table 8-1 can be simplified if we assert that the number of symbols $n$ is smaller than a certain value and we associate each symbol with a value in the range 0 to $n-1$. For example, if we assert $n \leq 128$, which actually applies to many video compression applications, then

1. each pointer can be represented by a byte, with a left child denoted by the upper byte of a 16-bit word and right child by the lower byte,
2. table locations signify symbol values and do not need extra entries to hold the symbols, and
3. table size $N_T$ is reduced to $n-1$.

The above Huffman tree example where the number of symbols is 5 can now be represented by a table with size of $5 - 1 = 4$ as shown below.

**Table 8-2**

| Table Index ( Symbol ) | Left Child | Right Child | Comments |
|---|---|---|---|
| 3 ( 8 ) | 0 ( a ) | 7 | left, right children of node 0 ( root ) |
| 2 ( 7 ) | 6 | 4 ( e ) | left, right children of node 1 |
| 1 ( 6 ) | 1 ( b ) | 5 | left, right children of node 2 |
| 0 ( 5 ) | 2 ( c ) | 3 ( d ) | left, right children of node 3 |

Table 8-2 only has 4 entries while Table 8-1 which has 13 entries. The symbols are represented by the table indices with 0 representing 'a', 1 representing 'b' and so on. To resolve the case whether a table entry holds a pointer or an actual symbol value, we've added the value $N_T$ to all table indices before saving them as pointers. Therefore, in a table entry, if the pointer value is smaller than $N_T$, we know that it is a terminal node ( symbol ). The following piece of code shows how to decode such a table that represents a Huffman tree; a left mask and right mask are used to extract the correct pointer value.

```
                              //N = # of symbols
   left_mask = 0xFF00;        //to extract upper byte(left child)
   right_mask = 0x00FF;       //to extract lower byte(right child)
   loc = ( N - 1 ) + N;       //start from root; add offset N to
                              // distinguish pointers from symbols
do {
   loc0 = loc - N;            //loc0 is real table location
   if ( read_one_bit( in ) == 0 ){  //a 0, go left
       loc = ( htree[loc0] & left_mask ) >> 8;
   } else{
       loc =  htree[loc0] & right_mask;
   }
} while ( loc >= N );         //traverse until reaches leaf
return loc;                   //symbol value = loc
```

# 8.4 Pre-calculated Huffman-based Tree Coding

The Huffman coding process has a disadvantage that the statistics of the occurrence of the symbols must be known ahead of the encoding process. Though we do not need to transmit the probability table to the decoder, we do need it before we can do any encoding. The probability table for a large video cannot be calculated until after the video data have been processed which may introduce unacceptable delay into the encoding process. Because of these, practical video coding standards define sets of codewords based on the probability distributions of generic video data. The following example is a pre-calculated Huffman table taken from MPEG-4 Visual ( Simple Profile ), which uses 3D run-level coding discussed before to encode quantized coefficients. A total of 102 specific combinations of ( *run, level, last*

) have variable-length codewords assigned to them and part of these are shown in Table 8-3. Each codeword can be up to 13 bits long and the last bit is the sign bit 's', which indicates if the decoded coefficient is positive ( 0 ) or negative ( 1 ). Any (*run, level, last* ) combination that is not listed in the table is coded using an escape sequence; a special ESCAPE code of 0000011 is first transmitted followed by a 13-bit fixed-length codeword describing the values of *run, level*, and *last*. A valid codeword cannot contain more than eight consecutive zeros. Therefore, a sequence consisting of eight or more consecutive zeros, "00000000..." indicates an error in the encoded bitstream or possibly a start code, which might contain a long sequence of zeros. We shall use Table 8-3 in our entropy-encoding stage shown in Figure 7-1. The full implementation of the Huffman encoding and decoding for our video codec is discussed in the next section.

Table 8-3

| Run | Level | Last | Code |
|---|---|---|---|
| 0 | 1 | 0 | 10s |
| 1 | 1 | 0 | 110s |
| 2 | 1 | 0 | 1110s |
| 0 | 2 | 0 | 1111s |
| 0 | 1 | 1 | 0111s |
| 3 | 1 | 0 | 01101s |
| 4 | 1 | 0 | 01100s |
| 5 | 1 | 0 | 01011s |
| 0 | 3 | 0 | 010101s |
| 1 | 2 | 0 | 010100s |
| 6 | 1 | 0 | 010011s |
| 7 | 1 | 0 | 010010s |
| 8 | 1 | 0 | 010001s |
| 9 | 1 | 0 | 010000s |
| 1 | 1 | 1 | 001111s |
| 2 | 1 | 1 | 001110s |
| 3 | 1 | 1 | 001101s |
| 4 | 1 | 1 | 001100s |
| 0 | 4 | 0 | 0010111s |
| 10 | 1 | 0 | 0010110s |
| 11 | 1 | 0 | 0010101s |
| 12 | 1 | 0 | 0010100s |
| 5 | 1 | 1 | 0010011s |
| 6 | 1 | 1 | 0010010s |
| 7 | 1 | 1 | 0010001s |
| 8 | 1 | 1 | 0010000s |
| ESCAPE | | | 0000011s |
| .. | .. | .. | .. |

# 8.5 Huffman Coding Implementation

Because Huffman coding involve reading and writing one bit at a time, we need to first develop some functions that can process an arbitrary number of bits of a file. We provide the program "BitIO.java" which consists of two classes, namely, **BitInputStream** and **BitOuput-Stream** that has functions to process data on a bit-basis. The file can be downloaded from this book's web site at *http://www.forejune.com/jvcompress/*. We do not intend to discuss the details of these classes as they do not directly relate to video compression. All we need to

124

know is how to use them, which is straightforward. The following is the class interface of BitInputStream class that can read data bits from an InputStream:

```
class BitInputStream
{
  private InputStream ins;
  ........
  public BitInputStream( InputStream in )
  {
      ins = in;
  }
  //read one bit
  synchronized public int readBit() throws IOException
  {
    .....
  }
  //read n bits
  synchronized public int readBits( int n ) throws IOException
  {
  }
};
```

The interface of the corresponding output class, BitOutputStream that sends data bits to an OutputStream is shown below:

```
class BitOutputStream
{
  private OutputStream outs;
  ........

  public BitOutputStream( OutputStream out )
  {
    outs = out;
  }
  synchronized public void writeBit(int bit) throws IOException
  {
    ........
  }
  synchronized public void writeBits(int data, int n)
                                    throws IOException
  {
    ........
  }
};
```

The main purpose of the Huffman code here is to encode the run-level codewords of the DCT coefficients after forward quantization and reordering. Recall that we have defined a class to represent a 3D run-level codeword:

```
class Run3D {
  byte   run;
  short  level;
  byte   last;
};
```

Each Run3D object represents a run-level codeword, and the Huffman code is used to encode these codewords. We define a class called **RunHuff** that will help encode and decode run-level codewords. This class "has-a" run3D class. As you'll see, we'll insert **RunHuff** objects into a **map**, which involves the ordering of nodes. **Maps** and **multimaps** are data structures that are useful in problems in which multiple collections naturally occur.

A **map**, sometimes also referred to as a dictionary or a table is an associative container where records ( data ) are specified by key values. It is an indexed collection; the key can be used to generate an index to access the corresponding record. A map can be considered as a collection of associations of key and value pairs. The key is used to find the value as shown below:

$$key_1 \rightarrow value_1$$

$$key_2 \rightarrow value_2$$

$$key_3 \rightarrow value_3$$

$$\dots$$

$$key_n \rightarrow value_n$$

For example, we can use the telephone number as the key to lookup the information of a person. The keys in a map must be ordered and unique. A multimap is similar to a map except that a multimap permits multiple entries to be accessed using the same key value. ( i.e. The keys in a multimap do not need to be unique. )

In java, elements are found via the keys; we cannot use an iterator to traverse a map. To traverse all the elements ( values ) in a map, we have to put the elements in a set. Therefore, another data structure we need to use in our implementation is a **set**. A **set** is an unordered collection of elements in which each element is unique. It is also a container. A **bag** ( also called a multiset ) is similar to a set except that duplicated elements are allowed. Actually, the concept of a **set** underlies much of mathematics and is as well an integral part of many computing algorithms. The fundamental operations of a set include adding and removing elements, testing for inclusion of an element, and forming unions, intersections and differences of other sets. A set does not require ordering. Therefore, we cannot find an element in a set using a key like what a map does. On the other hand, we can traverse a set and perform the standard operations on sets. ( Note that unlike java, the C++ Standard Template Library slightly modifies the concept of a set so that its elements are ordered. ) The following figure shows a set of 3D run-level codewords:

Java provides several implementing classes of map interface, including HashMap, Hashtable, IdentityHashMap, RenderingHints, TreeMap, and WeakHashMap. We choose **TreeMap** in our implementation. The function "put( Object *key*, Object *value* )" associates the specified value with the specified key and inserts them into the map. If the map previously contained a mapping for the key, the old value is replaced. On the other hand, the function "public Object get ( Object key )" returns the value to which the map associated with the specified key.

In our implementation of the Huffman codec ( encoder-decoder ), we make both the **key** and the **value** to be RunHuff objects for the convenience of programming. Since the keys are ordered, to utilize a map properly, we must define the keys in a way that they can be compared with each other. Therefore, our class **RunHuff** implements **Comparable<RunHuff>** as shown in Listing 8-1. The parameter inside the angular brackets <> specifies the key type and in our case the key type is a RunHuff object. Actually, as a RunHuff object "has-a" Run3D object, we order the objects using the values of ( $run, level, last$ ) of the Run3D objects. ( Aternatively, one can specify the key type of Comparable as a Run3D object rather than a RunHuff object. ) We first try to determine the "smaller" relation of two RunHuff objects by comparing the $runs$ of their Run3D objects; the one with smaller run values is the smaller RunHuff object and the comparison is done. If the $runs$ are equal, we compare the $levels$ and if the $levels$ are equal, we compare the the $lasts$. If the $runs$, $levels$ and $lasts$ of the two objects are equal, we assume that the keys are equal. This concept is presented in the compareTo function of Listing 8-1 shown below.

**Program Listing 8-1**:   Class Containing Run-level Codewords

```
/*
 * RunHuff.java
 * For the use of constructing a pre-calculated Huffman tree.
 */

/*
 * Need to implement Comparable so that a RunHuff object
 * can be inserted into a TreeMap which will contain the
 * Huffman Table used for encoding.
 */
class RunHuff implements Comparable<RunHuff>
{
  Run3D r = new Run3D();
  int codeword;
  byte hlen; //length of Huffman code
  short index; //table index where codeword saved

  RunHuff() {} //constructors

  RunHuff ( Run3D a, int c, byte len, short idx )
  {
    r.run = a.run; r.level = a.level; r.last = a.last;
    codeword = c; hlen = len; index = idx;
  }

  //A run tuple is used as a key for comparison
  public int compareTo ( RunHuff right ) throws ClassCastException
  {
    if ( r.run < right.r.run )
      return 1;      //smaller
    if ( r.run > right.r.run )
      return -1;    //larger
```

```
    //run equals
    if ( r.level < right.r.level )
      return 1;
    if ( r.level > right.r.level )
      return -1;
   //both run and level equal
    if ( r.last < right.r.last )
      return 1;
    if ( r.last > right.r.last )
      return -1;
    return 0;    //The two objects equal
  }
};
```

We assume that a pre-calculated Huffman Table like the one shown in Table 8-3 is provided. Listing 8-2 presents the class **Hcodec** that makes use of a pre-calculated Huffman Table to build the encoder and decoder. We declare a variable *htable* to be a map to collect **RunHuff** objects, each of which contains a 3D run-level tuple and the corresponding Huffman codeword ( Table 8-2 ). The statement

```
TreeMap<RunHuff,RunHuff>htable = new TreeMap<RunHuff,RunHuff>();
```

constructs a TreeMap object with *htable* pointing to this new object. The first and second argument enclosed by the anugular brackets <> of TreeMap specify the key type and value tppe respectively. In our case, both the key type and value type are RunHuff objects.

The function **build_htable()** of the class Hcodec has all codewords and run-level tuples hard-coded in the code and saved in variables *hcode, runs, levels,* and *last* respectively. The function collects all these pre-calculated run-level tuples and Huffman codewords and saves them in the map *htable*. The TreeMap member function **put** is used to insert the RunHuff objects into the map. In the function, the special run value 127 is used to represent the ESC ( escape ) symbol:

**Program Listing 8-2**:   Class for Building Huffman Coder Decoder

```
//Hcodec.java
//Building a Huffman Encoder-Decoder
import java.util.Set;
import java.util.Map;
import java.util.TreeMap;
import java.util.Iterator;
import java.io.*;

class Hcodec
{
  private final int NSymbols = 256;    //maximum symbols allowed
  private final short ESC = 0x60;      //Escape code
  private boolean tableNotBuilt = true;
  TreeMap<RunHuff, RunHuff>  htable = new TreeMap<RunHuff,RunHuff>();

  //use a map ( htable ) to collect all pre-calculated run-level
  //  and Huffman codewords
  void build_htable ()
  {
    //N = number of pre-calculated codewords with positive levels
    //In practice, N should be larger than 100
```

```
short i, j, k, N = 10;
//lengths of Huffman codewords (not including sign-bit)
byte hlen[] = { 2, 3, 4, 4, 4, 5, 5, 5, 6, 7 };
//Huffman codewords, 0x60 is ESC
short hcode[] = {0x01,0x3,0x7,0xf,0xe, 0x16, 0x6, 0x1a, 0x2a, ESC};

//data of 3D run-level tuples ( codewords )
byte runs[] = {0, 1, 2, 0, 0, 3, 4, 5, 0, 127};  //127 signifies ESC
short levels[] = {1, 1, 1, 2, 1, 1, 1, 1, 3, 0 };
byte lasts[] = {0, 0, 0, 0, 1, 0, 0, 0, 0, 0 };

Run3D r = new Run3D();              //a 3D run-level codeword (tuple)
RunHuff rf[] = new RunHuff[128];    //table containing RunHuff objects

//inserting RunHuff objects into Map htable
k = 0; j = 0;
for ( i = 0; i < N-1; i++ ) {
  r.run = runs[i];
  r.level = levels[i];
  r.last = lasts[i];
  //construct a RunHuff object, positive level, so sign=0
  rf[k++] = new  RunHuff ( r, hcode[i] << 1,  hlen[i], j++ );
  //do the same thing for negative level, sign = 1
  r.level = (short) -r.level;
  rf[k++] = new RunHuff ( r, (hcode[i]<<1) | 1, hlen[i], j++ );
}
//special handling for ESC code
r.run = runs[N-1];
r.level = levels[N-1];
r.last = lasts[N-1];
rf[k] = new RunHuff ( r, hcode[N-1] << 1, hlen[N-1], j );
//insert all (positive & negative levels) RunHuff objects into htable
k = (short) ( 2 * N - 1 );     //2N - 1 RunHuff objects
for ( i = 0; i < k; i++ )
  htable.put ( rf[i], rf[i] );
tableNotBuilt = false;
  }
  ........
};
```

As we mentioned earlier, we cannot use an iterator to traverse a map directly in java but TreeMap provides the function **entrySet**() to return a set view of the mappings in the map. Therefore, we can make use of the set's iterator and functions to process the map's data. The set's iterator returns the mappings in ascending key order. Each element in the returned set is a Map.Entry. The returned set is bound to this map, so changes to this map are reflected in the set, and vice-versa. The set supports element removal, which removes the corresponding mapping from the TreeMap, through the **Iterator.remove, Set.remove, removeAll, retainAll** and **clear** operations. Listing 8-3 shoows how to use the set view and functions to print all the entries of TreeMap *htable*. ( In Java or C++, an iterator is an object that can access members of an array or a container class. It has the ability to traverse the elements in a certain range using certain operators. Very often, it is used in a manner similar to pointers. ).

**Program Listing 8-3**:  Print TreeMap Entries Using Set View and Functions

```
class Hcodec
```

```
{
  ....

  void print_htable()
  {
    // Use an Iterator to traverse the mappings in the TreeMap.  Note
    // that the mappings are in sorted order (with respect to the keys).
    Iterator itr = htable.entrySet().iterator();
    RunHuff rfs[] = new RunHuff[htable.size()];
    System.out.printf("\n(run,level,last),\tCodeword\tHCode Length,index");
     while ( itr.hasNext() )
     {
        Map.Entry entry = (Map.Entry) itr.next();
        RunHuff rhuf = (RunHuff) entry.getValue();
        rfs[rhuf.index] = rhuf;
     }
     for ( int i = 0; i < htable.size(); i++ ) {
        RunHuff rhuf = rfs[i];
        System.out.printf("\n(%4d, %4d, %d), \t%8x \t%x\t    %d, \t%4d",
            rhuf.r.run, rhuf.r.level, rhuf.r.last, rhuf.codeword,
            rhuf.codeword >> 1, rhuf.hlen, rhuf.index );
     }
  }
}
```

After we have collected all the pre-calculated run-level Huffman codewords in the **map** *htable*, the encoding of 3D run-levels tuples becomes simple. To encode a run-level codeword, all we need to do is to lookup the **map** *htable*; if the run-level codeword is in the map, we output the Huffman codeword along with the sign-bit; if it is not in the map, we "escape" and output the run-level codeword "directly".

Suppose the array *runs*[] contains all the run-level codewords of a macroblock; the following piece of code shows how to encode them using the pre-calculated Huffman codewords saved in *htable*. In the code, we use the member function **containsKey**() of TreeMap to determine if the run-level tuple is in *htable*. If yes, we retrieve the RunHuff object which contains the Huffman codeword from *htable* using the function **get**() and the run-level tuple as key. It then outputs the Huffman codeword and the sign-bit, otherwise it escape-encodes the run-level tuple by first outputting the ESCAPE code followed by a fixed-length codeword for the tuple:

**Program Listing 8-4**:   Encode 3D run-level tuples with Huffman codewords

```
/*
  Inputs:
    runs[] contains the 3D run-level tuples of a macroblock of quantized
    DCT coefficients
  Outputs:
    bitstreams of codewords ( Huffman + sign or ESCAPE + 3D run-level )
    to BitOutputStream outputs
  Note that data member htable contains all the pre-calculated Huffman
    codewords of 3D run-level tuples
*/
void huff_encode ( Run3D runs[], BitOutputStream outputs )
{
  short i, j, k;
```

```
    if ( tableNotBuilt )
      build_htable();
    k = 0;  i = 0;
    while ( i < 64 ) {              //a macroblock has at most 64 samples
      try {
        //construct a RunHuff object; only runs[k] is relevant as it is
        //   used for searching (we've defined CompareTo in RunHuff class)
        RunHuff rf = new RunHuff( runs[k], 0, (byte) 0, (short) 0 );
        if ( htable.containsKey ( rf ) ){
          RunHuff rhuf = htable.get ( rf );
        } else {                           //not in table
          escape_encode( outputs, rf.r ); //need to 'escape encode' Run3D Object
        }
      } catch (IOException e) {
        e.printStackTrace();
        System.exit(0);
      }
      if ( runs[k].last != 0 ) break;    //end of run-level codewords
      i += ( runs[k].run + 1 );          //special case: whole run-block 0
      k++;
    }
  }
```

To encode a run-level tuple using the ESC symbol, we first check if the level is negative. If it is negative, we output a '1' bit otherwise we output a '0' bit. We then send the special code for the ESC symbol followed by the binary numbers representing the values of run, level and last. The following piece of code shows how to do this precisely.

```
//Encode codeword unsing ESC
void escape_encode ( BitOutputStream outputs, Run3D r )
{
  try {
    if ( r.level < 0 ) {         //value of level negative
      outputs.writeBit ( 1 );    //output sign-bit first
      r.level = (short) -r.level; //change level value to positive
    } else
      outputs.writeBit ( 0 );    //value of level positive
    outputs.writeBits ( ESC, 7 ); //ESCAPE code
    if ( r.run == 64 ) r.run = 63; //r.level differentiates between
                                   //   if last element nonzero
    outputs.writeBits ( r.run, 6 );    //6 bits for run value
    outputs.writeBits ( r.level, 8 );  //8 bits for level value
    outputs.writeBit ( r.last );       //1 bit for last value
  } catch (IOException e) {
      e.printStackTrace();
      System.exit(0);
  }
}
```

The functions **huff_encode**() and **escape_encode**() encode the 3D run-level tuples of a macroblock. In the encoding process, the Huffman tree is not needed. However, to decode the encoded bitstream, we have to use the Huffman tree to recover the 'symbols' ( run-level tuples ). We can easily construct the Huffman tree in the form of a table from the **map** *htable*. Note that here we build the Huffman tree from pre-calculated codewords, not from symbol weights as people normally do. Therefore, the process is a lot simpler as Huffman codewords have been provided. The following function **build_huff_tree**() builds the Huffman tree from *htable* and saves it in the table ( array ) *huf_tree*[] of data type short. An entry of *huf_tree*[] holds a node's pointer to a child or an index ( 'symbol' ) if the node is a leaf; the index points to an entry of another table, *run_table*[], which contains the actual run-level tuple ( see Table 8-3 ). For convenience of programming, we put *huf_tree*[] and *run_table*[] in a class called **Dtables**. Again we use the member function entrySet() of the class TreeMap to obtain a set view of the map *htable*; a set iterator is used to traverse the set and obtain all the RunHuff objects of the set. Keep in mind that a RunHuff object contains a 3D run-level tuple and the associated Huffman codeword.

**Program Listing 8-5**:   Constructing Huffman Tree

```
class Dtables {
  short huf_tree[] = new short[1024];   //table containing Huffman Tree
  Run3D run_table[] = new Run3D[512];   //table containing run-level codewords

  Dtables()
  {
    for ( int i = 0; i < 512; i++ )
      run_table[i] = new Run3D();
  }
};

class Hcodec
{
  ....

  void build_huff_tree ( Dtables d )
  {
    int i, j, n0, free_slot, loc, loc0, root, ntotal;
    int mask, hcode;

    n0 = NSymbols;       //number of symbols (=number of leaves in tree)
    ntotal = 2 * n0 - 1; //Huffman tree has  n0 - 1  internal nodes
    root = 3 * n0 - 3;   //location of root, offset n0 has been added
    free_slot = root - 2; //next free table entry for filling in with a
                         //   pointer or an index
                         //   (note:root has root_left, root_right)
    for ( i = 0; i < ntotal; ++i )   //initialize the table
      d.huf_tree[i] = -1;            //all entries empty

    Iterator itr = htable.entrySet().iterator();
    RunHuff rfs[] = new RunHuff[htable.size()];
    while ( itr.hasNext() ) {
        Map.Entry entry = (Map.Entry) itr.next();
        RunHuff rhuf = (RunHuff) entry.getValue();
        rfs[rhuf.index] = rhuf;
    }
    for ( int ii = 0; ii < htable.size(); ii++ ) {
        RunHuff rhuf = rfs[ii];
        if ( rhuf.r.level < 0 ) continue;//only save positive levels
                               //  of run-level codeword
        d.run_table[rhuf.index/2]=rhuf.r;//save run-level codeword;index
                         //  divided by 2 as only postive levels saved
        loc = root;                  //always start from root
        mask = 0x01;                 //for examining bits of Huffman codeword
```

```
          hcode = rhuf.codeword >> 1;//rightmost bit is sign-bit,not Huffman
          for ( i = 0; i < rhuf.hlen; ++i ){ //traverse the Huffman codeword
            loc0 = loc - n0;          //everything shifted by offset n0
            if ( i == ( rhuf.hlen - 1 ) ){//last bit, should point to leaf
              if ( (mask & hcode) == 0 )  //a 0, save it at 'left' leaf
                d.huf_tree[loc0] = (short) (rhuf.index/2);
              else                        //a 1, save it at 'right' leaf
                d.huf_tree[loc0-1] = (short) (rhuf.index/2);
              continue; //get out of for-i for loop, consider next codeword
            }
            if ( (mask & hcode) == 0 ){     //a 0 ( go left )
              if (d.huf_tree[loc0] == -1){  //slot empty
                d.huf_tree[loc0] = (short)free_slot;//point to left new child
                free_slot -= 2;             //next free table entry
              }                             //else : already has left child
              loc = d.huf_tree[loc0];       //follow the left child
            } else {                        //a 1 ( go right )
              if (d.huf_tree[loc0-1]== -1){ //slot empty
                d.huf_tree[loc0-1]= (short)free_slot;//point to right new kid
                free_slot -= 2;
              }                             //else: already has right child
              loc = d.huf_tree[loc0-1];     //follow the right child
            }
            mask <<= 1;                     //consider next bit
          } //for i
        } //while
    } //build_huff_tree()
}
```

After we have built the Huffman tree, decoding becomes simple. We read in a bitstream and traverse the tree starting from the root. If the bit read is a 0, we traverse left, otherwise we traverse right until we reach a leaf where we recover a symbol. If the symbol is an ESCAPE code, we need to further read in a fixed-number of bits to determine the 'symbol' ( the run-level tuple ). Then we read in another bit and start the tree-traversal from the root again. The details are shown in the function **huff_decode**() listed below.

**Program Listing 8-6**: Huffman Decoder

```
/*
  Inputs: inputs, the encoded bitstream to be decoded
          d.huf_tree[], table containing the Huffman tree
          d.run_table[], table containing the actual run-level codewords
  Output: runs[], table containing the run-level tuples of a macroblock
*/
short huff_decode( BitInputStream inputs,  Dtables d,  Run3D runs[] )
{
  short n0, loc, loc0, root, k;
  int c, sign;
  boolean done = false;
  Run3D rp;
  n0 = NSymbols;              //number of symbols
  root = (short)(3 * n0 - 3); //points to root of tree
  k = 0;
  try {
    while ( !done ) {
      loc = root;             //starts from root
```

```
                sign = inputs.readBit(); //sign-bit
                do {
                  loc0 = (short) (loc - n0);
                  c = inputs.readBit();              //read one bit
                  if (c < 0) {done = true; break;}   //no more data, done
                  if ( c == 0 )                      //a 0, go left
                    loc = d.huf_tree[loc0];
                  else                               //a 1, go right
                    loc = d.huf_tree[loc0-1];
                } while ( loc >= n0 );               //traverse until reaches leaf
                if ( loc >= n0 ) break;              //done
                rp = d.run_table[loc];

                Run3D r3d = new Run3D();
                if ( rp.run == -1 ) { //ESCAPE code, read actual run-level tuple
                  r3d.run   = (byte) inputs.readBits ( 6 );   //read 6 bits for run
                  r3d.level = (byte) inputs.readBits ( 8 );//read 8 bits for level
                  r3d.last = (byte) inputs.readBit();       //read 1 bit for last
                  if ( sign == 1 )          //if sign is 1, level should be negative
                    r3d.level = (byte) -r3d.level;
                } else {                           //not ESCAPE code
                  r3d.run = rp.run;
                  r3d.level = rp.level;
                  r3d.last = rp.last;
                  if ( sign == 1 )                 //1 => negative
                    r3d.level = (byte) -r3d.level;
                }
                if ((r3d.run == 63)&&(r3d.level == 0))
                  r3d.run = 64;                      //whole block 0
                runs[k++] = r3d;                     //save tuple in table runs[]
                if ( r3d.last != 0 )                 //end of macroblock
                  break;
              } //while
            } catch (IOException e) {
              e.printStackTrace();
              System.exit(0);
            }

            if ( done ) return -1;                   //if ( done ) => no more data
            else return 1;
          }
```

Putting all these together, we provide two driver programs,

```
        Test_huf_encode.java, and
        Test_huf_decode.java
```

for you to do the testing of the concepts discussed above. ( The programs can be downloaded from the web site of this book, *http://www.forejune.com/jvcompress/*. ) You can copy the files along with the ".dct" files and put them in the same directory. Since the classes discussed here need to use other classes discussed in previous chapters, you need to setup the CLASSPATH properly using a command like the following:

```
        export CLASSPATH=$CLASSPATH:../5/:../6/:../7/
```

Then compile all the java programs in the current directory with the command "javac *.java". Java byte codes will be generated and you may use the command,

```
$java Test_huf_encode t.dct t.huf
```

to encode the DCT coefficients of the file "t.dct" and save the Huffman codeword bitstream in "t.huf". The command

```
$java Test_huf_decode t.huf t.dec
```

decodes the Huffman codeword bitstream saved in "t.huf" and saves the decoded DCT coefficients in the file "t.dec".

# Chapter 9    Image Prediction and Motion Compensation

## 9.1 Introduction

In previous chapters, we combined various well-developed techniques which are shown in Figure 7-1 to compress image data. You may be amazed to see that the techniques can achieve high compression ratios with high-quality reproduced decompressed images. Actually, the best is yet to come. So far, we have only considered static images and have used .ppm files in our examples; the techniques employed in Figure 7-1 have only exploited the correlations between pixels ( or spatial redundancy ). These techniques are very similar to those used by the JPEG standard to compress static images. Actually, they can be applied to encode a sequence of images, compressing each image individually. This method of compressing each frame independently is known as motion JPEG or M-JPEG. Obviously, M-JPEG has not made use of the correlations between frames ( temporal redundancy ) to achieve higher compression. M-JPEG is usually used in very high quality video captures and the scenes are normally captured in the raw data format which are then edited and compressed into another format. Encoding each frame individually is also referred to as *intra-frame* coding, where at a certain instance, data processing is applied only to the data of the current frame but not to any other frame in the video sequence. This contrasts with *inter-frame* coding, where processing is applied simultaneously to the data of the current frame and the adjacent frames. If you watch a movie played by a DVD player and at some point change it to play at a slow-motion mode, you would notice that most consecutive frames within a sequence are very similar to the frames both before and after the frame of interest. By exploiting the inherent temporal, or time-based redundancies between frames, considerably more compression efficiency can be obtained.

Intra-frames are often referred to as I-frames and inter-frames are called P-frames. P here refers to 'prediction'. This is because people use motion estimation and a technique known as block-based motion compensated prediction to exploit the temporal correlations between frames in order to reduce the redundancies. Indeed, in Chapter 2 we have discussed that the information conveyed by a set of data closely relates to its predictability. A perfectly predictable message conveys no information. Actually, besides temporal prediction, we can also use spatial prediction to reduce data redundancies.

## 9.2 Temporal Model

A temporal model exploits inter-frame correlations to reduce redundancies. Very often, a predicted frame is calculated or formed by certain procedures and is subtracted from the current frame, producing a residual or difference frame. The more accurate the prediction, the less information the residual data contain and the higher compression we can achieve. The residual data are encoded in the usual way as presented in Figure 7-1. Besides decoding the encoded residual data, the decoder has to recreate the predicted frame and adds it to the decoded residual to reconstruct the current frame ( usually this is a lossy process; the reconstructed frame is not identical to the original one ). The predicted frame is often created from one or more past or future frames which are referred to as 'reference frames'. Predictions in general can be improved by compensating for motion between the current frame and reference frames. We will discuss motion compensation in detail in the next section.

For instance, MPEG predicts images from previous frames (P frames) or bidirectionally from previous and future frames (B frames). After predicting frames using motion compensation, the coder calculates the residual which is then compressed using the methods shown in Figure 7-1.

# 9.3 Block Based Motion Estimation and Motion Compensation

A simple and commonly used method for temporal prediction is to use the previous frame as the predictor for the current frame. However, very often for many frames of a video scene, the main difference between one frame and another is the result of either the camera moving or an object in the frame moving. This means much of the information that represents one frame will be the same as the information used in the next frame. A direct subtraction of the previous frame ( predictor ) from the current frame could produce substantial nonzero residual values. For instance, consider an example where the images are shown in Figure 9-1 and Figure 9-2 ( for simplicity, we assume that a white pixel has a zero value and a black pixel has a nonzero value ). The objects in the two figures are identical except that one is displaced with respect to the other. Direct calculation of the difference between the two frames yields substantial residual values as shown in Figure 9-3. Actually, this example is quite extreme as the difference has more nonzero values than Frame 1 and Frame 2, resulting in a less efficient compression. However, if we make compensation for the motion by translating the object in Frame 1 to the position of the object in Frame 2 before carrying out the subtraction, then the residual will consist of all zeros, which result in a very efficient compression.

The residual can be compressed and decompressed as usual ( Figure 7-1 ). *But how do we recover the current frame ( Frame 2 )?* To reconstruct the current frame, the decoder needs to know the the image data of the previous frame ( Frame 1 ) and the displacement of the object, which is known as **motion vector**. The process of obtaining the motion vector is known as **motion estimation**, and using the motion vector to remedy the effects of motion is known as **motion compensation**.

Once we have reconstructed Frame 2, we can use it as the predictor for Frame 3 and the reconstructed Frame 3 is used as the predictor for Frame 4 and so on. Therefore, we only need to send one complete frame to be used as the predictor along with the residual and motion vectors at the very beginning. After that, the predictor ( reference frame ) is reconstructed from other information.

Of course in reality, the objects in two different frames are rarely identical. Moreover, many objects in a scene are deformable and it is very difficult to identify all the objects in a large number of frames. *Then in practice, how do we do motion compensation?*

**Figure 9-1**. Frame 1

**Figure 9-2**. Frame 2

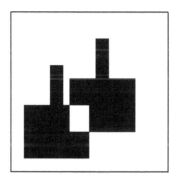

**Figure 9-3**. Residual = Frame 1 - Frame 2

**Figure 9-4**. Motion Compensated Residual

The most commonly used technique in motion compensation is the block-based motion estimation. In this method, a current frame is divided into rectangular sections or 'blocks'. We handle each block independently and search in the reference frame a block that matches this block best. The following procedures explain more precisely how the search is carried out for each block of size $M \times N$:

1. Search a region in the reference frame that best matches the $M \times N$ sample block. This is done by comparing the $M \times N$ block of the current frame with some or all

of the possible $M \times N$ regions of the reference frame. The best matched region can be determined using an objective quality measure such as the minimum absolute difference ( MAD ) or sum of absolute difference ( SAD ) discussed below. That is, we want to find an $M \times N$ block in the reference frame so that the sum of absolute difference ( SAD ) between it and the given sample block is minimized. This is the motion estimation procedure.

2. Set the selected block in the reference frame to become the predictor for the $M \times N$ sample block of the current frame and subtract it from the current block to form a residual $M \times N$ block. Also, calculate the motion vector ( displacement ) between the two blocks. This is the motion compensation procedure.

3. Encode the residual block using methods discussed in previous chapters ( Figure 7-1 ). We may also encode the motion vector using a pre-calculated Huffman code. Send the encoded values to the decoder.

The decoder first decodes the encoded motion vector and residual block. It uses the motion vector to identify the predictor region in the reference frame and adds the predictor to the residual to reconstruct a version of the original block.

From the above discussions, we see that encoding one frame usually involves more than one motion vector. This is the reason that we encode a motion vector with a Huffman code. Figure 9-5a presents the video compression that extends Figure 7-1 to include temporal prediction, motion estimation and motion compensation; the steps of RGB-YCbCr transformation and down sampling are omitted in the diagram. The corresponding diagram for decoding the encoded stream is shown in Figure 9-5b.

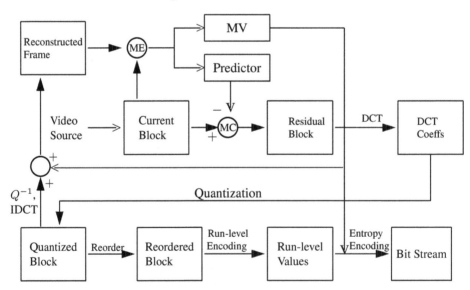

**Figure 9-5a**. Video Compression with ME and MC

In Figure 9-5, the terms MV, ME, MC, and $Q^{-1}$ represent motion vector, motion estimation, motion compensation, and inverse quantization respectively. Block-based motion compensation ( MC ) is commonly used in video compression. This is because it is simple and straightforward to implement. The algorithm could be efficient, depending on the choice of block size and search details. The method also fits well with commonly used rectangular video frames and the block-based Discrete Cosine Transform ( DCT ). On the other hand, there are some drawbacks in using block-based MC. Objects in a scene are often non-rectangular and their boundaries rarely match well with rectangular edges. Very often, an object may move by a fraction of the distance between pixels from one frame to another; the motion may not be simple translations but more complex motions like shrinking, rotation, and vibration. Also, objects like animals and liquid could be deformable and some objects such as clouds, smoke and fire may not even have any regular shape .

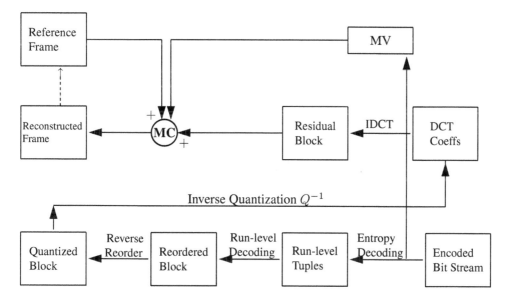

**Figure 9-5b**. Decoding of Compressed Stream with ME and MC

# 9.4 Matching Criteria

Before we perform any search, we need some criteria to determine which is the best match. Some of these criteria are simple to evaluate, while others are more involved. Different kinds of algorithms may use different criteria for comparison of blocks. The commonly used criteria are the "Sum of Differences" (SAD), the "Mean Absolute Difference" (MAD), and the "Mean Squared Difference" (MSD). If the compensation block size is $N \times N$ samples, and $I_{ij}$ and $I'_{ij}$ are the current and reference sample values respectively at location $(i, j)$, the formulas for these criteria are presented in equations (9.1a), (9.1b), and (9.1c) below:

$$SAD = \sum_{i=0}^{N-1} \sum_{j=0}^{N-1} |I_{ij} - I'_{ij}| \qquad (9.1a)$$

$$MAD = \frac{1}{N^2} \sum_{i=0}^{N-1} \sum_{j=0}^{N-1} |I_{ij} - I'_{ij}| \qquad (9.1b)$$

$$MSD = \frac{1}{N^2} \sum_{i=0}^{N-1} \sum_{j=0}^{N-1} (I_{ij} - I'_{ij})^2 \qquad (9.1c)$$

The functions SAD, MAD, and MSD presented in (9.1) are also referred to as distortion functions. Because of its simplicity, SAD is probably the most commonly used measure to determine the best match. In subsequent discussions, we shall also use "minimizing SAD" as our criterion to find the best match.

In practice, instead of searching in the RBG space, we search in the YCbCr space. The residuals are actually the differences of the YCbCr components between two frames. Also, we need to send the motion vectors to the decoder. Very often, small vectors occur more frequently, and a pre-calculated Huffman coder 'bias' towards smaller values. Therefore, we usually encode smaller vectors with less number of bits than larger vectors. Consequently, it may be useful to 'bias' the choice of a vector towards the location of the current block which is assumed to be at $(0, 0)$. We can accomplish this by subtracting a constant from the SAD at location $(0, 0)$.

## 9.5 Choice of Block Size

The next question arises on motion compensation is what block size should we use in the search. Intuitively, a smaller block size would give smaller SADs, yielding 'better' residual results ( more zeros and small values ). However, a smaller block size requires more search operations and motion vectors encoding. Encoded motion vectors increase the overhead bits required for decoding and the increase in bits may outweigh the benefits of improved residual compression. For instance, consider the extreme case that we were to use a block consisting of only a single pixel ( i.e. block size = 1 ). Then in the searching process, a pixel with the same intensity value would result in a perfect match and produce a motion vector. However, we would not gain any compression in this situation because instead of encoding a set of pixel values, we would encode the same number of two dimensional motion vectors, which could be less correlated and make the compression worse.

On the other hand, a large block size requires much less search and motion vectors. However, a large block may contain small moving objects, giving rise to a poor predictor block and thus poor residual results. The larger the block, the less likely we will find a predictor block that matches reasonably well with the current block.

One effective way to compromise between choosing a large block size and a small block size is to adapt the block size to the image characteristics. For example, we choose a large block size in flat, and homogeneous areas of a frame and choose a small block size in regions of rapid or complex motion. In practice, video compression standards, including MPEG-1, MPEG-2, MPEG-4, H.261, H.263 and H.264 use a macroblock as the basic block for motion compensation. H.264 also uses adaptive motion compensation block sizes which are organized in a tree structure. In Chapter 5, we discussed that a macroblock is a $16 \times 16$ region of a frame. It shows in Figure 5-1 that a 4:2:0 formatted macroblock consists of a $16 \times 16$

luminance ( Y ) sample block, an $8 \times 8$ blue chrominance ( Cb ) sample block and an $8 \times 8$ red chrominance ( Cr ) sample block. Motion estimation is done by searching a $16 \times 16$ sample region in a reference frame that best matches the current macroblock consisting of Y, Cb, and Cr samples. The Minimum Absolute Difference ( MAD ) criterion or the Sum of Absolute Differences ( SAD ) is usually used to determine the best-match. Motion compensation is done by subtracting the chosen best matching region in the reference frame from the current macroblock to generate a residual macroblock, which is encoded in the usual manner ( Figure 7-1 of Chapter 7 ) and sent to the decoder along with an encoded motion vector that describes the position of the selected region relative to the current macroblock. Within the encoder, we have to decode encoded residual macroblock and make use of the motion vector to add it to the matching region to form a reconstructed macroblock frame which is stored as a reference for future motion compensation operations (see Figure 9-5). You may wonder why we obtain the reference frame by reconstructing the macroblock rather than using one from the video source. This is because the encoder and decoder need to use an identical reference frame for motion compensation otherwise errors will accumulate over time. Sometimes, if there is a rapid scene change, causing a significant difference between adjacent frames, it is better not to use motion compensation in the encoding. To carry out the compression effectively, one can allow the encoding to switch between *intra* mode that encodes without motion compensation and *inter* mode that uses motion compensation for each macroblock. Also, objects may move by a fraction of the distance between two pixels rather than an integral value. In this case, we may be able to find better predictions by first interpolating the reference frame to sub-pixel positions before searching a best-match of these positions.

# 9.6 Motion Estimation Algorithms

Often motion estimation ( ME ) is the most computationally intensive part of a video encoder. Reduction of the required computational complexity is one of the most challenging issues for motion compensation. It is the state of the art in video encoding and is particularly critical in real-time video compression. On the other hand, nonreal-time applications can do the compression offline and can afford to spend more time on optimizing the compression. The decoder does not need to do any motion compensation and in general runs a lot faster than the encoder. Moreover, in many applications such as the distribution of a video clip, compression has to be done only once but decompression will be done many times. Therefore, these applications may afford to pay the cost of computation even if they are very high during the compression process.

As mentioned in the previous section, a common way to do motion estimation is to find a region in the reference frame that best matches the current macroblock and compute the motion vector between the two regions. *How do we find the best-matched region?* A model that is commonly used in searching is the *block-translation* model, where an image is divided into non-overlapping rectangular blocks. Each block in the predicted image is formed by translating a similar source region from the reference frame. This model does not consider any rotation or scaling of the block. The brute-force exhaustive search, which is also known as full search is one of such models.

### 9.6.1 Full Search

In a full search ( or exhaustive search ), we test every block within a defined range against the block it is defined to match ( target block ). In terms of minimizing SAD, exhaustive search always finds the optimal motion vector because the method compares all possible displacements within the search range. The following java-like pseudo code shows this algorithm:

```
for ( int i = 0; i < 256; ++i ) {
  x[i] = pixel in current macroblock
  y[i] = pixel in a 16x16 block in reference frame
  for each k = 16x16 block in reference frame {
    D[k] = sum of distortion( x[i], y[i][k] )
  }
}

return k-th 16x16 block in reference frame that minimizes D
```

If the search window size is 2S + 1, and its center ( 0, 0 ) is at the position of the current macroblock, the search window is typically a rectangular region with lower-left and upper-right corners defined by the coordinates $(-S, -S)$, and $(+S, +S)$. Full search evaluates SAD at each point of the window, for a total of $(2S + 1)^2$ points. A simple full search strategy is to start from the upper-left corner at $(-S, +S)$ and proceed in raster scan order, from left to right and top to bottom until SADs at all positions have been evaluated. However, in a typical video sequence, movements of objects between frames are small and small SAD positions are concentrated around ( 0, 0 ). It is not likely that we find a minimum SAD near the corners of the search window. Therefore, we can simplify a full search by starting the search at the center ( 0, 0 ) and proceeding to evaluate points in a spiral pattern as shown in Figure 9-6. Of course, if we evaluate the SAD at every position as usual, we do not gain an advantage. However, we can make a short cut by adopting an early termination strategy, in which the evaluation of a SAD terminates once its value is larger than the previous SAD minimum ( note that we just terminate the SAD evaluation at the position but we do **not** terminate the search until all positions in the window have been covered ). By using this early termination strategy, it is increasing likely that the search will terminate early as the search pattern expands outward, and thus saving a significant amount of time in calculating SADs.

There are various strategies to decide on the search range. The search range usually depends on how fast objects move in the image sequence, and how well we want to track the fastest objects. If our reference frames are adjacent frames, it is not possible to track an object that moves more than an image width or height between successive frames. It might be reasonable to track an object that moves about half an image width between successive frames but in terms of TV, this corresponds to an object that appears in a frame and might disappear in the subsequent frame in one tenth of a second, which is faster than what we need. If we aimed at tracking an object that traverses a frame in about half a second, and the video dimension is about $512 \times 512$ and is played at a rate of 40 frames per second ( fps ). we would need to accommodate a movement of about 12 pixels per frame. If we wish to make predictions from two successive frames instead of one, we would need to double the search range to about 24 pixels.

Search Window

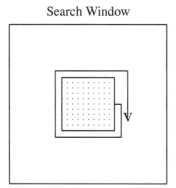

**Figure 9-6**. Full Search with Spiral Scan

Also, in real-world scene, there are usually more and faster movements in the horizontal direction than in the vertical direction. People found that it was best to search the width about twice as much as the height.

Full search is rather easy to implement. However, the best match as determined by a criterion like minimum SAD may not represent the real match of the object that appears in two frames. Good matches tend to minimize the residual errors, resulting in good compression, but if the matches do not represent true motion, the motion vectors of subsequent matching blocks may not correlate well, and encoding these vectors become inefficient.

## 9.6.2 Fast Searches

Though full search gives optimal results for a given criterion, it is computationally intensive. There are suboptimal search algorithms, usually referred to as fast search algorithms that trade the quality of the image prediction with the efficiency of searching. These algorithms evaluate the search criterion at a subset of the locations of the search window.

## Three Step Search ( TSS )

The Three Step Search ( TSS ),introduced by Koga et al in 1981 is a popular and robust search algorithm that gives near-optimal results. The N-Step Search ( NSS ) is a modified version of the TSS that calculates the SADs at a specified subset of locations within the search window. It searches for the best motion vectors in a coarse to fine search pattern. Figure 9-7 illustrates the search positions of this algorithm. Suppose the origin (0, 0) is at the center of the figure. We start by choosing the origin as our center of searching and pick a step size b, which is 4 in Figure 9-7. In the first stage, in addition to the origin, we choose eight locations of blocks at a "distance" of b from the center for comparison; in Figure 9-7 these first 9 search locations are labeled '1'. We pick the location that gives the smallest SAD as our new center of search, which is marked by a concentric circle in Figure 9-7. In the second stage search, the step size is halved and a further 8 locations around the new center are chosen with the new step size which is 2 in this example. The search locations for this stage is labeled '2' in

Figure 9-7. Once again, we pick the best-matched location to be the new search center and repeat the procedure until the step size cannot be subdivided further.

In an N-step search, the step size in general is $2^{(N-1)}$ and there are N searching levels. The number of searches is only $8N+1$ as compared to $(2^{N+1}-1)^2$ in a corresponding full search. However, NSS uses a uniformly allocated checking point pattern in the first step, which could be inefficient for small motion estimation.

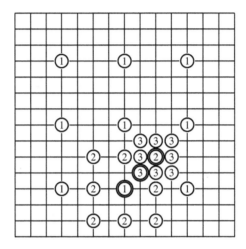

**Figure 9-7**. Three Step Search ( TSS )

## Hierarchical Search

Hierarchical search employs the coarse-to-fine approach to reduce computations at the coarse levels. At a coarse level, a 'large' block may contain many pixel positions but only a small number of searching locations; the sample value at a location may be the average ( filtered value ) of many adjacent pixel values. The algorithm first searches a large block to obtain a first approximation of the motion, which can be successively refined by searching smaller regions using smaller blocks, each block being appropriately filtered. The method has a better chance of getting the "real" motion vector because we first establish the general trend of motion using large filtered blocks and accomplish more accurate measurement using small blocks. It has been shown that motion vectors obtained by hierarchical search has significantly lower entropy, implying that they require less number of bits to encode.

For example, the mean pyramid method constructs different pyramidal images by subsampling, and estimates motion vectors starting from higher levels ( coarse levels ) and proceeding to lower ones. We can reduce the noise at higher levels by constructing the image pyramids using low pass filters, and use a simple averaging to construct the multiple-level pyramidal images. For instance, suppose $g_L(x, y)$ is the gray level value at the position $(x, y)$ of the L-th level and $g_0(x, y)$ represents the original image at level 0. We obtain the pixel value at a level by averaging the four pixel values in a nonoverlapping window of the next lower level as shown in Equation (9.2):

$$g_L(x,y) = \lfloor \frac{1}{4} \sum_{i=0}^{1} \sum_{j=0}^{1} g_{L-1}(2x+i, 2y+j) \rfloor \tag{9.2}$$

where $\lfloor x \rfloor$ denotes the floor function of $x$, which truncates $x$ to the nearest integer. If there are totally three levels in the pyramid, one pixel at level 2 corresponds to a $2 \times 2$ block and a $4 \times 4$ block at level 1 and level 0 respectively. Therefore, a block of size $16 \times 16$ at level 0 produces a block of size $16/2^L \times 16/2^L$ at level $L > 0$. After constructing the mean pyramid, we can search the images starting at level 2 using the minimum SAD ( Sum of Absolute Differences ) criterion; we select the motion vector with the smallest SAD as the coarse motion vector at that level. We send the motion vector detected at the higher level to the next lower level ( level 1 ), which uses the received motion vector to guide the refinement step at that level. We repeat the motion estimation process once more down to level 0. Since SAD's are computed at the highest level based on relatively small blocks, the same values are likely to appear at several points. To solve this problem, we can use more than one candidate at the highest level (level 2 for our special case). A number of motion vectors at level 2 are propagated to the lower one. Full search in a small window around the candidates is used at level one to find the minimum difference location as the search center at layer 0. Figure 9-8 shows the search locations of the algorithm. At level 2 of the figure, three best matched points are selected as centers for search windows in the next level, which are shown at level 1 of the figure. Level 0 shows the search window where we search for the best match.

Level 2

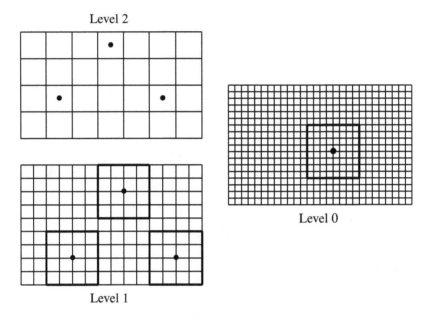

Level 0

Level 1

**Figure 9-8**. Search Locations for Hierarchical Search

## Nearest Neighbours Search

One problem of the TSS, Hierarchical Search and many other suboptimal searches is that the searches may quickly get trapped in local minima, as the distortion function does not necessarily increase monotonically as we move away from the global minimum distortion candidate. This could result in a significant loss in estimation accuracy, and hence compression performance as compared to Full Search. This problem can be alleviated by incorporating prediction into a fast-search algorithm. We can predict the the current motion vector ( MV ) from previously coded motion vectors that represent spatially or temporally neighbouring macroblocks. Localizing the search origin in this way reduces the possibility of getting trapped in local minima, as the predicted motion vector is usually closer than the vector (0, 0) to the global minimum candidate. If the predicted MV is accurate, we can quickly find the "optimal" MV by searching a relatively small neigbourhood.

Nearest Neighbours Search ( NNS ) makes use of the above-mentioned motion vector prediction method and highly localized search pattern to give estimation accuracy approaching that of Full Search in many applications but with much lower computational complexity. The algorithm offers a more reliable MV prediction that detects potential non-motion changes in the video sequence. In the algorithm, we predict an MV based on previously coded MVs and transmit the difference ( MVD ) between the current MV and the predicted MV. NNS exploits this property by giving preference to MVs that are close to the predicted MV, and thus minimize the MVD. Figure 9-9 shows an example of search positions of NNS, which first evaluates the SAD at the search origin ( labeled '0' ) and then calculates the SAD at the locations of the predicted MV as well as the SADs of the surrounding points in a diamond shape ( labeled '1' ). If the SAD at '0' or the center of the diamond is lowest, the search terminates, otherwise the location that gives the smallest SAD is chosen ( double-circled '1' in Figure 9-9 ), and becomes the center of a new diamond-shaped search pattern ( labeled '2' ) and the search process continues. In the example, the next search center is double-circled '2' and the final selected location is double-circled '3'.

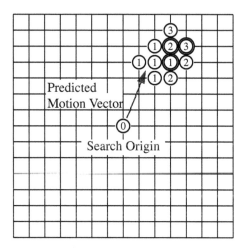

**Figure 9-9**. Nearest Neighbours Search ( NNS )

## Others

Many other fast search algorithms have been proposed. More popular ones include Binary Search (BS), Two Dimensional Logarithmic Search (TDL), Four Step Search (FSS), Orthogonal Search Algorithm (OSA), One at a Time Algorithm (OTA), Cross Search Algorithm (CSA), and Spiral Search (SS). In each case, we can evaluate its performance by comparing it with Full Search. We can compare the time an algorithm used and the compression ratio achieved against that of Full Search. Sometimes, an algorithm may be good for certain applications but not for others. For example, algorithms such as Hierarchical Search are more easily to be implemented with customized hardware than others.

# 9.7 Frame Types

There are two types of video frames concerning motion compensation. An **intraframe** or **I-frame** is a frame that is encoded using only the information from within that frame. On the other hand, **inter-** or non-intra frames are encoded using information from within that frame as well as information from other frames. Inter-frames can be further classified as P-frames and B-frames.

## 9.7.1 Intraframes (I-frames)

Intra frames are coded without motion estimation and compensation. That means it is encoded spatially with no information from any other frame. In other words, no temporal processing is performed outside of the current picture or frame. Coding an I-frame is similar to coding an image in JPEG. Compressing a video using I-frames only is similar to the techniques in motion JPEG. The compression ratio obtained is in general significantly lower than that of compressing with inter-frame coding.

Spatial prediction can be used in intra-frame coding. In spatial prediction, we make use of previously-transmitted samples to predict an image sample in the same image or frame. Figure 9-10 shows a pixel $d$ that is to be encoded. If the pixels in the frame are processed in the order from left to right and top to bottom, then the neighbouring pixel values at $a, b$, and $c$ have been processed and are available in both the encoder and decoder. The encoder predicts a value $P(d)$ for the current pixel $d$ based on some combinations of previously coded pixel values, $I(a), I(b)$, and $I(c)$. It then subtracts the actual pixel value $I(d)$ of $d$ from $P(d)$ and encodes the residual ( the difference resulted from the subtraction ). The decoder uses the same prediction formula and adds the decoded residual to construct the pixel value.

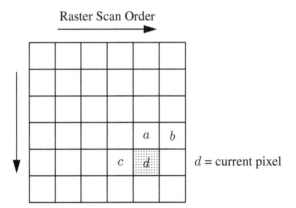

**Figure 9-10**. Spatial Prediction

The following is an example of spatial prediction for Figure 9-10. In the example, pixel $c$ has a larger weight than $b$ and $a$ because it is the most recently scanned pixel. We also assume that the encoding of the residuals is a lossless process, which means that the pixel values can be recovered exactly from the decoded residuals.

**Example 9-1**   Spatial Prediction for Figure 9-10.

Encoder prediction: $P(d) = \dfrac{2I(c) + I(b) + I(a)}{4}$

Residual: $R(d) = I(d) - P(d)$ is encoded and transmitted.

Decoder decodes $R(d)$, and

obtain $P(d)$ using same prediction formula: $P(d) = \dfrac{2I(c) + I(b) + I(a)}{4}$

Reconstruct sample value at $d$: $I(d) = R(d) + P(d)$

If the residual encoding involes lossy operations such as quantizations, the decoded sample values, $I'(a), I'(b)$, and $I'(c)$ may not be identical to the original sample values, $I(a), I(b)$, and $I(c)$ of pixels $a$, $b$, and $c$. In this case, the decoder does not know the values of $I(a), I(b)$, and $I(c)$ and if we still use $I(a), I(b)$, and $I(c)$ to calculate $P(d)$ in the encoder as it does in the example, the process could lead to a cumulative error between the encoder and decoder. Therefore, in this situation, the encoder should first reconstruct the sample values $I'(a), I'(b)$, and $I'(c)$ from the previous residuals before calculating the current prediction $P(d)$. The encoder uses the reconstructed sample values to form the prediction in the above example:

$$\begin{aligned} P(d) &= \frac{2I'(c) + I'(b) + I'(a)}{4} \\ R(d) &= I(d) - P(d) \\ R'(d) &= Decode(Encode(R(d))) \\ I'(d) &= P(d) + R'(d) \end{aligned} \tag{9.3}$$

In this way, just like what we discussed in Section 9.5, where we obtain the reference frame by reconstructing the macroblock rather than using one from the video source, the encoder and decoder use the same sample values in calculating $P(d)$, and the cumulative error can be avoided. The prediction equation of (9.3) is a special case of the more general linear prediction:

$$P(d) = C_a I'(a) + C_b I'(b) + C_c I'(c) \tag{9.4}$$

where $C_x$ is a constant for pixel $x$. In the example of (9.3), the constants for pixels $a, b$, and $c$ are 0.25, 0.25, and 0.5 respectively. For things to work properly, the sum of the constants in the linear prediction of (9.4) must be equal to 1. If the predicted values $I'$ have been scaled in the process, the original sample value $I(d)$ of the current pixel $d$ must be scaled accordingly before subtracting $P(d)$ from it to form the residual $R(d)$.

In practice, we may perform intra-prediction after DCT transformation at a block-based level with block size $8 \times 8$. Very often, the low-frequency DCT coefficients of neighbouring blocks are correlated. Therefore, we can predict the DC coefficient ( i.e. $F_{00}$ of Chapter 6) and AC coefficients of the first row and column ( $F_{0i}, F_{i0}$, $0 < i < 8$) from neigbouring coded blocks. Table 9-1 shows the DCT coefficients for each of the four luma $8 \times 8$ block of a mcaroblock. The data are obtained from the same PPM file, "beach.ppm" that we have used for testing in the previous chapters. The DC coefficients ( 629, 637, 653, and 662 ) are clearly similar but it is less obvious if there is correlation between the first row and first column of the AC coefficients in the blocks.

**Table 9-1**  Four $8 \times 8$ luma blocks of a DCT Macroblock

| 629 | -5 | -1 | -1 | 1 | -1 | -2 | -1 | 637 | -5 | 0 | 1 | 2 | 0 | 0 | -1 |
|---|---|---|---|---|---|---|---|---|---|---|---|---|---|---|---|
| -8 | -5 | -1 | 0 | 0 | -1 | -2 | -2 | -4 | 2 | -1 | -2 | -1 | 1 | 0 | 0 |
| 2 | -3 | -1 | -1 | -4 | -4 | -3 | -2 | 4 | -1 | 1 | -2 | 1 | 2 | 1 | 1 |
| -3 | -4 | -3 | -1 | 1 | -2 | -4 | -3 | 2 | 0 | -3 | -1 | 0 | 1 | 0 | 0 |
| -1 | -6 | 0 | -1 | -1 | 1 | 0 | 0 | 2 | -1 | -1 | 0 | -1 | 1 | -1 | 3 |
| -4 | -5 | -3 | 0 | 2 | -1 | -1 | 0 | 2 | -2 | -1 | -1 | -1 | 0 | -1 | 0 |
| -1 | -2 | -2 | -1 | -1 | -1 | -1 | -2 | 0 | 0 | 1 | 2 | 1 | -1 | 0 | -2 |
| 1 | -1 | 0 | 0 | 0 | -2 | -2 | -1 | -1 | -1 | 1 | 1 | 0 | 0 | 0 | -1 |
| 653 | 1 | 0 | 0 | -1 | 1 | -1 | 0 | 662 | -6 | 1 | -1 | 0 | -2 | 0 | 0 |
| -9 | 1 | 1 | -2 | -1 | 0 | -1 | 2 | -7 | 1 | 1 | -2 | 0 | 1 | 0 | 1 |
| 0 | 1 | 0 | 0 | 0 | 0 | 0 | -1 | 1 | 1 | 1 | 1 | -1 | 0 | -1 | -1 |
| -2 | 0 | -2 | 1 | 1 | -1 | 2 | 0 | 0 | -1 | -1 | 1 | -1 | -2 | 0 | 0 |
| 0 | -1 | -1 | 0 | -1 | 0 | 0 | 0 | 2 | 1 | 1 | 0 | -1 | -1 | 1 | 0 |
| 1 | -1 | 1 | -1 | 0 | 0 | -1 | 1 | 0 | 0 | -1 | -1 | -1 | 0 | 0 | 1 |
| 0 | -1 | 1 | 0 | 0 | 0 | 0 | 0 | -1 | -1 | -2 | -1 | 0 | 2 | -2 | 0 |
| 0 | 0 | 1 | 2 | 2 | 0 | 1 | -2 | 1 | 0 | -1 | 0 | 1 | 1 | -2 | 0 |

Suppose $F_{ij}^X$ represent the coefficient of block $X$ at location $(i, j)$. Figure 9-11 presents an example of prediction for the current block $D$ from neigbouring blocks. We predict $F_{00}^D$, the DC coefficient of the current block from the DC coefficients of the previously coded neigh-bouring $8 \times 8$ blocks, A, B, and C. The question is which block should we choose to form the prediction. *Should we choose A, B or C, or a combination of them?* A simple solution is to use either B or C as they are adjacent to the current block D. This is shown in Figure 9-11. In determining if we should choose B or C, we can examine the *gradients* of the DC values between the blocks. We choose the block that gives the smaller gradient. That is, the choice of prediction is determined by:

$$\text{if } |F_{00}^A - F_{00}^C| < |F_{00}^A - F_{00}^B|$$

Predict from Block B;

$$(9.5)$$

otherwise

Predict from Block C;

The prediction value $P_{00}^D$ of block D is set to the DC coefficient of the chosen block and is subtracted from the actual DC value of the current block. For example, if block C is chosen,

$$P_{00}^D = F_{00}^C$$
$$R_{00}^D = F_{00}^D - P_{00}^D$$

$$(9.6)$$

The residual $R_{00}^D$ is then coded and transmitted.

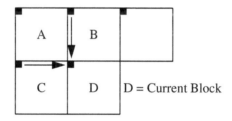

**Figure 9-11.** Prediction of DC of $8 \times 8$ DCT Block

We predict the AC coefficients in a similar way as shown in Figure 9-12, with the first row or column predicted in the direction determined by gradients of DC coefficients of (9.5). For example, if the prediction direction is from Block B, we predict the first row of AC coefficients of Block D from the first row of Block B. If the prediction direction is from Block C, we predict the first column of Block D from the first column of Block C.

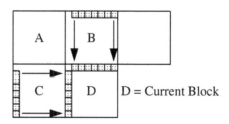

**Figure 9-12.** Prediction of AC of $8 \times 8$ DCT Block

## 9.7.2 Inter-frames

In addition to the techniques used in intra-frame coding, Inter-frame ( or nonintra-frame ) coding utilizes motion estimation and compensation to improve the compression of videos; it exploits the temporal correlations to make good predictions to reduce data redundancies. There are two types of inter-frames, **predicted frames** (**P-frames**) and **bidirectional frames**

(**B-frames**). The difference between P-frames and B-frames is that they use different kinds of reference frames to make predictions. These two kinds of frames and I-frames usually join in a GOP ( Group of Pictures ), which is often required to synchronize the encoder and decoder, when the encoded data are transmitted over a network and errors may occur. We can use an I-frame as a reliable reference for synchronization as it does not require information from other frames to be decoded. I-frames are also important for random access of compressed video files. Because of these, I-frames are also known as key frames or access points.

## P-frames

Starting with an I-frame, we can forward-predict a future frame, which is commonly referred to as a P-frame. We can also use a P-frame to predict other P-frames in the future. Therefore, a P-frame is always predicted from a past frame, a frame that has been coded earlier.

As an example, consider a GOP that has 6 frames. The ordering of the frames will be:

$$I, P, P, P, P, P, I, P, P, P, P, P, \ldots$$

We predict each P-frame in the sequence from the frame immediately preceding it, whether it is an I-frame or a P-frame. The I-frame can be used for synchronization.

## B-frames

B-frames are bidirectionally predicted frames. They can be predicted or interpolated from earlier and/or later frames. That is, we not only search a past frame to find the best match but also a future frame to find the optimal result. It is easy to understand making predictions using information of a previously coded frame. *But how do we make predictions from a future frame, something that has not happened?* The trick is that the terms "past" and "future" are artificial; we call the frames occurred before the current frame the past frames and frames occur after the current one, the future frames. To make predictions from a future frame, we must look ahead and buffer it, encoding and decoding it for it to be used as a reference frame. This is called backward prediction. Therefore, if video compression and decompression is to be done in "real time", there must be a time delay between the compression and decompression process if B-frames are used. Figure 9-13 shows various prediction modes for inter-frames.

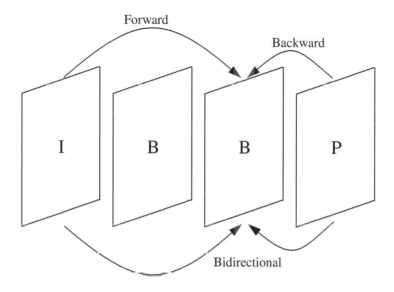

**Figure 9-13.** Prediction Modes of Inter-frames

## 9.8 Typical GOP Structure

Figure 9-14 shows a typical group of picture ( GOP ) structure, "IBBPBBP...". We can categorize the I-frames and P-frames as *anchor frames*, because they may be used as reference frames in the coding of other frames. On the other hand, B-frames are not anchor frames as they are never used as a reference. Note that the structure starts with an I-frame; it is essential to start coding with an I-frame as there is no previous information that can be used for reference in motion estimation.

Figure 9-15 shows a prediction scheme of the GOP structure. We use the I-frame to predict the first P-frame, and use these two frames ( I and P ) to predict the first and second B-frame. Then we use the first P-frame to predict the second P-frame. The first and second P-frames are joined to predict the third and fourth B-frames.

As you can see from the prediction scheme, we need the fourth frame ( P-frame ) to predict the second and the third ( B-frames ). So we need to transmit the P frame to the decoder before the B-frames and consequently we have to delay the transmission in order to keep the P-frame or to buffer the frames.

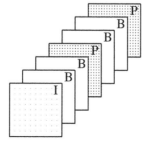

**Figure 9-14.** A Typical Group of Pictures ( GOP )

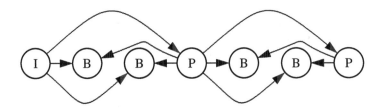

**Figure 9-15**. A Prediction Scheme for GOP of Figure 9-14

## 9.9 Rate Control

In many video compression applications, compressed data are sent over a network as bit-streams. The traffic in a large network is usually bursty. It may be idle for some of the time but may have congestion at some other time. This may make available bandwidth to clients change from time to time. Also, if the encoding parameters of a video codec are kept constant, the number of coded bits may change for each macroblock, depending on the video content; this will lead to variations of the output bit rate of the encoder. Typically, high-motion scenes or scenes with fine details generate more bits and low motion or coarse-detail scenes produce fewer bits. These can cause problems in delivering video data and it is necessary for the video encoder to adjust the bit rate to match the available bit rate of the transmission channel.

One simple way to control bit rate is to buffer the encoded data before transmission, which can 'smooth' the impact of fluctuations in the available bandwidth. Figure 9-16 shows a block diagram explaining this mechanism. The variable bit rate output is buffered by a queue, which is first-in first-out ( FIFO ). The data in the queue are deleted at a constant rate to match the available bandwidth of the delivering channel. Another queue at the receiving end of the channel is used to buffer data to the decoder which deletes the data from the queue at variable bit rate; this is because for the same number of input bits, the decoder may produce a different number of output bits depending on the context of the data. If the decoder needs to produce data at a constant frame rate, it has to consume input bits at a variable rate to counter the variations in the amount of data produced for a given number of bits. Of course, if the fluctuations in the channel capacity or the data context is too large, queues with limited size may not be able to maintain a constant bit rate, but at least the queues can 'smooth' the fluctuations.

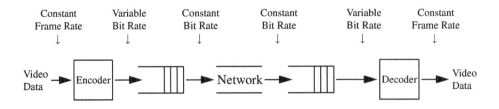

**Figure 9-16**. Controlling Bit Rate Using Queues

Another way to control the bit rate of the bitstream generated by a video encoder is to vary the encoding parameters from time to time in order to maintain a target bit rate. One important parameter that can change the encoding bit rate is the quantization parameter ( $Q_p$ ). The encoder can control the bit rate by analyzing the rate at which the encoder is producing data and comparing it with the desired target bit rate. If the encoder is producing too much data, it simply raises the $Q_p$. If too little data is being produced, it lowers the $Q_p$. Note that the larger the $Q_p$, the better the compression but the lower the quality. There are many different algorithms for varying $Q_p$ depending on the criteria of performance. Some of these algorithms also use the option of dropping frames of video as well as adjusting $Q_p$. The trade-off of the quality of each frame with the jerkiness in the video caused by frame dropping determines the extent to which we adjust the $Q_p$ and the number of frames we want to drop. Alos, the bit rate profiles and characteristics of these algorithms will differ, and often the choice of algorithm is dependent on the network and target application.

## 9.10 Implementations

We shall discuss the implementation of motion estimation and motion compensation in the next few chapters. We do not intend to cover many of the search algorithms and the prediction methods. We shall only discuss two simple cases, the encoding of the residual between two frames without any motion estimation, and the use of Three Step Search ( TSS ) to improve upon the encoding.

# Chapter 10    Video Programming

## 10.1 Introduction

In order to experiment with the encoding and decoding of video data, we need to have a way to play the video on a PC. We need some well-developed tools to help us achieve this goal. Java has very powerful and complex tools to manipulate images and graphics. We also need some tools to process some video files that you can find in Internet and download them to carry out the tests and experiments. There exists a lot of video formats but we do not intend to address all of them; exploring video formats is **not** a goal of this book. Rather, we shall only discuss in detail the relatively simple AVI ( Audio Video Interleaved ) format and we use it as an intermediate format that we can read and save video data. There are also a lot of free utilities that we can use to change AVI files to other video formats and vice versa. To simplify things, we shall also make use of an open source AVI ( Audio Video Interleaved ) library that can help us process AVI files.

The Abstract Windowing Toolkit (AWT) is a class library introduced in Java 1.0 for basic GUI interface. It also has image processing functions. A GUI interface created using AWT may look slightly different for different platforms. Later a user interface library code named "Swing" ( or "Swing set" ) was created to provide platform-neutral GUI interface. Swing is the official name for the non-peer-based GUI toolkit that is part of the Java Foundation Classes (JFC), which are a set of classes that allow developers to write graphics and image applications. JFC is vast and is an integrated and core technology in the Java 2 platform (also code-named JDK 1.2). To enhance the image processing capabilities, java provides further libraries which may be huge to process images.

The **Java 2D API** is a set of classes for advanced 2D graphics and imaging, encompassing line art, text, and images in a single comprehensive model. The API provides extensive support for image compositing and alpha channel images, a set of classes to provide accurate color space definition and conversion, and a rich set of display-oriented imaging operators.

The **Java Advanced Imaging API** (JAI) provides a set of object-oriented interfaces to support a simple, high-level programming model. It extends the java 2 platform by allowing sophisticated, high-performance image processing to be incorporated into java applets and applications. It is a set of classes providing imaging functionality beyond that of Java 2D and the Java Foundation classes, though it is designed for compatibility with those APIs. JAI is complex and is a high-level API; it hides from users the details of image processing which may be complex. For example, using JAI, a user does not need to have any knowledge about the format of a JPEG image in order to render it.

The **Java Image I/O API** provides a pluggable architecture for working with images stored in files and accessed across the network. The JAI Image I/O Tools classes provide additional plugins for other stream types and for advanced formats such as JPEG-LS, JPEG2000, and TIFF.

The **Java Media Framework API** (JMF) enables audio, video and other time-based media to be added to applications and applets built on java platform technology.

All these java tools, libraries or APIs are huge and complex. We are not interested to study or use many of them. Our goal is to study the techniques and principles of compressing data, not the java APIs. Interestingly, java tries to hide data processing details from users and image data are operated at a very high level. It is inconvenient to use java to do something very simple like sending some data to the graphics framebuffer for rendering. Beginners may have to go through the maze of the APIs, tracing the functions of classes after classes to get to the right ones. Here we only discuss the classes and related ones for rendering. We try to make the process as simple as possible.

In this chapter, we shall first use the JAI to develop a simple video player ( without audio part ). Our goal of course is to decode the compressed data and render them on the screen. *Can we integrate the decoder and player seamlessly? Could we separate the decoder and the player functionalities so that changing the decoder would not affect the rendering and vice versa?* It turns out that this can be easily handled by the concept of the producer-consumer problem, which is a well-studied synchronization problem in Computer Science. In this case, the decoder is the producer which provides data and the player is the consumer that consumes the data. To accomplish these, they have to be run using different threads. Java provides simple thread functions that allow us to implement all these with relative ease. We shall discuss the principles and implementations of the player and related issues in the following sections.

## 10.2 Java Image Rendering

JAI is not the only API in java that provides image manipulating capabilities. AWT also provides functions to render and manipulate images. Actually, JAI is defined in a way that it is backward compatible with AWT imaging APIs defined by the **java.awt.image.Image** interface. The most fundamental and significant class in this API maybe the **java.awt.image. BufferedImage** class, which provides a 'framebuffer' for image data and relevant color models. Figure 10-1 shows the BufferedImage class and its encapsulated classes.

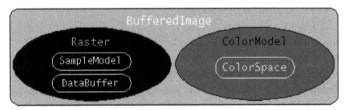

**Figure 10-1** AWT BufferedImage Class

### ColorModel

The **ColorModel** class shown in Figure 10-1 is an abstract class. An abstract class in java is a class declared *abstract* and cannot be instantiated (i.e. we cannot create objects of the class directly). However, we can extend it to a subclass (child class), which is not abstract and can be instantiated. An abstract class may or may not include abstract methods. An abstract method (function) is a method that is declared without an implementation; usually the implementations will be provided by subclasses. Though it cannot be instantiated, an abstract class can have static fields and methods, which can be referenced directly. ( See the example in the section of **ColorSpace** below. ) This class encapsulates methods for translating a pixel value to color components, red, green, and blue, and an alpha component, which denotes the degree of transparency at the pixel. In order to render an image to the screen, pixel values must be converted to color and alpha components. As arguments to or return values from methods of this class, pixels are represented as 32-bit ints or as arrays of primitive types. A **ColorSpace** class is used to specify the number, order, and interpretation of color components for the ColorModel. A ColorModel used with pixel data that does not include alpha information treats all pixels as opaque, which have an alpha value of 1.0. Java 2 provides three direct subclasses for ColorModel, namely, ComponentColorModel, IndexColorModel, and PackedColorModel. We shall only disucss and use the **ComponentColorModel** subclass here.

**ComponentColorModel** is a ColorModel class that works with pixel values representing color and alpha information as separate samples; each sample is stored in a separate data element. This class can be used with an arbitrary ColorSpace. The number of color samples in the pixel values must be the same as the number of color components in the ColorSpace. There may be a single alpha sample. For those methods that use a primitive array pixel representation of type *transferType*, the array length is the same as the number of color and alpha samples. Color samples are stored first in the array followed by the alpha sample, if present. The order of the color samples is specified by the ColorSpace. Typically, this order reflects the name of the color space type. For example, for TYPE_RGB, index 0 corresponds to red, index 1 to green, and index 2 to blue. ComponentColorModel has two constructors and we shall only use the following constructor in our applications:

```
public ComponentColorModel(ColorSpace colorSpace,
                   int[] bits,
                   boolean hasAlpha,
                   boolean isAlphaPremultiplied,
                   int transparency,
                   int transferType)
```

This constructor constructs a ComponentColorModel from the specified parameters. Color components will be in the specified ColorSpace. The supported transfer types are:

```
DataBuffer.TYPE_BYTE,
DataBuffer.TYPE_USHORT,
DataBuffer.TYPE_INT,
DataBuffer.TYPE_SHORT,
DataBuffer.TYPE_FLOAT, and
DataBuffer.TYPE_DOUBLE.
```

If not null, the *bits* array specifies the number of significant bits per color and alpha component and its length should be at least the number of components in the ColorSpace if there is no alpha information in the pixel values, or one more than this number if there is alpha information. When the *transferType* is DataBuffer.TYPE_SHORT, DataBuffer.TYPE_FLOAT, or DataBuffer.TYPE_DOUBLE the *bits* array argument is ignored. *hasAlpha* indicates whether alpha information is present. If *hasAlpha* is true, then the boolean *isAlphaPremultiplied* specifies how to interpret color and alpha samples in pixel values. If the boolean is true, color samples are assumed to have been multiplied by the alpha sample. The transparency specifies what alpha values can be represented by this color model. The acceptable transparency values are OPAQUE, BITMASK or TRANSLUCENT. The *transferType* is the type of primitive array used to represent pixel values. The following is an example of using this constructor:

```
int[] bits = { 8, 8, 8 };
ColorModel  colormodel = new ComponentColorModel(colorspace, bits,
        false, false, Transparency.OPAQUE, DataBuffer.TYPE_BYTE);
```

In this example, the red, green, and blue components are 8-bit samples. The ColorSpace class is discussed below.

## ColorSpace

ColorSpace is also an abstract class which serves as a color space tag to identify the specific color space of a Color object or, via a ColorModel object, of an Image, a BufferedImage, or a

GraphicsDevice. For purposes of the methods in this class, colors are represented as arrays of color components represented as floats in a normalized range defined by each ColorSpace. For our programs here, we shall use the sRGB color space. sRGB ( or standard RGB ) color space is a proposed standard that uses the ITU-R BT.709 primaries, the same as are used in studio monitors and HDTV, and a transfer function (gamma curve) typical of CRTs. It is similar to the usual RGB color space but with more flexibilities, optimizing for the vast majority of computer monitors, operating systems and browsers.

As mentioned above, we can reference a static method of an abstract class without creating any class object. ColorSpace provides the static method **getInstance()** for us to create a ColorSpace object in a convenient way. The following is an example of creating an sRGB color space:

```
ColorSpace colorspace = ColorSpace.getInstance ( ColorSpace.CS_sRGB );
```

In the example, we can think of *colorspace* as a pointer pointing to a ColorSpace object. Note that though an abstract java class does not provide implementations to its abstract methods, it does provide implementations to its nonabstract methods. We can always access the nonabstract methods of an abstract class object. For example, the following piece of code makes use of the methods of ColorSpace to find out more information about the color space sRGB:

```
ColorSpace cs = ColorSpace.getInstance ( ColorSpace.CS_sRGB );
int n = cs.getNumComponents();
int dataType = cs.getType();
System.out.printf("\nNumber of Components in sRGB color space=%d",n);
System.out.printf("\nComponent  MinValue  MaxValue  DataType  Name\n");
for ( int i = 0; i < n; i++ ) {
  float minValue = cs.getMinValue( i );
  float maxValue = cs.getMaxValue( i );
  String name =  cs.getName( i );
  System.out.printf("\n %d\t    %4.2f\t  %4.2f\t      %d \t    %s",
                          i,  minValue, maxValue, dataType, name);
}
System.out.println();
```

When executed, the above piece of code will produce some outputs similar to the following:

```
Number of Components in sRGB color space = 3

Component   MinValue    MaxValue   DataType   Name

0            0.00        1.00        5         Red
1            0.00        1.00        5         Green
2            0.00        1.00        5         Blue
```

We can use this ColorSpace in the ColorModel discussed above to create color models. The following piece of code is an example of using the ColorModel to convert a color to a pixel sample:

```
int[] bits = { 8, 8, 8 };
ColorModel colormodel = new ComponentColorModel(cs, bits,
            false, false, Transparency.OPAQUE, DataBuffer.TYPE_BYTE);
Color color = new Color ( cs, new float [] {1.0f, 0.5f, 0.25f}, 0 );
float [] components = color.getComponents ( null );
int [] unnormalized = colormodel.getUnnormalizedComponents(
                                        components, 0, null, 0);
byte[] pixels =(byte[])colormodel.getDataElements(unnormalized, 0, null);
//convert to an unsigned byte
for ( int i = 0; i < 3; i++ ) {
```

```
        int pixelvalue = 0x000000ff & pixels[i];
        System.out.printf( "%d ", pixelvalue );
    }
```

The code prints out the values "255 128 64" corresponding to the normalized red, green, and blue color values "1.0f, 0.5f, 0.25f". In the code, we first create a ColorModel object using the subclass ComponentColorModel and sRGB color space as discussed above. A Color with normalized red, green, and blue values equal to 1.0f, 0.5f, and 0.25f respectively are created in the color space. Then the normalized color components are retrieved using **getComponents**(), which returns a float array, with the three elements, 1.0, 0.5, and 0.25. Next, these components are "unnormalized" using the **getUnnormalized**() method of the ColorModel class. Finally, the unnormalized components are converted to pixel samples using ColorModel's getDataElements() method, which returns an array of the ColorModel's transfer type (byte, in this case) containing the unnormalized component values. The last for-loop is to convert a signed 8-bit integer ( byte ) to an unsigned integer.

## SampleModel

**SampleModel** is also an abstract class.    It defines an interface for extracting samples of pixels in an image.  All image data are expressed as a collection of pixels.  Each pixel consists of a number of samples.  A sample is a datum for one band of an image and a band consists of all samples of a particular type in an image.  For example, a pixel might contain three samples representing its red, green and blue components; there are three bands in the image containing this pixel.  One band consists of all the red samples from all pixels in the image.  The second band consists of all the green samples and the remaining band consists of all of the blue samples.  **ComponentSampleModel** is a subclass of SampleModel.  It provides the implementations of the abstract methods of SampleModel.  In our application, instead of using ComponentSampleModel to create SampleModel objects, we use a subclass of ComponentSampleModel, named **BandedSampleModel** to do the task. Figure 10-2 shows the relations between these classes:

---

**java.lang.Object**

      extended by **java.awt.image.SampleModel**

         extended by **java.awt.image.ComponentSampleModel**

           extended by **java.awt.image.BandedSampleModel**

---

**Figure 10-2** Class BandedSampleModel

**BandedSampleModel** class represents image data which are stored in a band-interleaved fashion and for which each sample of a pixel occupies one data element of the DataBuffer. Accessor methods are provided so that image data can be manipulated directly. Pixel stride is the number of data array elements between two samples for the same band on the same scanline. The pixel stride for a BandedSampleModel is one. Scanline stride is the number of data array elements between a given sample and the corresponding sample in the same column of the next scanline. Band offsets denote the number of data array elements from the first data array element of the bank of the DataBuffer holding each band to the first sample of the band. The bands are numbered from 0 to N-1. Bank indices denote the correspondence between a bank of the data buffer and a band of image data. This class supports TYPE_BYTE, TYPE_USHORT, TYPE_SHORT, TYPE_INT, TYPE_FLOAT, and TYPE_DOUBLE data types. The constructor

```
public BandedSampleModel ( int dataType, int w, int h, int numBands)
```

constructs a BandedSampleModel with the specified parameters. The pixel stride will be one data element. The scanline stride will be the same as the width. Each band will be stored in a separate bank and all band offsets will be zero. The following are the parameter specifications:

```
dataType - The data type for storing samples.
w - The width (in pixels) of the region of image data described.
h - The height (in pixels) of the region of image data described.
numBands - The number of bands for the image data.
```

The following is an example of using this constructor:

```
SampleModel  samplemodel =
        new BandedSampleModel ( DataBuffer.TYPE_SHORT, 128, 192, 3 );
```

In the example, the width of the image is 128 pixels, and the height is 192 pixels; the image data consists of 3 bands, red, green, and blue.

## DataBuffer

**DataBuffer** is another abstract class, which exists to wrap one or more data arrays. Each data array in the DataBuffer is referred to as a bank. Generally, a DataBuffer object will be cast down to one of its data type specific subclasses to access data type specific methods for improved performance. Currently, the Java 2D API image classes use TYPE_BYTE, TYPE_USHORT, TYPE_INT, TYPE_SHORT, TYPE_FLOAT, and TYPE_DOUBLE DataBuffers to store image data; all of these data types are static fields and thus can be accessed in a form like "DataBuffer.TYPE_BYTE".

## Raster

**Raster** is a class representing a rectangular array of pixels. A Raster object encapsulates a DataBuffer object that stores the sample values and a SampleModel object that describes how to locate a given sample value in a DataBuffer object.

A Raster defines values for pixels occupying a particular rectangular area of the plane, not necessarily including (0, 0). The rectangle, known as the Raster's bounding rectangle, which can be obtained through the getBounds() method, is defined by *minX, minY, width,* and *height* values. The *minX* and *minY* values define the coordinate of the upper left corner of the Raster.

One may use a SampleModel to describe how samples of a Raster are stored in the primitive array elements of a DataBuffer. Samples may be stored one per data element, as in a PixelInterleavedSampleModel or BandedSampleModel, or packed several to an element, as in a SinglePixelPackedSampleModel or MultiPixelPackedSampleModel classes.

The following is an example of using Raster and DataBuffer:

```
//allocate array to hold RGB data
int samples []  = new int[3*128*192];
.....
Byte[] bandValues = new Byte[1];
bandValues[0] = 3;
param1.add(new Float( 128.0 ));   // The width
param1.add(new Float( 192.0 ));   // Height
param1.add(bandValues);           // The band values
RenderedOp image = JAI.create("constant", param1 );
```

```
Raster ras = image.getData();
DataBuffer data = ras.getDataBuffer();
//output n sample data to raster
for ( int i = 0; i <  n; ++i )
  data.setElem ( i, samples[i] );
```

In the code, we have made use of the class RenderedOp, a node in a rendered imaging chain defined in Java Advanced Imaging (JAI), to create an "empty image". We then copy the data stored in the array *samples*[] to the raster of this image using the method "data.setElem(i, samples[i])".

# TiledImage

**TiledImage** is the main class for writable images in JAI. It provides a straightforward implementation of the WritableRenderedImage interface, taking advantage of that interface's ability to describe images with multiple tiles. It may be the most efficient class that can create an image out of some given data. In Java2D, a tile is one of a set of rectangular regions that span an image on a regular grid.

The tiles of a WritableRenderedImage must share a SampleModel, which determines their width, height, and pixel format. The tiles form a regular grid, which may occupy any rectangular region of the plane. The contents of a TiledImage are defined by a single RenderedImage source provided by means of one of the set() methods or to a constructor which accepts a RenderedImage. The set() methods provide a way to selectively overwrite a portion of a TiledImage, possibly using a region of interest (ROI).

TiledImage also supports direct manipulation of pixels by means of the getWritableTile() method. This method returns a WritableRaster that can be modified directly.

Another way to modify the contents of a TiledImage is through calls to the object returned by createGraphics(), which returns a Graphics2D object that can be used to draw line art, text, and images in the usual Abstract Window Toolkit (AWT) manner.

### Example

Putting all these together, we present a complete program that renders data to the screen. In this example, we hard-coded the image width and image height, and use BandedSample-Model to create a SampleModel object with the width and height and three bands. The sRGB color space is used in creating a ColorModel. The SampleModel and ColorModel objects are then used to create the TiledImage object outImage which will be used for rendering. Artificial data corresponding to an image which is half-red and half-white are saved in the integer array *samples*[]. The data are then assigned to *outImage* using the method setSample(). ScrollingImagePanel is used to render the *outImage*. The code is shown in Program Listing 10-1 and the corresponding output image is shown in Figure 10-3.

**Program Listing 10-1**:   Example of Rendering Data

```
/*
  DataToImage.java
  Demonstrates how to render data as an image on the screen.
*/
import java.io.*;
import java.awt.Frame;
import java.awt.image.*;
import java.awt.image.ColorModel;
import java.awt.color.ColorSpace;
import java.awt.*;

import javax.media.jai.widget.ScrollingImagePanel;
import javax.media.jai.*;

public class DataToImage {

   public static void main(String[] args) throws InterruptedException {

      int width = 128;      //image width
      int height = 192;     //image height

      //create a SampleModel object
      SampleModel  samplemodel = new BandedSampleModel
                              ( DataBuffer.TYPE_BYTE, width, height, 3 );
      //use sRGB as our color space
      ColorSpace colorspace = ColorSpace.getInstance ( ColorSpace.CS_sRGB );

      //create a color model using our color space (sRGB), 8-bit components,
      // no alpha, no alpha premultiplied, opaque, data type is BYTE
      int[] bits = { 8, 8, 8 };
      ColorModel colormodel = new ComponentColorModel(colorspace,bits,false,
          false, Transparency.OPAQUE, DataBuffer.TYPE_BYTE );

      //allocate array to hold RGB data
      int samples [] = new int[3*width*height];

      //create a TiledImage using sample model and color model defined above
      TiledImage outImage;
      outImage = new TiledImage(0,0,width,height,0,0,samplemodel,colormodel);

      int isize = width * height;    //image size
      int bands = 3;                 //3 bands: Red, Green, Blue
      int k = 0;

      //create some artificial sample data for rendering
      for ( int i = 0; i < isize; i++, k+=3 ){
         samples[k] = 255;            //red
       if ( i < isize / 2 ) {         //first half red
         samples[k+1] = 0;            //green
         samples[k+2] = 0;            //blue
       } else {                       //second half white
         samples[k+1] = 255;          //green
         samples[k+2] = 255;          //blue
       }
      }
      //assign data to the image
      k = 0;
      for (int y = 0; y < height; y++)
```

```
    for (int x = 0; x < width; x++)
      for (int band=0; band < bands; band++)
        outImage.setSample(x, y, band, samples[k++] );

  /* Attach image to a scrolling panel to be displayed. */
  ScrollingImagePanel panel =
           new ScrollingImagePanel( outImage, width, height );

  /* Create a frame to contain the panel. */
  Frame window = new Frame("Red and White");
  window.add(panel);
  window.pack();
  window.show();
  Thread.sleep( 10000 ); //sleep for ten seconds
  window.dispose();      //close the frame
}
```

**Figure 10-3** Image Created using TiledImage and Artificial Data

# 10.3 Threads

The effective use of threads is very important in modern programming. It allows a program to execute multiple parts of itself simultaneously in the same address space. In many cases, we basically cannot accomplish the tasks without using threads. For instance, consider a game program that needs to accept inputs from the mouse and keyboard, and at the same time has to play music at the background and generate some special sounds at various stages; it will be extremely difficult if not impossible to achieve these effects without using threads. Of course, we use threads only when we have to. We are not replacing simple nonthreaded programs with fancy, complex, threaded ones. Threads are just one more way we can use to make our programming tasks easier. The main benefits of using threads in programming include the following:

- gaining performance from multiprocessor hardware,
- easier programming for jobs with multi-tasks,

    o increasing job throughput by overlapping I/O tasks with computational tasks,
    o more effective use of system resources by sharing resources between threads,
    o using only one binary to run on both uniprocessors and multiprocessors,
    o creating well-structured programs, and
    o maintaining a single source for multiple platforms.

## 10.3.1 What Are Threads

A thread is also referred to as a **light weight process** ( **LWP** ). A process is a program (object code stored on some media) in execution. It is a unit of work in a modern time-sharing system. You can create several processes from the same program. A process not only includes the program code, which is sometimes referred to as the text section, but also the current activities and consumed resources including the program counter, processor registers, the process stack ( which contains temporary data such as function parameters, return address, and local variable ), and the data section, which contains global variables. A process may also have a heap, which is the memory dynamically allocated to it during run time.

Threads of execution, often shortened to threads, are the objects of activity within the process. Each **thread** is a basic unit of CPU utilization, comprising a **thread ID**, a **program counter**, a **register set**, and a **stack**. It shares with other threads of the same process its code section, data section, and other operating-system resources, such as open files, signals, and global variables. The various states of a thread can be represented by Figure 10-4, where quantum refers to the time the computer allocated to run a thread before switching to running another thread.

## 10.3.2 Pthreads

IEEE defines a POSIX standard API, referred to as **Pthreads** ( IEEE 1003.1c ), for thread creation and synchronization. It is defined in C language. Many contemporary systems, including Linux, Solaris, and Mac OS X implement Pthreads. To use Pthreads in your program, the user must include **pthread.h** and link with **-l pthread**. The following C/C++ exmaple, **pthreads.cpp** of Listing 10-2 shows how to use Pthreads:

    **Program Listing 10-2**: Pthread Example in C/C++

```
/*
  pthreads.cpp
  A very simple example demonstrating the usage of pthreads.
  Compile: g++ -o pthreads_demo pthreads_demo.cpp -lpthread
  Execute: ./pthreads_demo
*/

#include <pthread.h>
#include <stdio.h>

using namespace std;

//The thread
void *runner ( void *data )
```

```
{
  char *tname = ( char * )data;

  printf("I am %s\n", tname );

  pthread_exit ( 0 );
}

int main ()
{
  pthread_t id1, id2;           //thread identifiers
  pthread_attr_t attr1, attr2;  //set of thread attributes
  char *tnames[2] = { "Thread 1", "Thread 2" }; //names of threads

  //get the default attributes
  pthread_attr_init ( &attr1 );
  pthread_attr_init ( &attr2 );

  //create the threads
  pthread_create ( &id1, &attr1, runner, tnames[0] );
  pthread_create ( &id2, &attr2, runner, tnames[1] );

  //wait for the threads to exit
  pthread_join ( id1, NULL );
  pthread_join ( id2, NULL );

  return 0;
}
```

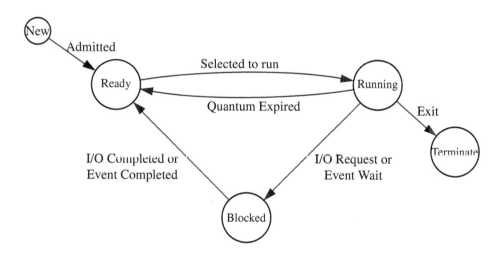

**Figure 10-4**. States of a Thread

In the example of **pthread.cpp** shown in Program Listing 10-2, we use **pthread_tid** to declare the identifiers for the threads we are going to create. Each thread has a set of attributes containing information about the thread like stack size and scheduling information. We use **pthread_attr_t** to declare the attributes of the threads and set the attributes in the function called by **pthread_attr_init()**. As we did not explicitly set any attributes, the default attributes will be used. The function **pthread_create()** is used to create a separate thread. In addition to passing the thread identifier and the attributes to the thread, we also pass the name of the function, *runner*, where the new thread will begin execution. The last argument passed to **pthread_create()** in the example is a string parameter containing the name of the thread. At this point, the program has three threads: the initial parent thread in **main()** and two child threads in **runner()**. After creating the child threads, the **main()** thread will wait for the **runner()** threads to complete by calling **pthread_join()** function.

Pthreads specification has a rich set of functions, allowing users to develop very sophisticated multithreaded programs. In the applications discussed here, we do not need to use many of the Pthread functions. Besides POSIX threads, different crucial thread programming schemes exist in the market. MS Windows has its own threading interface which is very different from POSIX threads. Though Sun's Solaris supports Pthreads, it also has its own thread API. Other UNIX systems may also have their own thread APIs. If you program in C/C++, an alternative way of creating threads is to use SDL threads which are platform independent. SDL solves the inconsistency of various thread-programming schemes with its own set of portable threading functions.

Java threads are relatively simpler and they are platform-independent as java byte codes run on java virtual machines.

## 10.3.3 Java Threads

Every thread in java is created and controlled by the **java.lang.Thread** class, which is a subclass of **java.lang.Object**. A java process can have many threads, and these threads can run concurrently, either asynchronously or synchronously. The following table shows some member methods of the Object class and Thread class:

| Object | Thread |
|---|---|
| notify()<br>notifyAll()<br>wait() | sleep()<br>yield() |

Every java thread has a priority; threads with higher priority are executed in preference to threads with lower priority. When code running in some thread creates a new thread object, the new thread has its priority initially set equal to the priority of the creating thread. There are two standard ways to create a new thread of execuation:

- o implementing the Runnable interface ( java.lang.Runnable ) ,
- o extending the Thread class ( java.lang.Thread ) and overriding its Run() method.

### Implementing the Runnable Interface

The following example presents the code of creating a thread by declaring a class that implements the Runnable interface. The class then implements the run() method. An object of the class can then be allocated.  In the example, the thread computes the modulo of an integer $m$ with respect to an integer $n$ and prints out the result:

```
class ModRun implements Runnable {
  int m, n;
  ModRun ( int x, int y ) {
  m = x;
  n = y;
  }

  public void run() {
    System.out.printf ("%d mod %d is %d\n", m, n, m % n );
  }
}
```

The following piece of code would then create a thread and start running it:

```
public class RunnableExample {
  public static void main(String[] args) {
    ModRun modthread = new ModRun( 8, 3);
    //Start the thread
    new Thread ( modthread ).start();
    try {
      //delay for two second
      Thread.currentThread().sleep(2000);
    } catch (InterruptedException e) {
    }
    //Display info about the main thread
    System.out.println(Thread.currentThread());
  }
}
```

This code generates the following output:

```
8 mod 3 is 2
Thread[main,5,main]
```

## Extending Thread Class

The other way to create a new thread of execution is to declare a class to be a subclass of Thread.  This subclass should override the run() method of class Thread.  An object of the subclass can then be allocated and started.  The above example of computing the modulo between two integers using this method could be written as follows:

```
class ModThread extends Thread {
  int m, n;
  ModThread ( int x, int y ) {
    m = x;
    n = y;
  }

  public void run() {
    System.out.printf ("%d mod %d is %d\n", m, n, m % n );
  }
}
```

The following code would then create a thread and start running it:

```
public class ThreadExample {
  public static void main(String[] args) {
    ModThread modthread = new ModThread( 8, 3);
    //Start the threads
    modthread.start();
    try {
      //delay for two second
      Thread.currentThread().sleep(2000);
    } catch (InterruptedException e) {}
    //Display info about the main thread
    System.out.println(Thread.currentThread());
  }
}
```

This code generates the same output as the first method.

Usually the first method ( implementing Runnable interface ) is a preferrable way of creating threads. This is because we can then save our 'subclassing' of Thread for other purposes. Also, if for some reason our class is a final class so that we couldn't make it a subclass, we must implement the Runnable interface to create thread execution. Moreover, a class might only be interested in being runnable, and therefore, inheriting the full overhead of the Thread class would be excessive.

## 10.4   The Producer-Consumer Problem

In Section 10.1, we have discussed how to render data as an image. We can modify it to a "video player" by adding a loop in **main**() to display a sequence of images: it reads in the image data from a file and saves it in a buffer *ibuf*, points the framebuffer to the data buffer, render the data to the screen, waits for a fixed period of time, and repeats the process by reading in another set of image data. Such a "video player" is single-threaded and is very inflexible. The whole program is dedicated to a single task, reading and displaying images. It cannot do other things like playing music or accepting inputs. If we add a decoder in the loop, it becomes difficult to synchronize the displaying speed and the decoding speed. We can overcome these shortcomings by changing the program to multi-threaded, and we will use the producer-consumer concept to handle the synchronization between decoding and rendering.

The producer-consumer problem is a common paradigm for thread synchronization. A **producer** thread produces information which is consumed by a **consumer** thread. This is in analog with whats happening in a fast-food restaurant. The chef produces food items and put them on a shelf; the customers consume the food items from the shelf. If the chef makes food too fast and the shelf is full, she must wait. On the other hand, if the customers consume food too fast and the shelf is empty, the customers must wait.

To allow producer and consumer threads to run concurrently ( simultaneously ), we must make available a buffer that can hold a number of items and be **shared** by the two threads; the producer fills the buffer with items while the consumer empties it. A producer can produce an item while the consumer is consuming another item. Trouble arises when the producer wants to put a new item in the buffer, which is already full. The solution is for the producer to go to sleep, to be awakened when the consumer has removed one or more items. Similarly, if the consumer wants to remove an item from the buffer and finds it empty, it goes to sleep until the producer puts something in the buffer and wakes the consumer up. The **unbounded-buffer** producer-consumer problem places no practical limit on the size of the buffer. The consumer may have to wait for new items, but the producer can always produce new items without waiting. The **bounded-buffer** producer-consumer problem puts a limit on the buffer size; the consumer must wait when the buffer is empty, and the producer must wait when the buffer is full.

The approach sounds simple enough, but if not properly handled, the two threads may **race** to access the buffer and the final outcome depends on who runs first. There is a simple technique to resolve the *race conditions*. E.W. Dijkstra introduced the concept of **semaphore** to handle synchronization problems in 1965. A semaphore is an integer variable associated with two operations, *down* and *up*, a generalization of *sleep* and *wakeup*, respectively. The *down* operation checks if the semaphore value is greater than 0. If yes, it decrements it and continues; if the semaphore value is 0, the thread is put on sleep. Checking the value, changing it, and possibly going to sleep are all done in a single, indivisible, **atomic action**. This it to guarantee that once a semaphore operation has started, no other thread can access the semaphore until the operation has completed or blocked.

Java uses a high-level synchronization technique called "monitors" to do synchronization; only one thread can be active inside a monitor. That is, only one thread can execute any of the methods at any time. In other words, a monitor is simply a lock that serializes access to an object. To gain access, a thread first acquires the necessary monitor, then proceeds. One can implement a semaphore using a monitor. A java monitor is signified by two basic synchronization idioms: *synchronized methods* and *synchronized statements*.

To make a method synchronized, we need to add the **synchronized** keyword to the declaration of a class like the following example:

```
class SynchronizedBuffer {
    private int buf = 0;

    public synchronized void write( int a ) {
      buf = a;
    }

    public synchronized void reset() {
      buf = 0;
    }

    public synchronized int value() {
      return buf;
    }
}
```

If *sharedBuffer* is an object of SynchronizedBuffer, then making these methods synchronized has two effects:

1. It is not possible for two invocations of synchronized methods on the object to interleave. That is, when one thread is executing a synchronized method for the object, all other threads that invoke synchronized methods for the same object will be blocked until the first thread has finished using the object.
2. When a synchronized method exits, it automatically establishes a happens-before relationship with any subsequent invocation of a synchronized method for the same object. This ensures that changes to the state of the object are known to all threads.

Note that we cannot use the synchronized keyword in a constructor. If we do, a syntax error occurs. When a thread invokes a synchronized method, it automatically acquires the intrinsic lock of the associated object; the thread releases the lock when the method returns. The lock-release occurs even if the return was caused by an uncaught exception.

Another way to create synchronized code is to use *synchronized statements*. Unlike synchronized methods, *synchronized statements* must specify the object that provides the intrinsic lock like the following example:

```
class AddBuffer {
    private int buf = 0;

    public int addValue ( int a ) {
      synchronized ( this ) {
        buf += a;
      }
      return buf;
    }
}
```

Putting these together, we present the code of a simple program adopted from the official java web site in Lising 10-3, Listing 10-4, and Listing 10-5. The program simulates the producer-consumer problem.

Listing 10-3 presents the SingleBuffer class. The *buffer* variable of SingleBuffer holds one piece of item, which will be accessed by both the producer and consumer. Mutual exclusion of accessing *buffer* must be established between a procuder thread and a consumer thread. Therefore, the methods of SingleBuffer that access the shared variable *buffer* is "synchronized", which ensures that only one object can access each method at one time. The **wait**() function sends the accessing thread to sleep and allows another thread to access the Single-Buffer object; the sleeping thread will be wakened up by the second thread when it executes the function **notifyAll**(). In summary, the producer produces an item and puts it in the single buffer. (It is in analogy of a chef producing a hamburger and put it on a plate.) A consumer 'removes' the item from the single buffer. (This is in analogy of a customer removing the hamburger from the plate.) If the buffer is occupied (full), the producer goes to sleep and will be wakened up by the consumer. If the buffer is empty, the consumer goes to sleep and will be wakened up by the producer.

**Program Listing 10-3**:   SingleBuffer object is shared

```
/*
  SingleBuffer.java
  The buffer variable is shared.  So it has to be synchronized.
  That is, only one object can access the synchronized method at a time.
*/
public class SingleBuffer
{
  private int buffer = -1;     //shared by producer and consumer
  private int count = 0;       //counts occupied buffers

  public synchronized void set( int value )
  {
    String name = Thread.currentThread().getName();
    while ( count == 1 ) {
      try {
        System.err.println( name + " tries to write." );
        System.out.println( "Buffer full. " + name + " waits. \t" +
                             buffer + "\t" + count);
        wait();               //sleep if necessary
      } catch ( InterruptedException e ) {
        e.printStackTrace();
```

```
      }
   } //end while

   buffer = value;
   ++count;
   System.out.println( name + " writes \t\t" + buffer + "\t" + count );

   notifyAll();               //wake up other threads
   }  //end set()

 public synchronized int get()
 {
   String name = Thread.currentThread().getName();

   while ( count == 0 ) {
     try{
       System.err.println( name + " tries to read." );
       System.out.println( "Buffer empty. " + name + " waits. \t" +
                               buffer + "\t" + count );
       wait();                //sleep if necessary
     } catch ( InterruptedException e ) {
       e.printStackTrace();
     }
   }  //while
   --count;
   System.out.println( name + " reads \t\t\t" + buffer +
                           " \t" + count );
   notifyAll();          //wake up sleeping threads
   return buffer;
   }  //get()
} //SingleBuffer
```

The Producer and Consumer classes are presented in Listing 10-4. A shared SingleBuffer object is passed in as the argument to the Producer constructor. (More precisely, a pointer to the object is passed in.) The Producer thread puts a value in the *buffer* variable of the shared SingleBuffer object via the set() method. Similarly, the same SingleBuffer object is passed to a Consumer thread as the argument of the Consumer constructor. The Consumer 'removes' the value from *buffer* via the get() method. To simulate a real producer-consumer problem, both the Producer and Consumer thread sleeps a random amount of time between 0 to 3 seconds after performing a task; each thread performs its task for six times and then terminates:

**Program Listing 10-4**:   Producer and Consumer Classes using a Single Buffer

```
/*
 *Producer-Consumer.java
 *Producer thread and Consumer thread shares a single buffer.
 *Only one thread can access the shared buffer at one time.
 */
class Producer extends Thread
{
  private SingleBuffer sharedBuffer;
  private int nTimes = 6;

  public Producer( SingleBuffer shared )
  {
```

```
      super ( "Producer" );
      sharedBuffer = shared;
   }
   public void run()
   {
      for ( int i = 1; i <= nTimes; i++ )
      {
          //sleep 0 to 3 seconds, then place value in Buffer
          try {
            Thread.sleep( (int) ( Math.random() * 3000 ) );
            sharedBuffer.set ( i ); //write to buffer
          } catch ( InterruptedException e ) {
            e.printStackTrace();
          }
      }//for
      System.err.println( getName() + " done producing." +
             "\nTerminating " + getName() + "." );
   }//end run
} //end class Producer

class Consumer extends Thread
{
   private SingleBuffer sharedBuffer;
   private int nTimes = 6; //number of times to run a loop

   public Consumer( SingleBuffer shared )
   {
      super( "Consumer" );
      sharedBuffer = shared;
   }
   public void run()
   {
      int sum = 0;

      for ( int i = 1; i <= nTimes; i++ )
      {
          //sleep 0 to 3 seconds, then reads value from Buffer
          try {
            Thread.sleep( (int) ( Math.random() * 3000 ) );
            sum += sharedBuffer.get(); //read from buffer
          } catch ( InterruptedException e ) {
            e.printStackTrace();
          }
      }//for
      System.err.println( getName() + " read values totaling: " + sum +
          "\nTerminating " + getName() + "." );
   } //end run
} //end Consumer
```

Listing 10-5 is a sample program that can be used to test the Procuder and Consumer classes which share a common SingleBuffer object. The SingleBuffer variable *sharedLocation* is used to construct a Procuder object and a Consumer object. The Producer thread puts a value in *sharedLocation* and the Consumer thread reads it.

**Program Listing 10-5**:   Testing Producer and Consumer classes

```
//SharedBuffetTest creates producer and consumer threads
```

```
public class SharedBufferTest
{
  public static void main( String [] args )
  {
    SingleBuffer sharedLocation = new SingleBuffer();

    StringBuffer header = new StringBuffer( "Operation" );
    header.setLength( 40 );
    header.append( "\t\t\tBuffer\tCount");
    System.err.println( header );

    Producer p = new Producer( sharedLocation );
    Consumer c = new Consumer( sharedLocation );
    p.start(); //start producer thread
    c.start(); //start consumer thread
  } //main
}//SharedBufferTest
```

The following is a sample output of the program:

```
Operation                          Buffer   Count
Consumer tries to read.
Buffer empty. Consumer waits.      -1       0
Producer writes                    1        1
Consumer reads                     1        0
Producer writes                    2        1
Consumer reads                     2        0
Producer writes                    3        1
Producer tries to write.
Buffer full. Producer waits.       3        1
Consumer reads                     3        0
Producer writes                    4        1
Consumer reads                     4        0
Consumer tries to read.
Buffer empty. Consumer waits.      4        0
Producer writes                    5        1
Consumer reads                     5        0
Consumer tries to read.
Buffer empty. Consumer waits.      5        0
Producer writes                    6        1
Consumer reads                     6        0
Producer done producing.
Terminating Producer.
Consumer read values totaling: 21
Terminating Consumer.
```

In the above example, the buffer we use is a single buffer which can hold only one item. In many practical applications, we may use a circular queue to hold more than one item at a time. The producer inserts an item at the tail of the queue and the consumer removes an item at the head of it. We advance the tail and head pointers after an insert and a remove operation respectively. The pointers wrap around when they reach the "end" of the queue. If the tail reaches the head, the queue is full and the producer has to sleep. If the head catches up with the tail, the queue is empty and the consumer has to sleep. Actually, such a queue may handle the situation of multiple producers and multiple consumers. This concept is illustrated in Figure 10-5:

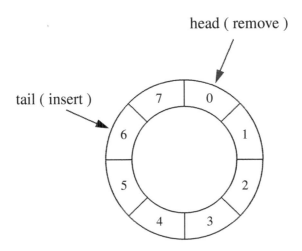

**Figure 10-5**. Circular Queue with Eight Slots

## 10.5   A Multi-threaded Raw Video Player

In this section, we put together what we have learned to develop a simple multi-threaded video player. Our concern here is to illustrate the concept of playing video data in an effective way. To simplify things, we hard-code the dimensions of a frame and assume that there's no compression in the data. We shall see that we can easily generalize the player to accommodate encoded data and data attributes.

A single-threaded raw video player is easy to implement: it just sits in a main loop to read in the video data and blit (bit-block transfer) them to the screen, wait for a while and repeat the data reading and blitting. In practice, a player has to handle various tasks besides blitting data on the screen. It may have to decode the data or to process the audio; a single-threaded player tangles all the tasks together and one needs to worry about the coordination between various tasks. On the other hand, a multi-threaded program can handle these tasks much better, as playing data ( sending data to screen ) can be cleanly separated from other tasks. The following section describes how to develop a multi-threaded program to play raw video data. The program and the sample raw data can be downloaded from this book's web site at *http://www.forejune.com/jvcompress/*.

In its simplest form, our multi-threaded player needs two threads, one for sending data to the screen and one for 'decoding' data ( at this moment, 'decoding' is simply reading data from the file ). Suppose we name these threads **Player** and **Decoder** respectively. This becomes a classical producer-consumer problem. Here, **Decoder** is the producer which produces resources ( video data ) and **Player**() is the consumer which consumes resources ( video data ). As discussed above, in the producer-consumer problem, to allow producer and consumer threads to run concurrently, we must have available a buffer of items that can be filled by the producer and emptied by the consumer. A producer can produce zero or more items while the consumer is consuming an item; the number of items that can be produced or consumed depends on the production rate as well as the consumption rate and other factors that may influence the production and consumption operations. The producer and consumer must be synchronized, so that the consumer does not try to consume an item that has not yet been produced and the producer suspends production when the buffer is full as there will not be any space to hold the produced item. Therefore, the producer ( **Decoder** ) must wait when the buffer is full and the consumer ( **Player** ) must wait when the buffer is empty. In our implementation, the Decoder (producer) and Player (consumer) will operate independently by sharing a circular queue. The Decoder dumps data into the circular queue while the Player removes them from the queue. So our first task is to implement a circular queue that will be shared by the Player and Decoder.

Listing 10-6 presents the code of the class **CircularQueue** that implements a circular queue. The queue may have more than one slot and each slot can hold the data of one image frame. We assume that an RGB model is used for processing the image data. The length of the queue is passed in as a parameter of the constructor. Operations on the *head* and *tail* variables are synchronized. When the difference between the *tail* and the *head* is equal to the queue length, the queue is full. On the other hand, if the *tail* and the *head* point to the same slot (i.e. *tail = head* ), the queue is empty. After producing an item, the producer has to increment *tail* and wakes up the consumer if it is sleeping by calling "notifyAll()"; these are implemented in the **tailInc**() method. On the other hand, after consuming an item, the consumer has to increment *head* and wakes up the producer if it is sleeping; these are implemented in the **headInc**() method. The operations "tail % length" and "head % length" implement the wrapping mechanism of the queue.

Note that in the class CircularQueue, the methods **setSamples**() and **putSamples**() are **not** synchronized. This is because when a consumer thread is reading the image data from the shared queue, we do not want to block the producer thread from writing data to it as long as they operate on different slots of the queue. Similarly, we do not block the consumer when the producer processes data from the queue.

**Program Listing 10-6**: CircularQueue Shared by Producer and Consumer

```
/*
 * CircularQueue.java
 * Implements a circular queue that may have more than
 * one slot.  Each slot may hold the data of an image frame.
 * Because setSamples() and putSamples() are not synchronized,
 * two threads can access the queue data simultaneously as
 * long as they are in different slots.
 * Assume an RGB model for the image.
 */
import java.io.*;
import javax.media.jai.*;

class CircularQueue
{
  private long head = 0;
  private long tail = 0;
  private int length;       //length of queue
  public int width;         //image width
  public int height;        //image height
  public byte buffer[][];   //the data queue
  public boolean quit = false;

  public CircularQueue ( int queueLength, int w, int h )
```

```
{
  if ( queueLength > 0 )
    length = queueLength;
  else
    length = 1;
  width = w;
  height = h;
  int frameSize = 3 * width * height;
  buffer = new byte[length][frameSize];
}

public synchronized void headInc()
{
  head++;
  notifyAll();    //wake up other threads
}

public synchronized void tailInc()
{
  tail++;
  notifyAll();    //wake up other threads
}

public synchronized void waitIfBufferFull()
{
   if ( tail >= head + length ){
     try {
       System.out.println( "Buffer full, producer waits." );
       wait();
     } catch ( InterruptedException e ) {
         e.printStackTrace();
     }
   }
}

public synchronized void waitIfBufferEmpty()
{
  if ( tail <= head ){
    try {
      System.out.println( "Buffer empty, consumer waits." );
      wait();
    } catch ( InterruptedException e ) {
        e.printStackTrace();
    }
  }
}

//consumes data
public void setSamples ( TiledImage outImage )
{
  int bands = 3;
  int k = 0;
  int h = (int) ( head % length );      //wrap-around
  for (int y = 0; y < height; y++)
    for (int x = 0; x < width; x++)
       for (int band=0; band < bands; band++)
         outImage.setSample(x, y, band, buffer[h][k++] );
}

//produces data
```

```
public int putSamples ( InputStream in )
{
   int t = (int) ( tail % length );       //wrap-around
   int size = 3 * width * height;
   int num = 0;
   try {
       if (  ( num = in.read( buffer[t], 0, size ) )  < 0 )
         quit = true;
   } catch (IOException e) {
           e.printStackTrace();
           System.exit(0);
   }
   return num;   //return number of bytes read,-1 for end of data stream
}
}
```

Typically, when the buffer is empty, the consumer goes to sleep and when the producer has finished producing an item and put it in the buffer, it is responsible to wake up the consumer. On the other hand, when the buffer is full, the producer goes to sleep and the consumer is responsible to wake up the producer after it has consumed an item. These mechanisms are implemented in the methods waitIfBufferFull(), waitIfBufferEmpty(), headInc(), and tail-Inc().

Once the CircularQueue class has been implemented, the implementations of the Player class ( consumer ) and the Decoder class ( producer ) are fairly straightforward. Listing 10-7 presents the code of the Player class. As discussed in Section 10.2, it uses the sRGB color space to create a color model, which in turn is used to create a TiledImage with the predefined image width and height. The TiledImage object ( *outImage* ) is attached to a ScrollingImagePanel, and the ScrollingImagePanel object ( *panel* ) is attached to a Frame object ( *window* ). The Player shares a CircularQueue with the Decoder. The CircularQueue method **setSamples**() is used to put the image data of a frame in *outImage*. The **set**() method of ScrollingImagePanel is utilized to send the image data of *outImage* to *panel* for display. The image frames are played at a rate of 20 frames per second (fps), which implies that the duration between two frames is 50 ms. To accomplish this frame rate, we use the function **System.currentTimeMillis**() to get the current time in milliseconds and insert a delay between playing frames estimated by the statement "delay = 50 - (int) ( current_time - prev_time );":

**Program Listing 10-7**: Player Class is a Consumer

```
//A consumer, CircularQueue buf is shared
class Player extends Thread
{
  private CircularQueue buf;
  private TiledImage outImage;
  private int width;
  private int height;
  private Frame window;
  private ScrollingImagePanel panel;

  //Constructor
  public Player( CircularQueue q )
  {
```

```
      super("Player");
      buf = q;                    //shared CircularQueue
      width = buf.width;
      height = buf.height;

      //create a SampleModel object
      SampleModel  samplemodel = new BandedSampleModel (
                              DataBuffer.TYPE_BYTE, width, height, 3);
      //use sRGB as our color space
      ColorSpace colorspace = ColorSpace.getInstance ( ColorSpace.CS_sRGB );

      //create a color model using our color space (sRGB), each color 8-bit,
      // no alpha, no alpha premultiplied, opaque, data type is BYTE
      int[] bits = { 8, 8, 8 };
      ColorModel  colormodel = new ComponentColorModel( colorspace, bits,
            false, false, Transparency.OPAQUE, DataBuffer.TYPE_BYTE );

      //create a TiledImage using above the sample model and color model
      outImage = new TiledImage(0,0,width,height,0,0,samplemodel,colormodel);
      /* Attach image to a scrolling panel to be displayed. */
      panel = new ScrollingImagePanel( outImage, width, height );

      /* Create a frame to contain the panel. */
      window = new Frame("Raw Video Player");
      window.add(panel);
      window.pack();
      window.show();
   }

   public void run()
   {
      long prev_time = System.currentTimeMillis();    //time in ms
      long current_time;
      int delay;

      while ( !buf.quit ) {
        buf.waitIfBufferEmpty();
        //consumes the data
        buf.setSamples ( outImage );
        buf.headInc();   //advance head pointer
        current_time = System.currentTimeMillis();     //time in ms
        if (current_time - prev_time < 50)     //20 fps = 50 ms / frame
          delay = 50 - (int) ( current_time - prev_time );
        else
          delay = 0;
        prev_time = current_time;
        try { Thread.sleep( delay );} catch ( InterruptedException e ){}
        panel.set ( outImage );
      } //while
      window.dispose();
   }
}
```

---

The code of the Decoder class is particularly simple and is presented in Listing 10-8. The Decoder is a producer. At this point, the Decoder does not decode anything. It simply reads the image data from a file and puts them in the buffers of the shared CircularQueue. It shares a CircularQueue with the Player. If the queue is full, it goes to sleep and will be wakened up by the Player when it calls the method **headInc**() of CircularQueue. Otherwise Decoder calls the **putSamples**() method of CircularQueue to deposit image data at the slot pointed by the variable *tail* of CircularQueue. After depositing the data, it calls **tailInc**() of CircularQueue to increment *tail* and wake up the Player if it is sleeping. The variable *quit* of CircularQueue is set to true when there is no more data.

In later chapters, we shall modify the Decoder class to include the task of decoding compressed data before putting the data in the queue.

**Program Listing 10-8**: Decoder is a Producer

```
//A Producer, CircularQueue buf is shared
class Decoder extends Thread
{
  private DataInputStream in;
  private CircularQueue buf;

  //Constructor
  public Decoder(DataInputStream ins,   CircularQueue q)
  {
    in = ins;
    buf = q;
  }

  public void run()
  {
     while ( !buf.quit ) {
       buf.waitIfBufferFull();
       //produce data
       buf.putSamples ( in );     //quit if out of data
       buf.tailInc();             //advance tail
     } //while
  }
```

Listing 10-9 presents a simple program for testing the Player and Decoder classes which share a common CircularQueue. In the program, the height and width of an image frame are hard-coded ( 320 × 240 ). The program creates a shared CircularQueue, a Player thread and a Decoder thread. Itreats the data in the file as a DataInputStream and passes the handle of the DataInputStream to the Decoder thread for "decoding":

**Program Listing 10-9**: A Simple Multi-threaded Raw Video Player

```
/*
  RawPlayer.java
  Simple program for testing Player and Decoder which share
  a CircularQueue.  The height and width of an image frame
  are hard-coded ( 320 x 240 ).  It reads raw RGB video data
  from a file that has saved the data in raw 8-bit format.
*/
import java.io.*;

public class RawPlayer
{
```

```
public static void main( String [] args )
{
  if (args.length < 1) {
    System.out.println("Usage: java " + "RawPlayer" +
      " filename_of_raw_video_data\n" +
      "e.g. java RawPlayer ../../data/jvideo.raw" );
    System.exit(-1);
  }

  //queue size, width, height
  CircularQueue sharedQueue = new CircularQueue( 4, 320, 240 );
  DataInputStream in;
  try {
    File f = new File ( args[0] );
    InputStream ins = new FileInputStream( f );
    in = new DataInputStream ( ins );
    //producer
    Decoder p = new Decoder( in, sharedQueue );
    p.start();                    //start producer thread
  } catch (IOException e) {
     e.printStackTrace();
     System.exit(0);
  }
  //consumer
  Player c = new Player( sharedQueue );
  c.start();               //start consumer thread
} //main
}
```

The user has to supply a file that has saved raw **RGB** video data in 8-bit format and the dimension of each frame is $320 \times 240$ in order to use the program. Again, a sample data file is provided in the web site of this book. For example, to excute the program, one can issue a command similar to the following:

```
java RawPlayer ../data/jvideo.raw
```

This plays the raw video saved in "jvideo.raw". Figure 10-6 shows a sample output frame.

The program **RawPlayer.java** shown in Listing 10-9 uses hard-coded parameters and plays video data that are not compressed. If we need to play compressed data, we only have to change the **Decoder** thread, which decodes data and acts as the producer. Instead of using hard-coded parameters, we need to read in the parameters from the file containing the encoded data. Also, in order to test or perform experiments on our encoder and decoder, we need to download from the Internet some video files which are saved in a standard video format. We shall address these problems in the next chapter.

**Figure 10-6** A Frame of Sample Raw Video

# Chapter 11 Video File Formats and Codec Player

## 11.1 Introduction

In Chapter 10, we have discussed how to play a video using data saved in the raw format of a file. In reality, video data are saved in a predefined format. There have been numerous video formats around and the data of most of them are saved in compressed form. In this Chapter, we shall give a brief discussion on some popular formats and do a case study on the **.avi** file format. Just as raw pixel data are often saved in **.bmp** format, and raw PCM sound samples in **.wav** format, raw video data are often saved in **.avi** format. We shall learn how to extract the raw video data from a .avi file so that we can play the video that we discussed in Chapter 10 or process them in our own way. There exists utilities in the Internet that allows one to convert from other video formats to uncompressed .avi format. With the help of those utilities, we can download a video file saved in any format from the Internet, convert it to uncompressed .avi and experiment the converted uncompressed data with our own encoder, decoder, and video player.

## 11.2 Video Storage Formats

### 11.2.1 Requirements of Video File Format

There exists a large number of video file formats in the market not only because competing companies create their own formats, hoping to push out competitors and to make their formats standards, but also because there are legal needs of not overstepping competitors' so called intellectual property. The following sections examine some common characteristics between the popular file formats. We summarize the requirements for a video file format to be successful as follows. A video file format should be able to

1. store video and audio data,
2. provide fast, real-time playback on target viewing platforms,
3. provide efficient scrubbing ( fast-forward and rewind while previewing ),
4. store metadata ( e.g. copyright, authorship, creation dates ... ),
5. store additional tracks and multimedia data like thumbnails, subtitle tracks, alternate language audio tracks ...,
6. allow for multiple resolutions,
7. provide file locking mechanisms,
8. allow for video editing,
9. provide integrity checking mechanism, and
10. perform segmentation of audio and video portions into packets for efficient Internet transmission.

### 11.2.2 Common Internet Video Container File Format

A container file format is hierarchical in structure, and can hold different kinds of media ( audio, video, text .. ) synchronized in time. The following are some popular container formats, which can save various types of media data:

185

1. AVI ( Audio Video Interleaved ) – standard audio / video file format under Windows; not suited for streaming as it does not have any standard way to store packetization data.
2. MOV – Apple's Quick Time format, better than AVI in synching audio and video; also supports Windows, and Linux.
3. ASF ( Advanced Streaming Format ) – Microsoft's proprietary format ( .WMV, .WMA ), designed primarily to hold synchronized audio and video.
4. NSV ( NullSoft Video ) – by NullSoft ( a division of AOL ) for streaming.
5. RM ( RealMedia ) – Real's streaming media files; can be extended to hold all types of multimedia; supports Windows, and Linux platforms and many standards, including MPEG-2, MPEG-4, Real, H263.
6. MP4 ( MPEG-4 ) – almost identical to MOV but MPEG-4 players can handle only MPEG-4 related audio, video and multimedia.
7. SWF, SWV ( Shockwave Flash ) – for Flash movies, typically containing vector-drawn animations with scripting controls; also supports video codecs, JPEG still images, remote loading of SWF files, XML data and raw text.

### 11.2.3 Simple Raw or Stream Video Format

Simple raw storage or stream formats store the compressed data without extra headers or metadata. These are essentially live audio-video streams saved to disk. Below are some examples:

1. MPEG-1, MPEG-2 – streams are composed of interleaved audio and video data arranged into groups of pictures.
2. MP3 – encode audio; part of MPEG-1.
3. DV ( Digital Video ) – used by modern digital cameras and video editing software.
4. .263 – video compressed with H.263 codec.
5. .RTP – Real Time Protocol data.

### 11.2.4 Internet Playlist, Index, and Scripting Format

Index formats have pointers linking to other resources. The following are some of this kind:

1. MOV – has several formats that do not contain actual video or audio data, but merely point to other files.
2. RAM ( RealAudio Metafile ) – points to the URL of the actual media file ( RealMedia .RM or RealAudio .RA ).
3. ASX ( Active Streaming Index ) – indexes files that work in Windows Media system and point to the content held in an ASF media file.
4. SMIL ( Synchronized Multimedia Integration Language ) – provides instructions to a media player on how to present a multimedia interface and what content to display.

## 11.3 Case Study: AVI Files ( .avi )

**AVI** ( Audio Video Interleaved ) is a file format defined by Microsoft for use in applications that capture, edit and play back audio-video sequences. Just as raw pixel data are often saved in .bmp format, and raw PCM sound samples in .wav format, raw video data are often saved in .avi format. It is a special case of **RIFF** (Resource Interchange File Format) and is the most commonly used format for storing audio/video data in a PC. An AVI file can be embedded in a web page using a link like:

< A HREF="http://www.*somedomain*.com/movie.avi" > A Movie </A>

In order that your Apache Web server is able to handle avi files, you need to add in the configuration file the following statement.

AddType video/avi .avi

AVI is considered as an obsolete video/audio file format as it lacks many contemporary and crucial features to support streaming and image processing. However, it has been extended by OpenDML to include some of those features.

## 11.3.1 RIFF File Format

The AVI file format is based on the RIFF (resource interchange file format) document format. A RIFF file consists of a RIFF header followed by zero or more lists and chunks; it uses a FOURCC ( four-character code ) to denote a text header. A FOURCC is a 32-bit unsigned integer created by concatenating four ASCII characters. For example, 'abcd' = 0x64636261. The AVI file format uses FOURCC code to identify stream types, data chunks, index entries, and other information. The RIFF file format has the following form.

1. A RIFF header consists of
   'RIFF' *fileSize fileType* (*data*)
   where

   ○ 'RIFF' is the literal FOURCC code 'RIFF',

   ○ *fileSize* is a 4-byte value indicating the size of the data in the file including the size of the *fileType* plus the size of the data that follows,

   ○ *fileType* is a FOURCC that identifies the specific file type,

   ○ *data* consists of chunks and lists in any order.

2. A **chunk** consists of
   *chunkID chunkSize chunkData*
   where

   ○ *chunkID* is a FOURCC that identifies the data contained in the chunk,

   ○ *chunkSize* is a 4-byte value giving the size of data in chunkData not including padded values,

   ○ *chunkData* is zero or more bytes of data, padded to nearest WORD boundary.

3. A **list** consists of
   'LIST' *listSize listType listData*
   where

○ 'LIST' is the literal FOURCC code 'LIST',

○ *listSize* is a 4-byte value, indicating the size of the list,

○ *listType* is a FOURCC code specifying the list type,

○ *listData* consists of chunks or lists, in any order.

Table 11-1 shows some sample data from an AVI file. The data are displayed in hexadecimal; the corresponding ASCII characters are printed on the right if they are printable otherwise a dot is printed. Some comments are shown at the far right to indicate what the data represent.

**Table 11-1**    Sample AVI Data

```
 0  1  2  3  4  5  6  7  8  9 10 11 12 13 14 15   0123456789012345]
52 49 46 46 DC 6C 57 09 41 56 49 20 4C 49 53 54  |RIFF.lW.AVI LIST|RIFF fileSize
                                                                 fileType LIST
CC 41 00 00 68 64 72 6C 61 76 69 68 38 00 00 00  |.A..hdrlavih8...|listSize
                                                                 listType avih structSize
50 C3 00 00 00 B0 04 00 00 00 00 00 10 00 00 00  |P...............|
                                                            microSecondPerFrame maxBytesPerSec
A8 02 00 00 00 00 00 00 01 00 00 00 00 84 03 00  |................|totalFrames
                                                  initFrames streams suggestedBufferSize
40 01 00 00 F0 00 00 00 00 00 00 00 00 00 00 00  |@...............|width height
00 00 00 00 00 00 00 00 4C 49 53 54 74 40 00 00  |........LISTt@..|
73 74 72 6C 73 74 72 68 38 00 00 00 76 69 64 73  |strlstrh8...vids|
00 00 00 00 00 00 00 00 00 00 00 00 00 00 00 00  |................|
64 00 00 00 D0 07 00 00 00 00 00 00 A8 02 00 00  |d...............|
00 84 03 00 10 27 00 00 00 00 00 00 00 00 00 00  |.....'..........|
40 01 F0 00 73 74 72 66 28 00 00 00 28 00 00 00  |@...strf(...(...|
40 01 00 00 F0 00 00 00 01 00 18 00 00 00 00 00  |@...............|
00 84 03 00 00 00 00 00 00 00 00 00 00 00 00 00  |................|
00 00 00 00 69 6E 64 78 F8 3F 00 00 04 00 00 00  |....indx.?......|
01 00 00 00 30 30 64 62 00 00 00 00 00 00 00 00  |....00db........|
00 00 00 00 0C 44 00 00 00 00 00 00 40 00 00 00  |.....D......@..|
.
.
.
4C 49 53 54 38 F9 56 09 6D 6F 76 69 69 78 30 30  |LIST8.V.moviix00|LISTlistSize
                                                                 listType indexBlock
F8 3F 00 00 02 00 00 01 A8 02 00 00 30 30 64 62  |.?..........00db|
                                                            ....00db(uncompress frame)
```

As we can see from the sample avi data of Table 11-1, a two-character code is used to define the type of information in the chunk:

| Two-character code | Description |
|---|---|
| db | Uncompressed video frame |
| dc | Compressed video frame |
| pc | Palette change |
| wb | Audio data |

For example, if stream 0 contains audio, the data chunks for that stream would have the FOURCC '00wb'. If stream 1 contains video, the data chunks for that stream would have the

FOURCC '01db' or '01dc'.

## 11.3.2 AVI RIFF Format

As shown in Table 11-1, the FOURCC 'AVI ' in a RIFF header identifies the file to be an AVI file. An AVI file has two mandatory LIST chunks, defining the format of the streams and the stream data, respectively. An AVI file might also include an index chunk, indicating the address of the data chunks of the file; it has the following form ( Table 11-2 ):

**Table 11-2    AVI RIFF Format**

```
RIFF ('AVI '
        LIST ('hdrl' ... )
        LIST ('movi' ... )
        ['idx1' () ]
        )
```

The 'hdrl' list defines the format of the data and is the first mandatory LIST chunk. The 'movi' list contains the data for the AVI sequence and is the second required LIST chunk. An optional index ('idx1') chunk can follow the 'movi' list. The index contains a list of the data chunks and their location in the file. If we expand 'hdrl' and 'movi' in Table 11-2, we shall get a form as shown below:

```
RIFF ('AVI '
        LIST ('hdrl'//header length
            'avih'()
            LIST ('strl'//stream length
                'strh'()
                'strf'()
                [ 'strd'() ]
                [ 'strn'() ]
                ...
                )
            ...
            )
        LIST ('movi'
            {SubChunk | LIST ('rec '
                            SubChunk1
                            SubChunk2
                            ...
                            )
            ...
            }
            ...
            )
        ['idx1' () ]
        )
```

The 'hdrl' list begins with the main AVI header, which is contained in an 'avih' chunk. The main header contains global information for the entire AVI file, such as the number of streams within the file and the width and height of the AVI sequence. This main header structure is shown below:

```
typedef struct _avimainheader {
    FOURCC fcc;      //'avih'
    DWORD  cb;          //size of structure, not including 1st 8 bytes
    DWORD  dwMicroSecPerFrame;
    DWORD  dwMaxBytesPerSec;
    DWORD  dwPaddingGranularity;
    DWORD  dwFlags;
    DWORD  dwTotalFrames;
    DWORD  dwInitialFrames;
    DWORD  dwStreams;
    DWORD  dwSuggestedBufferSize;
    DWORD  dwWidth;
    DWORD  dwHeight;
    DWORD  dwReserved[4];
} AVIMAINHEADER;
```

One or more 'strl' lists follow the main header. A 'strl' list is required for each data stream. Each 'strl' list contains information about one stream in the file, and must contain a stream header chunk ('strh') and a stream format chunk ('strf'). In addition, a 'strl' list might contain a stream-header data chunk ('strd') and a stream name chunk ('strn'). The stream header chunk ('strh') consists of an AVISTREAMHEADER structure as shown in Table 11-3.

**Table 11-3** AVI Main Stream Header

```
typedef struct _avistreamheader {
    FOURCC fcc;
    DWORD  cb;
    FOURCC fccType;//'vids'-video, 'auds'-audio, 'txts'-subtitle
    FOURCC fccHandler;
    DWORD  dwFlags;
    WORD   wPriority;
    WORD   wLanguage;
    DWORD  dwInitialFrames;
    DWORD  dwScale;
    DWORD  dwRate;
    DWORD  dwStart;
    DWORD  dwLength;
    DWORD  dwSuggestedBufferSize;
    DWORD  dwQuality;
    DWORD  dwSampleSize;
    struct {
        short int left;
        short int top;
        short int right;
        short int bottom;
    }  rcFrame;
} AVISTREAMHEADER;
```

One can also express Digital Video ( DV ) data in the AVI file format. The following example shows the AIFF RIFF form for an AVI file with one DV data stream, expanded with completed header chunks.

```
                     Example AVI File With One DV Stream

00000000 RIFF (0FAE35D4) 'AVI '
0000000C    LIST (00000106) 'hdrl'
00000018        avih (00000038)
                    dwMicroSecPerFrame      : 33367
                    dwMaxBytesPerSec        : 3728000
                    dwPaddingGranularity    : 0
                    dwFlags              : 0x810 HASINDEX|TRUSTCKTYPE
                    dwTotalFrames           : 2192
                    dwInitialFrames         : 0
                    dwStreams               : 1
                    dwSuggestedBufferSize : 120000
                    dwWidth                 : 720
                    dwHeight                : 480
                    dwReserved              : 0x0
00000058        LIST (0000006C) 'strl'
00000064            strh (00000038)
                        fccType                 : 'iavs'
                        fccHandler              : 'dvsd'
                        dwFlags                 : 0x0
                        wPriority               : 0
                        wLanguage               : 0x0 undefined
                        dwInitialFrames         : 0
                        dwScale            : 100 (29.970 Frames/Sec)
                        dwRate                  : 2997
                        dwStart                 : 0
                        dwLength                : 2192
                        dwSuggestedBufferSize : 120000
                        dwQuality               : 0
                        dwSampleSize            : 0
                        rcFrame                 : 0,0,720,480
000000A4            strf (00000020)
                        dwDVAAuxSrc     : 0x........
                        dwDVAAuxCtl     : 0x........
                        dwDVAAuxSrc1    : 0x........
                        dwDVAAuxCtl1    : 0x........
                        dwDVVAuxSrc     : 0x........
                        dwDVVAuxCtl     : 0x........
                        dwDVReserved[2] : 0,0
000000CC    LIST (0FADAC00) 'movi'
0FADACD4    idx1 (00008900)
```

## 11.4 Utility Program for Reading AVI Files

In order to extract the data from an AVI file, we need a program that can understand the AVI format. Rather than reinventing the wheel and developing such a program, which is not directly related to video compression, we shall make use of some existing open-source libraries and code to help us do the job.

We shall utilize the **ImageJ** library to help us read uncompressed .avi files. ImageJ is a public domain java image processing and analysis program. You may download it from the site,

```
http://rsb.info.nih.gov/ij/
```

which also contains detailed documentation of the package. You may also obtain it from the web site of this book. The package is commonly referred to as **ij** and comes as a jar file named **ij.jar**.

You may run ImageJ, either as an online applet or as a downloadable application, on any computer with java1.5 or later installed. It can display, edit, analyze, process, save and print 8-bit, 16-bit and 32-bit images. It can read many image formats including TIFF, GIF, JPEG, BMP, DICOM, FITS and 'raw'. It supports 'stacksx' (and hyperstacks), a series of images that share a single window.

Actually, we only have to use one of the programs, **AVI_Reader.java** in the package. AVI_Reader is written by Michael Schmid, base on a plugin by Daniel Marsh and Wayne Rasband. It only has very limited support for processing .avi files but the functions are rich enough for our purpose, which is mainly to read the data of an uncompressed .avi file. As of this writing, AVI_Reader only supports the following formats:

1. uncompressed 8 bit with palette (=LUT)
2. uncompressed 8 and 16 bit grayscale
3. uncompressed 24 and 32 bit RGB (alpha channel ignored)
4. uncompressed 32 bit AYUV (alpha channel ignored)
5. various YUV 4:2:2 compressed formats
6. png or jpeg-encoded individual frames.

It also has the following limitations:

1. Most MJPG (motion-JPEG) formats are not read correctly.
2. Does not read avi formats with more than one frame per chunk.
3. Palette changes during the video are not supported.
4. Out-of-sequence frames (sequence given by index) not supported.
5. Different frame sizes in one file (rcFrame) are not supported.
6. Conversion of (A)YUV formats to grayscale is non-standard: all 255 levels are kept as in the input (i.e. the full dynamic range of data from a frame grabber is preserved).

The above information of AVI_Reader can be found at the site *http://rsbweb.nih.gov/ij/plugins/avi-reader.html*. The relations of AVI_Reader class to other java classes are shown below:

```
java.lang.Object
  1-- ij.ImageStack
        1-- ij.VirtualStack
              1--ij.plugin.AVI_Reader
```

AVI_Reader extends Virtual_Reader and implements PlugIn of ij. It has only one constructor, "AVI_Reader()". The following are some of the commonly used methods of AVI_Reader:

```
public int getWidth()

  Returns the image width of a frame
  ----------------------------------------------------------
public int getHeight()

  Returns the image height of a frame
  ----------------------------------------------------------
public int getSize()
```

```
    Returns the number of frames in the video
    ---------------------------------------------------------
public ImageStack makeStack(java.lang.String path,
                            int firstFrameNumber,
                            int lastFrameNumber,
                            boolean isVirtual,
                            boolean convertToGray,
                            boolean flipVertical)

    Create an ImageStack from an avi file with given path.

    Parameters:
      path - Directoy+filename of the avi file
      firstFrameNumber - Number of first frame to read (starts from 1)
      lastFrameNumber - Number of last frame to read or 0 for reading all,
                        -1 for all but last...
      isVirtual - Whether to return a virtual stack
      convertToGray - Whether to convert color images to grayscale
    Returns:
      Returns the stack; null on failure. The stack returned may be
         non-null, but have a length of zero if no suitable frames were
         found
```

Listing 11-1 shows a simple example of using AVI_Reader to play an uncompressed .avi file and to print out some parameters of the .avi file. It uses the the method **getPixels**() to read the RGB pixel values from the file and put them into an integer array:

**Program Listing 11-1**: PlayAVI Plays Uncompressed AVI Video Using AVI_Reader

```
/*
  PlayAVI.java
  Demonstrates the use of AVI_Reader of ImageJ to
  play an uncompressed .avi file.
*/
import java.io.*;
import java.awt.Frame;
import java.awt.image.*;
import java.awt.image.ColorModel;
import java.awt.color.ColorSpace;
import java.awt.*;
import javax.media.jai.widget.ScrollingImagePanel;
import javax.media.jai.*;
import ij.plugin.AVI_Reader;

public class PlayAVI {

  public static void main(String[] args) throws InterruptedException {
    if (args.length != 1) {
      System.out.println("Usage: java " +
                                 "AVI_input_image_filename");
      System.exit(-1);
    }

    AVI_Reader avi = new AVI_Reader();
    //read images from AVI file to virtual stack
    avi.makeStack ( args[0], 0, 0, true, false, false  );

    int vsize = avi.getSize();     //number of images in the virtual stack
    int width = avi.getWidth();    //image width
```

```
    int height = avi.getHeight();  //image height
    System.out.printf("total frames=%d, width=%d, height=%d \n",
                                          vsize, width, height );

    //create a TiledImage using a ColorModel and a SampleModel
    ColorSpace colorspace = ColorSpace.getInstance ( ColorSpace.CS_sRGB );
    int[] bits = { 8, 8, 8 };
    ColorModel  colormodel = new ComponentColorModel( colorspace, bits,
        false, false, Transparency.OPAQUE, DataBuffer.TYPE_BYTE );
    TiledImage outImage;
    SampleModel  samplemodel = new BandedSampleModel(DataBuffer.TYPE_BYTE,
                                          width, height, 3);
    outImage = new TiledImage(0,0,width,height,0,0,samplemodel,colormodel);
    ScrollingImagePanel panel = new ScrollingImagePanel(outImage,width,height);
    Frame window = new Frame("AVI_Reader Demo");
    window.add(panel);
    window.pack();
    window.show();

    //render the AVI images
    for ( int s = 1; s < vsize; ++s ) {
      Object obj = avi.getPixels ( s );
      if ( obj instanceof int[] ) {
        int[] pixels = (int[]) obj;
        int k = 0;
        for (int y = 0; y < height; y++) {
          for (int x = 0; x < width; x++) {
            int c, n = 16;
            //consider colors R, G, B
            for ( int i = 0; i < 3; ++i ) {
              c = (int)( 0x000000ff & (pixels[k]>>n) );
              outImage.setSample(x, y, i, c );
              n -= 8;
            }
            k++;
          }
        }
        panel.set ( outImage );
        Thread.sleep ( 60 );
      } else {
        System.out.println("Only supports integer pixels\n");
        System.exit ( -1 );
      }
    }
    Thread.sleep( 4000 ); //sleep for four seconds
    window.dispose();     //close the frame
  }
}
```

---

You can simply compile the program with the command "javac PlayAVI.java". However, you must point your class path to the correct location of the ImageJ library. The following are typical commands to set the class path, compile and run the program,

> export CLASSPATH=$CLASSPATH:*/path_to_library/*ImageJ/ij.jar
> javac PlayAVI.java
> java PlayAVI ../data/jvideo.avi

where *path_to_library* is the path to the directory that saves the ImageJ library, and "jvideo. avi" is a sample uncompressed .avi file which can be downloaded from the web site of this book.

# 11.5 A Simple Video Codec for Intra Frames

In previous chapters, we have discussed the coding and decoding of intra-frames of a video as well as playing videos using a solution for the producer-consumer problem. In this section, we combine all the code and put together a simple video codec ( coder-decoder ) that does intra-frame coding and decoding. At this point, our codec does not consider inter-frame coding that utilizes Motion Estimation ( ME ) and Motion Compensation ( MC ). Also, the pre-calculated Huffman code is very brief and is far from optimized.

Like what we did before, we use integer arithmetic in the implementation to speed up the computing process; we utilize the ImageJ and Java Imaging packages to simplify the program and make it more robust. The codec can compress an uncompressed AVI file and play it back. We assume that the video data of the avi file are saved using the 24-bit RGB colour model. Most of the code presented here have been discussed in previous sections or chapters.

## 11.5.1 Compressed File Header

We first define our own header of the compressed file. The header contains the basic information of the compressed data and consists of 24 bytes as listed in Table 11-4.

| Table 11-4 | |
|---|---|
| **Bytes** | **Information** |
| 0 - 9 | contains "FORJUNEV" as I.D. of file |
| 10 - 11 | frame rate ( frames per second ) |
| 12 - 15 | number of frames |
| 16 - 17 | width of an image frame |
| 18 - 19 | height of an image frame |
| 20 | bits per pixel |
| 21 | quantization method |
| 22 | extension, 0 for uncompressed data |
| 23 | dummy |

The default extension of such a compressed file is **.fjv**. The dummy byte in the header is used for byte-alignment so that the header makes up 24 bytes rather than 23 bytes; it may be used for other purposes in the future. This header can be implemented by defining a class like the following:

```
class Vheader {
  public byte  id[] = new byte[10]; //I.D. of file, ``FORJUNEV"
  public short fps;        //frame per second
  public int   nframes;    //number of frames
  public short width;      //width of video frame
  public short height;     //height of video frame
  public byte  bpp;        //bits per pixel
  public byte  qmethod;    //quantization method
  public byte  ext;        //extension
  public byte  dummy;      //for byte alignment,make header size=24

  //Constructor
  Vheader ()
  {
    byte src [] = {'F', 'O', 'R', 'J', 'U', 'N', 'E', 'V', 0, 0};
    System.arraycopy(src, 0, id, 0, src.length);//set header I.D.
  }

  //Constructor
  Vheader (short w, short h, short frameRate, int numVideoFrames)
  {
    this();      //call the other constructor
    //System.out.printf( "%s\n", id );
    fps = frameRate;        //frame per second
    nframes = numVideoFrames;  //number of frames
    width = w;               //image width
    height = h;              //image height
    bpp = 8;                 //number of bits per pixel
    qmethod = 1;             //quantization method
    ext = 1;                 //file contains compressed data
    dummy = 0;
  }
  ......
}
```

At present, we set the quantization method variable *qmethod* to 1. The extension variable *ext* is set to 0 if the **.fjv** data are uncompressed and 1 if they are compressed. In summary, at this point the encoding and decoding processes consist of the following steps:

1. **Encoding**:

   1. Read a 24-bit RGB image frame from an uncompressed avi file.

   2. Decompose the RGB frame into $16 \times 16$ macroblocks.

   3. Transform and down-sample each $16 \times 16$ RGB macroblock to six $8 \times 8$ YCbCr sample blocks using YCbCr 4:2:0 format.

   4. Apply Discrete Cosine Transform ( DCT ) to each $8 \times 8$ sample block to obtain an $8 \times 8$ block of integer DCT coefficients.

   5. Forward-quantize the DCT block.

   6. Reorder each quantized $8 \times 8$ DCT block in a zigzag manner.

7. Run-level encode each quantized reordered DCT block to obtain 3D ( run, level, last ) tuples.

8. Use pre-calculated Huffman codewords along with sign bits to encode the 3D tuples.

9. Save the output bit stream of the Huffman coder in a file.

2. **Decoding**:

1. Construct a Huffman tree from pre-calculated Huffman codewords.

2. Read a bit stream from the encoded file and traverse the Huffman tree to recover 3D run-level tuples to obtain $8 \times 8$ DCT blocks.

3. Reverse-reorder and inverse-quantize each DCT block.

4. Apply Inverse DCT ( IDCT ) to resulted DCT blocks to obtain 8x8 YCbCr sample blocks.

5. Use six $8 \times 8$ YCbCr sample blocks to obtain a $16 \times 16$ RGB macroblocks.

6. Combine the RGB macroblocks to form an image frame.

We have discussed all of the above steps and their implementations in detail in previous chapters. We just need to make very minor modifications to accomplish the task. The two files **Encoder.java**, and **Decoder.java** discussed in Chapter 6 need some modifications. The file **CircularQueue.java** also needs modification because we now use **AVI_Reader** to put samples into the circular queue. On the other hand, the following files can be used without any any modifications:

| Table 11-5 | |
|---|---|
| **Files** | **Chapter** |
| RgbYcc.java | 5 |
| common.java | 5 |
| DctVideo.java | 6 |
| Quantizer.java | 7 |
| Reorder.java | 7 |
| Run3D.java | 7 |
| Run.java | 7 |
| BitIO.java | 8 |
| Hcodec.java | 8 |
| Dtables.java | 8 |

Of course, to use the the classes of the files, we need to point the class path to the directories that contain those classes. Suppose our current working directory is **11/** and the ImageJ package is in **11/avi/**. The following is a typical command that may be used to set the class path to point to the necessary classes discussed above:

*export CLASSPATH=$CLASSPATH:../5/:../6/:../7/:../8:../10/:avi/ImageJ/ij.jar*

The files that we need to modify or develop in this section ( in the direcotry **11/** ) include the following:

| AviFrameProducer.java | Decoder.java | Encoder.java | Vheader.java |
|---|---|---|---|
| CircularQueue.java | Display.java | Vcodec.java | |

We are going to discuss these new files briefly below. Again, the whole package along with a couple of sample AVI files are provided in the book's web site at:

*http://www.forejune.com/jvcompress/.*

1. **Vheader.java**

   The class **Vheader** reads and writes the header of a **.fjv** file defined in Table 11-4. Its data members and constructors are shown above in section 11.5.1.

2. **Display.java**

   The class **Display** simply displays a frame in the window. It uses the ColorModel, ColorSpace and SampleModel discussed in Chapter 10 to create a TiledImage which is attached to a ScrollingImagePanel. It gets the image data from the head of the shared circular buffer and send the data to the panel using the method **set()**:

**Program Listing 11-2**: Display Class Renders the Image of a Frame

```
public class Display {
 private CircularQueue buf;
 private int height;
 private int width;
 private TiledImage outImage;
 private ScrollingImagePanel panel;
 private Frame window;

 //constructor
 public Display ( CircularQueue q, int w, int h )
 {
   buf = q;
   width = w;
   height = h;

   //create a TiledImage using a ColorModel and a SampleModel
   ColorSpace colorspace=ColorSpace.getInstance(ColorSpace.CS_sRGB);
   int[] bits = { 8, 8, 8 };
   ColorModel  colormodel = new ComponentColorModel(colorspace,
       bits,false,false,Transparency.OPAQUE, DataBuffer.TYPE_BYTE);
   SampleModel samplemodel=new BandedSampleModel
                     (DataBuffer.TYPE_BYTE, width, height, 3);
   outImage=new TiledImage(0,0,width,height,0,0,samplemodel,
                                                   colormodel);
```

```
      panel = new ScrollingImagePanel(outImage,width,height);
      window = new Frame("Player");
      window.add(panel);
      window.pack();
      window.show();
   }

   public void display_frame()
   {
      //render the  images
      int h = buf.getHead();
      int k = 0;
      for (int y = 0; y < height; y++) {
        for (int x = 0; x < width; x++) {
          int c;
          //consider colors R, G, B
          for ( int i = 0; i < 3; ++i ) {
            c = (int)( buf.buffer[h][k++] );
            outImage.setSample(x, y, i, c ),
          }
        }
      }
      panel.set ( outImage );
   }

   public void close_window()
   {
      window.dispose();      //close the frame
   }
}
```

3. **AviFrameProducer.java**:

The class **AviFrameProducer** makes use of **AVI_Reader** to read frames from an avi file and put the frames in the shared circular buffer. It acts as a producer which produces uncompressed frames for consumers to consume:

**Program Listing 11-3**: AviFrameProducer is a Producer of Image Frames

```
import ij.plugin.AVI_Reader;

//producer
class AviFrameProducer extends Thread {

  private AVI_Reader avi;
  private CircularQueue buf;

  //constructor
  public AviFrameProducer(AVI_Reader aviReader, CircularQueue q)
  {
    avi = aviReader;
    buf = q;
  }

  public void run()
  {
```

```
    //get number of images in the virtual stack
    int vsize = avi.getSize();
    int nFrame = 1;
    while ( !buf.quit ) {
      buf.waitIfBufferFull();
      //produces data
      buf.putSamples ( avi, nFrame );   //put samples in buffer
      buf.tailInc();
      ++nFrame;
      if ( nFrame > vsize )
        buf.quit = true;
    }
  }
}
}
```

4. **Vcodec.java**:

The class **Vcodec** consists of the entry point **main** () function. The **main**() asks for an AVI file as input to encode. If a switch "-d" is provided, it tries to decode the input file whose data are saved in the **.fjv** format; it plays the video data using the **Display** class. It utilizes **Encoder** to encode uncompressed video data and **Decoder** to decode compressed data. In the encoding process, **AviFrameProducer** acts as a producer and puts image data in the shared circular buffer; the **Encoder** acts as a consumer which gets data from the circular buffer and encodes them. It also uses **Display** to render the frames; if you do not want to render the frames while encoding, simply comment out the statement "display.display_frame();" in the run() method of the file "Encoder.java".

In the decoding process, the **Decoder** is a producer and puts data in the shared circular buffer; we have not written a player class which acts as a consumer to fetch data from the buffer and plays them on the screen; instead the **Decoder** renders the frame itself after decoding it.

You may compile all the java programs in the directory **11/** using the command, "javac *.java" after setting the CLASSPATH correctly. The following are two examples of using **Vcodec** to compress and decompress video data. The following command compresses the avi file "t.avi" in the directory:

```
java Vcodec t.avi
```

It encodes the video data and saves the compressed data in the file "t.fjv". The following command decodes the compressed data and renders the images on the screen:

```
java Vcodec -d t.fjv
```

The programs presented here are for intra-frame coding. No temporal correlations have been considered. However, the code presented here forms the basis for implementations of more advanced compression techniques. In the next two chapters, we discuss the implementations of inter-frame coding and codecs that exploit temporal redundancies. A lot of the code presented here will be reused in those implementations.

# Chapter 12　DPCM Video Codec

## 12.1 Introduction

There is a simple technique called frame differencing that we can exploit temporal redundancy in a video sequence to achieve good compression. In the method, we code the difference between one frame and the next. In other words, the predicted frame for the current frame is equal to the previous frame. We code the difference between the two frames. Again, as we discussed before, if the encoding process is lossy, we obtain the predicted frame by reconstructing it from the decoded difference so that both of the encoder and decoder use the same predicted frame. We refer to this method as differential pulse code modulation ( **DPCM** ) coding, a term borrowed from signal processing. Figure 12-1a shows a block diagram of DPCM encoding and Figure 12-1b shows the corresponding decoder.

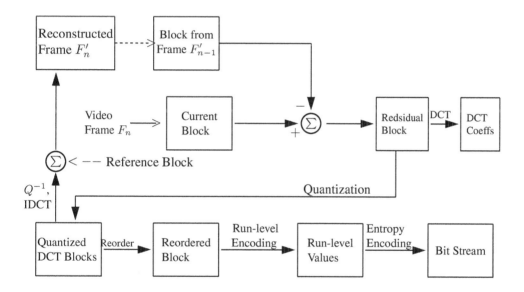

**Figure 12-1a**. DPCM Video Encoder

If there is little motion between successive frames, DPCM yields a difference image that is mostly uniform and can be coded efficiently. However, if there is rapid motion between frames or when a scene changes sharply, DPCM does not give good results.

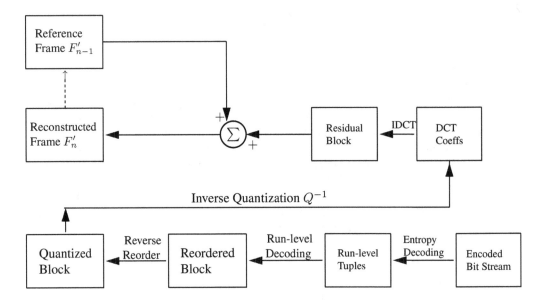

**Figure 12-1b**. DPCM Video Decoder

# 12.2 DPCM Encoding and Decoding

As shown in Figure 12-1, the DPCM encoder processes the n-th video frame $F_n$ to produce a compressed bitstream, and the decoder decompresses the encoded bitstream to the n-th reconstructed video frame $F_n'$, which is usually not identical to the original source video frame $F_n$. Many of the decoding functions are actually contained within the encoder as the encoder needs to reconstruct $F_n'$ to be used as the predictor for the next source frame. The following steps describe the encoding and decoding processes of such a codec.

**Encoder:**

1. **Forward Encoding**:

    1. Read a 24-bit RGB image frame from an uncompressed avi file.

    2. Decompose the RGB frame into $16 \times 16$ macroblocks.

    3. Transform and down-sample each $16 \times 16$ RGB macroblock to six $8 \times 8$ YCbCr sample blocks using YCbCr 4:2:0 format.

    4. Calculate the differences between the current sample blocks and the corresponding sample blocks from the previously encoded-and-reconstructed frame.

    5. Apply Discrete Cosine Transform ( DCT ) to each 8x8 difference sample block to obtain an $8 \times 8$ block of integer DCT coefficients.

    6. Forward-quantize the DCT block; reconstruct the block as described in **reconstruction process**.

    7. Reorder each quantized $8 \times 8$ DCT block in a zigzag manner.

**8.** Run-level encode each quantized reordered DCT block to obtain 3D ( run, level, last ) tuples.

**9.** Use pre-calculated Huffman codewords along with sign bits to encode the 3D tuples.

**10.** Save the output bitstream of the Huffman coder in a file.

2. **Reconstruction Process**:

**1.** Inverse-quantize each quantized DCT block. ( Note that quantization is a lossy process and therefore, the recovered block is not identical to the one before quantization. )

**2.** Apply Inverse DCT ( IDCT ) to resulted DCT blocks to obtain $8 \times 8$ YCbCr difference sample blocks.

**3.** Add the difference sample blocks to the corresponding reference sample blocks that were previously encoded and reconstructed.

**4.** Save the reconstructed sample blocks which will be used as the reference blocks when we encode the next frame.

**Decoder:**

1. Construct a Huffman tree from pre-calculated Huffman codewords.

2. Read a bit stream from the encoded file and traverse the Huffman tree to recover 3D run-level tuples to obtain $8 \times 8$ DCT blocks.

3. Reverse-reorder and inverse-quantize each DCT block.

4. Apply Inverse DCT ( IDCT ) to resulted DCT blocks of Step 3 to obtain $8 \times 8$ YCbCr difference sample blocks.

5. Add the difference sample blocks to the corresponding reference sample blocks that were previously encoded and reconstructed.

6. Save the decoded sample blocks which will be used as the reference blocks when we decode the next frame.

7. Use six $8 \times 8$ YCbCr sample blocks to obtain a $16 \times 16$ RGB macroblock.

8. Combine the RGB macroblocks to form an image frame.

The above descriptions and Figure 12-1 clearly present the requirement of a decoding path in the encoding process. This is necessary to ensure that the encoder and decoder use the same reference sample blocks to calculate residuals.

# 12.3 Implementation of DPCM Codec

To implement the DPCM codec, we just need to make minor modifications to the codec presented in the previous chapter ( Chapter 11 ). Actually, the main difference between the current codec and the previous one is that the current codec encodes the residuals ( differences ) between two adjacent frames as opposed to encoding the frame directly in the previous case. Note that we calculate the residuals in the YCbCr space rather than in the RGB space. A simple way to accommodate this feature is to reconstruct the YCbCr macroblock from the quantized difference DCT blocks and save it using a vector; the saved macroblock will be used as the reference block when we process the next frame. Initially, the reference block sample values are set to zero.

**Java Vector**

The java Vector class implements a growable array of objects. It is in the java.util package and thus to utilize the class, one has to add the statement "import java.util.*" at the beginning of the program. Unlike arrays, vectors expand automatically when new data is added to them. The Java 2 Collections API introduced a similar data structure called ArrayList. ArrayLists are unsynchronized and therefore works faster than Vectors, but they are less secure in a multithreaded environment. The Vector class was changed in Java 2 to add the additional methods supported by ArrayList.

Vectors can hold only Objects but not primitive types like int and char. If you want to put a primitive type in a Vector, you have to embed it inside an object. For example, to save an integer value, you may use the Integer class or define your own class that contains an int. If you use the Integer wrapper, you will not be able to change the integer value, so it may be more useful to define your own class.

The Vector class was updated in Java 2 to implement the List interface. Some old methods have changed. For example, old methods **addElement**(), **elementAt**(), and **setElementAt**() have been changed to **add**(), **get**() and **set**() respectively. We will use the new methods in our programs.

**Reference Vector**

We use java Vector to construct the class **RefVector** that rebuilds the reference frames. The constructor of **RefVector** creates a vector (*ycc_refv* ) that is big enough to hold all the YCbCr macroblocks of one frame; it also sets all sample values in each block to zero. The member function **calculate_diff**() calculates the residuals of a YCbCr macroblock in the current frame as compared to a corresponding one in the previous frame. This member function is used only by the **Encoder** class. The member function **reconstruct_macro**() reconstructs the YCbCr macroblock from the quantized DCT coefficients. As discussed above both the encoding and decoding processes need to reconstruct the reference frames. Thus this function is used by both the Encoder and Decoder classes. Note that inverse DCT and inverse quantization take place at this function. Therefore, the Decoder class does not need to perform these operations any more. Listing 12-1 presents the code of this class:

**Program Listing 12-1** Reference Vector

```
class RefVector {
```

```
private CircularQueue buf;   //shared buffer
private YCbCr_MACRO m;
public Vector<YCbCr_MACRO>  ycc_refv; //vector holding YCbCr macroblocks

//constructor
public RefVector ( CircularQueue q )
{
  buf = q;
  //initialize the YCbCr Macro reference vectors
  //calculate the number of macroblocks in one frame
  int n = ( buf.width/16 ) * ( buf.height / 16 );
  //set reference frame values to 0
  ycc_refv = new Vector<YCbCr_MACRO>();
  for ( int i = 0; i < n; i++ ){
    m = new YCbCr_MACRO();
    for ( int ii = 0; ii < 256; ii++ ){
      m.Y[ii] = 0;
      if ( ii < 64 )
        m.Cb[ii] = m.Cr[ii] = 0;
    }
    ycc_refv.add( m );    //push_back, capacity automatically expanded
  }
}

//Calculates residuals of macroblock pointed by mp.
//Returns results through diff.
public void calculate_diff (  YCbCr_MACRO mp, YCbCr_MACRO diff, int nm )
{
  for ( int i = 0; i < 256; ++i ) {
    diff.Y[i] = mp.Y[i] -  ycc_refv.get(nm).Y[i];
  }
  for ( int i = 0; i < 64; ++i ) {
    diff.Cb[i] =  mp.Cb[i] -  ycc_refv.get(nm).Cb[i];
    diff.Cr[i] =  mp.Cr[i] -  ycc_refv.get(nm).Cr[i];
  }
}

//reconstructs YCbCr macroblock from quantized DCT coefficients
//saves reconstructed block in ycc_refv[nm]
public void reconstruct_macro ( short dctcoefs[][][], int nm )
{
  int [][] X = new int[8][8], Y = new int[8][8];
  YCbCr_MACRO diff_macro = new YCbCr_MACRO();
  short py;
  int i, j, k = 0;
  Quantizer quantizer = new Quantizer();
  DctVideo dct_idct = new DctVideo();

  for ( int b = 0; b < 4; ++b ){          //Y blocks
    quantizer.inverse_quantize_block ( dctcoefs[b] );
    for ( i = 0; i < 8; i++ )
      for ( j = 0; j < 8; j++ )
        Y[i][j] = dctcoefs[b][i][j];
    dct_idct.idct ( Y, X );
    k = 0;
    if ( b < 2 )
      k = 8 * b;                     //points to beginning of block
    else
      k = 128 + 8 * ( b - 2 );  //points to beginning of block
    for ( i = 0; i < 8; i++ ) { //one sample-block
```

```
          if ( i > 0 ) k += 16;      //advance by 1 row of macroblock
          for ( j = 0; j < 8; j++ ){
            diff_macro.Y[k+j] =  X[i][j];
          }
        }
      }  //for b

      //Cb
      quantizer.inverse_quantize_block ( dctcoefs[4] );
      for (  i = 0; i < 8; i++ )
          for ( j = 0; j < 8; j++ )
            Y[i][j] =  dctcoefs[4][i][j];
      dct_idct.idct( Y, X );
      k = 0;
      for ( i = 0; i < 8; i++ ) {
        for ( j = 0; j < 8; j++ ) {
          diff_macro.Cb[k] = X[i][j];
          k++;
        }
      }
      //Cr
      quantizer.inverse_quantize_block ( dctcoefs[5] );
      for (  i = 0; i < 8; i++ )
          for ( j = 0; j < 8; j++ )
            Y[i][j] =  dctcoefs[5][i][j];
      dct_idct.idct( Y, X );
      k = 0;
      for ( i = 0; i < 8; i++ ) {
        for ( j = 0; j < 8; j++ ) {
          diff_macro.Cr[k] = X[i][j];
          k++;
        }
      }

      YCbCr_MACRO aMacro;
      aMacro = ycc_refv.get(nm);
      for ( i = 0; i < 256; i++ ){
        aMacro.Y[i] += diff_macro.Y[i];
        if ( i < 64  ) {
          aMacro.Cb[i] += diff_macro.Cb[i];
          aMacro.Cr[i] += diff_macro.Cr[i];
        }
      }
      ycc_refv.set( nm, aMacro );
  }

  //return the requested YCbCr macroblock
  public YCbCr_MACRO get ( int nm )
  {
     return ycc_refv.get(nm);
  }
}
```

---

The encoding process has a reconstruction path. The function **reconstruct_macro()** shown above reconstructs the YCbCr macroblock from the DCT coefficients of the residuals of a current macroblock; it first inverse-quantizes the coefficients, applies IDCT to them to obtain the residuals, and then adds the residuals to the reference sample values to reconstruct the macroblock. The newly reconstructed macroblock replaces the one in the vector *ycc_refv*; this macroblock will be used as the reference block when we encode the next frame.

Note that we do **not** need to transform the YCbCr samples back to RGB values because in the DPCM codec, we always operate in the YCbCr space when we calculate the residuals.

**Encoding:**

We only need to make minor modifications to the function **encode_one_frame**() that encodes one frame of the video. We use **calculate_diff**() of **refVector** to obtain the residuals of the current macroblock from that of the reference frame. We apply DCT transform to the residuals; other encoding processes are the same as those discussed in Chapter 11. We then use the function **reconstruct_macro**() to reconstruct the macroblock and save it in the vector *ycc_refv* of **refVector**, which will be used as the reference block ( or predictor ) when we process the corresponding macroblock of the next frame.

**Program Listing 12-2** Modified encode_one_frame() of Encoder

```
private void encode_one_frame ()
{
  //encode the frame at the head of buf
  int h = buf.getHead();
  int row, col, i, j, k, r;
  int nm = 0;                       //for indexing macroblock

  RGB_MACRO rgb_macro = new RGB_MACRO();
  YCbCr_MACRO ycbcr_macro = new YCbCr_MACRO();//macroblock for YCbCr samples
  //difference between current and reference YCbCr macroblocks
  YCbCr_MACRO ycc_diff = new YCbCr_MACRO();

  RgbYcc rgbycc = new RgbYcc ();
  short dctcoefs[][][] = new short[6][8][8];
  short Yr[][] = new short[8][8];
  short Y[][] = new short[8][8];

  Quantizer quantizer = new Quantizer();
  Reorder reorder = new Reorder();
  Run3D runs[] = new Run3D[64];
  for ( i = 0; i < 64; i++ )
    runs[i] = new Run3D();
  Run run = new Run();

  for ( row = 0; row < buf.height; row += 16 ){ //scan all rows of image
    for ( col = 0; col < buf.width; col += 16 ){//scan all columns of image
        k = (row * buf.width + col) * 3;        //x3 for RGB
        r = 0;
        for ( i = 0; i < 16; i++ ) {
          for ( j = 0; j < 16; j++ ) {
            rgb_macro.rgb[r].B = 0x000000ff & (int) buf.buffer[h][k];
            rgb_macro.rgb[r].G = 0x000000ff & (int) buf.buffer[h][k+1];
            rgb_macro.rgb[r].R = 0x000000ff & (int) buf.buffer[h][k+2];
            ++r;
            k += 3;
          }
          k += ( buf.width - 16 )*3;//points to next row within macroblock
        }
```

```
        //convert from RGB to YCbCr
        rgbycc.macroblock2ycbcr( rgb_macro, ycbcr_macro );
        //obtain difference between current and reference
        refVector.calculate_diff ( ycbcr_macro, ycc_diff, nm );
        get_dctcoefs ( ycc_diff, dctcoefs );
        for ( int bn = 0; bn < 6; bn++ ) {
          //quantize one dct sample block
          quantizer.quantize_block ( dctcoefs[bn] );
          reorder.reorder ( dctcoefs[bn], Yr ); //reorder sample block
          run.run_block(Yr, runs); //encode DCT coefs with run-level code
          /*
            Encode the 3D runs with precalculated Huffman codes using the
            provided Huffman table htable. Save the encoded bit stream in
            file pointed by bitout.
          */
          hcodec.huff_encode ( runs, bitout );    //encode and save
        } //for bn
        //reconstruct YCbCr macroblock from quantized DCT coefficients;
        //  save block in ycc_refv[nm] of refVector
        refVector.reconstruct_macro ( dctcoefs, nm );
        nm++;                                    //next macroblock
      } //for col
    } //for row
}
```

---

**Decoding**:

The decoding process makes use of the function **reconstruct_macro**() of the **RefVector** class to decode the bitstream. We make minor modifications to the decoding code discussed in Chapter 11. The main change is in the **get_yccblocks**() function. It uses **get_dct_block()** to get a residual DCT sample block by reading from the input bitstream, and carrying out the Huffman decoding, run-level decoding and reverse-reordering. However, **get_dct_block()** does not perform the task of inverse-quantization, which has been moved to the function **reconstruct_macro**(). The function **get_yccblocks**() gathers six quantized sample DCT blocks into the array *dctcoefs* with the help of **copy_dct_block**() and calls **reconstruct_macro**() to reconstruct the corresponding YCbCr macro block which will be held by the Vector *ycc_refv* of **RefVector**. Vector *ycc_refv* contains all reference YCbCr macroblocks:

**Program Listing 12-3** Modified get_yccblocks of Decoder

---

```
private int get_yccblocks( YCbCr_MACRO ycbcr_macro, int nm )
{
  int r, row, col, i, j, k, n, b, c;
  byte  abyte;
  int [][] Y = new int[8][8], X = new int[8][8];
  short dctcoefs[][][] = new short[6][8][8];

  //read data from file and put them in four 8x8 Y sample blocks
  for ( b = 0; b < 4; b++ ) {
    if ( !get_dct_block ( Y ) )
      return 0;
    copy_dct_block ( Y, dctcoefs, b );
  } //for b
```

```
//now do that for 8x8 Cb block
if ( !get_dct_block ( Y ) )        //read in one DCT block
  return 0;
copy_dct_block ( Y, dctcoefs, 4 );

//now do that for 8x8 Cr block
if ( !get_dct_block ( Y ) )        //read in one DCT block
  return 0;
copy_dct_block ( Y, dctcoefs, 5 );

//Reconstruct current frame from DCT coefficients
refVector.reconstruct_macro ( dctcoefs, nm );
YCbCr_MACRO aMacro;
aMacro = refVector.get(nm);
for ( i = 0; i < 256; i++ ){
  ycbcr_macro.Y[i] = aMacro.Y[i];
  if ( i < 64  ) {
    ycbcr_macro.Cb[i] = aMacro.Cb[i];
    ycbcr_macro.Cr[i] = aMacro.Cr[i];
  }
}

n = 6 * 64;
return n;                  //number of bytes read
}
```

---

The function **decode_one_frame**() makes use of **get_yccblocks**() and **ycbcr2macroblock**() to recover the RGB samples. All other classes used are the same as before. Thus the class files that reside in the directory of this Chapter ( **12/** ) are: **Decoder.java**, **Encoder.java**, and **RefVector.java**. Again, you need to point CLASSPATH to the directories that contain classes developed in previous chapters and are used by the Encoder and Decoder classes. The following command will do the job:

*export CLASSPATH=$CLASSPATH:../5/:../6/:../7/:../8:../10/:../11/:../11/avi/ImageJ/ij.jar*

After setting the correct class paths, we can run Vcodec in the current directory **12/**. For example, the following command,

*java Vcodec ../data/jvideo.avi*

generates the compressed file "jvideo.fjv". ( The Vcodec class resides in directory **11/** but we have pointed the class path to that directory. ) We may check the file sizes with the "ls" command:

```
$ ls -l ../data/jvideo.*
-rw-r--r-- 1 user user  5762656 ../data/jvideo.avi
-rw-r--r-- 1 user user   446687 ../data/jvideo.fjv
```

To decode and play the video of "jvideo.fjv", we can run Vcodec with the "-d" switch:

```
java Vcodec -d ../data/jvideo.fjv
```

In the next chapter, we will discuss the implementation of a codec that includes more formal motion estimation and compensation.

# Chapter 13    Implementation of Video Codec with ME and MC

## 13.1 Introduction

The DPCM video codec introduced in the previous chapter can be considered as a simple inter-frame codec, which extends the intra-frame codec presented in Chapter 11. It usually gives better compression ratio compared to intra-frame coding. To make further improvement, we have to include both motion estimation ( ME ) and motion compensation ( MC ) in the coding process. This can be done by extending and making minor modifications to the DPCM codec. In the DPCM codec implementation, we do **not** have to reconstruct a reference frame in the RGB space. We only have to reconstruct it in the YCbCr space as we only have to find the residuals between macroblocks of two frames at fixed positions. Because of the inclusion of Motion Estimation, here we need to search for the 'best-matched' macroblocks for each frame and their positions may vary from frame to frame. Therefore, we need to reconstruct a reference frame in the RGB space to accommodate the searching; for each macroblock considered, it is transformed to the YCbCr space before calculating the residuals for comparison. You can see that motion estimation is computing intensive. As an illustration of the technique, we use a simple Three Step Search ( TSS ) as our searching algorithm. Motion estimation and compensation involve the search of locations and the transmission of motion vectors. We consider a location as a point and a motion vector as a vector. Before moving on, we discuss briefly the distinction between a point and a vector.

## 13.2 Points and Vectors

In our implementation, we shall use two classes to define points and vectors. You may ask: "Why do we need two classes? Isn't a point the same as a vector as both of them are specified by a 2-tuple (x, y)? Isn't one class good enough to describe both of them?"

First of all, a point is **not** the same as a vector. A **point** denotes a position or a location; it does not have any direction. On the other hand, a **vector** specifies a direction rather than a location; it has a magnitude and directional components. It makes sense to add two vectors but it does **not** make any sense to add two points. In some situations, a vector may be considered as a special point located at infinity. A common way to distinguish between a point and a vector denoted by (x, y) is to introduce an additional component, usually expressed as '$w$', with '$w = 1$' denoting a point and '$w = 0$' denoting a vector. Therefore, in two-dimensional space, (x, y, 1 ) represents a point and ( x, y, 0 ) represents a vector. If we consider three-dimensional situations, (x, y, z, 1 ) represents a point and ( x, y, z, 0 ) represents a vector. With this representation, the operations on points and vectors are consistent with our intuition or understanding of points and vectors. For example, a point $(x_1, y_1, 1)$ plus a vector $(x_2, y_2, 0)$ is a point $(x_1 + x_2, y_1 + y_2, 1)$, and a point $(x_1, y_1, 1)$ minus a point $(x_2, y_2, 1)$ is a vector $(x_1 - x_2, y_1 - y_2, 0)$. A point $(x_1, y_1, 1)$ plus another point $(x_2, y_2, 1)$ gives $(x_1 + x_2, y_1 + y_2, 2)$, which is an invalid representation and therefore, adding two points is an illegal operation. The operations may be summarized in the following table:

**Table 13-1**

| Operation | | | Result |
|---|:---:|---|---|
| Vector | + | Vector | Vector |
| Vector | - | Vector | Vector |
| Vector | + | Point | Point |
| Vector | - | Point | Illegal |
| Point | + | Point | Illegal |
| Point | - | Point | Vector |
| Point | + | Vector | Point |
| Point | - | Vector | Point |

Though it is illegal to add two points, we may form linear combinations of points:

$$P = c_0 P_0 + c_1 P_1 + ... + c_{n-1} P_{n_1} \tag{13.1}$$

where $P_i = (x_i, y_i, 1)$ is a point and $c_i$'s are constant coefficients. The combination is legitimate if the summing coefficients are summed up to 1, and the combination gives a valid new point. i.e.,

$$c_0 + c_1 + ... + c_{n-1} = 1 \tag{13.2}$$

This is the principle behind point interpolation and extrapolation. Linear combination of points satisfying (13.2) is in general referred to as affine combination of points. ( The word "affine" has the Latin root "affinis" meaning "connected with"; "finis" means border or end, and "af" means sharing a common boundary. ) To construct a valid interpolation or extrapolation of points, the combination must be affine.

From the above discussion, we see that actually we can use one class to define both points and vectors by introducing and incorporating a third component 'w' in the implementation. However, it is a lot clearer, especially for illustrating concepts discussed, to separate points from vectors, by declaring two classes, one defining points, and the other defining vectors. The users will not mix up the two types of variables and the program becomes easier to read and understand.

For the purpose of implementing the video codec, we define the **Point2** class to represent two-dimensional points and the **Vec2** class to represent two-dimensional vectors. (Alternatively, one can define a parent class **XY** that contains common attributes of points and vectors, and let both **Point2** and **Vec2** extend **XY**.) Since java does not support operator overloading, we define the operations using function names. The following is the implementation of the **Vec2** class:

**Program Listing 13-1** Implementation of Vec2 class

```
class Vec2 {
  public int x;
  public int y;
```

```
//constructor
public Vec2 ()
{
  x = y = 0;
}

public Vec2 ( int x0, int y0 )
{
  x = x0;    y = y0;
}

public Vec2 ( Vec2 v )
{
  x = v.x;
  y = v.y;
}

public void set ( int x0, int y0 )
{
  x = x0;    y = y0;
}

public void set ( Vec2 v )
{
  x = v.x;
  y = v.y;
}

public void neg ()
{
  x = -x;
  y = -y;
}

//vector - vector --> vector
public Vec2 minus ( Vec2 v )
{
  Vec2 v1 = new Vec2();

  v1.x = x - v.x;
  v1.y = y - v.y;

  return v1;
}

//vector + vector --> vector
public Vec2 plus ( Vec2 v )
{
  Vec2 v1 = new Vec2();

  v1.x = x + v.x;
  v1.y = y + v.y;

  return v1;
}

//vector + point --> point
public Point2 plus ( Point2 p )
{
```

```
    Point2 p1 = new Point2();

    p1.x = x + p.x;
    p1.y = y + p.y;

    return p1;
    }

}
```

---

Note the definition of the **set ( Vec2 v )** method in our implementation. Though it works even if the class does not have such a method, its inclusion is important for robust programming here. As we have mentioned throughout the book, besides the primitive data types, basically all java variables are pointers; if we assign one variable to another, we simply make this variable point to where the other variable is pointing at. For instance, consider three **Vec2** objects, *v1, v2,* and *v3.* The statement

   *v1 = v2;*
simply let *v1* point to where *v2* is pointing at; no new object is created or copied. Meanwhile,

   *v3 = v2;*
will make *v3* pointing to the object that *v2* is pointing at. Therefore, if we are not careful, when we change the *v3* object, we may unintentionally change the *v1* object also. On the hand, if we use

   *v1.set( v2 )*
and

   *v3.set( v3 )*
to set the values then *v1* and *v3* are operated on different object space and they will not interfere with each other. This makes life easier even though the program will run slower.

The implementation of **Point2** is very similar to that of **Vec2**. Of course, the implementations have to follow the rules shown in Table 13-1.


# 13.3 Three Step Search ( TSS )


As mentioned above, we use a simple three-step search ( TSS ) ( see Chapter 9 ) as our searching alogorithm in the motion estimation process. A search is divided into three stages. The adjacent searching centers are 4 pixels apart in the first stage, and are 2 and 1 apart in the second and third stages respectively. We label the searching positions from 0 to 8 as shown in Figure 13-1, which shows the searching coordinates of stage 1.

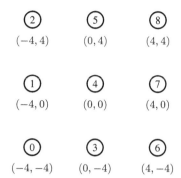

**Figure 13-1**. Stage 1 Searching Centers of TSS

The vector of a location is measured relative to the origin (0, 0) (node 4 in Figure 13-1). Therefore, the position and the vector of a searching center have the same values. For example, both the position and the vector of node 1 are represented by ( -4, 0 ) or if we include the 'w' component in our representation, the position of node 1 is ( -4, 0, 1 ) and the vector of node 1 relative to the origin is ( -4, 0, 0 ). We define a class called **Tss** to perform Three Step Search, where we use the method **setLevel**() to set the searching centers at the three different levels. It sets the coordinates of the searching positions with the origin (node 4 of Figure 13-1) as an input parameter. Another input parameter is for specifying one of the three levels that we want to set.

**Program Listing 13-2** Three Stage Search Implementation

```
//Tss.java:   Three Stage Search
//Upper-left corner of macroblock is location of macroblock
class Tss {
  private int width;      //frame width
  private int height;     //frame height
  public Point2 level[][];

  public Tss ( int w, int h )
  {
    width = w;
    height = h;
    level = new Point2[3][8];   //3 levels
  }

  //set the searching locations of stage n, p is the origin
  public void setLevel ( Point2 p, int n )
  {
    //searching centers for stage 0
    int rx[] = { -4,  0,  4,  -4,  4,  -4,  0,  4 };
    int ry[] = { -4, -4, -4,   0,  0,   4,  4,  4 };
    int m;                       //scaling factor of (rx, ry)
                                 //  for stage 0, 1, and 2
    if ( n == 0 ) m = 1;         //stage 0
    else if ( n == 1 ) m = 2;    //stage 1
    else m = 4;                  //stage 2
    if ( p.x < 0 || p.y < 0 ){   //not valid position
      for ( int i = 0; i < 8; ++i )
        level[n][i].set(-1, -1);
      return;
```

```
    }
    //set the searching locations
    for ( int i = 0; i < 8; ++i ) {
      int locx = p.x - rx[i] / m;
      int locy = p.y - ry[i] / m;
      //skip the out-of-bound locations
      if (locx < 0||locx >= (width-16)||locy < 0||locy >= (height-16))
        level[n][i].set( -1, -1 );
      else
        level[n][i].set ( locx, locy );
    }
  }
  .....
}
```

We use Sum of Absolute Difference (SAD) as our searching criterion. Its implementation is straightforward. We name it **sad**() in the **Tss** class:

```
class Tss {
  .....
  //Sum of absolute differences between macroblocks
  public int sad( YCbCr_MACRO p1, YCbCr_MACRO p2 )
  {
    int s = 0;
    for ( int i = 0; i < 256; ++i )
      s += Math.abs ( p1.Y[i] - p2.Y[i] );
    for ( int i = 0; i < 64; ++i ) {
      s += Math.abs ( p1.Cb[i] - p2.Cb[i] );
      s += Math.abs ( p1.Cr[i] - p2.Cr[i] );
    }

    return s;
  }
}
```

Note that we operate in YCbCr space rather than in RGB space. We define a method named **getRGBmacro**() to obtain an RGB macroblock at a specified location of an RGB image. The function basically copies the RGB data of a $16 \times 16$ region at the specified location of the RGB image to an RGB array:

**Program Listing 13-3** Method getRGBMacro() of Tss class

```
/*
  Obtain an RGB macroblock at the position p of an RGB image
    input: rgb_image, p
    ouput: rgb_macro
*/
void getRGBmacro ( RGBImage rgb_image, Point2 p, RGB_MACRO rgb_macro)
{
  int k, r;
```

```
//points to specified RGB macroblock
k = p.y * width + p.x;    //width is the image width
r = 0;
for ( int i = 0; i < 16; ++i ) {
  for ( int j = 0; j < 16; ++j ){
    rgb_macro.rgb[r].R = rgb_image.ibuf[k].R;
    rgb_macro.rgb[r].G = rgb_image.ibuf[k].G;
    rgb_macro.rgb[r].B = rgb_image.ibuf[k].B;
    ++r; ++k;
  }
  k += ( width - 16 );   //points to next row within macroblock
  }
}
```

Now we can implement the TSS search. The method **search**() of **Tss** presented in Listing 13-4 shows the implementation. An RGB image frame and the search origins are inputs to the method. It starts from the origin and uses the strategy discussed above to search the minimal point at each level. The difference between a minimal point and the search origin gives the desired motion vector. ( Note that the difference between two points is a vector as shown in Table 13-1. ) The resulted motion vectors (MVs) at the three levels are returned in the integer array mvs[]:

**Program Listing 13-4**  Method search() of Tss class

```
//Search for the best mactch using TSS.  The motion vectors of the
// 'minimal point' for stages 0, 1, and 2 are returned in mvs]0],
// mvs[1], and mvs[2] respectively.
void search (RGBImage ref_frame,Point2 origin,YCbCr_MACRO yccm,Vec2 mvs[])
{
  Point2 p = new Point2(), cp = new Point2();
  int d, dmin;
  int iwidth = ref_frame.width;
  int iheight = ref_frame.height;
  if ( iwidth != width || iheight != height ) {
    System.out.printf("\nsearch: Inconsistent image dimensions!\n");
    System.exit ( -1 );}
  RgbYcc rgbYcc = new RgbYcc();
  RGB_MACRO rgb_macro = new RGB_MACRO();
  YCbCr_MACRO yccm_ref = new YCbCr_MACRO();
  for ( int i = 0; i < 3; ++i )
   mvs[i].set ( 0, 0 );      //Set alll motion vectors to (0, 0)
   cp.set ( origin );        //Set current point to origin
   for (int k = 0; k<3; ++k){//Find minimal points at three levels
    p.set ( cp );
    setLevel ( cp, k );       //Calculate all search locations of stage k
    //Get an RGB macroblock from Reference frame
    getRGBmacro (ref_frame, cp, rgb_macro);
    rgbYcc.macroblock2ycbcr(rgb_macro,yccm_ref);//convert RGB to YCbCr
    //calculate SAD between the current and reference macroblocks
    dmin = sad (yccm, yccm_ref);
    for ( int i = 0; i < 8; ++i ) {      //test all valid search points
       if (level[k][i].x < 0 || level[k][i].y < 0)
          continue;                      //invalid search point
       getRGBmacro (ref_frame, level[k][i], rgb_macro);
```

```
      rgbYcc.macroblock2ycbcr (rgb_macro, yccm_ref); //RGB to YCbCr
      d = sad (yccm, yccm_ref);
      if ( d < dmin ) {
        p.set ( level[k][i] );
        dmin = d;
      }
    }
    //p is the 'minimal' point
    if ( p.x == cp.x && p.y == cp.y ) //origin is minimal, we're done
      break;
    //motion vector is difference between minimal point and origin
    mvs[k].set ( p.minus( cp ) );
    cp.set ( p );
  } //for k
}
```

Note that unlike the DPCM codec where we only need to reconstruct a reference frame in YCbCr, in **search**() of **Tss**, we have to reverse the transformations all the way to RGB to reconstruct a reference frame. It searches a fixed number of positions, specified by **setLevel** ( cp, k ) and obtain the RGB macroblock of the reference frame using **getRGBmacro**(); for each selected RGB macroblock, it transforms it to YCbCr using **macroblock2ycbcr**() of **RgbYcc** before calculating the SAD between the current and reference macroblocks.

# 13.4 Reconstructing Frame

We reconstruct an RGB frame from a vector of YCbCr macroblocks. Each time when we transform and encode a YCbCr macroblock of a frame, we reverse the transformations to reconstruct it and save the reconstructed YCbCr macroblock in a vector ( see also the reconstruction algorithm described in Section 13.6 below ). After we have gathered all the YCbCr macroblocks of one frame, we use the function **ycbcr2macroblock**() of **RgbYcc** to convert each YCbCr macroblock saved in the vector to an RGB macroblock; we then combine all the RGB macroblocks to form an RGB reconstructed frame. We write a class called **RefVectorMV** that extends **RefVector** discussed in Chapter 12 to implement these features:

**Program Listing 13-5** RefVectorMV extends RefVector for ME and MC

```
//RefRefVectorMV.java
//Reference Vector for inter-frame Encoding and Decoding with ME and MC
class RefVectorMV extends RefVector {
  public RGBImage ref_frame;
  public Tss tss;
  private Printer printer = new Printer();
  private int temp_count = 0;
  //constructor
  public RefVectorMV ( CircularQueue q )
  {
    super ( q );
    ref_frame = new RGBImage ( q.width, q.height );
    tss = new Tss ( q.width, q.height );
  }
```

```
//get the reference point
void get_ref_point ( Point2 cp, Vec2 mvs[], Point2 ref_point )
{
  Vec2 v = new Vec2();      //zero vector
  Point2 p = new Point2();
  p.set ( cp );
  for ( int i = 0; i < 3; i++ )
    p.plus( mvs[i] );
  ref_point.set( p );
}

//obtain difference between current and reference macroblock
//  update the reference macroblock
void current_ref_diff ( YCbCr_MACRO mp, Point2 ref_point,
                                    YCbCr_MACRO diff, int nm )
{
  RGB_MACRO rgb_macro = new RGB_MACRO();
  YCbCr_MACRO refm = new YCbCr_MACRO();
  RgbYcc rgbYcc = new RgbYcc();
  tss.getRGBmacro ( ref_frame, ref_point, rgb_macro );

  rgbYcc.macroblock2ycbcr ( rgb_macro, refm );   //convert RGB to YCbCr
  for ( int i = 0; i < 256; i++ )
    diff.Y[i] = (short) mp.Y[i] - (short) refm.Y[i];
  for ( int i = 0; i < 64; ++i ) {
    diff.Cb[i] = (short) mp.Cb[i] - (short) refm.Cb[i];
    diff.Cr[i] = (short) mp.Cr[i] - (short) refm.Cr[i];
  }
  //save the reference macroblock for reconstruction
  YCbCr_MACRO aMacro;
  aMacro = ycc_refv.get(nm);
  for ( int i = 0; i < 256; ++i ){
    aMacro.Y[i] = refm.Y[i];
    if ( i < 64 ) {
        aMacro.Cb[i] = refm.Cb[i];
        aMacro.Cr[i] = refm.Cr[i];
    }
  }
  ycc_refv.set( nm, aMacro );
}

//reconstruct frame from the vector of  reconstructed macros
void reconstruct_frame ( int number_of_macros )
{
  int row, col, i, j, k, r;
  RGB_MACRO rgb_macro = new RGB_MACRO();
  RgbYcc rgbYcc = new RgbYcc();
  int width = ref_frame.width, height = ref_frame.height;
  //ycc_refv is data member of parent
  row = col = 0;
  YCbCr_MACRO ycbcr_macro;
  for ( k = 0; k < number_of_macros; ++k ){
    ycbcr_macro = ycc_refv.get ( k ); //get k-th YCbCr macro
    rgbYcc.ycbcr2macroblock( ycbcr_macro, rgb_macro );//converts to RGB
    int offset = row * width + col; //points to beginning of macroblock
    r = 0;
    for ( i = 0; i < 16; ++i ) {
      for ( j = 0; j < 16; ++j ) {
        ref_frame.ibuf[offset].R  = rgb_macro.rgb[r].R;
        ref_frame.ibuf[offset].G  = rgb_macro.rgb[r].G;
```

```
        ref_frame.ibuf[offset].B  = rgb_macro.rgb[r].B;
        offset++;   r++;
      }
      offset += ( width - 16 );        //points to next row of macroblock
    }
    col += 16;
    if ( col >= width ){
      row += 16;                       //next row of frame
      col = 0;
    }
  }  //for k;
}
.....
}
```

## 13.5 Encoding Motion Vectors

Like encoding 3D run-level tuples, we use pre-calculated 'Huffman codes' to encode motion
vectors. We also use this as an example to elaborate more on our implementation of Huffman
Trees. Since objects are more likely to have left-right motion than up-down movements, we
assign higher probabilities to nodes 1 and 7 of the TSS searching positions shown in Figure
13-1. Eventually, we come up with the pre-calculated Huffman Tree for TSS motion vectors
of stage 0 shown in Figure 13-2. This tree is based on very brief estimates. Readers should be
able to improve it by gathering real statistics. The same tree structure is also used for stage 1
and stage 2.

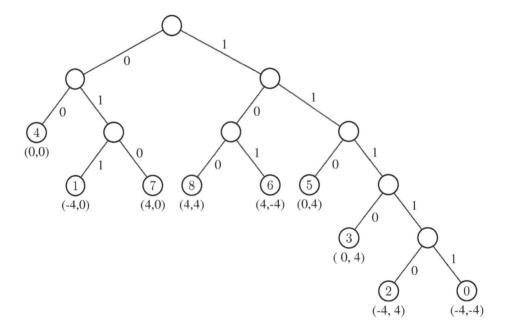

**Figure 13-2**. A Huffman Tree of Three Step Search ( TSS ) MVs

The codewords corresponding to the Huffman Tree of Figure 13-2 are shown in Table 13-2. In general, we express Huffman codeword bits from left to right corresponding to the traversal of the tree from the root to a leaf. However, in our program, we send out the rightmost bits first. Therefore, in Table 13-2, we flip the bits of each codeword to make things consistent. The flipped codewords are the ones we actually use to encode motion vectors.

**Table 13-2**    Pre-calculated Huffman Codewords of TSS Motion Vectors

| Index | MV | Codeword ( Binary ) | Flipped Codeword | Codeword in Hex | Codeword Length |
|-------|-----|------|------|------|------|
| 0 | (-4, -4) | 11111 | 11111 | 1f | 5 |
| 1 | (-4, 0) | 010 | 010 | 02 | 3 |
| 2 | (-4, 4) | 11110 | 01111 | 0f | 5 |
| 3 | ( 0, -4) | 1110 | 0111 | 07 | 4 |
| 4 | ( 0, 0) | 00 | 00 | 00 | 2 |
| 5 | ( 0, 4) | 110 | 011 | 03 | 3 |
| 6 | ( 4, -4) | 101 | 101 | 05 | 3 |
| 7 | ( 4, 0) | 011 | 110 | 06 | 3 |
| 8 | ( 4, 4) | 100 | 001 | 01 | 3 |

As shown in Table 13-2 and Figure 13-1, the total number of symbols is $n_0 = 9$. Based on the discussions of Chapter 8, there are $n_0 - 1$ internal nodes. If the table holds all internal node pointers and symbols, the size of the table $N_T'$ required to implement the Huffman tree is $N_T' = 2 \times (n_0 - 1) + n_0 = 3 \times n_0 - 2 = 3 \times 9 - 2 = 25$. As discussed in Chapter 8, actually we do not need to save the symbols. Under this situation, the table size required is :

$$N_T = N_T' - n_0 = 25 - 9 = 16 \qquad (13.1)$$

The locations of the table can be indexed as $N_T - 1, ...., 1, 0$ ( or $15, 14, ..., 1, 0$ here ). The root starts at location $N_T - 1$. However, to distinguish if a location contains an internal node or a symbol we need to add $n_0$ back to a saved pointer so that if its value is smaller than $n_0$, we know that it is a symbol, otherwise it is a pointer, and when we actually access a table location, we need to subtract $n_0$ from the pointer value. Thus, the initial value of the root is $root = (N_T - 1) + n_0 = 3 \times n_0 - 3 = 24$. We develop the class **MvCodec** which is similar to **Hcodec** discussed in Chapter 8 to handle the encoding of motion vectors using the Huffman code. Besides encoding different kinds of 'symbols' ( motion vectors vs. runs ), the main difference between **MvCodec** and **Hcodec** is that **MvCodec** needs three TreeMaps to handle the three levels of motion vectors, one for each level:

**Program Listing 13-6** Structure of Class MvCodec

```
class MvCodec {
  TreeMap<MvHuff, MvHuff> mvHtables[];
  public MVtables mv_decode_tables[] = new MVtables[3];

  //constructor
  public MvCodec()
  {
    //generic array creation not allowed in java
    mvHtables = (TreeMap<MvHuff, MvHuff>[]) new TreeMap[3];
    for ( int i = 0; i < 3; i++ ) {
      mvHtables[i] = new TreeMap<MvHuff, MvHuff>();
      mv_decode_tables[i] = new MVtables();
    }
    build_mvHtables();
    for ( int i = 0; i < 3; i++ )    //for decoding only
      build_huff_tree ( i );
  }

  //use a map ( mvHtable ) to collect all pre-calculated motion vector (MV)i
  // codewords. There are totally 9 motion vectors.
  void build_mvHtables ()
  {
    ......
  }

  void mv_encode (Vec2 mvs[], BitOutputStream outputs)
  {
    ......
  }

  //build the Huffman treel for level nlevel
  void build_huff_tree ( int nlevel )
  {
    ......
  }

}
```

In Listing 13-6, the constructor calls **build_mvHtables**() to build an array of three TreeMaps of **MvHuff**. They are used in both the encoding and decoding processes. The constructor also calls **build_huff_tree**() to build the Huffman trees of motion vectors for decoding; these trees are only used in the decoding process but not in the encoding process because in the encoding process we do not have to traverse a tree and we only need to encode a 'symbol' with its codeword. Actually, it is better not to build the trees in the constructor but build them in the **Decoder**.

The function **build_huff_tree**() takes the TreeMap that contains all pre-calculated Huffman codewords of motion vectors as the 'input parameter' to generate the Huffman tree for the motion vectors, which are interpreted as 'symbols' in Huffman encoding. The outputs are saved in the specified locations of the data member array *mv_decode_tables*[] with data type **MVtables** ( see below ).

The class **MVtables** uses a short array *mv_tree*[] to hold the Huffman tree and a Vec2 array *mv_table*[] to hold the motion vectors:

```
class MVtables
{
  public short mv_tree[];      //table containing Huffman Tree for MVs
  public Vec2  mv_table[];     //table containing MVs

  public MVtables()
  {
    mv_tree = new short[1024];
    mv_table = new Vec2[512];
    for ( int i = 0; i < 512; i++ )
      mv_table[i] = new Vec2();
  }
}
```

We define the class **MvHuff** to hold a row of information of Table 13-2 that contains the pre-calculated Huffman codes and motion vectors:

```
class MvHuff implements Comparable<MvHuff>
{
  Vec2 mv;
  int codeword;
  byte hlen;              //length of Huffman code
  short index;           //table index where codeword saved

  MvHuff()               //constructors
  {
    mv = new Vec2();
  }

  MvHuff ( Vec2 a, int c, byte len, short idx )
  {
    mv = a;
    codeword = c; hlen = len; index = idx;
  }
  //A Vec2 is used as a key for comparison
  public int compareTo ( MvHuff right ) throws ClassCastException
  {
    if ( mv.x < right.mv.x )
      return 1;
    if ( mv.x > right.mv.x )
      return -1;
    //x equals
    if ( mv.y < right.mv.y )
      return 1;
    if ( mv.y > right.mv.y )
      return -1;
    //both x and y values equal
    return 0;                      //The two objects equal
  }
}
```

We use a map of **MvHuff** objects to save the relevant information of all the entries of Table 13-2, which has a total of 9 entries. We also use the other two maps to save the corresponding information of the other two search levels ( Level 1 and Level 2 ) of TSS. These maps are input parameters of **build_huff_tree**() and are constructed by the function **build_mvHtables**(), where we use the variable *scale* to find the motion vectors of Level 1 and Level 2 from those of Level 0. For example, at Level 0, $scale = 1$ and $(x_0, y_0) = (-4, -4)$; at Level 1, $scale = 2$, and $(x_0, y_0) = (-4/2, -4/2) = (-2, -2)$; at Level 2, $scale = 4$, and $(x_0, y_0) = (-4/4, -4/4) = (-1, -1)$. The code of this function is shown below:

**Program Listing 13-7 Building MV Tables**

---

```
//use a map ( mvHtable ) to collect all pre-calculated motion vector
// ( MV ) codewords. There are totally 9 motion vectors.
void build_mvHtables ()
{
  short i, j, k, N = 9;            //N = # of possible motion vectors
  byte hlen[] = { 5, 3, 5, 4, 2, 3, 3, 3, 3 }; //lengths of MV codewords
  //Huffman codewords: no codeword is a prefix of another
  short hcode[] = {0x1f, 0x02, 0x0f, 0x07, 0x00, 0x03, 0x05, 0x06, 0x01};

  //Level 0  motion vectors (x, y)
  int x[] = { -4, -4, -4,  0, 0, 0,  4,  4,  4 };
  int y[] = { -4,  0,  4, -4, 0, 4, -4,  0,  4 };
  Vec2 mv;
  MvHuff mvf[][] = new MvHuff[3][128]; //table containing MvHuff objects

  int scale = 1;          //for calculating MVs of all levels
  for ( j = 0; j < 3; ++j ) {
    k = 0;
    for ( i = 0; i < N; ++i ) {
      mv = new Vec2();                //an MV vector
      mv.set( x[i]/scale, y[i]/scale );
      mvf[j][k] = new MvHuff ( mv, hcode[i], hlen[i], i );
      k++;
    }
    scale *= 2;
  }

  //insert all N MvHuff objects into the mvtable map
  for ( k = 0; k < 3; ++k ) {
    for ( i = 0; i < N; ++i )
      mvHtables[k].put ( mvf[k][i], mvf[k][i] );
  }
}
```

---

We then use the *mvtables*[] built by the function to encode the three motion vectors found by TSS:

```
void mv_encode (Vec2 mvs[], BitOutputStream outputs )
{
  int nlevels = 3;
  for ( int  i = 0; i < nlevels; ++i ) {
    TreeMap<MvHuff, MvHuff> htable = mvHtables[i];
    //construct an MvHuff object;only mvs[k] is relevant here
    MvHuff mvf = new MvHuff ( mvs[i], 0,(byte) 0, (short)0 );
     if ( htable.containsKey ( mvf ) ) {
       MvHuff mvhuf = htable.get ( mvf );
       try {
         outputs.writeBits( mvhuf.codeword, mvhuf.hlen );
       } catch (IOException e) {
         e.printStackTrace();
         System.exit(0);
       }
       if ( mvhuf.mv.x == 0 && mvhuf.mv.y == 0 )
         break;                  //best match at position 0, done
     }
  }
}
```

# 13.6 Encoding One Frame

After we have developed the utility functions discussed above, we are ready to implement a function that encodes a frame. As shown in Figure 9-5a, encoding of a frame consists of a forward path and a reconstruction path. The goal of the reconstruction process is to obtain a reference frame for motion compensations of the macroblocks of the next frame. Many of the reconstruction functions are also used in the decoding process. We present the algorithms of the two stages used in our implementations where we have used TSS in searching:

**Encoding:**

1. **Forward Encoding**:

    1. Read a 24-bit RGB image frame from an uncompressed avi file.

    2. Decompose the RGB frame into $16 \times 16$ macroblocks.

    3. Transform and down-sample each $16 \times 16$ RGB macroblock to six $8 \times 8$ YCbCr sample blocks using YCbCr 4:2:0 format.

    4. Use TSS to search the reference frame for a 'best-matched' YCbCr macroblock, which we call it reference macroblock.

    5. Encode the motion vector ( MV ) of the reference macroblock found by TSS using pre-calculated Huffman codes and transmit the codewords.

    6. Calculate the residuals between the current macroblock and the reference macroblock.

    7. Apply Discrete Cosine Transform ( DCT ) to the residuals.

    8. Forward-quantize the DCT block; reconstruct the block as described in **reconstruction path**.

    9. Reorder each quantized $8 \times 8$ DCT block in a zigzag manner.

**10.** Run-level encode each quantized reordered DCT block to obtain 3D ( run, level, last ) tuples.

**11.** Use pre-calculated Huffman codewords along with sign bits to encode the 3D tuples.

**12.** Transmit the codewords.

2. **Reconstruction Path**:

**1.** Inverse-quantize each quantized DCT block. ( Note that quantization is a lossy process and therefore, the recovered block is not identical to the one before quantization. )

**2.** Apply Inverse DCT ( IDCT ) to resulted DCT blocks to obtain $8 \times 8$ YCbCr residual sample blocks.

**3.** Add the residual sample blocks to the corresponding reference sample blocks that were previously encoded and reconstructed to obtain the reference macroblock.

**4.** Save the reconstructed reference macroblock in a vector which will be used to construct one frame.

**5.** Convert each of the YCbCr macroblock saved in the vector to an RGB macroblock, which is then saved in a buffer. The buffer is the reconstructed frame. ( See Section 13.4 for the implementation of reconstructing one frame. )

The function **encode_one_frame**() of the class **Encoder** implements the encoding of one frame. It walks through a frame to decompose it to $16 \times 16$ RGB macroblocks. It uses **macroblock2ycbcr**() to convert each RGB macroblock to a YCbCr macroblock in 4:2:0 format, and employs **search**() of the Tss class to find the three vectors ( or positions ) of the macroblocks in the reference frame that best-matches the current macroblock using TSS. ( Keep in mind that TSS is a three-level search and this is why we have three vectors. ) It then encodes the vectors and sends the codewords to the output file by **mv_encode**() of MvCodec. Given the three vectors, it obtains the point at which the reference block will be subtracted using **get_ref_point**() of RefVectorMV and uses this information to calculate the residuals between the current macroblock and the reference macroblock. After finding the residuals, it transforms them to DCT coefficients using **get_dctcoefs**() of Encoder, which are then quantized, reordered, and run-level encoded respectively by the functions **quantize_block**(), **reorder**(), and **run_block**() of various classes that we have discussed in previous chapters. Utilizing pre-calculated Huffman codewords, it employs **huff_encode**() to encode the 3D run-level tuples and to send the codewords to the output file. Each time it encodes a macroblock, **encode_one_frame**() uses **reconstruct_macro**() to reconstruct a YCbCr macroblock from the quantized DCT coefficients and save the macroblock in the vector *ycc_refv*. Finally, after it has finished encoding one frame, it reconstructs the next reference frame from the *ycc_refv* using **reconstruct_frame**():

**Program Listing 13-8** Encoding One Frame
───────────────────────────────────────────────────────────────

```
/*
   Method of class Encoder.
   Encode one image frame pointed by image using Huffman code.
   Note that the reference frame is in RGB space as we need to
   search at  various positions.
```

```
*/
private void encode_one_frame ()
{
 //encode the frame at the head of buf
 int h = buf.getHead();
 int row, col, i, j, k, r;

 RGB_MACRO rgb_macro = new RGB_MACRO();
 YCbCr_MACRO ycbcr_macro=new YCbCr_MACRO();//macroblock for YCbCr samples

 //difference between current and reference YCbCr macroblocks
 YCbCr_MACRO ycc_diff = new YCbCr_MACRO();

 RgbYcc rgbycc = new RgbYcc ();
 short dctcoefs[][][] = new short[6][8][8];
 short Yr[][] = new short[8][8];
 short Y[][] = new short[8][8];
 int nm = 0;                          //for indexing macroblock
 Point2 cp = new Point2();            //current point
 Point2 ref_point = new Point2();     //reference point
 Vec2 [] mvs = new Vec2[3],           //motion vectors

 Quantizer quantizer = new Quantizer();
 Reorder reorder = new Reorder();
 Run3D runs[] = new Run3D[64];
 for ( i = 0; i < 64; i++ )
   runs[i] = new Run3D();
 Run run = new Run();
 for ( i = 0; i < 3; i++ )
   mvs[i] = new Vec2();

 for (row = 0; row < buf.height; row += 16){ //scan all rows of image
   for ( col = 0; col < buf.width; col += 16 ){   //scan all columns
     k = (row * buf.width + col) * 3;        //x3 for RGB
     cp.set ( col, row );    //set x, y values of current position
     r = 0;
     for ( i = 0; i < 16; i++ ) {
       for ( j = 0; j < 16; j++ ) {
         rgb_macro.rgb[r].B = 0x000000ff & (int) buf.buffer[h][k];
         rgb_macro.rgb[r].G = 0x000000ff & (int) buf.buffer[h][k+1];
         rgb_macro.rgb[r].R = 0x000000ff & (int) buf.buffer[h][k+2];
         ++r;
         k += 3;
       }
       k += ( buf.width - 16 )*3;  //next row within macroblock
     }
     rgbycc.macroblock2ycbcr(rgb_macro,ycbcr_macro);//convert RGB to YCbCr

     //motion estimation and motion compensation
     tss.search ( refVectorMV.ref_frame, cp, ycbcr_macro, mvs );
     mvCodec.mv_encode ( mvs, bitout );
     //obtain the point at which the reference block is subtracted
     refVectorMV.get_ref_point ( cp, mvs, ref_point );

     //obtain difference between current and reference;
     //  save the reference YCC macro in  ycc_refv[nm]
     refVectorMV.current_ref_diff ( ycbcr_macro, ref_point, ycc_diff, nm);
     get_dctcoefs ( ycc_diff, dctcoefs );
     for ( int bn = 0; bn < 6; bn++ ) {
       quantizer.quantize_block ( dctcoefs[bn] ); //quantize one dct block
```

```
            reorder.reorder ( dctcoefs[bn], Yr ); //reorder the quantized block
            run.run_block ( Yr, runs ); //run-level encode reordered DCT coefs
            hcodec.huff_encode ( runs, bitout );   //encode and save
        } //for bn

        //reconstruct YCbCr macroblock from quantized DCT coefficients;
        //  save block in ycc_refv
        refVectorMV.reconstruct_macro ( dctcoefs, nm );
        nm++;                              //next macroblock
    } //for col
} //for row
//reconstruct frame from reconstructed macros
refVectorMV.reconstruct_frame ( nm );
}
```

## 13.7 Decoding a Frame

The process of decoding a frame is shown in Figure 9-5b. It consists of the following steps, some of which overlap with the reconstruction path of the encoding stage:

**Decoding:**

1. Construct a Huffman tree from pre-calculated Huffman codewords for decoding 3D run-level tuples.

2. Construct a Huffman tree from pre-calculated Huffman codewords for decoding motions vectors ( MVs ).

3. Read the bits of the bit stream from the encoded file and traverse the MV Huffman tree to recover the TSS MVs of a macroblock.

4. Read the bits from the encoded file and traverse the 3D run-level Huffman tree to recover 3D run-level tuples to obtain $8 \times 8$ DCT blocks.

5. Reverse-reorder and inverse-quantize each DCT block.

6. Apply Inverse DCT ( IDCT ) to resulted DCT blocks of Step 5 to obtain $8 \times 8$ YCbCr residual sample blocks.

7. Add the residual sample blocks to the corresponding reference sample blocks that were previously encoded and reconstructed. frame.

8. Save the reconstructed reference macroblock in a vector which will be used to construct one frame.

9. Convert each of the YCbCr macroblock saved in the vector to an RGB macroblock, which is then saved in a buffer. The buffer is the reconstructed frame.

In our implementation, the function **get_yccblocks**() of the Decoder class does most of the work in the decoding process. It fetches DCT data using the function **get_dct_block**() which does the Huffman decoding to obtain 3D run-level tuples, then performs run-level decoding, reverse ordering and inverse quantization. After obtaining a DCT block from **get_dct_block**(),

**get_yccblocks**() does IDCT to obtain YCbCr sample blocks and put them in a YCbCr macroblock structure. These are actually the residual values. The function add the residual values to the corresponding YCbCr macroblock in the reference vector:

**Program Listing 13-9**  Method get_yccblocks() of Decoder class

```
private int get_yccblocks( YCbCr_MACRO ycbcr_macro, Point2 cp, int nm )
{
 int r, row, col, i, j, k, n, b, c, py;
 int [][] Y = new int[8][8], X = new int[8][8];
 short dctcoefs[][][] = new short[6][8][8];
 //difference between current and reference YCbCr macroblocks
 YCbCr_MACRO ycc_diff = new YCbCr_MACRO();
 Point2 ref_point = new Point2(); //refer block subtracted at ref_point
 Vec2 [] mvs = new Vec2[3];         //motion vectors
 for ( i = 0; i < 3; i++ )
   mvs[i] = new Vec2();
 if ( mvCodec.mv_decode( bitin,  mvs ) < 0 ) {
     System.out.printf("\nOut of Data in mv_decode\n");
     return -1;
 }
 n = 0;
 //read data from file and put them in four 8x8 Y sample blocks
 for ( b = 0; b < 4; b++ ) {
   if ( !get_dct_block ( Y ) )
       return 0;
   dct_idct.idct ( Y, X );    //perform IDCT, output in X
   k = 0;
   if ( b < 2 )
     py = 8 * b;              //points to beginning of block
   else
     py = 128 + 8 * ( b - 2 );//points to beginning of block

   for ( i = 0; i < 8; i++ ){ //one sample-block
     if ( i > 0 ) py += 16;   //advance py by 16(row length macroblock)
       for ( j = 0; j < 8; j++ ) {
         ycc_diff.Y[py+j] = X[i][j]; //put sample value in macroblock
         n++;
       } //for j
     } //for
 } //for b
 //now do that for 8x8 Cb block
 if ( !get_dct_block( Y ) )   //read in one DCT block
     return 0;
 dct_idct.idct(Y, X);
 k = 0;
 for ( i = 0; i < 8; ++i ) {
   for ( j = 0; j < 8; ++j ) {
     ycc_diff.Cb[k]=X[i][j];  //put Cb sample value in macro block
     k++;
     n++;
   }
 }
 //now do that for 8x8 Cr block
 if ( !get_dct_block( Y ) )   //read in one DCT block
     return 0;
 dct_idct.idct(Y, X);
 k = 0;
 for ( i = 0; i < 8; ++i ) {
```

```
    for ( j = 0; j < 8; ++j ) {
      ycc_diff.Cr[k] = X[i][j];//put Cr sample value in macro block
      k++;
      n++;
    }
  }
  refVectorMV.get_ref_point ( cp, mvs, ref_point );
  refVectorMV.current_ref_sum ( ycbcr_macro, ref_point, ycc_diff, nm );
  //Reconstruct current frame from DCT coefficients
  YCbCr_MACRO aMacro;
  aMacro = refVectorMV.get (nm);
  for ( i = 0; i < 256; i++ ){
    aMacro.Y[i] = ycbcr_macro.Y[i];
    if ( i < 64 ) {
      aMacro.Cb[i] = ycbcr_macro.Cb[i];
      aMacro.Cr[i] = ycbcr_macro.Cr[i];
    }
  }

  refVectorMV.ycc_refv.set ( nm, aMacro );
    return n;                      //number of bytes read
  }
```

---

Finally, the function **decode_one_frame**() rounds up our implementation of decoding one frame. The function uses **get_yccblocks**() to fetch one YCbCr macroblock from the encoded bit-stream. It then employs **ycbcr2macroblock**() to convert the YCbCr macroblock to RGB. At the end, it uses **reconstruct_frame**() to reconstruct the next reference frame from the vector *ycc_refdv*.

**Program Listing 13-10** Method decode_one_frame() of Decoder

---

```
private int decode_one_frame ()
{
 int r, row, col, i, j, k, block;
 int n = 0;
 RGB_MACRO rgb_macro=new RGB_MACRO(); //assume 24-bit for each RGB pixel
 YCbCr_MACRO ycbcr_macro = new YCbCr_MACRO(); //YCbCr macroblock
 RgbYcc rgbycc = new RgbYcc();
 int nm = 0;
 Point2 cp = new Point2();  //current point
 for ( row = 0; row < image.height; row += 16 ) {
   for ( col = 0; col < image.width; col += 16 ) {
     cp.set ( col, row );
     int m = get_yccblocks( ycbcr_macro, cp,  nm++ );
     if ( m <= 0 )
       return m;
     n += m;
     rgbycc.ycbcr2macroblock( ycbcr_macro, rgb_macro );
     k = row * image.width + col;
     r = 0;
     for ( i = 0; i < 16; ++i ) {
       for ( j = 0; j < 16; ++j ) {
         image.ibuf[k].B = rgb_macro.rgb[r].R;
         image.ibuf[k].G = rgb_macro.rgb[r].G;
         image.ibuf[k].R = rgb_macro.rgb[r].B;
```

```
        k++;   r++;
      }
      k += (image.width - 16);    //points to next row of macroblock
    }
  } //for col
  }  //for row
  refVectorMV.reconstruct_frame ( nm );
  return n;
 }
}
```

The following are sample commands and outputs for checking classes in the directory of this chapter, setting the classpath, encoding, decoding, checking original and compressed file sizes:

```
$ ls *.class
  Decoder.class  MvCodec.class  MVtables.class  RefVectorMV.class
  Vec2.class     Encoder.class  MvHuff.class    Point2.class    Tss.class
$ export CLASSPATH=$CLASSPATH:../5/:../6/:../7/:../8:../10/:../11/
$ export CLASSPATH=$CLASSPATH:../11/avi/ImageJ/ij.jar:../12/:../util/
$ java Vcodec ../data/jvideo.avi
$ java Vcodec -d ../data/jvideo.fjv
$ ls -l ../data/jvideo.*
  -rw-r--r-- 1 user user  5762656 2010-12-09 11:37 ../data/jvideo.avi
  -rw-r--r-- 1 user user   483879 2011-01-16 23:07 ../data/jvideo.fjv
```

We see from the sample outputs that the originial video file size is 5762656 bytes and the compressed file size is 483879 bytes. This implies that the compression ratio $R$ is

$$R = \frac{5762656}{483879} = 11.9$$

Figure 13-3 below shows a frame of the original sample video (jvideo.avi) and Figure 13-4 shows the corresponding decoded frame from the compressed file (jvideo.fjv). A quantization factor of 12 has been used in the compression. The following are the classes we have developed or modified in this chapter and reside in the directory 13/ :

```
      Encoder    MvCodec    MVtables    RefVectorMV
      Decoder    MvHuff     Vec2        Point2  Tss
```

Besides these classes, the codec also uses other classes we have developed in previous chapters. The following are the classes that this codec needs to use:

```
    Chapter 5 : RGB  RgbYcc  YCbCr_MACRO  RGBImage  RGB_MACRO  YCbCr
    Chapter 6 : DctVideo
    Chapter 7 : Quantizer  Reorder  Run3D  Run
    Chapter 8 : BitInputStream    BitOutputStream    CompareRun
                Dtables           Hcodec             RunHuff
    Chapter 11: AviFrameProducer  CircularQueue
                Display           Vcodec             Vheader
    Chapter 12: RefVector
```

**Figure 13-3** Original Sample Image Frame

**Figure 13-4** Decoded Image Frame of Figure 13-3

# Chapter 14   Hybrid Coding

## 14.1 Introduction

In the past two decades, a new development in video compression is to utilize synthesized images to represent some natural scenes that do not change much for a substantial period of time. For example, in a TV news announcement like the one shown in Figure 14-1, the major scene change is the lip movement of the announcer. The background of the scene is fixed and in many cases may not be very important. This is also true for the situation of a video conference.

**Figure 14-1** News Announcer

To compress this kind of frames, one can use a graphics model to synthesize the announcer; the encoder just has to send the parameters of the lip movements of the announcer. Upon receiving the parameters, the decoder reconstructs the scene using the parameters and the graphics model. Of course, the parameters can be compressed before sending. One can easily see that this can give a very high compression ratio of the video as the encoder does not need to send the details of the images. It only has to send some parameters that will be used by the graphics model of the decoder to reconstruct the scene. The advance in computer graphics software and hardware technologies will make the use of graphics techniques play a more important role in video compression. The recent success of real 3D movies such as "Avatar" and "Alice and Wonderland" will further accelerate this trend.

In the 1990s, MPEG began to integrate synthetic audio and video data into audio and visual samples acquired from the natural world. The MPEG Synthetic-Natural Hybrid Coding was based on technologies developed by the Virtual Reality Modeling Language ( VRML ) Consortium ( now Web3D ). In the later versions of MPEG-4 International Standard, efficient coding of shape and animation of human faces and bodies is specified. The specifications include standardizing Facial Animation ( FA ) and Face and Body Animation ( FBA ). MPEG-4 Visual specifies support for animated face and body models within the Simple Face Animation and simple FBA. A face model described by Facial Definition Parameters ( FDPs ) and animated using Facial Animation Parameters ( FAPs ) is specified. The body is described by body animation parameters ( BAP ). The basic idea of these technologies is to use graphics models to create synthesized human bodies or faces which are modified or deformed by parameters extracted from the real scene. Figure 14-2 shows an example of such a model. ( The image is taken from *http://coven.lancs.ac.uk/mpeg4/* . ).

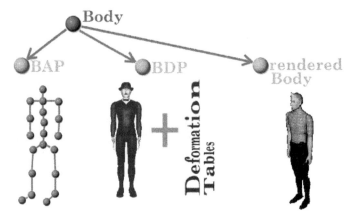

**Figure 14-2** MPEG-4 Body Animation

The next question is: *how do we generate synthesized human bodies or in general graphics objects?* It turns out that most 3D objects can be described using polygon meshes. Polygon meshes ( or simply meshes ) are collections of polygons that fit together to form the skin of the object. They have become a typical way of representing a broad class of solid graphical shapes. The simplest polygon is the triangle, which is one of the most useful geometric figures. The triangle is commonly used in the construction of buildings and bridges as it is the strongest geometric figure. Moreover, the vertices of a triangle always lie on the same plane. Therefore, it is the most popular polygon used to construct 3D graphical objects. The left image of Figure 14-3 shows the triangles that are used to construct a human face and the upper body. The right two images of Figure 14-3 show the use of triangles to represent a rabbit; by deforming a triangle, one can change the shape of the object.

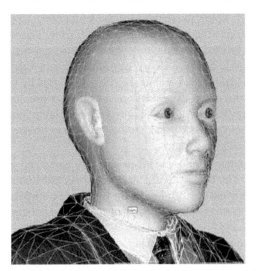 

**Figure 14-3** Human Face Formed by Polygon Mesh and Changing a Rabbit's Shape by Deforming a Polygon

There exist a lot of geometric modeling software packages that construct a model from some object, which can be a surface or a solid; it tries to capture the true shape of the object in a polygonal mesh. By using a sufficient number of polygons, a mesh can approximate the underlying surface to any desired degree of accuracy. For example, 3D Max is one of such 3D modeling software packages that run on Windows. Blender ( *http://www.blender.org/* ) is a popular free open-source 3D creation suite that lets users create sophisticated 3D graphical objects and do animation, and is available in all major operating systems, including Linux, Windows, and Mac OS/X. Typically, an artist creates an object using one of those packages and save it as a mesh in a file. A programmer writes programs in a computer language such as C/C++ or java to parse the polygons and manipulate the object. Artists may even post their graphical objects on some 3D graphics sites such as 3D Cafe ( *http://www.3dcafe.com/* ) for sale or for sharing. Specifically, **MakeHuman** ( *http://www.makehuman.org/* ) is an open-source tool for making 3D characters. Using MakeHuman, a photorealistic character can be modeled in less than 2 minutes and the character can be saved as a polygon mesh. MakeHuman is released under an Open Source Licence (GPL3.0) , and is available for Windows, Mac OS X and Linux. Xface is an MPEG4-based open-source toolkit for 3D facial animation. .

Figure 14-4 shows two more synthetic images for video compression taken from the web site *http://coven.lancs.ac.uk/mpeg4* that does Synthetic-Natural Hybrid Coding ( SNHC ) conformed to the MPEG-4 standard.

**Figure 14-4a** Animating Sign Language    **Figure 14-4b** Animating Business Meeting

## 14.2 MPEG-4 Facial Animation

To accomplish the representation of synthetic visual objects, MPEG-4 had to choose a scene description language to describe the scene structure. MPEG-4 selected Virtual Reality Modeling Language ( VRML ) standard as the basis with some additional new nodes to form the scene description language. Rather than constructing an object using purely triangles, the standard composes human face or body and other generic objects using a variety of geometric primitives such as cones, rectangles, triangles, and spheres. This makes the task of creating an object easier, and the object may look more realistic with the same number of polygons. To make the processing of the geometric primitives more efficient, the standard uses an indexed face set to define vertices and surface patches. It also uses nodes such as Transform to define rotation, scale, or translation and uses IndexedFaceSet nodes to describe the 3-D shape of an object. There are three problems that one has to address in animating human faces: a head needs to be specified; facial expressions have to be animated in real-time; animation and speech need to be synchronized.

MPEG-4 Facial Animation (FA) specifies the procedures to create a talking agent by standardizing various necessary parameters. The procedures of creating a talking agent consist of two phases. Phase one specifies the feature points on a static 3D model that defines the regions of deformation on the face. Phase two involves generation and interpolation of parameters that are used to modify the feature points to produce the actual animation. The two phases are cleanly separated from each other so that application developers can focus on their field of interest.

Face Definition Parameters (FDPs) and Face Animation Parameters (FAPs) are used to define head models and primitive facial expressions respectively. FDPs define the texture shape and face texture and FAPs are used to animate the face. FAPs are based on the study of minimal perceptible actions (MPA) and are closely related to muscle actions, including movements of lips, jaw, cheek and eyebrows. They make up a complete set of basic facial actions that represent the most natural facial expressions. Exaggerated parameter values may be used for Cartoon-like characters. Figure 14-5 shows some common facial expressions.

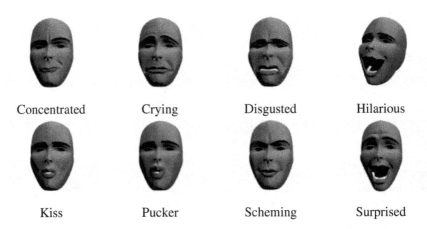

| Concentrated | Crying | Disgusted | Hilarious |

| Kiss | Pucker | Scheming | Surprised |

**Figure 14-5** Common Facial Expressions

The FAP values are usually defined and normalized in face animation parameter units (FAPUs) so that interpolations of the FAPs on any facial model are made in a consistent way. FAPUs measure spatial distances of facial expressions from its neutral state and are defined in terms of the fractions of distances between the marked key features. MPEG-4 defines a generic face model in its neutral state along with some feature points as shown in Figure 14-6. The neutral state of a face model may be defined by the following features:

1. gaze is along the Z-axis,
2. all face muscles are relaxed,
3. eyelids are tangent to the iris,
4. the pupil is one third of the diameter of the iris,
5. lips are in contact,
6. the mouth is closed and the upper teeth touch the lower ones,
7. the tongue is flat, horizontal with the tip of tongue touching the boundary between upper and lower teeth,
8. FAPUs (Face Animation Parameter Units) are defined as fractions of distances between key facial features in the neutral state as shown in the following table:

| Iris diameter | IRISD = IRISD0 / 1024 |
|---|---|
| Eye Separation | ES = ES0 / 1024 |
| Eye-nose Separation | ENS = ENS0 / 1024 |
| Mouth-nose Separation | MNS = MNS0 / 1024 |
| Mouth width | MW = MW0 / 1024 |
| Angle unit ( AU ) | $10^{-5}$ rad |

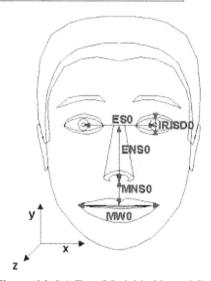

**Figure 14-6** A Face Model in Neutral State

For creating a standard conforming face, MPEG-4 specifies 84 feature points (FPs) on the neutral face. Feature points are arranged in groups such as cheeks, eyes and mouth. Applications need to define the locations of these feature points in order to conform to the standard. The feature points provide spatial references for defining FAPs as well as calibration between models when switched from one player to another. Figure 14-7 shows the set of FPs which are used to provide spatial reference for defining FAPs. The 68 FAPs are classified into 10 groups as shown in the following table:

**Table 14-1**  FAP Groups

| Group | Number of FAPs |
|---|---|
| 1. visemes and expressions | 2 |
| 2: jaw, chin, inner lowerlip, cornerlips, midlip | 16 |
| 3. eyeballs, pupils, eyelids | 12 |
| 4. eyebrow | 8 |
| 5. cheeks | 4 |
| 6. tongue | 5 |
| 7. head rotation | 3 |
| 8. outer lip positions | 10 |
| 9. nose | 4 |
| 10. ears | 4 |
| Total | 68 |

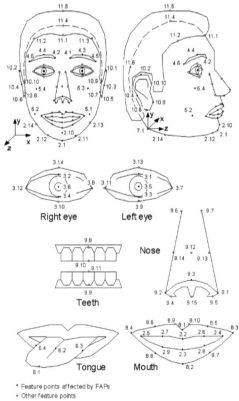

* Feature points affected by FAPs
• Other feature points

**Figure 14-7** MPEG-4 Feature Points

## 14.3 Computing Face Mesh Vertices

We use FAP values to animate a facial model, creating desired facial expressions. MPEG-4 further divides the FAPs into two subgroups. The first subgroup consists of FAPs that control simple motion of human face such as rotation, translation and scaling. The second subgroup FAPs are used for animating more complex motions that do not have any regular order such as frowning, blinking, and mouth-opening.

The first subgroup FAP values are fairly easy to process. For example, FAP23 is used to animate horizontal orientation of left eyeball. Suppose we have the following parameters,

$$
\begin{aligned}
\text{AU (Angle Unit)} &= 10^{-5} \, \text{rad} \\
\text{Rotation Axis} &= (0, -1, 0) \\
\text{Rotation factor } \theta &= 1 \\
\text{Value of FAP23} &= 10000
\end{aligned}
$$

then the left eyeball needs to be rotated by an angle $\alpha$ given by,

$$\alpha = 10^{-5} \times 10000 \times 1 = 0.1 \, radian$$

The mesh vertex coordinates are more difficult to obtain from the second subgroup of FAPs. We have to perform a piecewise linear interpolation to obtain the new vertex coordinates of the mesh in the affected region. Figure 14-8 shows two phases of a left eye blink along with the neutral phase. The eyelid motion is controlled by FAP19. In the blinking animation, the eyelid movement is along an acred trajectory but we can use 2D coordinates to specify the trajectory as shown in the figure.

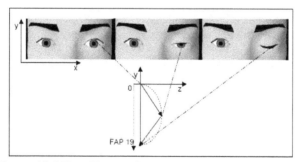

**Figure 14-8** Two Phases of Movement of Upper Left Eyelid

In general, we can compute the displacements of mesh vertices using piecewise linear interpolation. We approximate the motion trajectory of each mesh vertex as a piecewise linear one as shown in the figure below:

Suppose $P_m$ is the position of vertex m when the face is in neutral state (FAP = 0) and $D_{m,k}$ is the 3D displacement that defines the piecewise linear function in the $k$th interval as shown in Figure 14-9. If $P'_m$ is the new position of the same vertex after animation with the gvien FAP value, we can compute $P'_m$ according to the following algorithm which is slightly different from that of MPEG-4, which requires 0 to be on an interval boundary all the time.

1. Assume that the range of FAP is divided into $max$ intervals:

$$[I_0, I_1], [I_1, I_2], [I_2, I_3], ..., [I_{max-1}, I_{max}]$$

   where

$$I_0 = -\infty, \ I_{max} = +\infty$$

2. Assume that the received FAP is in the $j$th interval, $[I_j, I_{j+1}]$, and 0 is in the $k$th interval, $[I_k, I_{k+1}]$, with $0 \le j, k < max$. (See Figure 14-9.)

3. If $j > k$, we compute the new position $P'_m$ of the $m$th vertex by:

$$\begin{aligned} P'_m = \ & P_m + FAPU \times [(I_{k+1} - 0) \times D_{m,k} + (I_{k+2} - I_{k+1}) \times D_{m,k+1} \\ & + ... + (I_j - I_{j-1}) \times D_{m.j-1} + (FAP - I_j) \times D_{m,j}] \end{aligned}$$

(14.1)

4. If $j < k$, we compute $P'_m$ by:

$$\begin{aligned} P'_m = \ & P_m + FAPU \times [(I_{j+1} - FAP) \times D_{m,j} + (I_{j+2} - I_{j+1}) \times D_{m,j+1} \\ & + ... + (I_k - I_{k-1}) \times D_{m.k-1} + (0 - I_k) \times D_{m,k}] \end{aligned}$$

(14.2)

5. If $j = k$, we compute $P'_m$ by:

$$P'_m = P_m + FAPU \times FAP \times D_{m,k}$$

(14.3)

6. If the range of FAP contains only one interval, the motion is strictly linear, and we compute $P'_m$ by:

$$P'_m = P_m + FAPU \times FAP \times D_{m,0}$$

(14.4)

For example, suppose the FAP range is divided into three intervals:

$$[-\infty, 0], [0, 500], [500, +\infty].$$

The coordinates $(x, y, z)$ of the displacements of vertex m controlled by the FAPs in these intervals are:

$$\begin{pmatrix} 1 \\ 0 \\ 2 \end{pmatrix}, \quad \begin{pmatrix} 0.8 \\ 0 \\ 0 \end{pmatrix}, \quad \begin{pmatrix} 1.5 \\ 0 \\ 4 \end{pmatrix}$$

respectively. The coordinates of vertex m in neutral expression is $P_m$. Suppose the received FAP value is 600 and the corresponding FAPU is Mouth Width, MW = 0.1. Since this FAP value is in the third interval [500, $+\infty$] and 0 is in the second interval [0, 500], we have the situation $j > k$. Thus we apply (14.1) to calculate the new position $P'_m$ of vertex m:

$$P'_m = P_m + 0.1 \times [(500 - 0) \times \begin{pmatrix} 0.8 \\ 0 \\ 0 \end{pmatrix} + (600 - 500) \times \begin{pmatrix} 1.5 \\ 0 \\ 4 \end{pmatrix}] = P_m + \begin{pmatrix} 55 \\ 0 \\ 40 \end{pmatrix}$$

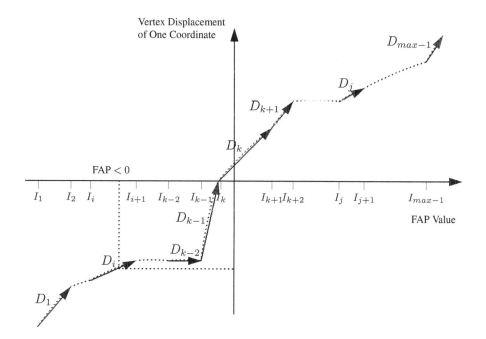

**Figure 14-9**. Piecewise Linear Interpolation of FAP Values

To speed up the animation process, we may save the relation between FAP intervals and 3D displacements in the so called *FaceDefTables*. When we get the value of an FAP, we need to look up the *FaceDefTables* to get information about the control region of the FAP and the three dimensional displacements of vertices within the control region to convert the FAP into facial animation as shown in the figure below:

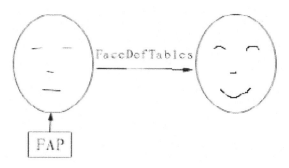

# 14.4 Keyframing

To animate realistic facial expressions, one can first calculate the animation parameters for key frames from photographs. A key frame in animation and film making is an image that defines the starting and ending points of any smooth transition. **Keyframing** is the process of creating animated motion by specifying objects at key frames and then interpolating the motion in intermediate frames. For traditional animation of movies, the key frames, also known as keys, are drawn by a senior artist. Other artists, *inbetweeners* and *inkers*, draw the intermediate frames and fill in the complete detailed drawings. The key frames are drawn for critical poses or when there is a sharp change in motion. At the beginning, the key frames could be very brief without fine details. The inbetweener would draw the intermediate poses to ensure that the motion appear fluid and natural.

Keyframing is particularly important in the animation of a full-length movie, which plays 24 frames per second. A 90-minute movie consists of 129,600 frames, which are way too many for a single artist to handle. On the other hand, if many artists draw different portions of the movie, the style or even appearance could be inconsistent. The movie has much better look if the production company employs a few senior animators to draw the key frames and a larger number of inbetweeners and linkers to draw the frames in between. A single senior animator can draw all the key frames of a particular character in a movie, producing more consistency of style.

In a similar spirit, computer animation uses interpolation to do keyframing. We specify the crucial parameters such as positions, orientations, and shapes of objects in the scene at key frames. Then, we obtain the parameters as smooth functions of time by using interpolating curves. This often can be done fully automatically but manual editing may be needed at some stages.

# 14.5 Extracting FAPs From Video

We have discussed how to use FAPs to animate facial expressions. This actually is a relatively easy part. When the animation parameters are given, one can basically use any appropriate model to perform animation. The more difficult problem is how to extract the FAPs from a given video. The extraction of facial parameters from video is not a completely solved problem. The process involves face detection, identification, recognition and tracking which are still active research topics in the academic and the industry. Automatic and accurate location of facial features is always difficult. The variety of human faces, expressions, facial hair, glasses, poses, and lighting contribute to the complexity of the problem.

A quick and simple way to find a human face in an image is to search for some common characteristics of human faces, such as color and shape. Some people use Delaunay triangulation and Voronoi diagrams to locate facial features of humans. However, this method is usually not very robust.

More sophisticated methods in general involve some statistical techniques and deformable models. A human is a deformable object and the tracking and recognition of it is usually tackled by making simplified assumptions concerning the motion or imposing constraints on it. Very often, the first step towards human tracking is to segment human figures from the background. A popular and relatively simple method to extract and track a deformable object in an image is the Active Contour Model ( also called "snake" ), which finds the contour of an object by balancing the effects of several energy terms. Variations of the Active Contour Model also exist. The gradient vector flow (GVF) snake is an improved model that includes the gradient vector flow, a new non-irrotational external force field. Another approach for tracking a deformable object is to employ deformable templates to automatically detect the objects. In general, retrieval by shape requires object detection and segmentation. Some researchers had used model-based region-grouping techniques to detect and retrieve deformable objects and found that using this method along with perceptually-motivated splitting strategy yields good image segmentation results of deformable shapes. In this section, we present a practical and popular technique for extracting FAPs from a video, the active appearance model (AAM).

## 14.5.1 Active Appearance Model (AAM)

An active appearance model (AAM) considers a face as a pattern in an image and makes use of a statistical model to match its appearance and shape with a pattern in the image. The approach is widely used for matching and tracking faces and for medical image interpolation.

AAM is an extension of the active shape model (ASM), which is a statistical model of the shape of objects that iteratively deform to fit to an example of the object in a new image. The shapes are constrained by the PDM (point distribution model) Statistical Shape Model to vary only in ways seen in a training set of labelled examples.

The shape of an object can be represented by a mesh of polygons or represented by a set of points (controlled by the shape model). Typically, it works by alternating the following steps:

1. Look in the image around each point for a better position for that point.
2. Update the model parameters to best match these new found positions.

To locate a better position for each point one may need to look for strong edges, or a match to a statistical model of what is expected at the point.

Usually, the points that represent a shape are referred to as *landmarks*. In general, a *landmark* is a distinguishable point present in most of the images under consideration and people use landmarks to locate features of an image. In our case, we locate facial features by locating landmarks. Figure 14-10 shows an image with correctly positioned landmarks.

**Figure 14-10** A face with correctly positioned landmarks

A set of landmarks forms a shape. Therefore, a shape s consists of a set of points. We can express s as an n-tuple:

$$s = \begin{pmatrix} p_1 \\ p_2 \\ \cdot \\ \cdot \\ \cdot \\ p_n \end{pmatrix} \tag{14.5}$$

where

$$p_i = \begin{pmatrix} x_i \\ y_i \\ z_i \end{pmatrix} \tag{14.6}$$

is a point with three coordinates if we consider 3D space. The $z_i$ component of (14.6) will be dropped if we consider 2D space. In general, the points of a shape are vertices of a mesh composed of triangles.

One can align one shape to another with an affine transformation (translation, scaling, or rotation) that minimizes the average Euclidean distance between shape points. The mean shape is the mean of the aligned training shapes, which are manually landmarked faces. (Note that the average of points is a linear affine combination of points and thus the average is also a valid point.) In general, a shape s is typically controlled by adding a linear combination of shape/deformation modes to the average shape $\bar{s}$:

$$s = \bar{s} + \Phi b \tag{14.7}$$

where $b$ is a set of vectors consisting of deformation parameters and $\Phi$ is a matrix whose columns contain the deformation modes. A deformation is a displacement of a point and can be regarded as a vector. The operation $\Phi b$ gives us another set of vectors. Therefore, in (14.7) we add a set of points to a set of vectors and the operation is legitimate.

We can generate various shapes with Equation (14.7) by varying the deformation parameters in $b$. By keeping the elements of $b$ within limits (determined during model building) we ensure that the generated face shapes are lifelike. Conversely, given a suggested shape $s$, we can calculate the parameter $b$ that allows Equation (14.7) to best approximate $s$ with a model shape $s'$. One can use an iterative algorithm to find $b$ and $T$ that minimize a 'distance' $D$ described by

$$D = ||s, T(\bar{s} + \Phi b)|| \tag{14.8}$$

where $T$ is an affine transformation that maps the model space into the image space.

ASM is relatively fast but it is too simplistic, not robust when new images are introduced. It may not converge to a good solution. Another disadvantage of ASM is that it only uses shape constraints and does not take advantage of all the available information like the texture of the target object.

It turns out that an equation similar to (14.7) can be also used to describe the texture of objects based on statistical models. A texture $t$ of an object is also a set of points at various locations of the objects:

$$t = \bar{t} + \sigma w \tag{14.9}$$

where $\bar{t}$ is the average texture, $\sigma$ describes texture modes and $w$ is a set of texture parameters.

Active appearance models (AAMs), also known as "smart snakes" as they conform to some explicit shape constraints like what an active contour model ( snake ) does, combine shape and texture into a single statistical model. We can express an AAM as

$$
\begin{aligned}
s &= \bar{s} + \phi\mathbf{v} = \bar{s} + \sum_{j=1}^{n}\phi_{ij}v_j \\
t &= \bar{t} + \sigma\mathbf{v} = \bar{t} + \sum_{j=1}^{n}\sigma_{ij}v_j
\end{aligned}
\tag{14.10}
$$

That is, we use the same displacement vectors to control both shape and texture. In (14.10), each $v_i$ is a vector and the coefficients $\phi_i$ and $\sigma_i$ are shape and texture parameters respectively. Note that

$$
v_i - \begin{pmatrix} v_{ix} \\ v_{iy} \\ v_{iz} \end{pmatrix}
$$

AAMs are normally computed from training data. The standard approach is to apply Principal Component Analysis (PCA) to the training meshes. The mean shape $\bar{s}$ is usually referred to as the base shape. Figure 14-11 shows an example of AAM, where $\bar{s}$ is the average shape and $v_i$'s are shape vectors.

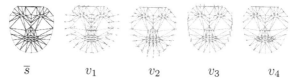

$$\bar{s} \qquad v_1 \qquad v_2 \qquad v_3 \qquad v_4$$

**Figure 14-11** An Example of AAM. $\bar{s}$ is the average shape. $v_i$'s are shape vectors.

## 14.5.2 An AAM Search Algorithm

Face modeling has been the most frequent application of AAMs. Typically an AAM is first fit to an image of a face. That is, we search for model parameters that maximize the "match" between the model instance and the input image. The model parameters are then used in whatever the application is. Fitting an AAM to an image is a non-linear optimization problem. The usual approach is to iteratively solve for incremental additive updates to the parameters (the shape and appearance coefficients.) We breifly describe an AAM search algorithm here that is based on such an iterative update.

For an input image $I$ and a model parameter vector $\mathbf{v}$, we can map the image onto the model and reshape the model to the standard shape to create a normalized image $J$:

$$
J = J(I, s(\mathbf{v}))
\tag{14.11}
$$

For simplicity, we assume that the input image $I$ is fixed. Therefore, the normalized image $J$ is a function of $\mathbf{v}$ only. The residual image $R$ is given by

$$
R(\mathbf{v}) = J(\mathbf{v}) - s(\mathbf{v})
\tag{14.12}
$$

We want to find **v** so that the error measure

$$E(\mathbf{v}) = ||R(\mathbf{v})||^2 \tag{14.13}$$

is minimized. Suppose we roughly know that the optimal **v** is near $\mathbf{v_0}$. Then the optimization process can be approximated by finding $\delta\mathbf{v}$ so that $E(\mathbf{v_0} + \delta\mathbf{v})$ is optimized. We can make a Taylor expansion of $R(\mathbf{v_0} + \delta\mathbf{v})$ and simplify the expression by retaining only the first two terms:

$$R(\mathbf{v_0} + \delta\mathbf{v}) \approx R(\mathbf{v_0}) + D\delta\mathbf{v} \tag{14.14}$$

where

$$D = \frac{\partial R(\mathbf{v})}{\partial \mathbf{v}}$$

is evaluated at $\mathbf{v} = \mathbf{v_0}$. Thus, our optimization is reduced to minimizing

$$E(\mathbf{v_0} + \delta\mathbf{v}) \approx ||R(\mathbf{v_0}) + D\delta\mathbf{v}||^2 \tag{14.15}$$

The least square solution to Equation (14.15) is

$$\delta\mathbf{v} = -(D^T D)^{-1} D^T R(\mathbf{v_0}) \tag{14.16}$$

We can use Equation (14.16) to update **v** in the search space; we use the $\delta\mathbf{v}$ to compute a new vector **v** and a new error measure:

$$\mathbf{v}' = \mathbf{v_0} + \delta\mathbf{v}$$
$$E' = E(\mathbf{v}') \tag{14.17}$$

If $E' < E$, we update **v** accordingly ( $\mathbf{v}' \rightarrow \mathbf{v_0}$ ) and repeat the steps until convergence occurs. If $E' > E$, we do not perform the update but try smaller update steps. If the smaller steps still do not improve the error measure, we assume that convergence has reached.

We can estimate the gradient matrix $D$ from a set of training data. For example, the $ith$ row of $D$ can be estimated as:

$$D_i = \sum_k [R(\mathbf{v} + \delta\mathbf{v}_{ik}) - R(\mathbf{v})] \tag{4.18}$$

where $\delta\mathbf{v}_{ik}$ is a vector that perturbs **v** in the $ith$ component to the amount of $k \times c$ for some suitable constant $c$. We can then compute the update matrix $U$ as the negative pseudoinverse of D:

$$U = -D^* = -(D^T D)^{-1} D^T \tag{14.19}$$

We can apply a similar procedure to the texture of Equation (14.10).

Some tools for studying AAM can be downloaded from the web site of Professor Tim Cootes ( *http://personalpages.manchester.ac.uk/staff/timothy.f.cootes/* ).

## 14.6 3DS File Format

We mentioned in the Introduction of this chapter that a 3D graphical object is composed of polygons and we can deform, rotate, scale or translate the object by changing the polygons. In general the tasks of creating nice-looking 3D objects are done by artists using some software such as the open-source 3D suite Blender. After creating the objects, the artists would pass them to software developers who could write programs to parse the objects that can be used for the 3D animation modeling discussed above. Or sometimes, a programmer may simply purchase or download the objects from the Internet, which may be sold as finished 'products' by the creators. In order that the programmers can use files created by artists effectively, they need to communicate in a standard agreed upon way. There are quite a lot of 'standard' 3D graphical object formats. Though MPEG-4 chose VRML as their scene description language, we shall discuss one of the more pupular ones, the 3ds file format so that readers can start doing experiments on this topic and may better integrate their work with the 3D graphics community.

File format of 3ds Max ( formerly 3D Studio Max ), is a full-featured 3D graphics animation package developed by Autodesk Media and Entertainment. The native file format used by 3D Studio for storing the 3D vector animations are binary files with the extension .3ds. The 3ds-file contain all information from the 3D editor and the keyframer (meshes, materials, cameras, tracks, etc.). The internal structure of the 3ds-file is hierrchical. The hirearchy is made up of data chunks, which can contain subchunks which in turn can contain new subchunks. Each data chunk starts with a 6-byte header which consists of a 2-byte id field and 4-byte length field. The length field includes the size of the header (6 byte). After the header follows an optional payload field that can contain new subchunks or data related to the 3D vector animation.

In addition to its modeling and animation tools, the latest version of 3ds Max also features advanced shaders (such as ambient occlusion and subsurface scattering), dynamic simulation, particle systems, radiosity, normal map creation and rendering, and global illumination. The open-source 3D grahics package Blender also supports this format. Figure 14-12 shows a 3ds image, which is made up of numerous number of triangles:

**Figure 14-12** 3ds max living room rendered with V-Ray

As mentioned above, 3ds data are organized into chunks with each chunk containing a 2-byte chunkname and a 4-byte length, and each chunk may have subchunks. The following list shows some of the chunks and subchunks:

1. MAIN3DS

    0x4D4D : The main chunk in the .3ds file, containing all other chunks

2. EDIT3DS

0x3D3D : Most interested, containing EDIT_OBJECT chunks, which define the objects in the .3ds scene (lights, geometry, etc...)

3. EDIT_OBJECT

0x4000 : Containing data and OBJ_TRIMESH; immediately followed by an object name, which is a NULL terminated string

4. OBJ_TRIMESH

0x4100 : Containing the geometric information about the object: the vertices, triangles, and texture coordinate chunks

5. TRI_VERTEXL

0x4110 : Containing a list of vertices, a 2-byte unsigned integer vertex count followed by vertex count float triplets that define the x, y, z coordinates

6. TRI_FACEL1

0x4120 : Defining the triangles of the model, similar to the vertex list, starting out with a 2-byte unsigned integer that gives a count of how many triangles there are, followed by sets of four 2-byte unsigned integers, the first three in-dixing to one of the vertices in the vertex list, the last containing a few bit-flags; a triangle consists of three vertices in counter-clockwise order

7. TRI_TEXCOORD

0x4140 : Giving a series texture coordinates, starting out with a 2-byte unsigned integer like the last couple lists which defines how many entries are in this list

The following is an example of some sample data of a 3ds file:

```
00000:  4D 4D 29 D2 00 00            |MAIN3DS chunk length
        02 00 0A 00 00 00            |BOTTOM subchunk length
        03 00 00 00                  |LEFT
00016:  3D 3D 39 D1 00 00 3E 3D      |EDIT3DS sibling chunk length
        0A 00 00 00 03 00 00 00

00032:  00 01 0A 00 00 00 00 00 80 3F 00 40 1F D1 00 00  |.........?.@....|
00048:  54 6F 72 75 73 20 4B 6E 6F 74 00 00 41 0E D1 00  |Torus Knot..A...|
00064:  00 10 41 C4 49 00 00 25 06 3D 09 61 42 40 3E 05  |..A.I..%.=.aB@>.|
00080:  C0 E7 75 01 42 6A 93 6D 42 F2 1F 0E C1 38 E3 1C  |..u.Bj.mB....8..|
00096:  42 C5 E3 67 42 40 BC 5D C1 D5 D4 3F 42 59 80 51  |B..gB@.]...?BY.Q|
00112:  42 97 CF 7A C1 C6 ED 60 42 DF 68 30 42 87 8F 5D  |B..z...`B.h0B..]|
00128:  C1 BA 4F 77 42 46 7B 0D 42 7C D2 0D C1 5C FB 7C  |..OwBF{.B|...\.||
00144:  42 E2 26 E4 41 81 D8 03 C0 B3 6B 70 42 88 12 CB  |B.&.A.....kpB...|
00160:  41 81 B4 97 40 64 FE 54 42 D0 71 D6 41 8F 76 1B  |A...@d.TB.q.A.v.|
00176:  41 C7 0C 32 42 53 9C 01 42 E9 89 38 41 D6 F3 10  |A..2BS..B..8A...|
00192:  42 CC B3 22 42 DD 49 1B 41 C1 23 F5 41 66 A1 45  |B.."B.I.A.#.Af.E|
00208:  42 AC 19 97 40 7C CC E9 41 3B 09 61 42 13 3E 05  |B...@|..A;.aB.>.|
00224:  C0 E5 75 01 42 AD 0E 6E 42 04 51 AA 3F 38 97 0D  |..u.B..nB.Q.?8..|
00240:  42 BA 90 7B 42 F4 63 84 C0 C9 08 2D 42 A6 99 76  |B..{B.c....-B..v|
        [ 0  1  2  3  4  5  6  7  8  9 10 11 12 13 14 15  0123456789012345]
```

In the example,

(a)  Chunk name = "MAIN3DS" ( 0x4D4D )
(b)  Length of main chunk = 0x0000D229 = 53801 bytes (equals length of file)
(c)  Subchunk name = "BOTTOM" ( 0x0002 )
(d)  Length of subchunk = 0x00000A = 10 ( bytes )
(e)  Sibling subchunk = "LEFT" ( 0x0003 )
(f)  Sibling subchunk = "3DSEDIT" ( 0x3D3D )
(g)  Length of "3DSEDIT" = 0x3D3E0000 = 15678 ( bytes )

It is not too difficult to write a program to parse a 3ds file. However, again we are not interested in studying file formats in details. We shall use existing free java libraries to parse 3ds files; we discuss this in the next section.

## 14.7 Parsing 3DS Files

Free java 3ds file parsers are available in the Internet. The package that we use to process 3ds files is "mri.v3ds", a simple 3D Studio 3ds file loader in Java written by Mats Byggmastar (*http://www.multi.fi/ mbc/v3ds/*). The package is intended to be used for importing 3D animations that are created with 3D Studio R4 into a 3D engine. The mri.v3ds package does not load every single data chunk from a 3ds-file. It only loads the chunks that the author considers important and useful to his 3D engines. The top level class of the package, Scene3ds, parses the input 3ds file and builds a memory image of it, using other classes such as Mesh3ds, Camera3ds, Vertex3ds, and TexCoord3ds. While the file is being parsed, textural decode of the data can be extracted. The parameters not decoded are shown as hex bytes. At this point, the package is not totally open-source but readers can download the classes archived in a jar file ( "mri-v3ds.jar" ) from its author's web site. The following table lists all the classes that the package has:

| Camera3ds | Exception3ds | Face3ds |
|-----------|--------------|---------|
| FaceMat3ds | HideKey3ds | HideTrack3ds |
| Material3ds | Mesh3ds | MorphKey3ds |
| MorphTrack3ds | PKey3ds | PTrack3ds |
| RotationKey3ds | RotationTrack3ds | Scene3ds |
| SplineKey3ds | TexCoord3ds | TextDecode3ds |
| Track3ds | Vertex3ds | XYZKey3ds |
| XYZTrack3ds |  |  |

Scene3ds is the top level class in this package. It has constructors that takes an input 3ds-file as parameter. The Scene3ds class parses the data chunks in the input file and builds a memory representation of the various parameters using the helper classes, Vertex3ds, Face3ds, Mesh3ds, Camera3ds, etc. After the file has been parsed and the Scene3ds object created successfully, the object can be passed to a 3D engine for further processing and visualization. Program listing 14-1 shows a simple piece of java code that makes use of the Scene3ds class of "mri.v3ds" to load a .3ds file and print out all the chunk information of the file.

**Program Listing 14-1** Loading and Parsing 3ds File Using "mri.v3ds"

```
/*
  Test3ds.java
*/
import java.io.*;
import mri.v3ds.*;

public class Test3ds {
  public static void main(String[] args) throws InterruptedException
  {
    if (args.length < 1) {
      System.out.println("Usage: java " + "Test3ds" +
        " 3DS_input_filename " );
      System.exit(-1);
    }
    TextDecode3ds decode = new TextDecode3ds();
    try {
        File f = new File ( args[0] );
        Scene3ds scene = new Scene3ds( f, decode, 2 ); //level 2 decode
    } catch ( Exception3ds e ) {}
    System.out.printf ( "%s\n", decode.text() );//print out all chunk info

    return;
  }
}
```

The program takes the file name of a .3ds as input. For example you can run the program using the command,

java Test3ds ../data/objects.3ds

which loads and parses the 3ds file "objects.3ds" residing in the directory "../data/". It prints out all the chunk information and data in text format. Of course, to compile and run the program properly, you need to point your CLASSPATH to the jar file "mri-v3ds.jar".

## 14.8 Conclusions

We have introduced video compression theories and and the corresponding implementations in java code. The description is far from complete. We have only introduced some basic concepts that help you to establish a solid foundation for further studies in the field. Audio compression and more advanced compression techniques have not been discussed. Though the programs presented are self-contained and executable, they should not be considered as end-applications. They are implemented in a way to help readers to understand the theories and concepts. Actually, we have hard-coded some of the parameters and ignored error-checking in a number of places for simplicity and clarity of illustration. The pre-calculated Huffman codes for 3D run-level tuples are very brief and incomplete. Nevertheless, the programs help readers understand basic video compression concepts and interested readers can use the programs as the basis for further development.

The field of video compression is still evolving. However, besides the hybrid coding, the basic techniques are fairly mature. There exists open-source software that compress and decompress videos along with sound using various standards. If your interest is mainly on utilizing existing video compression libraries, you may use open-source video codecs for your applications. One can make use of the libraries to easily integrate videos in a graphics or video game application. The use of these open-source video compression libraries will tremendously shorten your software development cycle. On the other hand, an understanding of the basic principles of video compression helps you more effectively use the libraries or even modify and improve them. Because of the huge advancement and demand of Internet and multi-media applications, the utilization of video compression technologies is ubiquitous. The technologies will be even more important in the coming decades. Their applications are only limited by your imagination.

# Chapter 15   Principal Component Analysis

## 15.1 Introduction

We have mentioned in Chapter 14 that people use the techniques of Principal Component Analysis (PCA) to model face features. Actually, PCA is a common statistical technique used in finding patterns in high-dimension data. It has applications in various fields such as image processing and face recognition. Before discussing PCA, we need to have a basic knowledge about the tools and techniques involved in PCA. Therefore, this chapter first introduces the mathematical tools that will be used in PCA, starting from a discussion on matrix operations. It then discusses standard deviation, covariance, eigenvectors and eigenvalues. If you are already familiar with these basic tools and concepts, you can skip them and go directly to the PCA section.

Some of the examples of this chapter are adopted from the college textbook *Linear Algebra with Applications* by *Steven J. Leon*.

## 15.2 Matrix Algebra

A matrix is a rectangular array of numbers. An $m \times n$ matrix, read "$m$ by $n$ matrix", has $m$ rows and $n$ columns. Let $A$ be an $m \times n$ matrix with $a_{ij}$ denoting the element in the $i$th row and $j$th column. Then

$$A = (a_{ij}) = \begin{pmatrix} a_{11} & a_{12} & \cdots & a_{1n} \\ a_{21} & a_{22} & \cdots & a_{2n} \\ . & . & \cdots & . \\ a_{m1} & a_{m2} & \cdots & a_{mn} \end{pmatrix} \tag{15.1}$$

The elements $a_{11}, a_{22}, a_{33}$... are called the elements of the *main diagonal* of $A$. Two matrices $A = (a_{ij})$ and $B = (b_{ij})$ are equal if they have the same number of rows and columns and the elements are equal, i.e. $a_{ij} = b_{ij}$. The following are examples of a $3 \times 1$ matrix, a $2 \times 3$ matrix, and a $3 \times 3$ matrix respectively.

$$\begin{pmatrix} 3.1 \\ 4.1 \\ 5.9 \end{pmatrix}, \quad \begin{pmatrix} 1 & -2 & 3 \\ 9 & 8 & 5 \end{pmatrix}, \quad \begin{pmatrix} 3 & 1 & 4 \\ 1 & 5 & 9 \\ 2 & 6 & 5 \end{pmatrix}$$

The transpose of $A$ in (15.1) is obtained by interchanging rows and columns, and is denoted by $A^T$. That is,

$$A^T = \begin{pmatrix} a_{11} & a_{21} & \cdots & a_{m1} \\ a_{12} & a_{22} & \cdots & a_{m2} \\ \cdot & \cdot & \cdots & \cdot \\ a_{1n} & a_{2n} & \cdots & a_{mn} \end{pmatrix} \qquad (15.2)$$

and $A^T$ has $n$ rows and $m$ columns. For example,

$$\begin{pmatrix} 1 & -2 & 3 \\ 9 & 8 & 5 \end{pmatrix}^T = \begin{pmatrix} 1 & 9 \\ -2 & 8 \\ 3 & 5 \end{pmatrix}$$

Maxtrix $X = (x_1, x_2, ..., x_n)$ is a $1 \times n$ matrix; it has one row and $n$ columns, and we call it an $n$th order row vector. Its transpose

$$X^T = \begin{pmatrix} x_1 \\ x_2 \\ \cdot \\ \cdot \\ \cdot \\ x_n \end{pmatrix}$$

is an $n \times 1$ matrix, consisting of $n$ rows and one column, and will be called a column vector in contrast to $X$ itself.

We note that, if $A$ is any matrix and $A^T$ its transpose, then $A$ is the transpose of $A^T$ so that $(A^T)^T = A$. We call a matrix that has the same number of rows as columns a *square matrix*. The transpose of a square matrix is also a square matrix. A square matrix with $n$ rows and $n$ columns is referred to as a matrix of *order* $n$. If the transpose of a square matrix is equal to itself (i.e. $A^T = A$), then it is called a *symmetric* matrix. An important property of symmetric matrix is that we can diagonalize any symmetric matrix $A$, which means that $A$ is similar to a diagonal matrix. That is, there exists an invertible matrix $P$ such that $P^{-1}AP$ is a diagonal matrix, where $P^{-1}$ is the inverse of $P$.

The *row rank* of a matrix $A$ is the maximum number of linearly independent row vectors of $A$ and the *column rank* is the maximum number of linearly independent column vectors. A matrix $A$ has full column rank if its column vectors are independet and it has full row rank if its row vectors are independent. One can show that the row rank is always equal to the column rank of a matrix. Therefore, we define that the *rank* of a matrix $A$ is the maximum number of linearly independent row (or column) vectors of $A$ and is denoted by $rank(A)$. The rank of an $m \times n$ matrix cannot be greater than $m$ nor $n$. That is $rank(A) \leq min(m, n)$. A matrix that has a rank as large as possible is said to have *full rank*, otherwise the matrix is *rank deficient*. If $A$ is a square matrix (i.e., $m = n$), then $A$ is invertible (i.e., its inverse exists) if and only if $A$ has rank $n$ (i.e., $A$ has full rank).

An identity matrix $I$ is an $n \times n$ square matrix with $I = (\delta_{ij})$, where

$$\delta_{ij} = \begin{cases} 1 & \text{if } i = j \\ 0 & \text{if } i \neq j \end{cases}$$

is the Kronecker delta. An identity matrix has 1's on the main diagonal and 0's elsewhere.

## Matrix Multiplication

If $A$ is an $m \times n$ matrix and $B$ is an $n \times r$ matrix, we can form the product of $A$ and $B$, which is an $m \times r$ matrix; if $C$ is the product of $A$ and $B$, we write $C = AB$ and

$$c_{ij} = \sum_{k=1}^{n} a_{ik} b_{kj} \qquad 1 \leq i \leq m, 1 \leq j \leq r \qquad (15.3)$$

One can easily show that matrix multiplication is *associative*. That is, if $A, B, C$ are any three matrices of types $(m, n), (n, r)$ and $(r, s)$, respectively, then

$$(AB)C = A(BC) \qquad (15.4)$$

One can also show that the transpose of the product of two matrices $A$ and $B$ is equal to the product of their transposes in *reverse order*. That is,

$$(AB)^T = B^T A^T \qquad (15.5)$$

For any $n \times n$ matrix $A$,

$$IA = AI = A$$

## Matrix Addition

If two matrices $A$ and $B$ are of the same type $(m, n)$, their sum $C = A + B$ is obtained by adding corresponding elements of $A$ and $B$:

$$c_{ij} = a_{ij} + b_{ij} \qquad (15.6)$$

Clearly, addition of matrices is commutative, $A + B = B + A$, and associative, $(A + B) + C = A + (B + C)$. Moreover, the zero matrix $O$ satisfies the law $A + O = A + O = A$ for every matrix $A$. For every matrix $A = (a_{ij})$, there corresponds a *negative* $-A = (-a_{ij})$ with property $A + (-A) = O$.

One can also easily prove that matrix multiplication is distributive with respect to matrix addition. That is, if matrices $A$ and $B$ are of type $(m, n)$, $C$ of type $(r, m)$ and $D$ of type $(n, s)$, then

$$C(A + B) = CA + CB \qquad (15.7)$$

and

$$(A + B)D = AD + BD \qquad (15.8)$$

## Determinant

The determinant of a square matrix is a value associated with the matrix and is computed from the entries of the matrix. It provides valuable information for the matrix operations such as computing the inverse. The determinant of a matrix $A$ is denoted det $(A)$ or $|A|$.

Let $A = (a_{ij})$ be a square matrix of order $n$. We can form a product of elements of $A$ by multiplying together one and only one element from each row and each column, which will be in the form,

$$a_{1i_1} a_{2i_2} \cdots a_{ni_n} \tag{15.9}$$

where $i_1, i_2, \cdots, i_n$ is a permutation of the numbers $1, 2, \cdots, n$. The numbering and permutation ensure that one and only one element is chosen from each row and each column. The determinant of $A$ is the sum of some of products in the form of (15.9). We say that an inversion occurs in the permutation $i_1, i_2, \cdots, i_n$ whenever a larger subscript precedes a smaller one. For example, consider $n = 4$; the product

$$a_{14} a_{22} a_{31} a_{43}$$

has a total of 4 inversions because $i_1 i_2 i_3 i_4 = 4213$, so 4 precedes $1, 2$, and 3 (3 inversions), and 2 precedes 1 (1 inversion); the product

$$a_{11} a_{22} a_{33} a_{44}$$

has zero inversion. We say that a permutation $i_1 i_2 \cdots i_n$ of the numbers $1, 2, \cdots, n$ is even if the number of inversions is even and it is odd if the number of inversions is odd. We can now define the determinant of a square matrix.

We denote the determinant associated with the square matrix $A$ by $|A|$ or by

$$\begin{vmatrix} a_{11} & a_{12} & \ldots & a_{1n} \\ a_{21} & a_{22} & \ldots & a_{2n} \\ . & . & \ldots & . \\ a_{n1} & a_{n2} & \ldots & a_{nn} \end{vmatrix} \tag{15.10}$$

The determinant is a polynomial of the elements of $A$ defined by

$$|A| = \sum \pm a_{1i_1} a_{2i_2} \cdots a_{ni_n} \tag{15.11}$$

where we sum over all $n!$ permutations $i_1, i_2, \cdots, i_n$ of $1, 2, \cdots, n$; the sign before a term is $+$ if the permutation is even, and $-$ for odd permutations. One can prove that the determinant $|A|$ of an $n \times n$ square matrix $A$ has the following properties.

1. $|A^T| = |A|$.
2. If the elements of two rows (or two columns) are identical, $|A| = 0$.
3. If matrix $B$ is obtained by interchanging two rows or two columns of $A$, then $|B| = -|A|$.
4. If matrix $B$ is obtained by multiplying all the elements of a row or a column of $A$ by a constant $c$, then $|B| = c|A|$.

5. If $c$ is a constant, then $|cA| = c^n |A|$.
6. If $B$ is an $n \times n$ matrix, then $|AB| = |A||B|$.
7. If all the elements of a row or a column of $A$ are 0, then $|A| = 0$.
8. If matrix $B$ is obtained by multiplying a row (or column) vector of $|A|$ by a constant $c$ and adding the result to another row (or column) vector, then $|B| = |A|$.
9. If $I$ is the identity matrix, then $1 = |I| = |AA^{-1}| = |A||A^{-1}|$, where $A^{-1}$ is the the inverse of $A$, which is discussed below. Therefore

$$|A^{-1}| = \frac{1}{|A|}$$

10. The determinant of the similarity transformation of $A$ is equal to $|A|$:

$$|BAB^{-1}| = |B||A||B^{-1}| = |B||A|\frac{1}{|B|} = |A|$$

For example, a $2 \times 2$ matrix can be calculated as,

$$\begin{vmatrix} a & b \\ c & d \end{vmatrix} = ad - bc \tag{15.12}$$

The calculation can be represented graphically as shown in Figure 15-1 below, where an arrow crosses the elements of a diagonal of the matrix, giving rise to a term of (15.11). We put a '−' sign in front of the term if the arrow points upward, and a '+' sign for the arrow pointing downward. The determinant is given by the sum of the terms.

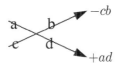

**Figure 15-1**   Calculating $2 \times 2$ Matrix Determinant

We can similarly use this graphical method to calculate the determinant of a $3 \times 3$ matrix $A = (a_{ij})$. In this case, we copy the first two rows of the matrix and put them beneath the last row. We then cross out the diagonal elements as shown in Figure 15-2. Again, a '−' sign is added for an 'upward' term and a '+' sign is added for a 'downward' term. The determinant is the sum of all the terms thus obtained.

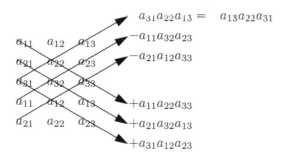

**Figure 15-2**   Calculating $3 \times 3$ Matrix Determinant

If we delete some rows and/or columns of a matrix $A$, the matrix of the remaining elements is referred to as a *submatrix* of $A$. In particular, if $A$ is a square matrix, and we delete the i-th row and j-th column of it, then we denote the remaining submatrix by $A_{ij}$. The determinant $|A_{ij}|$ is called the *minor* of of the element $a_{ij}$ in $A$, and $(-1)^{i+j}|A_{ij}|$ is called the *signed minor* or *cofactor* of $a_{ij}$ in $A$. With these notations, one can express the determinant of an $n \times n$ matrix $A$ as an expansion of determinants of minors as follows:

$$|A| = (-1)^{i+1}a_{i1}|A_{i1}| + (-1)^{i+2}a_{i2}|A_{i2}| + \cdots + (-1)^{i+n}a_{in}|A_{in}|$$

$$= (-1)^{1+j}a_{1j}|A_{1j}| + (-1)^{2+j}a_{2j}|A_{2j}| + \cdots + (-1)^{n+j}a_{nj}|A_{nj}|$$
(15.13)

where $i, j = 1, 2, \cdots, n$. For example, we can express the expansion along the first row as

$$
\begin{vmatrix} a_{11} & a_{12} & \cdot\cdot & a_{1n} \\ a_{21} & a_{22} & \cdot\cdot & a_{2n} \\ \cdot & \cdot & \cdot\cdot & \cdot \\ a_{n1} & a_{n2} & \cdot\cdot & a_{nn} \end{vmatrix}
= a_{11}
\begin{vmatrix} a_{22} & a_{23} & \cdot\cdot & a_{2n} \\ \cdot & \cdot & \cdot\cdot & \cdot \\ a_{n2} & a_{n3} & \cdot\cdot & a_{nn} \end{vmatrix}
- a_{12}
\begin{vmatrix} a_{21} & a_{23} & \cdot\cdot & a_{2n} \\ \cdot & \cdot & \cdot\cdot & \cdot \\ a_{n1} & a_{n3} & \cdot\cdot & a_{nn} \end{vmatrix}
$$

$$
+ \cdots + (-1)^{1+n}
\begin{vmatrix} a_{21} & a_{22} & \cdot\cdot & a_{2(n-1)} \\ \cdot & \cdot & \cdot\cdot & \cdot \\ a_{n1} & a_{n3} & \cdot\cdot & a_{n(n-1)} \end{vmatrix}
$$
(15.14)

In general, we can express the determinant of $A$ as

$$\boxed{|A| = \sum_{i=1}^{n} a_{ij}C_{ij}}$$
(15.15)

where $C_{ij}$ is the cofactor of $a_{ij}$, which is

$$C_{ij} = (-1)^{i+j}|A_{ij}|$$
(15.16)

and $A_{ij}$ is the submatrix formed by deleting row $i$ and column $j$ from $A$. One can also show that if $h \neq k$, then

$$\sum_{j=1}^{n} a_{hj}C_{kj} = 0 \quad \text{and} \quad \sum_{i=1}^{n} a_{ih}C_{ik} = 0$$
(15.17)

The left equation says that the sum of the elements from the $h$-th row times the cofactors from the $k$-th row is zero. The right equation is about columns.

We can combine equations (15.15) and (15.17) in the form

$$\sum_{j=1}^{n} a_{hj}C_{kj} = |A|\delta_{hk} \quad \text{and} \quad \sum_{i=1}^{n} a_{ih}C_{ik} = |A|\delta_{hk}$$
(15.18)

The following is an example of evaluating the determinant of a $3 \times 3$ matrix.

$$
\begin{vmatrix} 2 & -1 & 6 \\ 4 & 1 & 2 \\ 3 & 5 & 7 \end{vmatrix} = 2 \times \begin{vmatrix} 1 & 2 \\ 5 & 7 \end{vmatrix} - 4 \times \begin{vmatrix} -1 & 6 \\ 5 & 7 \end{vmatrix} + 3 \times \begin{vmatrix} -1 & 6 \\ 1 & 2 \end{vmatrix}
$$

$$
= 2(1 \times 7 - 5 \times 2) - 4(-1 \times 7 - 5 \times 6) + 3(-1 \times 2 - 1 \times 6)
$$

$$
= -6 + 148 - 24
$$

$$
= 118
$$

## Matrix Inverse

We denote $I = (\delta_{ij})$ as an $n \times n$ identity matrix, where $\delta_{ij}$ is a Kronecker delta. That is,

$$
I = \begin{pmatrix} 1 & 0 & \dots & 0 \\ 0 & 1 & 0.. & 0 \\ . & . & \dots & . \\ 0 & 0 & ..0 & 1 \end{pmatrix} \tag{15.19}
$$

We define the inverse of an $n \times n$ matrix $A$ as a square matrix $A^{-1}$ such that

$$
AA^{-1} = I \tag{15.20}
$$

A square matrix $A$ has an inverse iff its determinant $|A| \neq 0$. We say that a matrix is *nonsingular* or *invertible* if its inverse exists.

We can obtain the inverse of $A$ from the *adjoint* (matrix) of $A$, denoted as $A^{adj}$, which is defined as the transpose of the cofactor matrix $C_{ij}$. That is,

$$
A^{adj} = (C_{ij})^T = \begin{pmatrix} C_{11} & C_{21} & \dots & C_{n1} \\ C_{12} & C_{22} & .. & C_{n2} \\ . & . & \dots & . \\ C_{1n} & C_{2n} & .. & C_{nn} \end{pmatrix} \tag{15.21}
$$

From (15.18), we have

$$
AA^{adj} = |A|I \tag{15.22}
$$

Therefore, if $|A| \neq 0$, the inverse of $A$ is given by

$$
A^{-1} = \frac{1}{|A|} A^{adj} \tag{15.23}
$$

For a $2 \times 2$ matrix

$$A = \begin{pmatrix} a & b \\ c & d \end{pmatrix} \tag{15.24}$$

its adjoint is

$$A^{adj} = \begin{pmatrix} d & -b \\ -c & a \end{pmatrix} \tag{15.25}$$

So the inverse is

$$A^{-1} = \frac{1}{|A|} \begin{pmatrix} d & -b \\ -c & a \end{pmatrix}$$
$$= \frac{1}{ad-bc} \begin{pmatrix} d & -b \\ -c & a \end{pmatrix} \tag{15.26}$$

As an example, let us find the inverse of the $3 \times 3$ matrix

$$A = \begin{pmatrix} 2 & 1 & 3 \\ 2 & 4 & 0 \\ 1 & 2 & 1 \end{pmatrix}$$

In this example, $|A| = 6$, and

$$C_{11} = \begin{vmatrix} 4 & 0 \\ 2 & 1 \end{vmatrix} = 4, \quad C_{12} = -\begin{vmatrix} 2 & 0 \\ 1 & 1 \end{vmatrix} = -2, \quad C_{13} = \begin{vmatrix} 2 & 4 \\ 1 & 2 \end{vmatrix} = 0, \quad \cdots$$

and so on. So we have

$$A^{-1} = \frac{1}{|A|} A^{adj} = \frac{1}{6} \begin{pmatrix} 4 & 5 & -12 \\ -2 & -1 & 6 \\ 0 & -3 & 6 \end{pmatrix} = \begin{pmatrix} \frac{2}{3} & \frac{5}{6} & -2 \\ -\frac{1}{3} & -\frac{1}{6} & 1 \\ 0 & -\frac{1}{2} & 1 \end{pmatrix}$$

The following are some properties of matrix inverses:

1. If $A$ and $B$ are $n \times n$ matrices, we say that $B$ is **similar** to $A$ if there exists a nonsingular matrix $S$ such that $B = S^{-1}AS$. Obviously, if $B$ is similar to $A$, then $A$ is similar to $B$ as $A = U^{-1}BU$, where $U = S^{-1}$.

2. If matrices $A$ and $B$ are invertible, then their product $AB$ is also invertible and is

$$(AB)^{-1} = B^{-1}A^{-1}$$

3. A diagonal matrix has an inverse if no diagonal element is zero:

$$\text{If } \Lambda = \begin{pmatrix} \lambda_1 & 0 & \cdot\cdot & 0 \\ 0 & \lambda_2 & \cdot\cdot & 0 \\ \cdot & \cdot\cdot & \cdot & \cdot \\ 0 & \cdot\cdot & 0 & \lambda_n \end{pmatrix} \text{ then } \Lambda^{-1} = \begin{pmatrix} \frac{1}{\lambda_1} & 0 & \cdot\cdot & 0 \\ 0 & \frac{1}{\lambda_2} & \cdot\cdot & 0 \\ \cdot & \cdot\cdot & \cdot & \cdot \\ 0 & \cdot\cdot & 0 & \frac{1}{\lambda_n} \end{pmatrix}$$

where $\lambda_i \neq 0$.

4. If $A$ is an $n \times m$ matrix, then $AA^T$ is $n \times n$ and is a symmetric square matrix.

5. An **orthogonal** matrix is a square matrix with orthogonal unit column and row vectors $\mathbf{v_i}$ (i.e., orthonormal vectors where $\mathbf{v_i} \cdot \mathbf{v_j} = \delta_{ij}$). One can show that a matrix $A$ is orthogonal if and only if its transpose is equal to its inverse:

$$A^T = A^{-1}$$

or

$$AA^T = A^T A = I$$

## Left inverse

If $A$ is a nonsingular square matrix, it has a *2-sided inverse*, $A^{-1}$ for which $AA^{-1} = I = A^{-1}A$. This is what we have called the *inverse* of $A$. If $A$ is $m \times n$ and $m \neq n$, then it does not have a 2-sided inverse, but it can have a left inverse or a right inverse which are referred to as *pseudoinverse*.

If $A$ is $m \times n$ with full column rank (i.e. $r = rank(A) = n, m > n$), the matrix $A^T A$ is an invertible $n \times n$ symmetric matrix. Therefore, $(A^T A)^{-1} A^T A = I$. We can define the *left inverse* of $A$ to be

$$A_{left}^{-1} = (A^T A)^{-1} A^T$$

as $A_{left}^{-1} A = I$.

Note that $AA_{left}^{-1}$ is an $m \times m$ matrix which equals the identity matrix only if $m = n$. Actually,

$$P = AA_{left}^{-1} = A(A^T A)^{-1} A^T$$

is the matrix that projects $\Re^m$ onto the column space of $A$. This is the closest we can get to the matrix product $AB = I$.

## Right inverse

Similarly, if $A$ is $m \times n$ with full row rank (i.e. $r = rank(A) = m, m < n$), we can define its right inverse. In this case, $AA^T$ is an invertible $m \times m$ symmetric matrix. So, $AA^T(A^T A)^{-1} = I$. The *right inverse* of $A$ is

$$A_{right}^{-1} = A^T(AA^T)^{-1}$$

as $AA_{right}^{-1} = I$.

Also note that $A_{right}^{-1}A$ is an $n \times n$ matrix which equals the identity matrix only if $m = n$. The matrix

$$P = A_{right}^{-1}A = A^T(AA^T)^{-1}A$$

projects $\Re^n$ onto the row space of $A$. It is as close as we can get to the matrix product $BA = I$.

## Pseudoinverse

An $m \times n$ matrix $A$ has a left inverse if it is with full column rank ($r = rank(A) = n$) and has a right inverse if it is with full row rank ($r = rank(A) = m$). The left inverse or the right inverse of a matrix is a pseudoinverse. If $A$ has rank $r < min(m, n)$, then we need to consider the general **pseudoinverse**.

We can define the pseudoinverse $A^+$ of $A$ as the matrix for which $A^+A$ gives an identity operation on any row vector $\mathbf{x}$, i.e. $\mathbf{x} = A^+A\mathbf{x}$.

To find the pseudoinverse of $A$, we can start from the singular value decomposition,

$$A = U\Sigma V^T$$

where $\Sigma$ is an $m \times n$ matrix with zero entry values except the first $r$ row diagonal entries, which have nonzero values denoted by $\sigma_1, \sigma_2, \cdots, \sigma_r$. It is easy to find the inverses for $U$ and $V$ as they are orthonormal. So we only need to find the pseudoinverse for $\Sigma$. The best we can get to an inverse for $\Sigma$ is an $n \times m$ matrix $\Sigma^+$ which has nonzero elements $\sigma_1, \sigma_2, \cdots, \sigma_r$ along the diagonal in the first $r$ rows. The pseudoinverse for $A$ is

$$A^+ = (U\Sigma V^T)^+ = (V^T)^{-1}\Sigma^+U^{-1} = V\Sigma^+U^T$$

as $U$ and $V$ are orthogonal matrices and thus $U^{-1} = U^T$ and $V^{-1} = V^T$.

# 15.3 Discrete Data Sets

In science and engineering, we often encounter problems involving a large set of data. We would like to know whether the data set could be characterized by a few parameters and whether there are any correlations among the data. These can be analyzed using tools of discrete probability theory, which is a branch of statistics and deals with events that occur in countable sample spaces.

## 15.3.1  Standard Deviation

Standard deviation of a data set shows the degree of variation (or dispersion) from the average (mean, or expected value) of the data. A low standard deviation indicates that the data points tend to cluster near the mean, whereas a high standard deviation indicates that the data spread out over a wide range of values.

Consider a set of data samples $X$ with $n$ elements:

$$X = \{x_1, x_2, \cdots, x_n\} \tag{15.27}$$

The mean (average) $\mu$ of $X$ is given by

$$\mu = \frac{1}{n}\sum_{i=1}^{n} x_i = \frac{1}{n}(x_1 + x_2 + \cdots + x_n) \tag{15.28}$$

The standard deviation $s$ of the data set is defined as

$$s = \sqrt{\frac{1}{n-1}\sum_{i=1}^{n}(x_i - \mu)^2} \tag{15.29}$$

The value $var(X) = s^2$ is referred to as the *variance*. Note that the denominator in (15.29) is $n-1$ rather than $n$. People found that using $n-1$ in the formula of finding the standard deviation of a data sample set gives results closer to our intuition of of the dispersion of the data. However, if one calculates the standard deviation of the whole population of the data, one should use $n$ in the denominator of the formula and the mean is usually denoted as $\sigma$:

$$\sigma = \sqrt{\frac{1}{n}\sum_{i=1}^{n}(x_i - \mu)^2} \tag{15.30}$$

and the variance is $\sigma^2$.

## 15.3.2  Covariance and Correlation

Standard deviation is useful for analyzing data sets that are 'one dimensional' such as the heights or the ages of individuals of a nation. In many situations, we want to look at the correlation between two 'one dimensional' data sets such as the relation between cancer rate and the body weights of individuals. Covariance provides a good measure of this kind of correlation.

Consider two sample data sets, $X$ and $Y$. The size of each set is $n$:

$$X = \{x_1, x_2, \cdots, x_n\}$$
$$Y = \{y_1, y_2, \cdots, y_n\}$$

Suppose $\mu_X$ and $\mu_Y$ are the means of $X$ and $Y$ respectively. We can define the covariance for these two sample data sets as

$$cov(X,Y) = \frac{1}{n-1}\sum_{i=1}^{n}(x_i - \mu_X)(y_i - \mu_Y) \tag{15.31}$$

Note that if $X = Y$, the covariance is reduced to the variance. Also, $cov(X,Y) = cov(Y,X)$.

Another quantity that closely relates to covariance is *correlation*. Suppose we consider the two data sets $X'$, and $Y'$ obtained by subtracting the means $\mu_X$ and $\mu_Y$ from the elements of $X$ and $Y$ respectively so that their means are 0. We can imagine that $X'$ and $Y'$ represent two vectors, $\mathbf{X}$ and $\mathbf{Y}$. The correlation between these two vectors is the cosine of the 'angle' $\theta$ between these two vectors:

$$cor(X,Y) = \cos\theta = \frac{\mathbf{X} \cdot \mathbf{Y}}{||\mathbf{X}||\,||\mathbf{Y}||} \tag{15.32}$$

where $||\mathbf{X}||$, and $||\mathbf{Y}||$ are the norms (magnitudes) of the vectors, and

$$\mathbf{X} \cdot \mathbf{Y} = \sum_{i=1}^{n} x_i y_i$$

If $\cos \theta = 1$, the two vectors are 'pointing in the same direction', which means that the two data sets are perfectly correlated. If $\cos \theta = 0$, the two vectors are perpendicular, meaning that they are totally uncorrelated. Equation (15.32) can be expressed in the statistical form:

$$cor(X, Y) = \frac{\sum_{i=1}^{n}(x_i - \mu_X)(y_i - \mu_Y)}{(n-1)s_X s_Y} \tag{15.33}$$

where $s_X$ and $s_Y$ are the standard deviations of $X$ and $Y$ respectively.

### 15.3.3 Correlation and Covariance Matrices

Covariance is a measure for two one-dimensional data sets. (Unless otherwise stated, in this section we refer to a set of data as a one-dimensional data set.) If we have more than two data sets, we can calculate the covariance values of different data set pairs and put them in a matrix, which is referred to as a *covariance matrix*. For example, if we have 3 data sets, $X, Y$, and $Z$, we could calculate $cov(X, Y)$, $cov(Y, Z)$, $cov(Z, X)$. For $n$ data sets, there are $\binom{n}{2}$ covariance values. Another statistical quantity that closely relates to covariance matrix is the *correlation matrix*.

Let us consider a simple example to illustrate these concepts. Suppose we want to find out how closely blood sugar and cholesterol levels for a group of obese kids correlate with body weights. The data measured in relative units are shown in Table 15-1 below.

**Table 15-1** Health Data of Kids

| Person | Weight $X = (x_i)$ | Cholesterol $Y = (y_i)$ | Blood Sugar $Z = (z_i)$ |
|:------:|:------------------:|:-----------------------:|:-----------------------:|
| P1 | 198 | 200 | 196 |
| P2 | 160 | 165 | 165 |
| P3 | 158 | 158 | 133 |
| P4 | 150 | 165 | 91 |
| P5 | 175 | 182 | 151 |
| P6 | 134 | 135 | 101 |
| P7 | 152 | 136 | 80 |
| Mean | $\mu_X = 161$ | $\mu_Y = 163$ | $\mu_Z = 131$ |

We would like to measure obesity compared between each set of blood sugar level data or cholesterol level. We compute the deviations of each set of data from the means, and put the values in a matrix:

$$D = \begin{pmatrix} 37 & 37 & 65 \\ -1 & 2 & 34 \\ -3 & -5 & 2 \\ -11 & 2 & -40 \\ 14 & 19 & 20 \\ -27 & -28 & -30 \\ -9 & -27 & -51 \end{pmatrix} \tag{15.34}$$

The column vectors of $D$ represent the deviations from the mean for each of the three sets of data. The mean for each column vector of $D$ is 0; the first column represents $(x_i - \mu_X)$, the second column is $(y_i - \mu_Y)$, and the third column is $(z_i - \mu_Z)$. We can now easily calculate the covariance between two data sets. For example, $cov(X,Y)$, the covariance of $X$ and $Y$ is the dot product of the first two column vectors divided by $n$    1, $n$ being the number of rows. The square of the first column vector is essentially the variance of $X$, which is equal to $cov(X,X)$. The covariance matrix $C$ of this problem is a matrix in the form:

$$C = \begin{pmatrix} cov(X,X) & cov(X,Y) & cov(X,Z) \\ cov(Y,X) & cov(Y,Y) & cov(Y,Z) \\ cov(Z,X) & cov(Z,Y) & cov(Z,Z) \end{pmatrix} \tag{15.35}$$

From the definition of covariance of (15.31) and the properties of matrix multiplication, we can express the covariance matrix as

$$C = \frac{1}{n-1} D^T D \tag{15.36}$$

Evaluating all the covariance values using the data of (15.34), we obtain the covariance matrix:

$$C = \frac{1}{6} \begin{pmatrix} 37 & -1 & -3 & -11 & 14 & -27 & -9 \\ 37 & 2 & -5 & 2 & 19 & -28 & -27 \\ 65 & 34 & 2 & -40 & 20 & -30 & -51 \end{pmatrix} \begin{pmatrix} 37 & 37 & 65 \\ -1 & 2 & 34 \\ -3 & -5 & 2 \\ -11 & 2 & -40 \\ 14 & 19 & 20 \\ -27 & -28 & -30 \\ -9 & -27 & -51 \end{pmatrix}$$

$$= \begin{pmatrix} 417.7 & 437.5 & 725.7 \\ 437.5 & 546.0 & 830.0 \\ 725.7 & 830.0 & 1814.3 \end{pmatrix}$$

$$\tag{15.37}$$

The diagonal entries of $C$ are the variances of the three data sets, $X$, $Y$, and $Z$. The off-diagonal entries are the covariances.

We can also calculate the corresponding correlation matrix $R = (r_{ij})$ from $D$. Suppose $d_i$ is the $i$-th column vector of $D$. From (15.31) or (15.32), the $(i, j)$-th entry of $R$ is given by

$$r_{ij} = \frac{\mathbf{d_i} \cdot \mathbf{d_j}}{||\mathbf{d_i}|| \, ||\mathbf{d_j}||} \quad i, j = 1, 2, 3 \tag{15.38}$$

In this example,

$$R = \begin{pmatrix} 1.000 & 0.916 & 0.834 \\ 0.916 & 1.000 & 0.834 \\ 0.834 & 0.834 & 1.000 \end{pmatrix} \tag{15.39}$$

The three sets of data in our example are all positively correlated, because all entries in $R$ are positive. This means that obesity, cholesterol level and blood sugar level of a kid are all correlated. A value of 0 would mean that the vectors are orthogonal and are uncorrelated. A negative value would mean that the two data sets are negatively correlated. In image and speech problems, the data are usually highly correlated. Note that both $C$ and $R$ are symmetric.

In this example, we have considered three sample data sets $X$, $Y$, and $Z$. Each of them can be regarded a 1-dimensional data set. We can also group the data together to form one data set, say $S$. This newly formed data set $S$, consisting of $X$, $Y$, and $Z$, is 3-dimensional. If there is strong correlation between $X$, $Y$, and $Z$, we may be able to predict one from the other, and the dimension of the data set $S$ can be reduced.

## 15.4 Eigenvectors and Eigenvalues

To understand eigenvectors, we first consider operations in 2D Euclidean space. A transformation is represented by a $2 \times 2$ matrix and a vector is a $2 \times 1$ matrix. A transformation of a vector can be described by the multiplication of a transformation matrix and the vector, which gives us a new vector. Consider the example,

$$\begin{pmatrix} 1 & 2 \\ 3 & 4 \end{pmatrix} \begin{pmatrix} 1 \\ 1 \end{pmatrix} = \begin{pmatrix} 3 \\ 7 \end{pmatrix} \tag{15.40}$$

In this example, like most transformations, we cannot express the resulted vector $\begin{pmatrix} 3 \\ 7 \end{pmatrix}$, as a scalar multiple of the original vector $\begin{pmatrix} 1 \\ 1 \end{pmatrix}$.

Now consider another example with a $2 \times 2$ transformation matrix $A$ and a $2 \times 1$ vector $\mathbf{v}$:

$$A\mathbf{v} = \begin{pmatrix} 7 & 2 \\ 3 & 8 \end{pmatrix} \begin{pmatrix} -1 \\ 1 \end{pmatrix} = \begin{pmatrix} -5 \\ 5 \end{pmatrix} = 5 \begin{pmatrix} -1 \\ 1 \end{pmatrix} \tag{15.41}$$

In this example, the resulted vector $\begin{pmatrix} -5 \\ 5 \end{pmatrix}$ can be expressed as 5 times the original vector

$\mathbf{v} = \begin{pmatrix} -1 \\ 1 \end{pmatrix}$. This means that the transformed vector $A\mathbf{v}$ points in the same direction as the original vector $\mathbf{v}$. The vector $\mathbf{v}$ (and any scalar multiple of it, $\lambda\mathbf{v}$) is an *eigenvector* of the transformation matrix $A$; the scalar multiple $\lambda$ is an *eigenvalue* of the transformation. We can formally define these quantities as follow.

> Suppose $A$ is an $n \times n$ matrix. We call a scalar $\lambda$ an *eigenvalue* or a *characteristic value* of $A$ if there exists a nonzero vector $\mathbf{v}$ such that $A\mathbf{v} = \lambda\mathbf{v}$. We call the vector $\mathbf{v}$ an *eigenvector* or a *characteristic vector* belonging to $\lambda$.

The equation $A\mathbf{v} = \lambda\mathbf{v}$ can be expressed in the form

$$(A - \lambda I)\mathbf{v} - \mathbf{0} \tag{15.42}$$

where $\mathbf{0}$ is the zero vector whose entries are all equal to zero. Therefore, $\lambda$ is an eigenvalue of $A$ if and only if (15.42) has a nontrivial solution, which is true if and only if $A - \lambda I$ is singular (otherwise we can multiply (15.42) by the inverse and get $\mathbf{v} = \mathbf{0}$), or equivalently, its determinant is zero:

$$|A - \lambda I| = 0 \tag{15.43}$$

If we expand $|A - \lambda I|$, we obtain an $n$th degree polynomial in $\lambda$:

$$p(\lambda) = |A - \lambda I| = c_0 + c_1\lambda + \cdots + c_n\lambda^n \tag{15.44}$$

We call this polynomial the *characteristic polynomial*, and equation (15.43) the *characteristic equation*, for the matrix $A$. The eigenvalues of $A$ are the roots of the characteristic equation. An *eigenspace* of $A$ is the set of all eigenvectors with the same eigenvalue, together with the zero vector.

Here is a summary of the properties of eigenvectors and eigenvalues:

1. Eigenvectors can only be found for square matrices.
2. Not every square matrix has eigenvectors.
3. Given an $n \times n$ matrix that does have eigenvectors, there are $n$ of them; some of the eigenvalues may be complex numbers. So a $3 \times 3$ matrix has 3 eigenvectors.
4. The eigenvectors of a symmetric matrix (i.e. $A - A^T$) are 'perpendicular' to each other. That is, they are at right angles to each other. The mathematical term for 'perpendicular' is *orthogonal*.
5. People are more interested to find eigenvectors with unit lengths. The unit eigenvectors of a symmetric matrix may form an orthonormal basis of a coordinate system.

## Example 15.1

Find the eigenvalues and corresponding eigenvectors of the matrix

$$A = \begin{pmatrix} 4 & 3 \\ -2 & -1 \end{pmatrix}$$

## Solution

The characteristic equation is

$$\begin{vmatrix} 4-\lambda & 3 \\ -2 & -1-\lambda \end{vmatrix} = 0 \quad \text{or} \quad \lambda^2 - 3\lambda + 2 = 0 \tag{15.45}$$

The eigenvalues of $A$ are the roots of equation (15.45), which are $\lambda_1 = 1$ and $\lambda_2 = 2$. To find the eigenvector belonging to $\lambda_1 = 1$, we need to solve for $\mathbf{v}$ of equation (15.42). That is,

$$(A - \lambda_1 I)\mathbf{v} = \mathbf{0} \quad or \quad \begin{pmatrix} 3 & 3 \\ -2 & -2 \end{pmatrix} \begin{pmatrix} v_1 \\ v_2 \end{pmatrix} = \begin{pmatrix} 0 \\ 0 \end{pmatrix} \tag{15.46}$$

From this, we obtain the duplicate equations:

$$\begin{aligned} 3v_1 + 3v_2 &= 0 \\ -2v_1 - 2v_2 &= 0 \end{aligned} \tag{15.47}$$

which can be reduced to

$$v_1 + v_2 = 0 \tag{15.48}$$

If we let $v_2 = t$, then $v_1 = -t$. Therefore $\mathbf{e_1} = \begin{pmatrix} -1 \\ 1 \end{pmatrix}$ is an eigenvector of $A$ belonging to $\lambda_1 = 1$. Actually, all multiples of $\mathbf{e_1}$ are eigenvectors of $A$ for $\lambda_1$. We can claim that $\mathbf{e_1}$ is the basis of the eigenspace corresponding to $\lambda_1 = 1$. Similarly, with $\lambda_2 = 2$, we have the duplicate equations,

$$\begin{aligned} 2v_1 + 3v_2 &= 0 \\ -2v_1 - 3v_2 &= 0 \end{aligned} \tag{15.49}$$

An eigenvector of $A$ for $\lambda_2$ is $\mathbf{e_2} = \begin{pmatrix} -3 \\ 2 \end{pmatrix}$. The corresponding eigenspace for $\lambda_2 = 2$ is given by the span of $\mathbf{e_2}$.

For matrices with higher dimensions, we can solve for the eigenvectors using Gaussian elimination.

Consider another example, where $A$ is a $3 \times 3$ symmetric matrix:

$$A = \begin{pmatrix} 3 & 2 & 4 \\ 2 & 0 & 2 \\ 4 & 2 & 3 \end{pmatrix}$$

The roots for $|A - \lambda I| = 0$ are $\lambda_1 = -1, \lambda_2 = -1$, and $\lambda_3 = 8$. The corresponding eigenvectors are:

$$\mathbf{v_1} = \begin{pmatrix} 1 \\ -2 \\ 0 \end{pmatrix}, \quad \mathbf{v_2} = \begin{pmatrix} 4 \\ 2 \\ -5 \end{pmatrix}, \quad \mathbf{v_3} = \begin{pmatrix} 2 \\ 1 \\ 2 \end{pmatrix}$$

The eigenvectors $\mathbf{v_1}, \mathbf{v_2}$, and $\mathbf{v_3}$ are **orthogonal** to each other, which is a consequence of the property of a symmetric matrix mentioned above. For example, $\mathbf{v_2} \cdot \mathbf{v_3} = 4 \times 2 + 2 \times 1 + (-5) \times 2 = 0$.

Suppose we express the eigenvectors as row vectors $\mathbf{e_i}$'s and normalize them to unit vectors, i.e., $\mathbf{e_i} = \mathbf{v_i^T}/|\mathbf{v_i}|$. Then we have

$$\mathbf{e_1} = \frac{1}{\sqrt{5}}(1, -2, 0), \quad \mathbf{e_2} = \frac{1}{3\sqrt{5}}(4, 2, -5), \quad \mathbf{e_3} = \tfrac{1}{3}(2, 1, 2)$$

which form an orhtonormal basis (i.e., $\mathbf{e_i} \cdot \mathbf{e_j} = \delta_{ij}$). We can form an orthogonal matrix (see definition above) $P$ using the basis vectors:

$$P = \begin{pmatrix} \mathbf{e_1} \\ \mathbf{e_2} \\ \mathbf{e_3} \end{pmatrix} = \frac{1}{3\sqrt{5}} \begin{pmatrix} 3 & -6 & 0 \\ 4 & 2 & -5 \\ 2\sqrt{5} & \sqrt{5} & 2\sqrt{5} \end{pmatrix} = \begin{pmatrix} 0.45 & -0.89 & 0.00 \\ 0.60 & 0.30 & -0.75 \\ 0.67 & 0.33 & 0.67 \end{pmatrix}$$

As $P$ is an orthogonal matrix, its inverse is given by its transpose:

$$P^{-1} = P^T = \begin{pmatrix} 0.45 & 0.60 & 0.67 \\ -0.89 & 0.30 & 0.33 \\ 0.00 & -0.75 & 0.67 \end{pmatrix}$$

We will see in the next section that $P$ can be viewed as a projection matrix. If $B$ is a $3 \times n$ matrix, the operation $PB$ is to 'project' the $n$ column vectors of $B$ onto the new orthonormal basis, $\mathbf{e_1}, \mathbf{e_2}$, and $\mathbf{e_3}$.

One can regard that such an operation is a rotation of a 3D coordinate system. The oper ation of $P^{-1}$ is to rotate the coordinate system to the new basis. Imagine that a solid object consists of $n$ vertices and their original coordinates are given by the column vectors of $B$. The values of vertices in the rotated coordinate system are given by the columns of $PB$. Figure 15-3 below shows the original basis $(\mathbf{x}, \mathbf{y}, \mathbf{z})$, the new basis $(\mathbf{e_1}, \mathbf{e_2}, \mathbf{e_3})$ and the 8 vertices of a cube centered at the origin with length 0.2. By applying appropriate rotations about the axes $\mathbf{x}, \mathbf{y}$, and $\mathbf{z}$, we can rotate $(\mathbf{x}, \mathbf{y}, \mathbf{z})$ onto $(\mathbf{e_1}, \mathbf{e_2}, \mathbf{e_3})$. The columns of matrix $B$, which is now $3 \times 8$, are the coordinates of the 8 cube vertices:

$$B = \begin{pmatrix} -0.1 & 0.1 & 0.1 & -0.1 & 0.1 & 0.1 & -0.1 & -0.1 \\ -0.1 & -0.1 & 0.1 & 0.1 & -0.1 & 0.1 & 0.1 & -0.1 \\ 0.1 & 0.1 & 0.1 & 0.1 & -0.1 & -0.1 & -0.1 & -0.1 \end{pmatrix}$$

Each column of the matrix product $PB$ represents a vertex of the cube in the new coordinate system. Another interpretation of $PB$ is that we rotate the cube and the $PB$ columns are the vertex values of the rotated cube in the original coordinate system. This is shown in Figure 15-4. The rotated cube vertices are given by:

$$B' = PB = \begin{pmatrix} 0.05 & 0.13 & -0.05 & -0.13 & 0.13 & -0.05 & -0.13 & 0.05 \\ -0.16 & -0.05 & 0.02 & -0.10 & 0.10 & 0.16 & 0.05 & -0.02 \\ -0.03 & 0.10 & 0.17 & 0.03 & -0.03 & 0.03 & -0.10 & -0.17 \end{pmatrix}$$

Each column is a vertex.

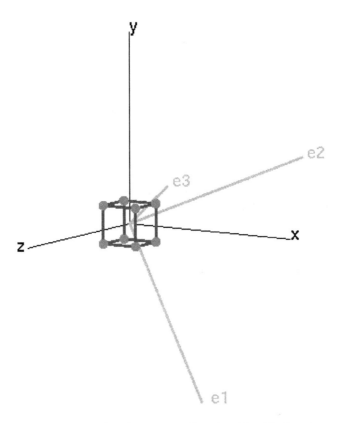

**Figure 15-3**  Eigenvectors Forming New Basis

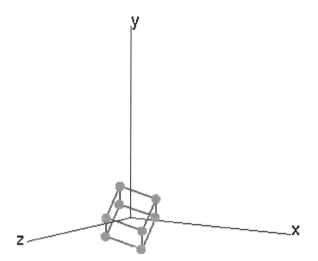

**Figure 15-4**  Rotated Cube with Vertex Values Given by $PB$

# 15.5 Principal Component Analysis

Principal Component Analysis (PCA) was invented by Karl Pearson in 1901, and was later popularized by Harold Hotelling.  PCA is a useful tool for analyzing high dimension data sets. It is effective for pattern search, dimensionality reduction, lossy data compression, feature extraction, and data visualization. Actually, PCA is a simple case of the eigenvector-based multivariate analysis. It also closely relates to factor analysis, which is a statistical method useful for reducing the number of variables in gathering data.

The goal of PCA is to identify the most meaningful basis to re-express a data set, hoping that the new basis will filter out the noise and reveal hidden structures. The technique uses an orthogonal transformation to convert a multi-dimension data set to a set of values of linearly uncorrelated variables called *principal components*. The number of principal components is less than or equal to the dimension of the original data set. We setup the transformation in such a way that the first principal component has the largest possible variance and each succeeding component is orthogonal to (i.e. uncorrelated with) the preceding components and in turn has the largest subsequent variance. In the process, we want to answer the question: *Can we find another basis, which can be expressed as a linear combination of the original basis, that best re-expresses our data set?*

Suppose $A$ is the original data set arranged as an $m \times n$ matrix. Suppose $P$ is an $m \times m$ matrix that transforms $A$ to another $m \times n$ matrix $B$. That is,

$$PA = B \qquad (15.50)$$

Suppose $a_i$ and $b_i$ are the $i$-th **column** vectors of $A$ and $B$, and $p_i$ is $i$-th **row** vector of $P$. We can interpret $\{p_1, \cdots, p_m\}$ as a set of new basis vectors for expressing the column vectors of

*A*:

$$PA = \begin{pmatrix} \mathbf{p_1} \\ \cdot \\ \cdot \\ \cdot \\ \mathbf{p_m} \end{pmatrix} \begin{pmatrix} \mathbf{a_1}, & \cdots, & \mathbf{a_n} \end{pmatrix} = \begin{pmatrix} \mathbf{p_1} \cdot \mathbf{a_1}, & \cdots, & \mathbf{p_n} \cdot \mathbf{a_n}, \\ \cdot & \cdots & \cdot \\ \cdot & & \cdot \\ \cdot & \cdots & \cdot \\ \mathbf{p_m} \cdot \mathbf{a_1}, & \cdots, & \mathbf{p_m} \cdot \mathbf{a_n}, \end{pmatrix} = B$$

(15.51)

We can see that a column vector $\mathbf{b_i}$ of $B$ has the form:

$$\mathbf{b_i} = \begin{pmatrix} \mathbf{p_1} \cdot \mathbf{a_i} \\ \cdot \\ \cdot \\ \mathbf{p_m} \cdot \mathbf{a_i} \end{pmatrix}$$

(15.52)

We recognize that each component of the vector $\mathbf{b_i}$ is a dot-product of $\mathbf{a_i}$ with the corresponding row in $P$. In another perspective, the $k$-th component of $\mathbf{b_i}$ is a projection on to the $k$-th row of $P$. We can therefore interpret the rows of $P$ as a new set of basis vectors for representing the column vectors of $A$. This concept has been illustrated in the example of the previous section. The row vectors $\mathbf{p_i}$'s become the *principal components* of $A$. The question that remains is how to make a good choice of $P$ to best re-express $A$? In a 2 variable case, we may use the least-square fitting method to find the line that best-fits the data. *How do we quantify and generalize these notions to arbitrarily higher dimensions?* The PCA technique makes use of covariance matrix and eigenvectors to address this question. The PCA technique is discussed below. We only present the steps of using PCA to find the best basis but we omit the proofs of some statements we claim to be true based on some simple examples.

### 15.5.1  PCA Procedures

**Calculate the Deviation Matrix**

The first step of the PCA procedures is to subtract the mean from the data for each of the data dimensions. Suppose we use the 3 dimensional health data for a group of kids of Table 15-1 above as example. After the subtraction, we obtain the deviation matrix $D$ of equation (15.34). The new mean for each column vector (data of each dimension) of $D$ is 0.

**Calculate the Covariance Matrix**

The second step is to calculate the covariance matrix, which is given by equation (15.36). (Alternatively, one can use the correlation matrix in the process.) In our example, $m = 3, n = 7$, and the covariance matrix is

$$C = \frac{1}{n-1} D^T D = \begin{pmatrix} 417.7 & 437.5 & 725.7 \\ 437.5 & 546.0 & 830.0 \\ 725.7 & 830.0 & 1814.3 \end{pmatrix}$$

(15.53)

Note that a covariance matrix is always **symmetric** (i.e. $C^T = C$). Therefore, the eigenvectors of a covariance matrix are always **orthogonal**.

### Calculate Eigenvectors

The next step is to calculate the eigenvalues and eigenvectors of the covariance matrix. We have discussed in the previous section how to find eigenvalues and eigenvectors of low-rank matrices. For the symmetric covariance matrix $C$ of (15.53), the eigenvalues are:

$$\lambda_1 = 39.57, \quad \lambda_2 = 180.29, \quad \lambda_3 = 2558.14$$

The corresponding normalized eigenvectors are:

$$\mathbf{e_1} = (0.770, \quad -0.638, \quad -0.016)$$
$$\mathbf{e_2} = (0.522, \quad 0.644, \quad -0.559) \tag{15.54}$$
$$\mathbf{e_3} = (0.367, \quad 0.422, \quad 0.829)$$

The eigenvectors of (15.54) have been normalized (i.e. length = 1) and are orthogonal. Therefore, the vectors $\{\mathbf{e_1}, \mathbf{e_2}, \mathbf{e_3}\}$ are orthonormal. The projection matrix $P$ and data matrix $A$ of (15.50) are given by

$$P = \begin{pmatrix} \mathbf{e_1} \\ \mathbf{e_2} \\ \mathbf{e_3} \end{pmatrix} \quad \text{and} \quad A = D^T \tag{15.55}$$

So

$$B = PA = \begin{pmatrix} \mathbf{e_1} \\ \mathbf{e_2} \\ \mathbf{e_3} \end{pmatrix} \begin{pmatrix} \mathbf{a_1}, & \cdots, & \mathbf{a_7} \end{pmatrix} \tag{15.56}$$

The square projection matrix of (15.55) is composed of unit row vectors which are orthogonal to each other. Therefore, it is an *orthogonal matrix*. As mentioned above, an important property of an orthogonal matrix is that its inverse is equal to its transpose (i.e. $P^{-1} = P^T$).

Figure 15 5 below shows a plot of the adjusted data (mean subtracted) of $X$, $Y$, and $Z$ of Table 15-1 and the eigenvectors. The axes labeled 1, 2, and 3 correspond to the eigenvectors for eigenvalues $\lambda_1$, $\lambda_2$, and $\lambda_3$ respectively.

From the figure, we see that most data points cluster around the axis of $\lambda_3$, which is the largest eigenvalue. When we project the data onto this axis, we'll get large values. So one should choose this axis to be the principal axis of the new basis. The axis of $\lambda_2$ has the second largest eigenvalue and it has less data points cluster around it. The axis of $\lambda_1$ has a much smaller eigenvalue and there is hardly any data point cluster around it. When we project the data onto this axis, we get values close to zero. From this simple example, we can see that the larger the eigenvalue, the more important the corresponding eigenvector is and the ones with the largest eigenvalues should be chosen as the principal components. It turns out that one can prove that this is generally true. The eigenvectors of the highest eigenvalues are the principal components of the data set.

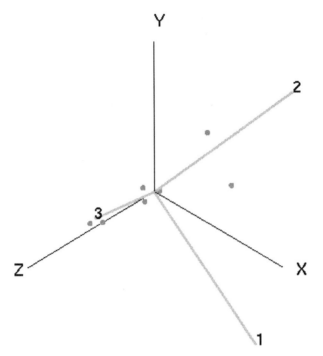

**Figure 15-5**   A Plot of Data of $D$ of (15.34) and the Eigenvectors

## Choosing Components

In general, once eigenvectors have been found from the covariance matrix, we order them according to their eigenvalues, from highest to lowest. This gives us the components in order of significance. At this point, if necessary we can discard the components of lesser significance, which may result in loss of some information, but if the eigenvalues are small, the loss is not significant. If we discard some components, the final data set is of lower dimension as compared to the original one. (As a consequence, PCA can be used in lossy data compression.) We obtain a lower dimension projection matrix by keeping the remaining eigenvectors. In our example, we can form a matrix $F$, for example, by throwing away $e_1$ and keeping only $e_2$ and $e_3$:

$$ F = \left( \begin{array}{c} e_3 \\ e_2 \end{array} \right) $$

Each vector $e_i$ of $F$ is sometimes called a feature vector because it is chosen to represent some characteristics or attributes of the original data set while still only partially describing it.

## Deriving New Data Set

A new data set with reduced dimension is obtained by projecting the original data onto the principal axes. This is achieved by multiplying the feature vector matrix $F$ by the matrix $A$

that contains the deviation data $(A = D^T)$. Suppose the new data matrix is $B$, then

$$B - FA \; - \; \begin{pmatrix} 0.367 & 0.422 & 0.829 \\ 0.522 & 0.644 & -0.559 \end{pmatrix} \begin{pmatrix} 37 & -1 & -3 & -11 & 14 & -27 & -9 \\ 37 & 2 & -5 & 2 & 19 & -28 & -27 \\ 65 & 34 & 2 & -40 & 20 & -30 & -51 \end{pmatrix}$$

$$= \begin{pmatrix} 83.078 & 28.663 & -1.553 & -36.353 & 29.736 & -46.595 & -56.976 \\ 6.807 & -18.240 & -5.904 & 17.906 & 8.364 & -15.356 & 6.423 \end{pmatrix}$$

$$(15.57)$$

The projection of (15.57) basically transforms our data so that they are expressed in terms of the lines where data tend to cluster around them.

**Recovering Data Set**

The transformation of (15.57) is a lossy transformation as we have thrown away one eigen-vector. We cannot recover the exact original data from the transformed data. On the other hand, the transformation using $P$ of (15.55) is lossless and reversible. If $B = PA$, then $A = P^{-1}B$. Since $P$ is an orthogonal matrix, $P^{-1} = P^T$. So

$$A = P^T B \qquad (15.58)$$

We can use this equation to recover the exact data transformed by $P$. However, if we have thrown away some components and the feature matrix $F$ of (15.57) is not the same as the projection matrix $P$, we cannot recover the exact data. Also, in this case $F$ is not a square matrix and does not have an inverse. Of course, the 'recovered' data will not be identical to that of the original set.

Without going into details of proving, we claim that the 'recovered' data can be approximated by $F^T B$. In this example, $F$ is $2 \times 3$. So $F^T$ is $3 \times 2$ and the 'recovered' data set is

$$A' = F^T B = \begin{pmatrix} \mathbf{e_3^T}, \mathbf{e_2^T} \end{pmatrix} B$$

$$= \begin{pmatrix} 0.367 & 0.522 \\ 0.422 & 0.644 \\ 0.829 & -0.559 \end{pmatrix} \begin{pmatrix} 83.08 & 28.66 & -1.55 & -36.35 & 29.74 & -46.60 & -56.96 \\ 6.80 & -18.24 & -5.904 & 17.91 & 8.36 & -15.36 & 6.42 \end{pmatrix}$$

$$= \begin{pmatrix} 34.81 & 1.00 & -3.65 & -3.99 & 16.05 & -25.12 & -17.56 \\ 38.80 & 0.35 & -4.46 & -3.81 & 17.30 & -29.55 & -19.91 \\ 65.05 & 33.96 & 2.01 & -40.15 & 19.96 & -30.04 & -50.82 \end{pmatrix}$$

$$(15.59)$$

Figure 15-6 shows a plot of the recovered data of (15.59) along with the original data and eigenvectors of Figure 15-5; the recovered data points are shown as black square dots. The recovered data here are the deviation data. If we want to get back the very original data of Table 15-1, we need to add the means $\mu_X, \mu_Y$, and $\mu_Z$ accordingly to the recovered data of (15.59).

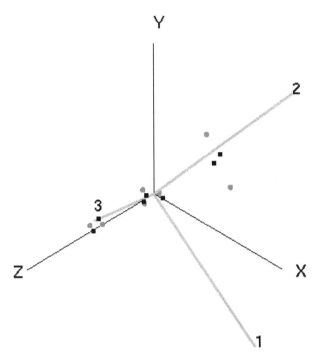

**Figure 15-6**  Recovered Data of Figure 15-5

## 15.6 Eigenvectors by Jacobi Method

We have discussed how to find egeinvalues and eigenvectors of a square matrix by solving a characteristic equation. This method works well for low-rank matrices as illustrated in the examples of section 15.4. However, for a large data set that involves large-size matrices, it is impractical to find eignevectors by solving characteristic equations. Instead, numerical methods are employed to find the eigenvectors and eigenvalues. There are a few popular numerical methods that can be used to give a general solution to the problem. However, here we are not interested in the general solutions of finding eigenvectors of a square matrix. We are interested in the problem of finding eigenvectors of a **symmetric** matrix as a covariance matrix is always symmetric. The solution to such a problem is a lot simpler as compared to solving the general problem. Again various numerical methods exist. The one that we will discuss is called the *Jacobi Method*, which diagonalizes a square symmetric matrix to obtain eigenvalues and eigenvectors.

We have discussed that a symmetric matrix is diagonalizable. Finding eigenvalues and eigenvectors of a diagonal matrix is trivial. For example, if $A$ is a $3 \times 3$ diagonal matrix, it is in the form

$$
A = \begin{pmatrix} a_{11} & 0 & 0 \\ 0 & a_{22} & 0 \\ 0 & 0 & a_{33} \end{pmatrix}
\tag{15.60}
$$

The eigenvalues of this matrix are $\lambda_1 = a_{11}, \lambda_2 = a_{22}$, and $\lambda_3 = a_{33}$, and the eigenvectors are

$$\mathbf{e_1} = \begin{pmatrix} 1 \\ 0 \\ 0 \end{pmatrix}, \quad \mathbf{e_2} = \begin{pmatrix} 0 \\ 1 \\ 0 \end{pmatrix}, \quad \mathbf{e_3} = \begin{pmatrix} 0 \\ 0 \\ 1 \end{pmatrix} \qquad (15.61)$$

The eigenvectors obviously form an orthonormal basis. Note that here we express eigenvectors as column vectors rather than row vectors as we did in the previous section.

The idea of the Jacobi method is to transform iteratively a symmetric matrix $A$ to a diagonal form through a sequence of 'rotations', which transform the original basis to the orthonormal basis formed by the eigenvectors of $A$. This concept can be visualized using an example of a 2D matrix as shown in Figure 15-7 below.

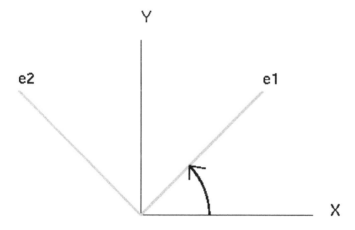

**Figure 15-7**   Rotating Orthonormal X-Y Basis to Orthonormal e1-e2 Basis

The 'rotations' are elementary orthogonal transformations that are often called *Jacobi rotations*, and have the form

$$U(p, q, \phi) = \begin{pmatrix} 1 & 0 & \cdots & & & \cdot & 0 \\ 0 & 1 & 0 \cdot\cdot & & \cdot & & \cdot & 0 \\ \cdot & \cdot & \cdot & \cdot & & & \cdot & \cdot \\ \cdot & \cdot & \cos\phi & & \sin\phi \cdot\cdot & \cdot & 0 \\ \cdot & \cdot & & 1 & & & \cdot & \cdot \\ \cdot & \cdot & -\sin\phi & & \cos\phi\cdot\cdot & \cdot & 0 \\ \cdot & \cdot & \cdot & \cdot & & & \cdot & \cdot \\ 0 & 0 & \cdots & & \cdot & & \cdot & 1 \end{pmatrix} \qquad (15.62)$$

The diagonal elements of $U(p, q, \phi) = (u_{ij})$ are all 1 except the two elements at rows and columns $p$ and $q$, which are equal to $\cos\phi$ (i.e. $u_{pp} = u_{qq} = \cos\phi$). All off-diagonal elements are 0 except $u_{pq} = \sin\phi$, and $u_{qp} = -\sin\phi$. Obviously, this matrix is orthogonal as $\sin^2\phi + \cos^2\phi = 1$.

Starting with a symmetric matrix $A_0$, in the $k$-th step of Jacobi rotations, a rotation matrix $U_k = U_k(p, q, \phi)$ of the form (15.62) is used to transform the matrix $A_k$ to $A_{k+1}$:

$$A_{k+1} = U_k^T A_k U_k \qquad (15.63)$$

The composite Jacobi rotations approximate the operation

$$A \to D = V^T A V \qquad (15.64)$$

where $D$ is a diagonal matrix and $V$ is orthogonal, $D$ being the limit of $A_k$ when $k \to \infty$; the matrix $V$ is the product of all Jacobi rotations:

$$V = U_0 U_1 U_2 \cdots \qquad (15.65)$$

Suppose we let $A = A_k$, $A' = A_{k+1}$, and $U = U_k(p, q, \phi)$. We can then express (15.63) as

$$A' = U^T A U \qquad (15.66)$$

The operation $U^T A$ only changes rows $p$ and $q$ of $A$, while $AU$ only changes columns $p$ and $q$. Therefore, only the elements of rows $p$ and $q$, and columns of $p$ and $q$ of $A$ will be changed in (15.66). The new matrix $A'$ is of the form

$$A' = \begin{pmatrix}
a_{11} & \cdots & a'_{1p} & \cdots & a'_{1q} & \cdots & a_{1n} \\
\cdot & \cdot & \cdot & \cdot & \cdot & \cdot & \cdot \\
\cdot & \cdot & \cdot & \cdot & \cdot & \cdot & \cdot \\
a'_{p1} & \cdots & a'_{pp} & \cdots & a'_{pq} & \cdots & a'_{pn} \\
\cdot & \cdot & \cdot & \cdot & \cdot & \cdot & \cdot \\
a'_{q1} & \cdots & a'_{qp} & \cdots & a'_{qq} & \cdots & a'_{qn} \\
\cdot & \cdot & \cdot & \cdot & \cdot & \cdot & \cdot \\
\cdot & \cdot & \cdot & \cdot & \cdot & \cdot & \cdot \\
a_{n1} & \cdots & a'_{np} & \cdots & a'_{nq} & \cdots & a_{nn}
\end{pmatrix} \qquad (15.67)$$

Multiplying out (15.66) and using the special form of $U$, we obtain the explicit formulas for the elements of $A'$:

$$a'_{rp} = a_{rp}\cos\phi - a_{rq}\sin\phi \qquad\qquad r \neq p, r \neq q \qquad (15.68a)$$

$$a'_{rq} = a_{rq}\cos\phi + a_{rp}\sin\phi \qquad\qquad r \neq p, r \neq q \qquad (15.68b)$$

$$a'_{pp} = a_{pp}\cos^2\phi + a_{qq}\sin^2\phi - 2a_{pq}\sin\phi\cos\phi \qquad (15.68c)$$

$$a'_{qq} = a_{pp}\sin^2\phi + a_{qq}\cos^2\phi + 2a_{pq}\sin\phi\cos\phi \qquad (15.68d)$$

$$a'_{pq} = a_{pq}(\cos^2\phi - \sin^2\phi) + (a_{pp} - a_{qq})\sin\phi\cos\phi \qquad (15.68e)$$

The idea of the Jacobi method is to make the off-diagonal elements of $A$ to become 0 through rotations. That is, we want the term $a'_{pq}$ in (15.68e) to be 0. As a consequence, we obtain the equation

$$0 = a_{pq}\cos 2\phi + (a_{pp} - a_{qq})\frac{1}{2}\sin 2\phi \qquad (15.69)$$

from which we can solve for the rotation angle $\phi$:

$$\cot 2\phi = \frac{\cos 2\phi}{\sin 2\phi} = \frac{a_{qq} - a_{pp}}{2a_{pq}} \qquad (15.70)$$

where we have used the trigonometric identities $\cos 2\phi = \cos^2\phi - \sin^2\phi$, and $\sin 2\phi = 2\sin\phi\cos\phi$. We can obtain $\phi$ from $\cot 2\phi$ and calculate other trigonometric quantities in (15.68). However, a simpler way is to solve for $\sin\phi$ and $\cos\phi$ directly from $\cot 2\phi$. If we let $t = \tan\phi$, then

$$\cot 2\phi = \frac{\cos 2\phi}{\sin 2\phi} = \frac{\cos^2\phi - \sin^2\phi}{2\sin\phi\cos\phi} = \frac{1}{2t} - \frac{t}{2} \qquad (15.71)$$

We can rewrite (15.71) as

$$t^2 + 2(\cot 2\phi)t - 1 = 0 \qquad (15.72)$$

The roots of the quadratic equation (15.72) are

$$t = -\cot 2\phi \pm \sqrt{\cot^2 2\phi + 1} \qquad (15.73)$$

We should choose the smaller root which corresponds to a rotation angle less than $\pi/4$ in magnitude. Such a choice at each iteration gives a stable reduction. This can be implemented by the following java code segment:

```
double cot_2phi =   ( A[q][q] - A[p][p] ) / (2 * A[p][q]);
double tan_phi;
double d = Math.sqrt ( cot_2phi * cot_2phi + 1 );
if ( cot_2phi > 0 )
   tan_phi = -cot_2phi + d;
else
   tan_phi = -cot_2phi - d;
```

Other trigonometric quantities in (15.68) can be then obtained from $\tan\phi$. By iterating the equation of (15.63), we eventually obtain a diagonal matrix $D = V^T AV$ as shown in equation (15.64). The diagonal elements of $D$ give the eigenvalues of the original matrix $A$. The column vectors of $V$ are the eigenvectors of $A$ as $AV = D(V^T)^{-1} = DV$. They can be computed by carrying out the same rotation operation as that on matrix $A$ at each iterative stage:

$$V_{k+1} = U_k^T V_k U_k \qquad (15.74)$$

where initially, $V_0$ is the identity matrix.

The following java class, *JacobiCyclic* shown in Listing 15-1 shows a full implementation of this method. The function **eigenVs** of this class takes an $n \times n$ symmetric matrix $A$ as a two dimensional array input. It returns $n$ eigenvalues in the array *evalues*. The function also returns $n$ eigenvectors, each with dimension $n$ in the 2D array *evectors*; each eigenvector is a column vector of the array.

**Program Listing 15-1**:  An Implementation of Finding Eigenvectors by Jacobi Method

---

```
import java.io.*;

class JacobiCyclic {
  private final static double eps = 1.0E-8;
  private static double threshold;
  private static double thresholdNorm;
```

```
    private static double max;

    // calculate eigenvalues and egienvectors
    // returns n eigenvectors as column vectors in evectors[][]
    // n eigenvalues are returned in evalues
    static boolean eigenVs (int n, double [][] A,
                            double [] evalues, double [][]  evectors )
    {
      if ( n < 1 ) return false;
      if ( n == 1 ) {
        evalues[0] = A[0][0];
        evectors[0][0] = 1.0;
        return true;
      }
      //start with identity matrix
      for ( int i = 0; i < n; i++ )
        for ( int j = 0; j < n; j++ )
          if ( i == j )
            evectors[i][j] = 1.0;
          else
            evectors[i][j] = 0.0;
      //calculate threshold and thresholdNorm
      threshold = 0.0;
      for ( int i = 0; i < n - 1; i++ )
        for ( int j = i + 1; j < n; j++ )   //consider upper triangle only
          threshold += A[i][j] * A[i][j];
      threshold = Math.sqrt ( threshold + threshold );
      thresholdNorm = threshold * eps;
      max = threshold + 1.0;
      while ( threshold > thresholdNorm ) {
        threshold /= 10.0;
        if (max < threshold) continue;
        max = 0.0;
        for ( int k = 0; k < n - 1; k++ ) {
          for ( int m = k + 1; m < n; m++ ) {
            if ( Math.abs ( A[k][m] ) < threshold ) continue;
            //calculate angle of rotation to make A[k][m] 0
            double cot_2phi =    ( A[k][k] - A[m][m] ) / (2 * A[k][m]);
            double tan_phi;
            double t1, t2, t3;
            double d = Math.sqrt ( cot_2phi * cot_2phi + 1 );
            if ( cot_2phi > 0 )
              tan_phi = -cot_2phi + d;
            else
              tan_phi = -cot_2phi - d;
            double tan2_phi = tan_phi * tan_phi;
            double  sin2_phi = tan2_phi / (1.0 + tan2_phi);
            double  cos2_phi = 1.0 - sin2_phi;
            double  sin_phi = Math.sqrt(sin2_phi);
            if (tan_phi < 0.0) sin_phi = - sin_phi;
            double cos_phi = Math.sqrt(cos2_phi);
            double sin_2phi = 2.0 * sin_phi * cos_phi;
            double cos_2phi = cos2_phi - sin2_phi;
            t1 = A[k][k];
            t2 = A[m][m];
            t3 = A[k][m];
            A[k][k] = t1 * cos2_phi + t2 * sin2_phi + t3 * sin_2phi;
            A[m][m] = t1 * sin2_phi + t2 * cos2_phi - t3 * sin_2phi;
            A[k][m] = A[m][k] = 0;
            for ( int i = 0; i < n; i++ ){
```

```
              if ( i == k  ||  i == m  ) continue;
              if ( i < k )
                t1 = A[i][k];
              else
                t1 = A[k][i];
              if ( i < m )
                t2 = A[i][m];
              else
                t2 = A[m][i];
              t3 = t1 * cos_phi + t2 * sin_phi;
              if ( i < k )
                A[i][k] = t3;
              else
                A[k][i] = t3;
              t3 = - t1 * sin_phi + t2 * cos_phi;
              if ( i < m )
                A[i][m] = t3;
              else
                A[m][i] - t3;
            } //for i

            for ( int i = 0; i < n; i++ ) {
              t1 = evectors[i][k];
              t2 = evectors[i][m];
              evectors[i][k] = t1 * cos_phi + t2 * sin_phi;
              evectors[i][m] = -t1 * sin_phi + t2 * cos_phi;
            }
          } //for m
          for ( int i = 0; i < n; i++ ) {
            if ( i == k ) continue;
            else if ( max < Math.abs ( A[k][i] ) )
              max = Math.abs ( A[k][i] );
          }
        }  // for k
      } //while
      for ( int i = 0; i < n; i++ )
        evalues[i] = A[i][i];

      return true;
    }
}
```

# Chapter 16    Active Shape Models (ASMs)

## 16.1 Introduction

Active shape models (ASMs) are statistical models for image processing and recognition, developed by Tim Cootes and Chris Taylor in the 1990s. ASM closely relates to the active appearance model (AAM), which is also known as a **smart snake** method. The formal name for **snake** model is **active contour model**.

A real-world image often consists of complex objects. Two image objects representing the same real-world object may vary in appearance and shape from one image to another. It is an inherent difficult task to recognize the existence of certain structures in an image. There are a lot of studies and methods of locating known objects in images. The method of using rigid models to represent image objects is well established. However, in many practical situations rigid models are not appropriate because objects of the same class are not identical. For example, in medical applications, the shape of organs may vary significantly through time and between individuals. In many industrial image processing applications, the images may involve assemblies with moving parts, and/or components with varying appearance. In such cases, we have to use flexible models, or deformable templates to allow for some degree of variability in the shape of the imaged objects. One may use trigonometric functions such as *sin* and *cos* to describe shapes. By varying the parameters and the number of terms used in a trigonometric series, one can generate different shapes. However, such methods are not suitable for describing general shapes. For example, using a finite number of terms, we can define a square corner only approximately. There is no clear relationship between variations in shape and variations in the parameters of the trigonometric expansion.

Utilizing models that cope with the variability, ASMs are able to remedy the defects of rigid models and are able to identify complex objects and special features of an image, and find examples of the structures that they represent.

An active shape model makes use of a set of annotated images of typical examples to build a statistical model of appearance. It requires one to first decide upon a suitable set of points (landmarks) to describe the shape of the target; the landmarks should be found reliably on each training image. The set of points representing each object or image structure may represent boundaries, internal features, or even external structures, such as the center of a concave boundary of a region. In the method, one has to manually place the points in the same way on each of a training set of examples of the object. The points that mark significant positions on an image object are usually referred to as *landmarks*. Each landmark point represents a distinguishable point on every example image. For example, when we build a model of the appearance of an eye of a human face image, we could choose the corners of the eye as landmarks as they are easy to identify and mark in an image. Such a requirement constrains the application of the method as the object shapes involve cannot change abruptly from image to image. Therefore, the method is not appropriate for highly amorphous objects such as some types of cells or simple organisms.

In our application, we use a simple OpenGL program to display an image, and use the mouse to click on the desired points, which are captured by the program and saved in a file. The program minimizes the variance in distance between equivalent points by automatically align the sets of points. The principal component analysis (PCA) technique discussed in the previous chapter is used to reduce data redundancy. By analyzing the point distribution, a model is derived to give the average positions of the points and a number of parameters to control the main modes of variation contained in the training sets.

Points at clear corners of object boundaries or 'T' junctions are good choices for landmarks. In practice, to make a good description of the shape of a target object, one needs to choose a large number of landmark points. Moreover, one should augment a landmark list with points along boundaries and these points should be placed equally spaced between well defined landmark points. However, in our examples here, landmarks are created very briefly without the augmented features; the main purpose of the examples is to illustrate some basic techniques and principles of ASM. Figure 16-1 below shows a face image annotated with landmarks.

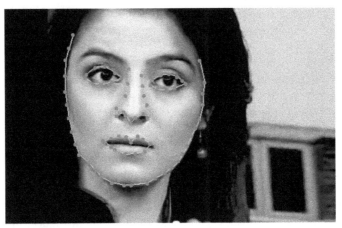

**Figure 16-1**   A Face Image Annotated with Landmarks

## 16.2 Statistical Models

We consider two dimensional images. We label significant points referred to as *landmarks* in images of interest in order to examine and measure shape changes which could be correlated with other factors. The landmarks, which are representative points may capture shape constraints and will be used to build models. We can then use the models to construct plausible new shape examples for use in image interpretation.

We define a point $p_i$ by its $x$-$y$ coordinates:

$$p_i = \begin{pmatrix} x_i \\ y_i \end{pmatrix} \tag{16.1}$$

We define a shape $S$ by a set of $n$ points:

$$S = \{p_1, p_2, \cdots, p_n\} \tag{16.2}$$

Each point in $S$ is usually referred to as a *landmark*, which "marks" a significant position of an image object.

We can form a linear affine combination of points by requiring the sum of the combining coefficients to be equal to 1. That is.

$$p = \alpha_1 p_1 + \alpha_2 p_2 + \cdots + \alpha_n p_n = \begin{pmatrix} \alpha_1 x_1 + \alpha_2 x_2 + \cdots + \alpha_n x_n \\ \alpha_1 y_1 + \alpha_2 y_2 + \cdots + \alpha_n y_n \end{pmatrix} \tag{16.3}$$

is a legitimate point if $\alpha_1 + \alpha_2 + \cdots + \alpha_n = 1$.

Suppose we have $N$ aligned shapes, and each shape $S_k$ is defined by an equation of (16.2); we can calculate the mean shape $\overline{S}$ by

$$\overline{S} = \frac{1}{N} \sum_{k=1}^{N} S_k \tag{16.4}$$

In (16.4), each combining coefficient is $\alpha_k = \frac{1}{N}$. Equation (16.4) means that for each point in the shape, we take the average of $N$ points from $N$ shapes. For example, the $i$-th point, $\overline{p}_i$ of $\overline{S}$ is given by

$$\overline{p}_i = \frac{1}{N} \sum_{k=1}^{N} p_i^k \tag{16.5}$$

where $p_i^k$ is the $i$-th point of the $k$-th shape, $S_k$.

We now consider a shape $S_k$ as one super-point with dimension $2n$. That is,

$$S_k = \left( x_1^k, \cdots, x_n^k, y_1^k, \cdots, y_n^k \right) \tag{16.6}$$

In the forthcoming discussions, when there is no confusion, we may simply refer to a super-point as a point. Therefore, a training set of $N$ shapes is composed of $N$ points in $2n$ dimensions. We can apply a principal component analysis (PCA) to these $N$ points in the usual manner discussed in the previous chapter. Each axis indicates a way that the landmark points tend to move together as the shape changes.

For each super-point (shape) $S_k$ in the training set we can calculate its deviation, $d_k$, from the mean, $\overline{S}$:

$$d_k = S_k - \overline{S} = \left( x_1^k - \overline{x}_1, \cdots, x_n^k - \overline{x}_n, y_1^k - \overline{y}_1, \cdots, y_n^k - \overline{y}_n \right) \tag{16.7}$$

Each $d_k$ is a $1 \times 2n$ row-vector. The deviation matrix $D$ is an $N \times 2n$ matrix given by

$$D = \begin{pmatrix} d_1 \\ d_2 \\ \cdot \\ \cdot \\ d_N \end{pmatrix} \tag{16.8}$$

Though $d_i$ is a row-vector, we can denote $d_{ij}$ as the $ij$-th element of matrix $D$ without confusion. Note that the transpose of $D$, denoted by $D^T$, is a $2n \times N$ matrix.

We can then calculate the $2n \times 2n$ covariance matrix $C$ using (15.36), where the denominator would be $N - 1$, the number of shapes minus 1. However, to be consistent with the calculations used by other authors in the field, we use $N$ in the denominator:

$$C = \frac{1}{N} D^T D \tag{16.9}$$

where $D^T$ is the transpose of $D$ and the $ij$-th element, $c_{ij}$, of $C$ is given by

$$c_{ij} = \frac{1}{N} \sum_{k=1}^{N} d_{ki} d_{kj} \tag{16.10}$$

Matrix $C$ is symmetric and is $2n \times 2n$; it has $2n$ eigenvectors. Following the conventions we have used in Chapter 15, each eigenvector $\mathbf{e_i}$ is a $1 \times 2n$ row vector. The projection matrix $P$ is given by

$$P = \begin{pmatrix} \mathbf{e_1} \\ \cdot \\ \cdot \\ \mathbf{e_{2n}} \end{pmatrix} \tag{16.11}$$

which is a $2n \times 2n$ square matrix. We define a training set $\mathbf{X_k}$ as the transpose of the shape $S_k$. So $\mathbf{X_k}$ is a $2n \times 1$ column vector:

$$\mathbf{X_k} = S_k^T = \begin{pmatrix} x_1^k \\ \cdot \\ \cdot \\ x_n^k \\ y_1^k \\ \cdot \\ \cdot \\ y_n^k \end{pmatrix} \tag{16.12}$$

and the mean of the training sets is $\overline{\mathbf{X}} = \overline{S}^T$. We can name the transpose of the deviation matrix $D$ as $A$, which is a $2n \times N$ matrix:

$$A = D^T = \left( \mathbf{X_1} - \overline{\mathbf{X}}, \cdots, \mathbf{X_N} - \overline{\mathbf{X}} \right) \tag{16.13}$$

As presented in (15.56) of Chapter 15, the projection of $A$ onto the new basis (eigenvectors) is given by:

$$
\begin{aligned}
B = PA &= \begin{pmatrix} \mathbf{e_1} \\ \cdot \\ \cdot \\ \mathbf{e_{2n}} \end{pmatrix} \left( \mathbf{X_1} - \overline{\mathbf{X}}, \cdots, \mathbf{X_N} - \overline{\mathbf{X}} \right) \\
&= \begin{pmatrix} \mathbf{e_1} \cdot (\mathbf{X_1} - \overline{\mathbf{X}}), & \cdots, & \mathbf{e_1} \cdot (\mathbf{X_N} - \overline{\mathbf{X}}) \\ \cdot & \cdots & \cdot \\ \cdot & \cdots & \cdot \\ \mathbf{e_{2n}} \cdot (\mathbf{X_1} - \overline{\mathbf{X}}), & \cdots, & \mathbf{e_{2n}} \cdot (\mathbf{X_N} - \overline{\mathbf{X}}) \end{pmatrix}
\end{aligned} \tag{16.14}
$$

which is a $2n \times N$ matrix. (Note that each $\mathbf{e_i}$ is $1 \times 2n$, and each $(\mathbf{X_i} - \overline{\mathbf{X}})$ is $2n \times 1$. So $e_i \cdot (X_i - \overline{X})$ is $1 \times 1$, which is a scalar.) If we apply PCA to the data and only retain the first

$t$ principal eigenvectors ($t < 2n$), the projection matrix $P$ becomes $F$, and (16.14) is reduced to:

$$B = FA = \begin{pmatrix} \mathbf{e_1} \cdot (\mathbf{X_1} - \overline{\mathbf{X}}), & \cdots, & \mathbf{e_1} \cdot (\mathbf{X_N} - \overline{\mathbf{X}}) \\ & & \\ \cdot & \cdots & \cdot \\ \cdot & \cdots & \cdot \\ & & \\ \mathbf{e_t} \cdot (\mathbf{X_1} - \overline{\mathbf{X}}), & \cdots, & \mathbf{e_t} \cdot (\mathbf{X_N} - \overline{\mathbf{X}}) \end{pmatrix} \qquad (16.15)$$

Here, $F$, $A$ and $B$ are $t \times 2n$, $2n \times N$, and $t \times N$ respectively. If we denote the $k$-th column vector of $B$ as $\mathbf{b_k}$, then

$$\mathbf{b_k} = \begin{pmatrix} \mathbf{e_1} \cdot (\mathbf{X_k} - \overline{\mathbf{X}}) \\ \cdot \\ \cdot \\ \mathbf{e_t} \cdot (\mathbf{X_k} \quad \overline{\mathbf{X}}) \end{pmatrix} = F(\mathbf{X_k} - \overline{\mathbf{X}}) \qquad (16.16)$$

The original shape $\mathbf{X_k}$ is approximated by

$$\mathbf{X_k} \approx \overline{\mathbf{X}} + F^T \mathbf{b_k} \qquad (16.17)$$

Conversely, the $t$-dimensional vector $\mathbf{b_k}$ can be expressed as

$$\mathbf{b_k} \approx F(\mathbf{X_k} - \overline{\mathbf{X}}) \qquad (16.18)$$

If $F = P$ (i.e. $t = 2n$), then $F^T = P^T = P^{-1}$ and the original data can be recovered exactly.

We can generalize $\mathbf{b_k}$ to a $t$-dimensional vector $\mathbf{b}$ which defines a set of parameters of a deformable model. A specific shape $\mathbf{X}$ (a $t$-dimensional column vector) can be obtained by varying the elements of $\mathbf{b}$; the shape is calculated by

$$\mathbf{X} = \overline{\mathbf{X}} + F^T \mathbf{b} \qquad (16.19)$$

We denote the $i$-th element of $\mathbf{b}$ as $b_i$. That is,

$$b_i = \mathbf{e_i} \cdot (\mathbf{X} - \overline{\mathbf{X}})$$

Note that $b_i$ is just one element of the column vector $\mathbf{b}$; do not confuse this with $\mathbf{b_k}$, which is simply a shape in the training set, a special $\mathbf{b}$. Suppose the variance of $b_i$ across the training set is $\delta_i$. We can ensure that the shape generated is similar to those of the original set by limiting $b_i$ to vary within the limits of 3 standard deviations, $\pm 3\sqrt{\delta_i}$. People usually call the model variation corresponding to $b_i$ as the $i$-th *mode* of the model. The feature vector matrix $F$, consisting of principal eigenvectors of the covariance matrix $C$, defines a rotated coordinate with each of its axis aligned with a cloud of the original shape vectors. The vector $\mathbf{b}$ defines points in this rotated coordinate system.

## 16.3 PCA with Fewer Samples than Dimensions

The above PCA technique works well when the number of training shapes $N$ is larger than the vector dimension ($2n$). However, if the number of shapes used is significantly smaller than the vector dimension, the method becomes inefficient as many of the eigenvector components are 0.

Suppose we wish to apply a PCA to $N$ points (shapes) each with $2n$ components, where $N < 2n$. The covariance matrix $C$, given by (16.9), is $2n \times 2n$, which may be very large. However, we can compute the eigenvalues and eigenvectors from a smaller matrix with order $N \times N$, derived from the data. Operations on a smaller matrix could save a significant amount of computing cost because such operations often go as the cube of the size of the matrix.

We start by subtracting each data vector $X_k$ of (16.12) from the mean $\overline{\mathbf{X}}$ and put them in the transpose of the deviation matrix $D^T$, which is the same matrix shown in (16.13):

$$D^T = \left( \mathbf{X_1} - \overline{\mathbf{X}}, \cdots, \mathbf{X_N} - \overline{\mathbf{X}} \right) \tag{16.20}$$

Matrix $D^T$ is $2n \times N$ and $D$ is $N \times 2n$.. The covariant matrix $C$ is given by

$$C = \frac{1}{N} D^T D \tag{16.21}$$

which is $2n \times 2n$. Normally, it has $2n$ eigenvectors and eigenvalues. However, if $N < 2n$, many of the eigenvalues are zero.

Suppose we calculate a matrix $T$ from

$$T = \frac{1}{N} D D^T \tag{16.22}$$

which is $N \times N$ and is much smaller than $C$. Let $\{\mathbf{e_1}, \cdot, \mathbf{e_i}, \cdot, \mathbf{e_N}\}$ be the set of $N$ eigenvectors of $T$ with corresponding eigenvalues $\{\lambda_1, \cdot, \lambda_i, \cdot, \lambda_N\}$. Each eigenvector $\mathbf{e_i}$ is a $1 \times N$ row vector. The product $\mathbf{e'_i} = \mathbf{e_i} D$ is a $1 \times 2n$ row vector. One can show that $\mathbf{e'_i}$ is an eigenvector of $C$ with corresponding eigenvalue $\lambda_i$. There are $N$ such eigenvectors; all the remaining $2n - N$ eigenvectors of $C$ have zero eigenvalues. The vector $\mathbf{e'_i}$ may not be of unit length; we may need to normalize it to make comparisons.

The feature vector matrix is given by

$$F = \begin{pmatrix} \mathbf{e'_1} \\ \cdot \\ \cdot \\ \mathbf{e'_t} \end{pmatrix} = \begin{pmatrix} \mathbf{e_1} D \\ \cdot \\ \cdot \\ \mathbf{e_t} \mathbf{D} \end{pmatrix} \tag{16.23}$$

which is $t \times 2n$.

## 16.4 Shape Model Example

Figure 16-2 below shows shapes from a training set of 6 landmarked faces. Each image is annotated with 81 landmarks and is displayed in a window of 500 pixels $\times$ 500 pixels.

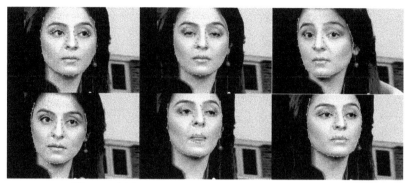

**Figure 16-2**   Shapes from a Training Set of Faces

Figure 16-3 shows the outlines of the 6 shapes drawn from the landmarks with the controid of each shape located at the same origin of the drawing coordinate system. The thick black outline in the figure is the average ($\overline{\mathbf{X}}$) of the 6 shapes.

In this example, the number of samples $N$ is 6 and the number of dimensions $2n$ is $2 \times 81 = 162$. So we shall use matrix $T$ given by equation (16.22) to determine the 6 eigenvectors and eigenvalues. As one can see from Figure 16-2, the landmarks can be separated into 5 groups: face, mouth, nose, left eye, and right eye. So we should expect that the data would cluster around 5 axes (eigenvectors) and thus one of the eigenvalues should be very small, close to 0.

**Figure 16-3**   Outlines of Six Shapes and Their Mean

We use the Jacobi Method discussed in the previous chapter to find eigenvectors and eigenvalues. The six eigenvalues, arranged from large to small, are found to be:

$$\lambda_1 = 13846.922, \quad \lambda_2 = 3538.559, \quad \lambda_3 = 2090.0279,$$

$$\lambda_4 = 968.843, \quad \lambda_5 = 618.593, \quad \lambda_6 = 0.000$$

As an example, the values of the normalized eigenvector $\mathbf{e_1}'$ for $\lambda_1$ are:

```
 0.089   0.086   0.093   0.083   0.078    0.077   0.046  -0.011  -0.075  -0.144
-0.176  -0.197  -0.208  -0.206  -0.186   -0.164  -0.117  -0.097  -0.069  -0.043
-0.016  -0.008   0.018   0.032   0.058    0.083   0.104   0.111   0.110   0.127
 0.004   0.009   0.005   0.002  -0.014   -0.022  -0.030   0.018   0.014  -0.004
```

```
-0.011 -0.017 -0.007 -0.018  0.003   0.004  0.054  0.055  0.051  0.053
 0.057  0.010 -0.001  0.014  0.027   0.054  0.037  0.030  0.020  0.037
 0.034  0.074  0.083  0.096  0.066   0.031  0.045  0.026  0.021 -0.001
 0.018  0.017  0.019 -0.012 -0.014  -0.012  0.008  0.012  0.006  0.020
 0.014  0.059  0.070  0.099  0.120   0.131  0.150  0.193  0.180  0.169
 0.162  0.129  0.096  0.040  0.007  -0.036 -0.069 -0.073 -0.101 -0.128
-0.151 -0.159 -0.178 -0.188 -0.171  -0.183 -0.178 -0.146 -0.123 -0.115
-0.063  0.030  0.024  0.024  0.017  -0.004  0.023  0.026  0.027  0.007
 0.005 -0.001  0.012  0.017  0.038   0.022  0.030  0.042  0.062  0.045
 0.024  0.015  0.015  0.028  0.047   0.054  0.042  0.018  0.017  0.016
 0.026  0.022  0.038  0.028  0.008   0.002  0.003  0.024  0.007  0.006
 0.008  0.009  0.048 -0.003 -0.025  -0.003  0.009 -0.035 -0.014 -0.016
-0.008 -0.012
```

Suppose we choose the first 3 eigenvectors $\mathbf{e_1}, \mathbf{e_2}$, and $\mathbf{e_3}$ to form the feature vector $F$:

$$F = \begin{pmatrix} \mathbf{e'_1} \\ \mathbf{e'_2} \\ \mathbf{e'_3} \end{pmatrix} \tag{16.24}$$

So $t = 3$ and $F$ is a $3 \times 162$ matrix. A shape projected onto these axes (eigenvectors) is given by

$$\mathbf{b} = F(\mathbf{X} - \overline{\mathbf{X}}) = \begin{pmatrix} \mathbf{e'_1} \cdot (\mathbf{X} - \overline{\mathbf{X}}) \\ \mathbf{e'_2} \cdot (\mathbf{X} - \overline{\mathbf{X}}) \\ \mathbf{e'_3} \cdot (\mathbf{X} - \overline{\mathbf{X}}) \end{pmatrix} \tag{16.25}$$

which is a $3 \times 1$ column matrix.

The original shape can be 'recovered' by (16.9) which is

$$\mathbf{X} = \overline{\mathbf{X}} + F^T \mathbf{b}$$

where $F^T$ is the the transpose of $F$ and is a $162 \times 3$ matrix. The outlines of the shapes 'recovered' in this way are shown in Figure 16-4 below.

**Figure 16-4**  Reconstructed Shapes using 3 Principal Eigenvectors

# Bibliography

1. N. Abramson, *Information Theory and Coding*, McGraw-Hill, 1963.

2. R.C. Agarwal, *An In-Place and In-Order WFTA*, ICASSP 83, pp. 190-193, Boston, 1983.

3. J.D. Bruguera and R.R. Osorio, *A United Architecture for H.264 Multiple Block-Size DCT with Fast and Low Cost Quantization*, Proceedings of the 9th EUROMICRO Conference on Digital System Design (DSD06), IEEE Computer Society, pp. 407-414, 2006.

4. D. Genzel and E. Charniak, *Entropy Rate Constancy in Text*, Proceedings of the 40th Annual Meeting of the Association for Computational Linguistics (ACL), Philadelphia, pp. 199-206, July 2002.

5. T. Budd, *Data Structures in C++: Using The Standard Template Library*, Addison Wesley, 1997.

6. S. R. Buss, *3-D Computer Graphics: A Mathematical Introduction with OpenGL*, Cambridge, 2003.

7. G.J. Chaitin, *Algorithmic Information Theory*, Cambridge University Press, 1987.

8. K. Chen, R. Kambhamettu, and D. Goldgof, *Extraction of MPEG-4 FAP Parameters from 3D Face Data Sequences*, CiteSeer, 1998.

9. W. Chen, C. Harrison, and S. Fralick, *A fast computational algorithm for the discrete cosine transform*, IEEE Trans. Com., Vol. COM-25 (9), pp. 1004-1011, Sept. 1977.

10. T. M. Cover and J.A. Cover, *Elements of Information Theory*, Second Edition, John Wiley, 2006.

11. P.F. Drucker, *The Essential Drucker*, Harper Business, 2001.

12. M. Ezhilarasan, and P. Thambidural, *A Hybrid Transform Coding for Video Codec*, 9th International Conference on Information Technology (ICIT06), IEEE Computer Society, 2006.

13. D. Genzel and E. Charniak, *Entropy Rate Constancy in Text*, Proceedings of the 40th Annual Meeting of the Association for Computational Linguistics (ACL), Philadelphia, pp. 199-206, July 2002.

14. A. Gersho and R.M. Gray, *Vector Quantization and Signal Compression*, Kluwer Academic Publishers, 1992.

15. R.G. Gonzalez and R.E. Woods, *Digital Image Processing*, Addison-Wesley, 1992.

16. E. L. Hall, *Computer Image Processing and Recognition*, Academic Press, 1979.

17. B. G. Haskell, A. Puri, and A. N. Netravali, *Digital Video: An introduction to MPEG-2*, Springer, 1996.

18. F.S. Hill, Jr. and S. M. Kelley, Jr., *Computer Graphics Using OpenGL*, Third Edition, Pearson Prentice Hall, 2007.

19. A.K. Jain, *Fundamentals of Digital Image Processing*, Prentice Hall, 1989.

20. R.W. Johnson and C.S. Burrus, *On the Structure of Efficient DFT Algorithms*, ICASSP 83, pp. 163-165, Boston, 1983.

21. T. Koga, K. Iinuma, et al., *Motion-Compensated Inter Frame Coding for Videoconferencing*, IEEE Nat. Telecomm. Conf. 4: pp. 15, 1981.

22. S. J. Leon, *Linear Algebra with Applications*, Eigth Edition, Prentice Hall, 2010.

23. J. Liang and T.D. Tran, *Fast Multiplierless Approximation of the DCT with the Lifting Schemes*, IEEE Transaction on Signal Processing, 49(12), pp. 3032-3044, December 2001.

24. Loki Software with J. R. Hall, *Programming Linux Games: Building Multimedia Applications with SDL, OpenAL, and Other APIs*, Linux Journal Press, 2001.

25. T. Luo et al., *An Improved Three-Step Search Algorithm with Zero Detection and Vector Filter for Motion Estimation*, International Conference on Computer Science and Software Engineering,Vol 2., pp. 967-978, 2008.

26. L. E. Mansfield, *Linear Algebra with Geometric Applications*, Marcel Dekker, Inc., 1976.

27. J.R. Masse and D. Cante, *General - N Winograd D.F.T. Programs with Inverse Option*, ICASSP 83, pp. 1164-1167, Boston, 1983.

28. D. C. Murdoch, *Linear Algebra for Undergraduates*, John Wiley & Sons, 1957.

29. A. V. Oppenheim and R. W. Schafer, *Digital Signal Processing*, Prentice Hall, 1975.

30. I.S. Pandzic and R. Forchheimer ( editors ), *MPEG-4 Facial Animation: The Standard, Implementation and Applications*, John Wiley & Sons, 2002.

31. M. Peder, *Lecture 6: Winograd's Small DFT: Implementation of DFT Using convolution*,

32. W. B. Pennebaker and J. L. Mitchell, *JPEG: Still Image Data Compression Standard*, Van Nostrand Reinhold, 1993.

33. Recommendations ITU-R BT.601-5, *Studio encoding parameters of digital television for standard 4:3 and wide-screen 16:9 aspect ratios*, ITU-T, 1995.

34. Iain E.G. Richardson, *H.264 and MPEG-4 Video Compression: Video Coding for Next-generation Multimedia*, John Wiley & Sons, 2003.

35. N. Sarris and M. G. Strintzis, *3D Modeling and Animation: Synthesis and Analysis Techniques for the Human Body*, IRM Press, 2005.

36. C. E. Shannon, *A Mathematical Theory of Communication*, The Bell System Technical Journal, 27:379-423, 623-656, July, October, 1948.

37. J. Shlens, *A Tutorial on Principal Component Analysis*, Systems Neurobiology Laboratory, Salk Insitute for Biological Studies La Jolla, CA 92037, April, 2009.

38. A. Silberschatz, P.B. Galvin, and G. Gagne, *Operating System Concepts*, Sxith Edition, John Wiley & Sons, 2004.

39. H. Tao and H. H. Chen et. al., *Compression of MPEG-4 Facial Animation Parameters for Transmission of Talking Heads*, IEEE Transactions on Circuits and Systems for Video Technology, 9(2), pp. 264-276, 1999.

40. J.F. Traub, G.W. Waslikowski, and H. Wozniakowski, *Information-Based Complexity*, Academic Press, 1988.

41. G. Wade, *Signal Coding And Processing*, Second Edition, Cambridge University Press, 1994.

42. S. Winograd, *On Computing the Discrete Fourier Transform*, Math. Comput., 32, pp. 175 199, January 1978.

43. T.L. Yu, *A Framework for Very High Performance Compression of Table Tennis Video Clips*, Proceedings of IASTED on Signal and Image Processing, pp. 167-172, Kailua-Kona, Hawaii, August 2008.

44. J. Ziv and A. Lempel, *A Universal Algorithm for Sequential Data Compression*, IEEE Transactions on Information Theory, 23(3), pp. 337343, May 1977.

45. J. Ziv and A. Lempel, *Compression of Individual Sequences Via Variable-Rate Coding*, IEEE Transactions on Information Theory, 24(5), pp. 530-536, September 1978.

46. M. Stokes, et al. *A Standard Default Color Space for the Internet - sRGB*, 1996, http://www.w3.org/Graphics/Color/sRGB.html

47. http://www.3dcafe.com/

48. http://www.blender.org/

49. http://coven.lancs.ac.uk/mpeg4

50. http://java.sun.com/javase/technologies/desktop/media/

51. http://www.makehuman.org/

52. http://personalpages.manchester.ac.uk/staff/timothy.f.cootes/

53. http://xface.fbk.eu

# Index

# Windows Fan, Linux Fan
by *Fore June*

*Windws Fan, Linux Fan* describes a true story about a spiritual battle between a Linux fan and a Windows fan. You can learn from the successful fan to become a successful Internet Service Provider ( ISP ) and create your own wealth.

Second Edition, 2002.
ISBN: 0-595-26355-0 Price: $6.86

# An Introduction to Video Compression in C/C++
by *Fore June*

The book describes the the principles of digital video data compression techniques and its implementations in C/C++. Topics covered include RBG-YCbCr conversion, macroblocks, DCT and IDCT, integer arithmetic, quantization, reorder, run-level encoding, entropy encoding, motion estimation, motion compensation and hybrid coding.

January 2010
ISBN: 9781451522273

# An Introduction to 3D Computer Graphics, Stereoscopic Image, and Animation in OpenGL and C/C++
by *Fore June*

This book explains 3D graphics and related topics using the open-source library OpenGL. Topics covered include affine transformations, projections, color blending, textures, depth perception, stereoscopic images, animations, meshes, and planar contours.

November 2011
ISBN: 978-1466488359

www.ingramcontent.com/pod-product-compliance
Lightning Source LLC
Chambersburg PA
CBHW080354060326
40689CB00019B/4002